WORLD ECONOMY

WORLD ECONOMY

GENERAL EDITOR

Stuart Corbridge

New York
OXFORD UNIVERSITY PRESS
1993

CONSULTANT EDITOR
Professor Peter Haggett, University of Bristol

Professor John Agnew, Syracuse University, New York, USA
Italy and Greece
Dr Morag Bell, Loughborough University of Technology, UK
Southern Africa
Dr Hans Blaas, University of Amsterdam, The Netherlands with Dr Alisdair Rogers, School of Geography, University of Oxford, UK
The Low Countries
Dr Richard Black, King's College, University of London, UK
Spain and Portugal
Dr Christopher Bramall, Sidney Sussex College, Cambridge, UK
China and its neighbors
Dr Colin Clarke, Jesus College, Oxford, UK
Central America
Dr John Connell, University of Sydney, Australia
Australasia, Oceania and Antarctica
Dr Stuart Corbridge, Sidney Sussex College, Cambridge, UK
The United States, The Economic Overview
Professor Christopher Dixon, City of London University, UK
Southeast Asia
Dr Michael Dunford, University of Sussex, UK
France and its neighbors
Professor Alan Gilbert, University College London, UK
South America
Dr Michael Heffernan, Loughborough University of Technology, UK
Northern Africa
Sarah Jewitt, Newnham College, Cambridge, UK
The Indian Subcontinent
Dr Gerard Kearnes, University of Wisconsin, USA
The Nordic Countries
Dr Gunter Krebs, London School of Economics and Political Science, UK with Dr Stuart Corbridge
Central Europe
Dr Andrew Leyshon, University of Hull, UK
Japan and Korea
Dr Ronald L. Martin, St Catherine's College, Cambridge, UK
The British Isles
Dr Simon Milne, McGill University, Canada
Canada and the Arctic
Dr Graham Smith, Sidney Sussex College, Cambridge, UK
Eastern Europe, Northern Eurasia
Dr Timothy Unwin, Royal Holloway and Bedford New College, UK
The Middle East
Paul D. Watson, United Nations Association International Service, UK
Central Africa

AN EQUINOX BOOK

Planned and produced by
Andromeda Oxford Limited
9-15 The Vineyard, Abingdon
Oxfordshire, England OX14 3PX

Published in the United States of America by
Oxford University Press, Inc.,
200 Madison Avenue,
New York, N.Y. 10016

Oxford is a registered trademark of
Oxford University Press

Library of Congress
Cataloging-in-Publication Data

World economy / edited by Stuart Corbridge.
p. cm.
Includes bibliographical references and index.
ISBN 0-19-520946-X
1. Economic history--Encyclopedias. I. Corbridge, Stuart.
HC15.W67 1993
330.9--dc20 93-6489
CIP

Volume Editor Fiona Mullan
Assistant Editors Lauren Bourque, Hilary McGlynn
Designers Chris Munday, Nigel Partridge
Cartographic Manager Olive Pearson
Cartographic Editor Andrew Thompson
Picture Research Manager Leanda Shrimpton
Picture Researchers David Pratt, Claire Lofting

Project Editor Susan Kennedy
Art Editor Steve McCurdy

ISBN 0-19-520946-X

Printing (last digit): 9 8 7 6 5 4 3 2 1

Printed in Singapore by C.S. Graphics Ltd

INTRODUCTORY PHOTOGRAPHS
Half title: *Money changer, Egypt (Hutchison, Melanie Friend)*
Half title verso: *Salerno harbor, southwest Italy (Hutchison, Robert Francis)*
Title page: *Children going to school, Barcelona, Spain (Robert Harding, Peter Scholey)*
This page: *Loans office in Seattle city center, Washington State, USA (Robert Harding, Robert Francis)*

Contents

Centre de Santé

PREFACE

ECONOMICS AS A SUBJECT IS KNOWN AS THE "DISMAL SCIENCE", BUT THE real world of economics has rarely been more exciting than it is at present. The second half of the 20th century has brought with it some profound changes in the organization of economic affairs in the world's rich and poor nations, with all countries coming to depend much more on trade and the flow of money between each other. The recent emergence of the newly industrialized economies of Southeast Asia lends further credibility to the view that we share one world economy; as do the emergence of massive international migrations of labor and business, and the assumption of greater economic powers by international institutions such as the World Bank and the International Monetary Fund.

World Economy explores this binding together of national and regional economies in three main ways. The introductory section sets the modern world economy in its historical context, paying particular attention to the economic effects of European expansionism and imperialism after 1492. We see that contemporary systems of production and exchange often have their roots in an earlier era of colonialism. The main body of the book goes on to examine the workings of the contemporary world economy in 22 of its constituent regions. The focus here is on trading patterns and on the relationships between financial and industrial systems and between the public and private sectors of the economy. Multinational corporations figure prominently in this analysis, as do the actions of various producer groups such as OPEC (the Organization of Petroleum Exporting Countries). The international debt crisis is identified as a major problem which continues to haunt large parts of the international economy today.

A third aim of *World Economy* is to explore the human dimensions of apparently abstract economic actions, theories and ideologies. What do we mean by economic growth and economic development and which countries and groups have benefited most from these processes, and why? How, and in what ways, are different economic systems – capitalism and socialism, for example – linked through to different economic outcomes? Who wins and who loses when it comes to wealth and welfare, access to healthcare and education or the way income is distributed? How precisely are these benefits shared out between different geographical regions and social classes, and between men and women?

These are some of the questions we will be asking to bring alive the real world of economics. Economics may not be the be-all and end-all of modern life, but it is difficult to think about the human condition without first addressing the events and processes that define the World Economy

Dr Stuart Corbridge
DEPARTMENT OF GEOGRAPHY, UNIVERSITY OF CAMBRIDGE

Mothers and children attending a field clinic, Zaire

Dealers working at the New York Stock Exchange (overleaf)

THE ECONOMIC OVERVIEW

THE WORLD ECONOMY TAKES SHAPE

THE WORLD ECONOMY AT WORK

GLOBAL PATTERNS

The World Economy in the 15th Century

TODAY, INTERNATIONAL TRADE AND CAPITAL flows bind together the most distant parts of the globe, and a handful of nations – notably Japan, the United States and Germany – exert a powerful influence over the workings of the world economy. From this perspective, it may be difficult to imagine a different economic order. Yet a global economy is a recent phenomenon, as is the existence of a United States of America or a united Germany.

A map of the world's economies in the 15th century would give a very different picture of the geography of international production and exchange. At this time, most production was carried out locally, for local use and using local resources. Although international trading was extensive, it was confined mainly to a handful of key cities and ports which traded in a few luxury items such as silver and spices. Even the relative prosperity of countries was different. The economies of China and India were more advanced in 1400 than those of northwestern Europe and North and South America.

The local limitations of the world economy in 1400 were partly dictated by geography. The Old World of Europe and Asia is crossed by a great chain of mountains running west to east from the Pyrenees in northeast Spain to the Kunlun mountains of southwest China. These mountains discouraged contact between areas to the north and south, except through a series of well-defined gaps in the chain. Pastoral economies were the norm in the extensive belt of dry country that runs from the Saharan and Arabian deserts to Mongolia. Local populations drove their herds to pastures along the desert margin and to oases. To the south of the dry zone lay the fertile areas of west Africa, the basin of the Ganges in India, Southeast Asia and southern China.

Rice and grain were the staff of life in these regions, as they are today. To the north of the deserts was the fertile land of central Europe, and above that the forested regions of Europe and Asia. The forests could not easily be farmed and so

Ancient artery of trade (*right*) Even today, the Chang river, China's principal waterway, is a major trading route and focus of local life. The local system of trade and commerce that still survives in many parts of contemporary China has remained essentially unchanged for hundreds of years.

Striking a bargain (*below*) market traders in Algeria consider carefully the worth of garments being offered for sale. In sealing bargains today, North African Arabs draw on a rich tradition of skillful negotiation passed on from father to son.

were secondary to the great arc of cultivable land and overland trade routes that linked Morocco to China.

Shifts of focus

The Chinese were renowned for their technical prowess at the beginning of the 15th century, not least in the military sphere, where they had already invented gunpowder. When Europe descended into the dark ages in the 5th century AD, China already had a unified political system, a productive and well-irrigated agricultural economy based largely on rice, and considerable maritime success in the waters of the Indian Ocean. Why, then, did China not become the focal point of the new colonial-based world economy that was to emerge in the early 16th century? Why did western Europe assume this lead? There are no definitive answers, though one explanation could be China's failure to exploit its economic opportunities overseas. China was an inward-looking country; its very size and riches reduced the incentive for foreign expansion. There is even evidence that the Imperial court, fearing uprisings, suppressed a local knowledge of gunnery.

Conditions in western Europe were very different. Most European economies depended on sheep, wheat and cattle, not rice. The desire for new pastureland gave Europe a strong impetus for territorial exploration and expansion. The Europeans were also geared to war – France and England had been engaged in the Hundred Years War from the mid 14th century to about 1450, a prolonged conflict that drove exhausted peasants from the countryside to the towns. In response, the growing towns and cities of Europe became centers for a social revolution that was ultimately to cause the breakdown of the feudal system. Protected by municipal rights, merchants could ply their trades and workers were free to combine in guilds. As feudalism dissolved from within, the towns of England and northwestern Europe began to act as sparking points for rural economies in which some bonded peasants were being set free to work as tenant farmers or paid laborers. At the same time, a new class of capitalist long-distance traders was beginning to emerge in northern Europe and in some parts of Italy and Iberia. These developments laid the foundations for European economic ascendancy over the next 500 years.

European Expansion

EUROPEAN EXPANSION OVERSEAS BEGAN IN 1415 when the Portuguese seized the Muslim port of Ceuta on the African side of the Straits of Gibraltar. In time, they ventured along the West African coast and round the Cape of Good Hope into the Indian Ocean and so to the East Indies. They also moved westward across the Atlantic to the New World of the Americas. By 1500 the Portuguese had landed in Brazil, where 20 years later the first sugar plantations were established, worked by slaves imported from Africa.

The Spanish had also mastered the arts of navigation. In 1492 Christopher Columbus (1451–1506) sailed to the New World. A few years later in 1519 the Spanish conquistador, Hernán Cortés (1485–1547) sailed to conquer Mexico for Spain, and in 1530 his countryman, Francisco Pizarro (1475–1541), set off from Panama to conquer Peru and founded the city of Lima. The Spanish also made conquests in the Philippines and Southeast Asia, where their main rivals were the Dutch. During this period the French and the British were also making territorial acquisitions. The British East India Company was chartered in 1600, just two years before its Dutch counterpart.

Building empires

The power of the Europeans to reshape the economic geography of the world soon became apparent in the main areas of international trade. Above all else, the conquistadors of the New World sought treasure or gold bullion to fill the royal coffers at home. In 1545 the Spanish discovered huge deposits of silver at Potosi in Bolivia, and set the indigenous people to work in the mines. In a pattern that was to be repeated elsewhere, the introduction of European labor regimes meant suffering or ill-treatment for local workers and slaves alike. Millions of people in the New World died as a result of forced labor or of the diseases the Europeans brought with them, against which they often had no immunity.

By the mid 16th century, large numbers of workers in the Americas had been pressed into the production of foodstuffs and raw materials for the benefit of peoples far away. The Spanish ensured that there was enough labor available to carry out the enterprises of the Spanish crown by setting up a system of large estates (haciendas) worked by bonded labor. Silver was not the only great trading commodity of these years. In North America, the British and French trapped beavers for their fur, which was highly prized at home. Here, too, the colonizing powers drove inland to map out new and exploitative trading relationships with diverse local populations.

Trading patterns were more established in Asia, especially routes involving silk and spices. The British, facing strong competition from the Dutch in the East Indies spice regions, fell back to the coasts of India, where they laid the foundations of a vast empire. Many British colonists – known as "nabobs" on their return home – made huge personal fortunes from their exploits in India. Revenues from the subcontinent also financed expanded British trade with China, where the British later traded Indian opium for Chinese tea. The British also took from India many thousands of indentured workers and put them to work in the plantations of the Empire in the Caribbean and in east and south Africa.

Trading in people

Europeans had begun taking slaves from Africa to work in their colonial plantations in the 15th century. An estimated 275,000 slaves were sent to Europe and America from Africa between 1450 and 1600. In the 17th century, 1.34 million slaves were exported, principally to the sugar plantations of the Caribbean. This figure was exceeded in the 18th century: between 1700 and 1810 about 6 million men and women were taken as slaves from Africa, mainly to work in British-held Jamaica and French-held Saint Domingue (Haiti). A European world economy was being born in these centuries even as local economies elsewhere were being bled to death.

Slavery formed one link of a three-way trade in which ships embarked from Europe for West Africa carrying woven cotton and metal goods and guns. These goods were exchanged for slaves who were then shipped to the European colonies. Finally, the ships returned to Europe carrying colonial produce such as sugar. By the mid 19th century, public disgust over the African slave trade led to its slow abolition.

Gold fever Centuries after European colonizers came to Latin America, driven by greed for its precious metals and prepared to use slaves to acquire it, Brazilian gold prospectors work on in the hope of a lucky strike.

The Age of Industrial Capitalism

THE EARLY EUROPEAN WORLD ECONOMY WAS not based on the principles of private ownership and control that we now know as capitalism. Capitalism and long-distance trade often go hand-in-hand, but they are not the same. Capitalism is better defined by the way people relate to the means of production (land and machines) to produce commodities for exchange. During the early years of European conquest, most colonial laborers were bound to the land (as in India), to an estate (as in the haciendas of South America) or to an owner. It was not until the 17th and 18th centuries in England, when men and women were freed to work as waged laborers, that modern labor relationships began to emerge, and with them the systems of industrial capitalism.

The rise of waged labor

Industrial capitalism emerged in Britain over a long period of time. Its formation was helped by the enclosure movements of the 18th and 19th centuries, when large numbers of people once tied to the land became divorced from the means of production. Meanwhile, the rich had accumulated cash surpluses to invest in industry as a result of new farming techniques or their success in the colonies. Huge amounts of public and private capital were invested in a network of turnpike roads, a canal system and later in railroads; at the same time new laws were introduced to protect private property rights and enforce new forms of labor contracts.

In response to these developments, Britain's cities became hives of industry. In a capitalist system, innovation is vital if companies are to maintain their competitive edge. The spirit of innovation that characterized the British industrial revolution transformed (among others) the English spinning industry, giving it a massive advantage over its rivals in global markets. By 1800 England's spinners could outproduce their Indian counterparts by as much as 25-fold.

New technologies that replaced skilled craftwork with machines were not the only sign of a new age in industry. More and more workers were brought together in factories where their jobs became increasingly specialized parts of mass production processes. Working and living conditions for the new urban labor force were extremely poor; consequently, many workers formed new combinations called trade unions. As industrial capitalism spread across northwest Europe and to North America, labor came to oppose capital on a large scale. Bitter battles were fought between workers and employers over working conditions and safety standards, the length of the working day, wages and employers' powers of dismissal.

Cutting sugar cane in Santa Cruz, Bolivia *(above)*
More than three centuries after sugar plantations were established in the South American Spanish colonies, sugar is still a major cash crop, though world demand is dropping.

Imperial trading routes c. 1770

British
Spanish
Portuguese
French
Dutch

Arrows indicate outward and homeward trade between the European powers and their overseas territories

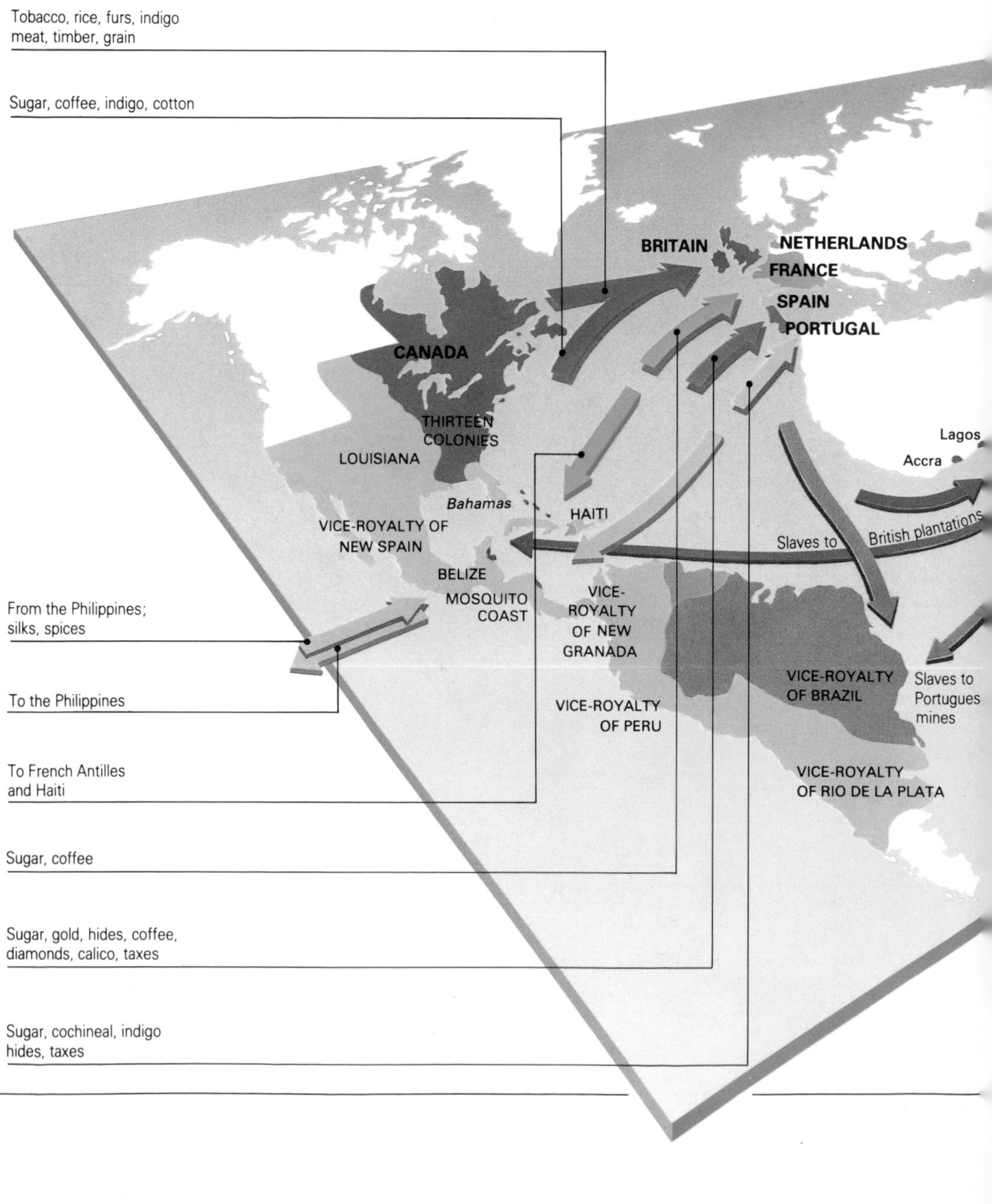

The drive for colonial expansion

By the 19th century, Europe's industrial prowess increased its ability to control the economies of its existing colonies. Europe was both the most important market for raw materials and the largest supplier of manufactured goods. It also gave the colonial powers a renewed incentive to secure distant lands as sources of labor and new outlets for the products that were streaming from European mills and factories. During the second half of the 19th century, the major European powers rushed to secure their former trading "partners" as colonies, to be ruled directly from London, Brussels or Paris. In 1857, even as Latin America was emerging from over two centuries of Spanish or Portuguese rule, India moved from the tutelage of the East India Company to being a colony of the British Empire.

THE SCRAMBLE FOR AFRICA

Before 1800 very few Europeans had penetrated the interior of Africa; this began to change in the early 19th century when several expeditions were mounted to explore the "dark continent". They were led by men such as the Scots explorer of the Niger, Mungo Park (1771–1806); British-born Hugh Clapperton (1788–1827) the first European explorer to reach northern Nigeria; the Scottish missionary Dr David Livingstone (1813–73), who made extensive expeditions through the African interior; and the French explorer Louis-Paul Caillie (1799–1838), the first European to survive a journey to the west African city of Timbuktu.

The European powers had agreed in 1884–85 to recognize certain "spheres of influence" as colonies or protocolonies, and by 1913 they had divided the territory of Africa between them, with the exception of Abyssinia and Liberia. The "scramble for Africa" as this period of colonization came to be known, was driven partly by missionary zeal to convert the continent to Christianity and partly by a desire to "civilize" Africans. Alongside these motives, however, was a strong economic imperative. Africa was a source of food, cheap labor, raw materials and minerals for Europe. The Kimberley diamond rush in South Africa in the 1870s typified European attitudes to their African colonies. The diamond company, De Beers, founded by the British colonist, Cecil Rhodes (1853–1902), brought thousands of black Africans to this small town to break the ground and haul and sift the earth. A white man wrote at the time that South Africa was a "veritable Tom Tiddler's ground" where prospectors could not only make a fortune but also have all the work done for them by local blacks.

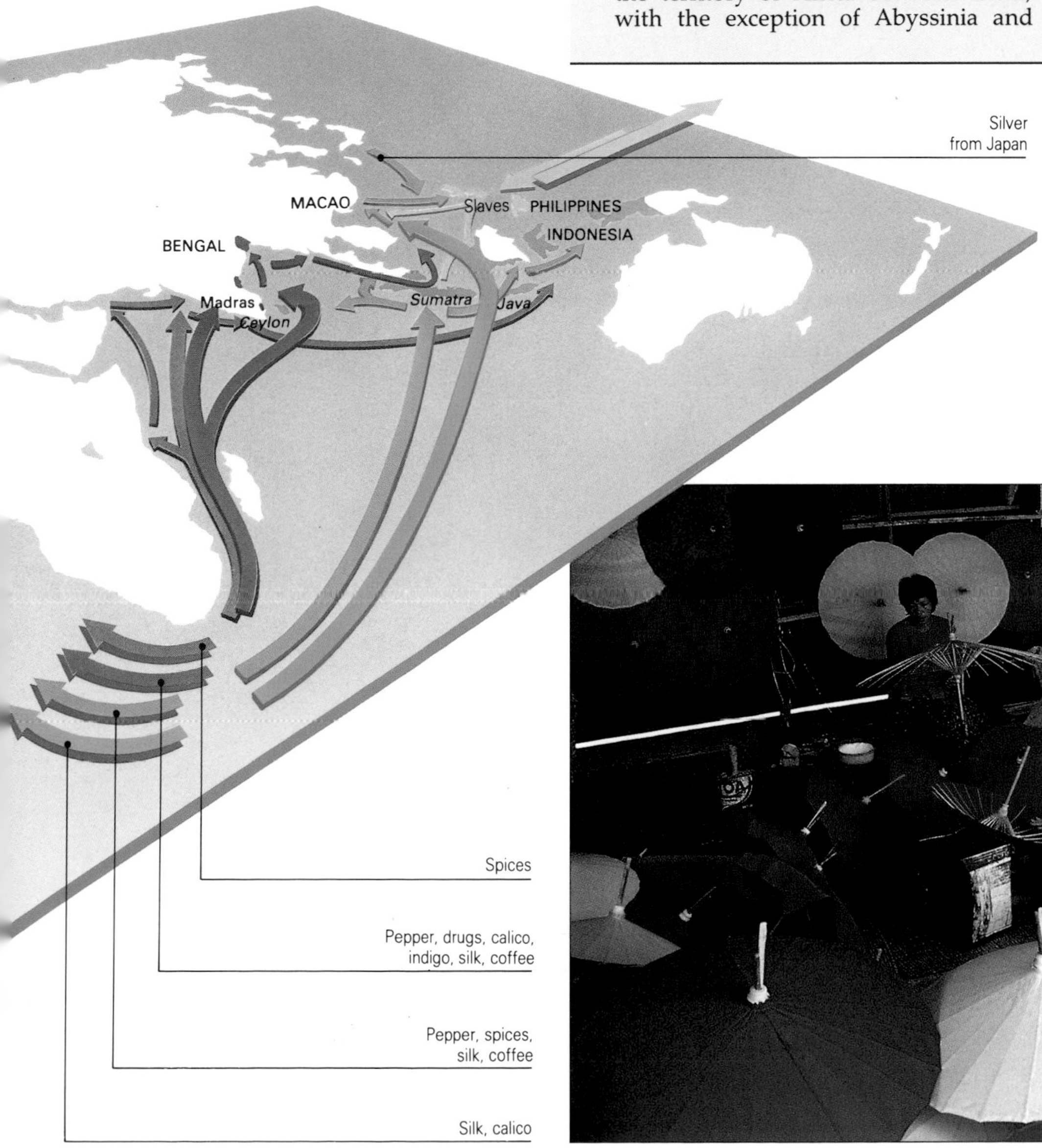

The pattern of 18th-century trade *(left)* By the middle of the century the major European powers had established their colonial spheres of influence, and exploiting the resources of the colonies was beginning to return substantial profits to them. Sugar, spices and slaves were the most profitable trading commodities, making South America, the Caribbean, Africa and India the most valuable sources of revenue.

The new silk road *(below)* Thai women make brightly colored miniature silk umbrellas for the local tourist trade and lucrative export market. Silk, one of the earliest and most precious commodities of Southeast Asia, is still a major export and foreign currency earner for the region.

Nationalism, Socialism and War

Hyperinflation made visible *(above)* In Berlin in 1923 inflation was running so high and German currency was worth so little that laundry baskets were used to deliver workers' weekly wages. In spite of a severe economic crisis following World War I, Germany recovered sufficiently to exercise its colonial ambitions in Europe again in 1939, provoking World War II.

Anticapitalist poster, 1931 *(right)* The original caption, in Russian, is a quotation from Lenin. It says that, though the bourgeoisie are currently free to torture and murder the oppressed, they cannot stop the imminent total liberation of the revolutionary proletariat.

The European age of empire proved to be short-lived. By the end of the 19th century deep rifts were beginning to open up, both between the colonial powers and within their empires. Some of these tensions were connected with the rise of Britain's main economic rivals, especially Germany and the United States. Others stemmed from the aspirations of the downtrodden and dispossessed. Nationalist and socialist struggles were set to become prominent features of the 20th-century world economy.

Britain's relative economic power was beginning to wane by the turn of the century. Its industrial revolution, the first in the world, had taken place over a period of 150 years. Subsequent industrial revolutions would not take so long. During the second half of the 19th century, the United States, France, Belgium and Germany each went through a period of rapid industrialization and moved into what economists called an era of "self-sustaining growth". In each case, these industrial revolutions were associated with the introduction of new products and technologies. Britain no longer showed the world an image of its future; other countries had industrialized their own means of production and caught up.

Where these countries lagged behind the British were in the matters of territory and empire. In the 20th century the Germans, Italians and Japanese would seek to emulate the conquests of Britain and France. In time these ambitions led to World War II, but not before a new era of economic mercantilism had taken its own toll. During the 1930s, an earlier European commitment to free trade was abandoned and nationalist economic policies

returned with a vengeance. As a result, the major economic powers became engaged in cut-throat competition through a succession of measures such as currency devaluation and wage-cutting. No one country was sufficiently dominant to impose a clear set of rules on the international economy.

Three Worlds

Meanwhile, the doctrines of Marx and Lenin and the rise of socialism were also threatening the old political and economic order. Socialist ideology rejected capitalist societies in which economic benefits were shared unfairly and unevenly. Instead, it looked toward a society where men and women would contribute according to their abilities, and receive according to their needs.

Marx expected that the working classes in Europe's industrial heartlands – Britain and Germany – would be the first to rebel against capitalism. Instead, the first socialist state was proclaimed in Russia in 1917 when the Bolsheviks seized power and established a Soviet socialist republic. This led to the emergence of a new type of economy within the world system. The Soviet Union (founded in 1923) sought to build a strong industrial economy on the back of collectivized agriculture and through state ownership and control of the means of production.

The founding of the Soviet Union was a triumph for socialism and nationalism. It was created as a largely self-sufficient economy (not least because it was attacked from the outset by the West) in which natural resources and local needs were put before the demands of the global marketplace. Some struggles against colonialism took a similar form. For example, the Indian National Congress movement – founded in 1885 – pressed for an end to colonial economic subordination. This movement became more radical in the 20th century, under the leadership of Mohandas Gandhi (1869–1948) and Jawaharlal Nehru (1899–1964).

India achieved independence from Britain in 1947. Most of Asia was decolonized in the 1950s and 1960s, with Africa following suit in the 1960s and 1970s. By the 1950s the outlines of a new world economy were emerging, divided into three main blocs: a First World of advanced industrialized countries; a socialist Second World; and a Third World of developing ex-colonial countries.

The Pax Americana

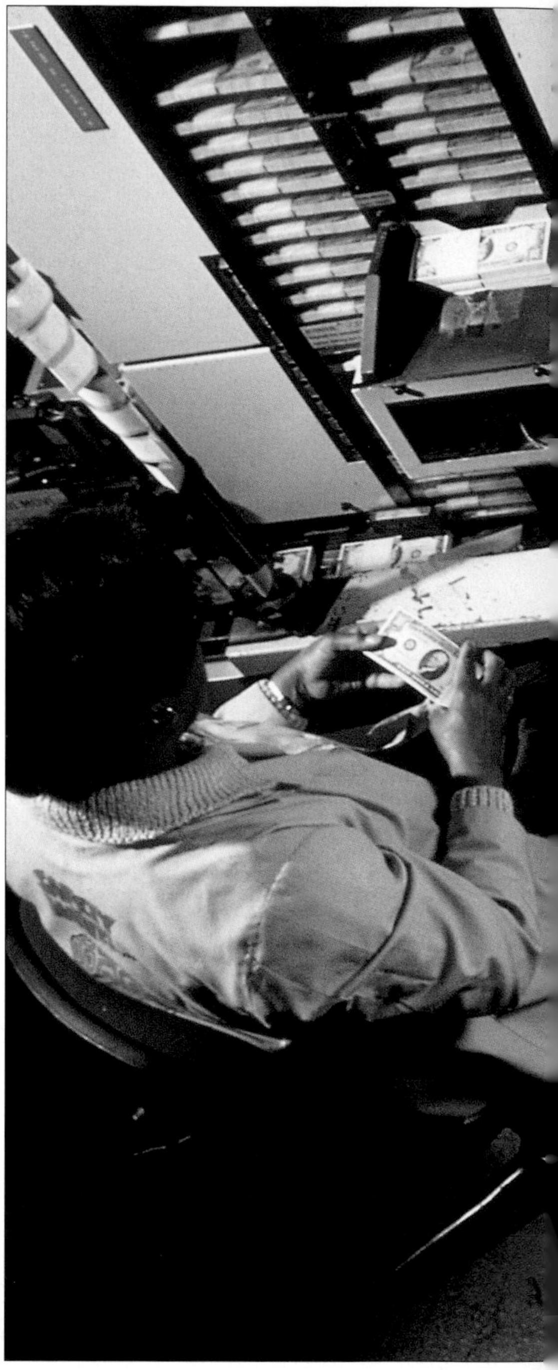

Defending the gold standard *(above)* Fort Knox, the almost impregnable military installation in Kentucky where American gold reserves are kept. Paper currency has not been freely convertible into gold in the domestic market since World War I.

THE UNITED STATES EMERGED FROM WORLD War II as the dominant world economic and political power. In 1945 it accounted for 50 percent of global production and controlled 75 percent of the world's gold reserves. The country was strongly situated to unveil a blueprint for the postwar international economic order. The Pax Americana – literally "American Peace" – was first made public at the 1944 United Nations Monetary and Financial Conference held in Bretton Woods, New Hampshire.

The Americans – represented by the economist Harry Dexter White (1892–1948) and the British – represented by John Maynard Keynes (1883–1946) – had contrasting views on how the world economy should be rebuilt after the war. Keynes wanted to see a world of independent national economies linked by international trade. Goods would be paid for by means of a new international unit of account, the *bancor*, issued by a central bank and independent of any one nation. However, as the dominant world power, the Americans wanted to ensure expanding international markets for American goods and industries. To this end, they were in favor of decolonization, free trade and a strong dollar. The American dollar would be the main international means of payment and would be issued by the American Treasury. To persuade other countries that the dollar was "as good as gold", the Americans agreed to maintain the value of their dollar at a fixed exchange rate against gold in order to guard against inflation. Other countries would then agree to maintain their currencies at a fixed exchange rate against the dollar.

The system of fixed exchange rates agreed at the Bretton Woods Conference lasted until the early 1970s. By 1960 most of the major currencies were bound into

KEYNESIANISM

The British economist John Maynard Keynes transformed economic and political thinking during the 1930s and 1940s. One of his most fundamental arguments was that in a time of recession government had to intervene to break the downward spiral. According to his theory there were no market forces that would automatically come into play to stop the economy shrinking. Keynes believed that low wages and high unemployment conspired to reduce demand in the economy as a whole; and that actions that made good financial sense for an individual company did not necessarily make sense for the wider economy. At a global level, Keynes believed that the depression of the 1930s was caused by individual countries acting selfishly and without regard to the need for international cooperation.

Keynesianism has come to be associated with state intervention in the economy. Although Keynes was a strong proponent of markets and liberty, he also believed that markets could fail and that governments should fine-tune their economies through measures such as keeping money cheap (by setting low interest rates) and investing in public works. Some economists considered his principles to be a charter for labor and a recipe for inflation, and his ideas lost favor during the 1970s and 1980s. However, the world economic depression of the early 1990s is reminiscent of the conditions that faced Keynes in the 1930s. Keynesianism may be set to make a comeback.

A license to print money Workers at the Bureau of Engraving and Printing in Washington DC handle millions of dollars and work within one of the tightest security systems in the world. This machine is banding newly printed $10 bills in stacks for distribution to United States' federal banks.

the system and most were convertible; for example, the citizens and officials of France could exchange francs for dollars at a fixed rate on the open market. The currencies of most developing countries were not convertible in this way, and this was still the case in the early 1990s.

Institutions of economic management

Global economic integration was supported by two international institutions established at Bretton Woods: the International Monetary Fund (IMF) and the International Bank for Reconstruction and Development (IBRD), later the World Bank. The IMF was charged with overseeing international trade and payments, a duty it has shared since 1947 with the committees meeting under the auspices of the General Agreement on Tariffs and Trade (GATT). The IBRD was set up to transfer funds from the United States to western Europe and Japan, both of which were vital markets for American goods.

Between 1947 and 1952 an estimated $700 million was transferred from the United States to the economies of its former allies and enemies through the IBRD. The rebuilding of Europe and Japan was further aided by the Marshall Plan for European Recovery (transfers of $13 billion between 1948 and 1952) and by United States' military budgets overseas during the Korean and Cold wars. In this way, western Europe and Japan were bolstered against communism, and were bound into an economic order that emphasized international exchanges over and above national economic policies.

By the early 1960s the First World was dominant enough to resist the international ambitions of the Soviet Union and the socialist Second World. Henceforth, a major economic battle would be to capture the hearts and minds of the developing Third World. The declared aims of the United Nations Development Decade, announced in 1960–61, enhanced the power and position of the World Bank, which pumped massive amounts of Western aid into Third World countries in a drive toward capitalist modernization. This was a period of economic optimism in which the West expected a developing world economy to unite around fast-growing flows of trade, aid, capital and skilled labor.

Aid and Trade

OFFICIAL DEVELOPMENT ASSISTANCE (OR foreign aid) has always been less important than trade between countries as a means of international economic integration. In relative terms, direct foreign aid reached its heyday in the 1950s and 1960s when it was simply given from one country to another (bilateral aid). During the 1970s and 1980s, aid from multinational institutions such as the World Bank or the European Community (EC) became more important (multilateral aid), supplemented by donations from nongovernmental agencies such as Oxfam.

There are three main reasons why aid is given. One is on a humanitarian impulse, particularly to combat famine or for disaster relief. A second motive is for economic reasons, some of which ultimately benefit the giver. During the 1950s and 1960s, Western governments believed that aid would help Third World economies to develop by providing foreign exchange (meeting the need for hard currencies), funding investment in industry and supplementing the skills of the local workforce with trained expatriate staff. The third reason is political. The geography of aid receipts does not correspond with the geography of need: Israelis have received more aid from the United States than Bangladeshis; Cubans have received more assistance from the Soviet Union than Haitians.

How effective aid is depends on how it is given (mostly in the form of a cheap loan), to whom and for what ends. The aid industry has improved its performance over the years. More aid is now given to rural areas, and local people have more say in how aid is used. Aid in the 1990s also tends to be given at lower interest rates with a longer repayment time than was the case 30 years ago.

A common objection to foreign aid is that it encourages dependency; the same is not supposed to be true of international trade, which is favored as a consequence. Western governments have increasingly promoted international trade alongside foreign aid as a means of stimulating economic development in low-income economies. In principle, free trade expands the international division of labor and encourages different areas or countries to specialize in the goods or services that they can produce relatively efficiently, such as cars in Japan or jute in Bangladesh. This is known as the "principle of comparative advantage".

The theory does not necessarily succeed in practice. In fact, some economists believe that free trade can impoverish developing countries. Although many Third World countries have a "comparative advantage" in resources and nonmanufactured products, the real price of raw materials and food products tends to remain relatively static in the global marketplace. On the other hand, manufactured goods tend to rise in price more quickly, with the result that industrialized countries have a significant trading advantage over developing countries.

Post-war expansion

The arguments for and against free trade are best examined in the context of postwar trading patterns. There was a massive expansion in international trade after the end of World War II, but since 1970, growth rates of world trade and the world

THE MARSHALL PLAN

The European Recovery Program – or Marshall Plan, as it came to be called after its initiator, the American general and statesman George Marshall (1880–1959) – was central to the rebuilding of an open international economy after 1945. Between 1948 and 1952 the United States transferred $13 billion – an estimated 4.5 percent of its gross national product (GNP) – to western Europe. Most of these transfers were in the form of government aid, as opposed to private credits. This ensured that the European countries were not faced with excessive reparation and a crippling deflation. The payments were made on a yearly basis on the condition that recipients made economic and political reforms in line with the United States' vision of a future Free Europe.

The Marshall Plan was only made possible by the defeat of isolationist politicians in the United States at the end of World War II. Its aims were political and ideological as much as economic; one underlying motive was the desire to bind western Europe to the United States and detach it from a burgeoning communism in eastern Europe. The Europeans understood this very well. One official of the British Treasury summed up the intentions of the Marshall Plan as: "The Americans want an integrated Europe looking like the United States of America". In this sense, the Pax Americana paved the way for the formation of the EC.

Distribution of aid *(above)* The map of official aid (excluding military aid) received by each country per head of population vividly illustrates the economic divide between the two hemispheres. South of the Equator only Australia and New Zealand are net donors. Africa is the most dependent on foreign aid.

THE WORLD'S LEADING RECEIVERS OF AID (1990)

	US$ (millions)	as % of GNP
Egypt	5,604	15.9
Bangladesh	2,103	9.2
China	2,076	0.6
Indonesia	1,724	1.6
India	1,586	0.6
Israel	1,374	2.6
Philippines	1,277	2.9
Turkey	1,264	1.2
Tanzania	1,155	48.2
Pakistan	1,152	2.9
Kenya	1,000	11.4
Morocco	970	3.8
Mozambique	946	65.7
Jordan	891	22.8
Ethiopia	888	14.6

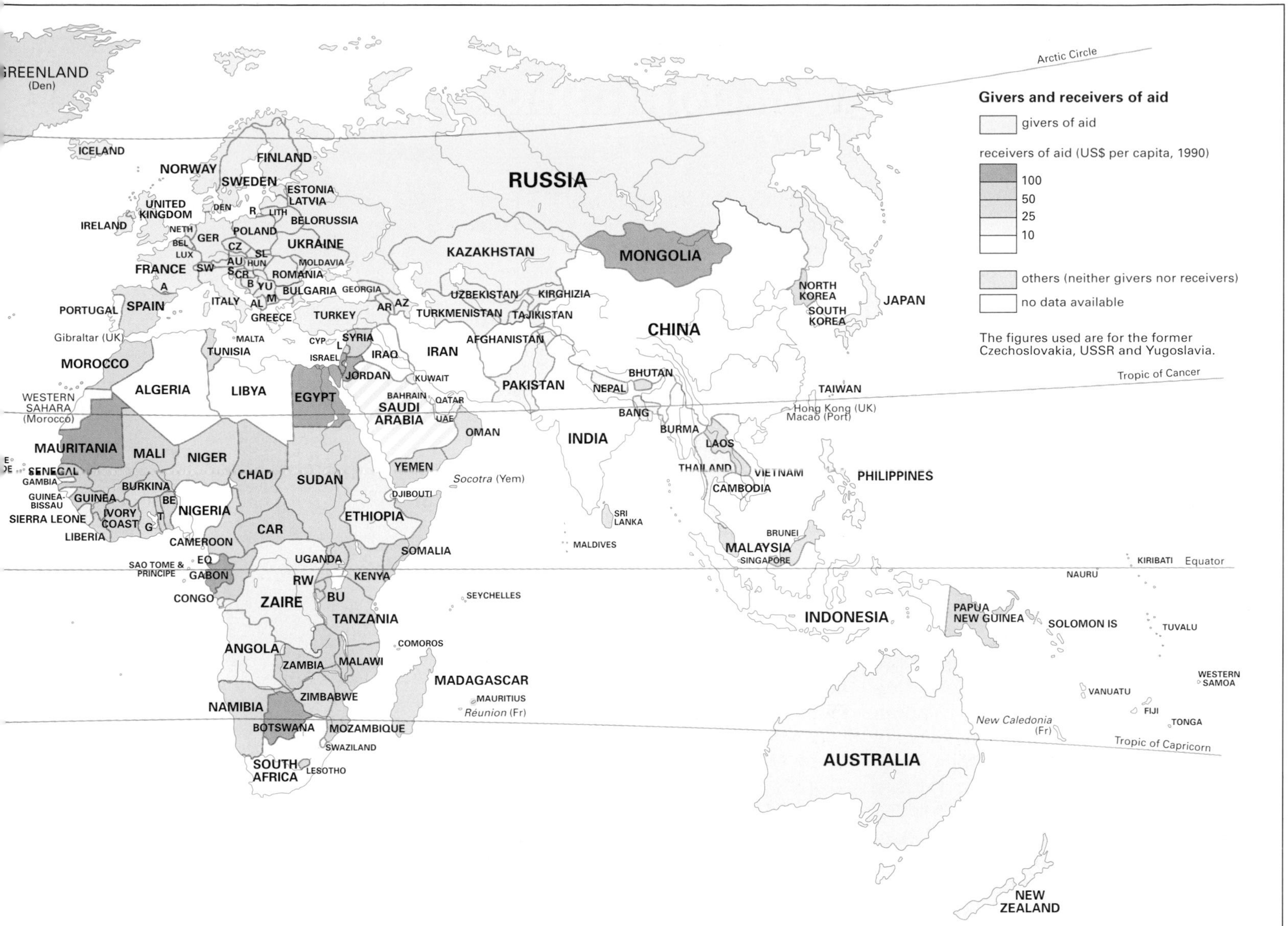

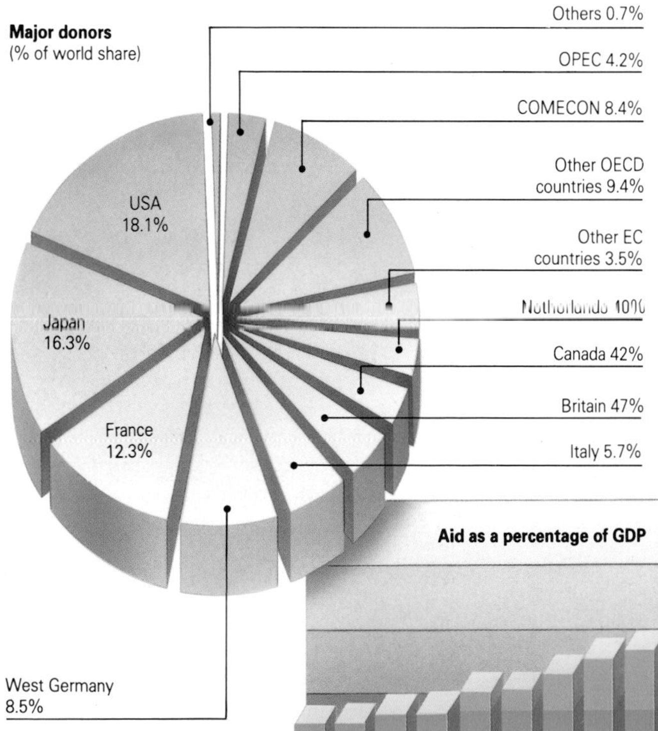

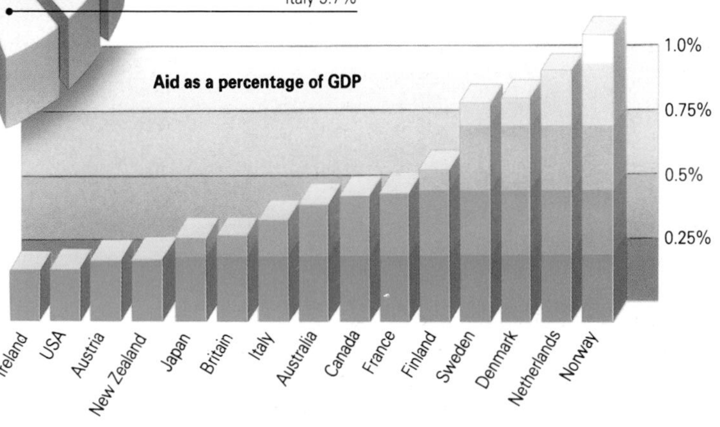

The donor countries *(left and below)* Over 70 percent of all foreign aid is donated by just eight countries: the United States, Japan, France, Germany, Italy, Britain, Canada and the Netherlands. However, the biggest donors are not necessarily the most generous. In 1988 the United States gives less aid as a percentage of the country's GDP than all the other seven countries, and barely more than Ireland. In these terms the northern European countries of Norway, the Netherlands, Denmark and Sweden are the most generous givers of aid.

economy have slowed down. Manufactured goods were by far the fastest growing sector, with a 16-fold increase since 1950. Countries dependent mainly on the production and exchange of foodstuffs and raw materials (except some fuels) did not enjoy such rapid increases in their exports. Not surprisingly, they continue to look to industrialization as the mainspring of development, even if it means protecting their economies in order to build up a manufacturing base.

One of the most significant aspects of the world trading system, and one that does not favor developing countries, is that international trade is still greatest between the developed market economies (about 70 percent of the total). Most of this trade is interindustry (for example, French Renaults exported to Germany, and German Audis exported to France), and an increasing share is between international branches of the same company. A world economy set up in 1944 as a world of trading countries is now more than ever an economy dominated by multinational trading corporations.

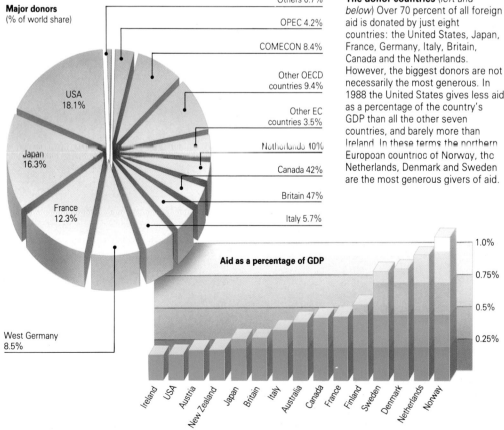

Multinational Corporations

IN THE EARLY 1990S, AN INCREASING SHARE of world trade (about 40 percent) was between branches of giant companies, or multinational corporations (MNCs). Also known as transnational companies, these largescale institutions are usually defined as enterprises that control and manage production in at least two countries. Such corporations, including the automobile giants Ford and General Motors; Mitsubishi, the loose consortium of Japanese companies; or the fuel, chemicals and metals company, Exxon; can operate with scant regard for national boundaries. Today's giant corporations think and act internationally and regularly have a dollar sales revenue that exceeds the gross domestic product (GDP) of all but 15 to 20 countries.

MNCs are not a product of the post-war era, but their scale and significance has expanded greatly since 1945. It has been estimated that 55 overseas subsidiaries of American companies were formed annually from 1946–52, a doubling of the rate in the interwar years. The rate doubled again between 1953 and 1955, until more than 300 new subsidiaries were being set up annually from 1959–62. This was the heyday of American MNCs. Companies such as General Motors, Ford, ITT (communications and defense) and Exxon opened plants throughout western Europe, and to a lesser extent in Japan.

Foreign subsidiaries offered American companies several advantages. European and Japanese markets were growing, and by producing in these markets the companies reduced the expensive transportation costs of exporting. Wages in Europe were lower than in the United States, though this advantage was somewhat offset by lower rates of labor productivity. In addition, because different countries levy different rates of corporate tax, a well-organized MNC can invoice its subsidiaries in such a way that low profits are declared in high tax countries and vice versa. This is known as transfer pricing.

The economic geography of MNC investment became more complex after the 1950s. European and Japanese MNCs began to rival those of the United States. Some MNCs also evolved in the Third World, while established MNCs began a major drive to enter the markets of developing countries. Multinationals including Ford or General Motors moved some of their operations to countries such as Mexico and Brazil to take advantage of cheaper labor and new domestic markets. Ford also serviced its new range of "global cars" – especially the Ford Escort – from such countries. This gave the corporation flexibility if workers became militant at another location, be it Detroit, Michigan in the United States or Dagenham in England. A major reason for MNC investment in the Third World was to escape the power of trade unions in the advanced industrial countries.

General Electric in Mexico This United States-owned domestic stove factory provides stable employment for hundreds of Mexican workers. Although accused of exploiting local labor, multinationals also help to stimulate the economy in developing countries.

Givers or takers?

MNC involvement in foreign economies is often controversial. Politicians and labor leaders are sometimes mistrustful of foreign direct investment in their economies. For example, there has been some resistance to Japan's investment in the automobile industries of western Europe and the United States. Often domestic

Japanese invaders Colorful ranks of Nissan trucks at one of the company's American plants in Tennessee. More popular and competitive than domestic manufacturers, the Japanese automobile giants are moving in their own production plants.

companies are damaged by the competition, especially if the high value-added activities of research and design are lost to the headquarters of the incoming companies. There are also fears that national economies will become dependent on managerial decisions taken by non-nationals in faraway locations. This is one of the principal objections to foreign MNCs in Third World countries, together with accusations of exploitation of local labor. MNC investment in the developing world has also been associated with the introduction of inappropriate products and technologies such as cigarettes or baby-milk powders.

Set against these arguments are others that emphasize the important contributions made by MNC investment in the host economy. They create new employment opportunities, and often pay higher wages than local companies, particularly in the Third World. MNCs also create exports, helping to improve the host country's balance-of-payments position. Finally, most MNCs make use of local suppliers and create local "multiplier effects" in the host economy (increasing employment and thereby generating more spending power and tax revenue). Japanese car firms in Britain, for example, have agreed to purchase up to 80 percent of their parts and components from companies based in Britain.

In short, the effects of individual MNCs on host economies vary widely. Some do take advantage of weak national governments – mining companies in Black Africa are often quoted as examples. Others will act more reasonably. Faced with competent governments, they are forced to strike bargains which can be to the advantage of all concerned.

Producer Power and Third Worldism

GIANT CORPORATIONS ARE NOT THE ONLY powerful players in the world economy. Some nation-states wield enormous influence, as do multinational economic groupings such as the Organization for Economic Cooperation and Development (OECD) and the G7 and G3 groups, which represent the world's most powerful economies. The G7 countries are the United States, Germany, Japan, the United Kingdom, France, Italy and Canada; the G3 countries are the United States, Germany and Japan. These countries dominate the meetings of the World Bank, the IMF and GATT (General Agreement on Tariffs and Trade) and set the agenda for new developments in the world economy. For example, the world's most important interest rates are set by the governments and banks of these countries. In Europe, key interest and exchange rates are also set within the terms of the European Monetary System. A pan-European currency might be in use by the turn of the century.

The United Nations Conference on Trade and Development (UNCTAD) is the major forum for Third World countries. The concept of a "Third World" was first embraced at the Bandung Conference of African and Asian countries in 1955. This gathering emphasized that developing countries have different priorities from both the capitalist First World and the socialist Second World, and agreed to take collective action on economic and political issues of common concern. For example, many developing countries are heavily dependent on one major product – tea in Sri Lanka, cotton in Sudan. As the global price of tea or cotton fluctuates sharply in response to climatic and other

The world's wealth (*above*) distributed geographically according to the four major income bands used by the World Bank. Countries are classified according to their gross national product per capita, which is generally regarded as the best indication of all-round economic strength. The high-income economies, predictably the developed Western nations, exert a powerful influence over the workings of the world economic system, especially through international organizations such as the World Bank and the IMF.

King Cotton (*left*) Bales of Sudanese cotton ready for ginning (removing the cotton fiber from the seeds). Cotton accounts for over 50 percent of Sudan's export earnings. Such heavy reliance on one commodity makes the economy very vulnerable to unfavorable climatic conditions, fluctuating prices or decline in global demand. This problem is common to many developing countries, which are pressing for higher, more stable world prices for their vital commodity exports.

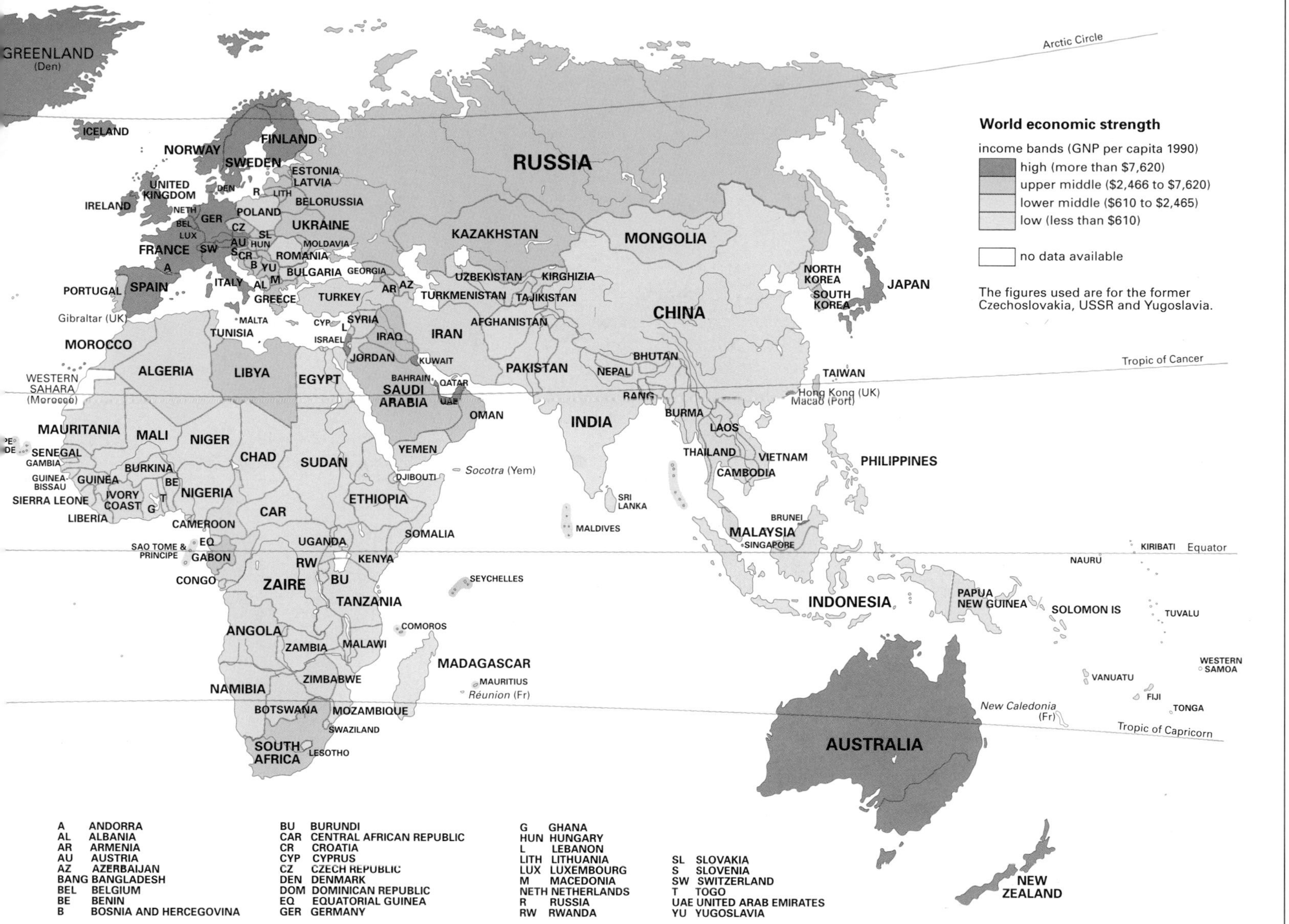

factors, economic planning is extremely difficult. Consequently, Third World demands have concentrated on achieving higher prices for their commodity exports and stabilizing the international market prices of raw materials.

The major forum for voicing these concerns was and remains UNCTAD. The first meeting was held in Geneva in 1964. At that time the Third World was represented by a caucus group of 77 countries. Later the group expanded to more than 120 countries. UNCTAD II was held in New Delhi in 1968, and UNCTAD III in Santiago, Chile in 1972.

The unequal balance of power

Third World producer power became more visible in the 1970s, when the developing countries pressed for a Charter of Economic Rights and Duties of States. This was intended to remind the developed countries of their obligations to poorer ex-colonies, and to provide some protection against the allegedly exploitative actions of MNCs. Third World countries wanted the right to nationalize some MNC operations or to receive guarantees over issues such as workers' rights, supply chains or taxation levies. Some of these demands were later incorporated into the Declaration on the Establishment of a New International Economic Order (NIEO), which was adopted without a vote at a special session of the United Nations (UN) General Assembly in 1974. The NIEO suggested a series of reforms to international trading and monetary systems, particularly greater stability in world commodity prices, increases in international aid transfers, regulation of technology transfers from the First World to the Third World and an increase of Third World influence within the IMF.

This last demand reflects a major problem facing the Third World. While Third World declarations usually pass easily through the UN (which has a one country, one vote system) the organization has no real influence on the world economy. Rather, power rests with large economic organizations such as the World Bank and IMF, where voting power is roughly proportional to the size of the subscription its members pay. Major subscribers, such as the United States, are therefore able to exercise considerable influence over policy-making. Furthermore, international economic conditions are established largely by the policies and actions of the G7 countries. If these countries are suffering from recession, the rest of the world suffers too.

Developing countries are not entirely powerless, especially when they can control the supply of a commodity much in demand in the West. For example, between 1973 and 1974 the Organization of Petroleum Exporting Countries (OPEC) caused the price of oil to almost quadruple, threatening oil-importing countries with recession and severe pressure on their balance of payments. The world economy was kept afloat mainly through a rapid recycling of OPEC's oil revenues (petrodollars) through the international banking system.

THE WORLD ECONOMY AT WORK/5

Banks, Money and International Finance

WHEN MOST PEOPLE THINK OF A MULTI-national corporation they call to mind a huge industrial enterprise such as the British- and Dutch-based company Unilever (producing household goods such as detergents) or the Japanese consortium Mitsubishi. However, big international banks are also MNCs of equal – if not greater – importance. Money-center banks such as Citibank or Chase Manhattan expanded massively in the 1960s and 1970s, returning rates of profit that were the envy of their industrial counterparts. Today, the dividing line between banks and other kinds of multinationals is less clear-cut. General Motors, for example, earns a sizable proportion of its income from financial activities. This income derives not only from automobile financing operations, but also from the American mortgage market where the corporation is a major trader. Pension funds are also important players in the modern world economy, together with savings and loan associations, building societies and insurance companies.

Changes in the structure of the financial services industry mirror wider changes in the postwar world economy, which became less regulated after 1970. For example, in the 1950s most banks operated within national boundaries: Citibank was an American bank; Barclays was a British bank, and so on. National governments could quite closely regulate the activities of "their" banks by influencing the rates of interest a bank could charge on its loans, or by requiring all banks within their jurisdiction to hold reserves at the country's central bank. If part of a bank's monetary base is on reserve, it can make fewer loans. Such a system allowed governments to exercise effective control over the domestic money supply.

Cambodia's link to the world economy *(above)* The Foreign Trade Bank in the capital Phnom Penh is an essential link to the international marketplace for this otherwise isolated and troubled state.

Solid banking *(right)* International financial houses dominate the skyline in Miami, now the banking capital of Central America as well as of the state of Florida. Authorities suspect that much of the profits from illegal drug dealing are lodged here, mixed with the profits from legitimate enterprise.

Offshore banking

Most large banks were unhappy with government controls in the postwar period. During the 1960s American banks began to circumvent the country's banking legislation by setting up branches overseas; this was known as moving offshore. These offshore deposits (usually counted as "Eurodollars", whether they were dollars outside the United States, or yen outside Japan) were gratefully accepted by most banks, precisely because they were not subject to national banking regulations. Banks were able to make loans on the basis of their Eurodollar accounts according to their own estimations of customers' credit status and ability to repay. Consequently, the offshore banking business expanded rapidly during the 1970s. These stateless funds grew three times more quickly than official reserves, with the result that international money markets and banks took over from governments as the main sources of international liquidity.

It was into this new banking system that OPEC's petrodollars were poured during the mid 1970s when oil prices rose dramatically. United States' and European banks on-lent the petrodollars, particularly to Latin American countries (Argentina, Brazil, Mexico and Venezuela) which were considered to be good credit risks. The loans had to be serviced or repaid in hard currencies at the prevailing rate of interest. Most loans were made for 5–7 years, whereas foreign aid loans are usually repayable over a 20–25 year period.

International banks made huge profits

THE IMF – IMPOSING MISERY AND FAMINE?

The original Articles of Agreement of the International Monetary Fund (IMF) were drafted at the 1944 Bretton Woods Conference, and the Fund began operations in April 1946 with a membership of 38 countries. Although the Articles of Agreement have been amended, the broad objectives of the IMF remain the same. It aims to promote international monetary cooperation; expand the balanced growth of international trade; and reduce inequalities in the international balance of payments of member countries. Since 1969 the IMF has sponsored the Special Drawing Right (SDR) as a new unit of international account. SDRs, together with the national currency and other reserve assets, make up a country's subscription to the IMF. Voting rights in the IMF vary according to the size of a country's subscription, with the result that the United States, Germany and Japan are able to outvote the remaining 150 or more countries which are now members of the IMF.

The IMF has contributed to international economic stability, but it has become an unpopular institution in some parts of the world. The fund has powers over debtor and deficit countries, but has no effective powers over countries that are in surplus on their balance of payments. This means that the IMF is frequently in conflict with developing countries, particularly since the international debt crisis of the 1980s. In return for rescheduling private or official debt, it has imposed "Structural Adjustment" programs that usually involve swingeing cuts in domestic public spending, devaluation, deregulation and efforts to improve export performance. These measures can impose great hardship on local populations. In some African countries, IMF is said to stand for "Imposing Misery and Famine".

from these activities. For example, Citibank earned 70 percent of its profits in the late 1970s from international operations, with 20 percent deriving from loans to Brazil alone. Nevertheless, the Eurodollar system, in which banks are free to make as many loans as they wish, is not without risk. The system is relatively stable when the world economy is healthy, but it can break down when borrowers are unable to repay their loans. This was what happened in many Latin American countries in the 1980s.

The International Debt Crisis

THE PRIVATE BANKING SYSTEM THAT HAD been expanding internationally since the end of World War II was thrown into disarray in August 1982 when Mexico defaulted on its loans. A gathering debt crisis was already apparent by this time. A number of African countries had been forced to reschedule their debt repayments in the late 1970s and early 1980s, but most of these debts were owed to official creditors such as the World Bank. The large Mexican default, and subsequent defaults in Brazil (1983), Venezuela (1983) and Peru (1985) threatened the stability of the big 10 United States' commercial banks, which found themselves contending with an international debt crisis on a massive scale. By the end of 1990 Western commercial banks were still owed $350 billion by debtor countries in the developing world.

Wealthy nations deep in debt (*above right*) Considered on a world scale, the debts of African, and even some South American, countries are dwarfed by those of the developed world. The essential difference is that the West has substantial assets as well as liabilities, and can easily service its debts.

The human cost (*left*) Almost unnoticed by passers-by, a homeless family begs on the streets of Salvador in eastern Brazil. Like other countries defaulting on international debts, Brazil was required to make massive cuts in public spending as part of austerity programs imposed by creditors. Housing and welfare services were the first to be cut, with harsh consequences for the needy.

How did it happen?

There is disagreement over the causes of the international debt crisis. Some believe that the banks themselves were to blame by lending unwisely during the loan-crazy years of the 1970s, when they had cash surpluses from the oil-producing countries to recycle. Others blame the debtor countries. It is significant that not all developing countries defaulted on their loans. For example, though South Korea was the developing world's fourth largest debtor in 1984, good economic

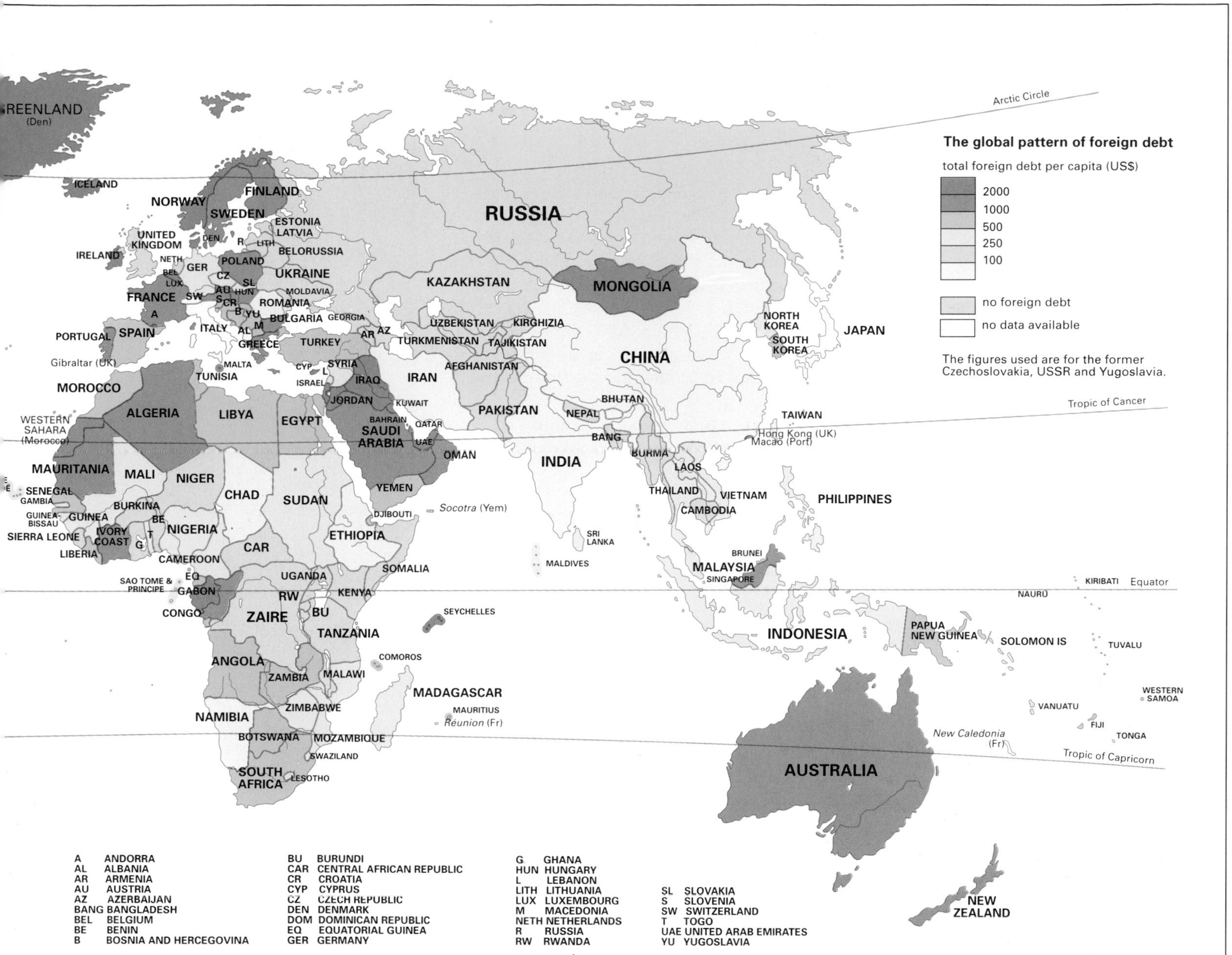

management ensured that the country met its debt repayments. Other developing countries did not manage their economies so well, and there have been accusations that loans were squandered on unviable projects, such as roads to nowhere in the Amazon jungle.

Although elements of both these arguments are true, neither gives the full picture. The debt crisis was also sparked by a downturn in international economic conditions between 1979 and 1983 which moved the world into its most severe recession since the 1930s. Real interest rates more than doubled during this period, just as commodity prices plummeted due to declining export markets in the West. The developing countries were caught in a two-way economic squeeze that was not of their own making.

Governments and banks responded to the debt crisis in three main ways. From 1982–85 the principal aim was to safeguard the international banking system. Loans to developing countries were rescheduled on condition that they took steps to boost their export earnings and cut domestic public spending. The introduction of the Baker Plan in 1985 promised to link economic reforms (structural adjustment) in the developing world to faster economic growth in the OECD world economy, allowing countries to grow out of debt. Since 1988 the Brady Plan has adopted a more pragmatic approach. Some banks have written off loans as bad debts. Other debts have been traded on the secondary debt market, often at a steep discount, and some have been swapped for equity or stakes in local nature reserves.

These measures brought the international debt crisis under control, albeit at massive cost to the debtor countries. Most households in Latin America were poorer in 1990 than they were in 1980; in sub-Saharan Africa the comparison is with 1960. Austerity measures imposed as part of IMF adjustment programs meant that education and health budgets have been slashed in some debtor countries, further threatening the process of development that the loans were intended to support. Moreover, there are signs that the debt crisis is spreading. India is now a major debtor, as is Eastern Europe and the former Soviet Union. Meanwhile, the biggest debtor of all is the United States. It owes foreign creditors approximately $1 trillion – or about as much as all the Third World debtors combined. The United States is, however, very unlikely to default on its debts.

The banks branch out

It seems that the world economy in the 1990s is built on credit, perhaps to a dangerous extent. Only the banks are happy with this situation, and then not wholeheartedly. In the mid 1980s the big commercial banks began to move away from lending to governments and back into sizable loans to businesses and home-buyers. The commercial banks have also diversified, becoming active in the financial services markets that had previously been the preserve of the merchant or investment banks.

Changing Ideologies

IN THE 1950s AND 1960s MOST GOVERNMENTS believed that they should intervene in the national economy to achieve certain goals, including full employment in the industrialized countries and development in the Third World. Such Keynesian doctrines were superseded by more free-market polices during the late 1970s and 1980s. The economies of the former socialist countries have undergone even more rapid changes in favor of market forces. By the early 1990s, only China retained a largescale socialist economy.

Detailed economic regulation along Keynesian (interventionist) lines seemed to make sense in the early postwar decades. Many economies had been seriously damaged by war and by the fiercely competitive pre-war policies of economic nationalism. Unemployment was a major blight; even those who were employed were often too poor to buy the products rolling off the assembly lines.

Western leaders considered the situation both economically depressive and politically dangerous. In a bid to make socialism less attractive to their workers,

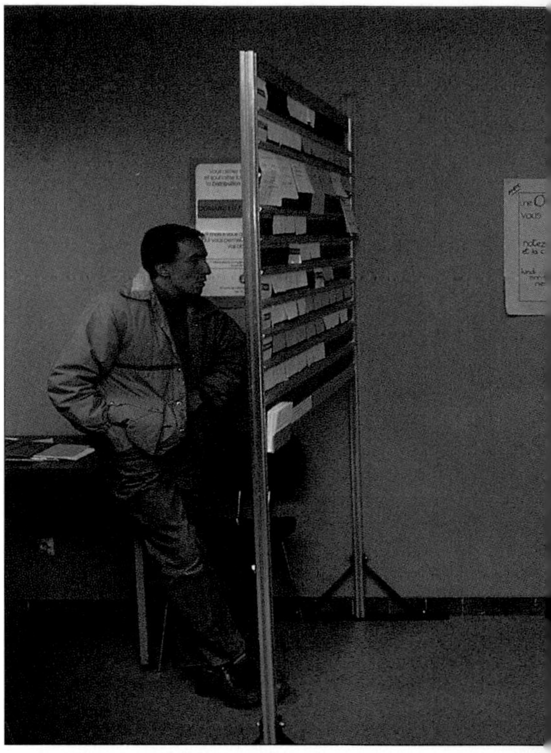

Victims of market forces (*right*) Young men anxiously search for work at a job center in France. Rising unemployment in Europe has prompted calls for a return to greater state intervention in the economy.

The free market at work (*below*) Traders do business in ordered chaos at a mercantile exchange in Chicago. Belief in self-regulating free markets underpinned the Reagan boom years of the 1980s when massive profits were made in this kind of trading.

most Western governments committed themselves to a policy of full employment. They put people to work directly through an expansion of public-sector industries, or indirectly by supporting the private sector. Workers – through their trade unions – negotiated annual wage settlements with their employers and the government, and as long as these deals were struck at reasonable levels, inflation was kept under control. Economic policies at this time expected rising wages (in real terms) to be paid for by increased labor productivity. Governments could then fine-tune the economy by raising taxes and interest rates in a boom and cutting them in a recession. Finally, the welfare state would care for those unable to provide for themselves through pensions, unemployment benefit, subsidized healthcare and education.

Keynesian economics worked well for 25 years after World War II, which is regarded by many as the golden age of Western capitalism. Unemployment and inflation were low, and ordinary people shared in the bounties of a modernizing industrial system. By 1960 most Americans owned a car, a house and any number of "white goods" (refrigerators, washing machines, and cookers).

MONETARISM

Monetarism was popularized in the 1970s and 1980s by the American economist Milton Friedman. He identified inflation as the major threat to the efficient working of a capitalist economy, because it distorts relative prices and erodes savings. Friedman also believed that the level of prices (or inflation) in an economy is determined directly by the rate of growth of the money supply. Governments that print or borrow money in excess of the real rate of growth are, therefore, bound to create inflation a few years later.

Aspects of monetarism were adopted by many Western governments during the 1980s, especially those of a right-wing persuasion. They published targets for the rate of growth of the money supply and promised to abide by these targets. For example, if the money supply was targeted to grow by 5 percent in a given year, and labor demanded pay increases of over 5 percent, these demands would be resisted. Workers were expected to form new expectations about the rate of inflation and to put forward more realistic pay demands. Having placed money on a sound footing, governments expected market forces to revive the economy.

New directions

However, by the 1970s the world economy was beginning to falter. The Third World wanted to develop its own industries and became less willing to supply the First World with cheap food, fuel and raw materials. Western workers, too, had become more militant, and there was a sharp increase in the number of industrial stoppages. Above all, inflation began to rise, threatening economic stability and the security of people's savings.

By 1980, new economic and political leaders – notably the United States' President Reagan, West Germany's Chancellor Kohl and Britain's Prime Minister Margaret Thatcher – had come to power determined to make money "sound" again, and to free their economies of government red tape. Their market-led economic policies were designed to encourage an expansion of the private sector and reduce the power of the trade unions; many countries embarked on largescale privatizations of their public sector activities during the 1980s. Monetarism became fashionable, along with an increasing emphasis on the supply side of the economy (encouraging workers to be productive and entrepreneurs to be entrepreneurial). These governments also put their faith in lower direct taxes and in self-regulating free market forces. Direct government control of the economy was substantially reduced as decisions regarding production and distribution were left to private individuals and firms – the state as nanny was a thing of the past.

There may yet be a backlash since markets create instabilities of their own. Those without power and money do not come to the marketplace as equals and some are left unprotected in a market economy. During the late 1980s and early 1990s, there were signs that a balance was being struck between Keynesian and market-led policies. The EC combines a free market with a social chapter that protects the rights of workers; and the Exchange Rate Mechanism (ERM) is reviving a system of fixed (or partially fixed) exchange rates. Even at the world level, the role of the free market is being reduced in the 1990s. The G3 and G7 countries regularly meet to coordinate their economic policies.

The Wealth of Nations

THE WORLD ECONOMY HAS CHANGED greatly since 1945 – this simple fact is evident in the way we talk about the world economy and its constituent parts. In the 1950s and the 1960s people generally spoke of a developed First World, a socialist Second World and an underdeveloped Third World. This obscured certain important distinctions between France and Japan, say, or India and China, but the broad distinctions were not hard to draw. Today, this is no longer the case. In its World Development Report (1992), the World Bank highlighted 41 Low-Income Economies (including separate information on India and China), 43 Lower-Middle-Income Economies, 17 Upper-Middle-Income Economies, 24 High-Income Economies and provided additional information on the OECD economies.

This classification confirms the growing complexity of the world economic system. Even a simple ranking of countries in terms of wealth can be misleading. For example, there are often pockets of poverty in rich countries and pockets of affluence in poor ones. Some of the urban areas of southern New Delhi in India are well-to-do by any standards, while the south Bronx and south-central Los Angeles areas of the United States have become symbols of urban degradation and social disadvantage within the developed world.

Nevertheless, it is possible to identify some broad geographical patterns in world wealth and poverty. The richest nations are mainly the advanced industrial powers of North America, Japan, Australia and Europe, whereas two-thirds of the population of the poorest countries live in India and China. Absolute poverty is also widespread throughout South Asia, due to the density of the population. Famine, by contrast, mostly affects sub-Saharan Africa, though even here the picture is far from uniform: the economies of Cameroon and Zimbabwe performed relatively well during the 1970s and 1980s.

Room for growth

The World Bank classifies a country's wealth by assessing its gross national product (GNP). GNP is calculated by adding the country's gross domestic product (GDP; the income earned by total

Breaking the stereotype (*right*) A mobile phone is a recent accessory for this young Mongolian businessman. The luxury of his traditionally designed yurt (tent) is in sharp contrast, but together they indicate significant wealth in pockets of this relatively poor region.

Abandoned by progress (*below*) This desolate urban wasteland in the south Bronx district of New York City is more reminiscent of the Third World than the greatest economic power on earth. Inner-city poverty has become a major blight in many of the United States' wealthiest areas.

domestic output and services) to net income earned from abroad by residents of the country. GNP is usually divided by the total population to show how much is earned on average by each resident of the country. According to 1990 data Low-Income Economies had a GNP per capita below $610; Lower-Middle-Income Economies had a GNP between $610 and $2,465; Upper-Middle-Income Economies between $2,466 and $7,619; and High-Income Economies above $7,620.

There are huge variations in GNP per capita throughout the world. For example, in 1990 the average GNP per capita in Switzerland was $32,680 compared with just $80 in Mozambique. Although the incomes of most people in most countries have probably increased in real terms since the 1950s, the gap between very rich and very poor countries continues to widen.

The outlook for poorer countries is not uniformly bleak. World Bank figures suggest that as many as 60 countries have climbed out of the low-income category since the end of World War II, though some have only just managed to make the transition: Angola's per capita income of $610 in 1989 allowed it to scrape into the next category up. Other countries have made more rapid progress. In 1990 Singapore's per capita income of $11,160 was higher than Spain's of $11,020, and the average income in South Korea was in excess of $5,300. Although this is still some way below the average income of $19,590 in the high-income countries, the relative gap between them is closing fast.

The rapid rise of Japan as an economic power since World War II is one of the most powerful indications of an increasingly diversified world economy. Japan is the second most powerful economy in the world and its citizens enjoyed an average per capita income in 1990 of $25,430. The rise of Japan also indicates that the "West" can no longer be used as another term for the First World. The center of gravity of the world economy is shifting from the Atlantic region to the Pacific basin, just as it is shifting in composition from individual countries to firms and markets. In the 1950s it was convenient to talk of a clear First World and a clear Third World. At the end of the millenium it is more accurate to refer to a staircase of economic wealth, which links cities, regions and countries in an interdependent world economy.

The Welfare of Nations

ECONOMIC INDICATORS SUCH AS GDP OR GNP per capita do not necessarily tell us very much about overall standards of living in different countries; there is often a significant difference between a country's rate of economic growth and its level of development. For example, Kuwait has a higher GNP per capita than the Netherlands, though the Netherlands is the more developed country. Kuwait's prosperity is based on large oil reserves that benefit only a very small section of the population; access to social services such as healthcare, housing and education is very limited compared with the Netherlands. At the other end of the scale, Mozambique may not be quite as badly off as its GNP suggests, as this measure often undervalues the contributions of subsistence farmers and people involved in household production.

The World Bank and other economic agencies have tried to take account of these anomalies by designing more accurate indicators of economic development. In 1991 the United Nations Development Program produced a survey of the world based on a Human Development Index (HDI). The HDI adjusts per capita incomes to take account of three variables: local purchasing power, life expectancy at birth, and educational standards (the average number of years spent at school and literacy levels). A country's final HDI is a weighted average score of the three variables expressed as a value between 0 and 1. In 1990, Japan scored the highest on this scale (0.993) followed by Canada and Iceland (0.983), and then by Sweden and Switzerland (0.982 and 0.981 respectively). Countries scoring over 0.8 are considered to have high human development, those scoring between 0.5 and 0.8 have medium human development and those scoring under 0.5 have low human development.

The unequal distribution of rights

The HDI is not a foolproof welfare indicator. Although it offers some insights into the disparities between economic growth and development, there are significant social factors that it fails to take into account. For example, if respect for human rights had been included in the HDI calculations, it is likely that Albania and China's scores would have been lower. On the other hand, China's score might have improved if the HDI had included an assessment of the position of women within society.

Despite rapid economic development throughout the world since World War II, women still perform roughly two-third's of the world's work for one-third of the pay, and own less than 1 percent of the world's property. Even in the "developed" world, the citizenship rights of women are not always equal in practice to those of men. Women are often paid less than men for doing the same job, are more likely to be employed on a part-time basis and frequently have to combine domestic work with waged labor.

Map of the Human Development Index *(above)* By combining economic statistics with healthcare and education factors, the HDI aims to provide a more comprehensive indication of basic standards of living around the world. The highest possible score is 1.

Next time lucky? *(right)* American FBI agents arrest Mexicans crossing the border illegally to get into the United States. Many would-be immigrants from Latin America are so desperate to enter the "land of opportunity" that they make repeated – sometimes dangerous – attempts.

Migrant workers in developed countries, such as the Turkish community in Germany, sometimes also lack full economic citizenship rights, such as pensions, holiday pay or sick leave. The plight of migrant workers in western Europe is likely to become more acute as a result of largescale migration from Eastern Europe and the former Soviet Union following the collapse of these socialist economies. The border between Mexico and the United States is another pressure point in a divided world economy. Although world trade is now more open than ever before, the free movement of people from one country to another is still restricted by policies of economic nationalism.

THE WIDENING GAP

Although most developing countries have made economic progress since 1950, the gap in global opportunities between the very rich countries and the very poor countries continues to widen. According to the United Nations Development Programme (UNDP), the richest 20 percent of the world's population had a joint income 30 times as great as the joint income of the poorest 20 percent of the world's population in 1960. This ratio widened to 32:1 in 1970, to 45:1 in 1980 and to 59:1 in 1989.

To put it another way, between 1960 and 1989, the countries with the richest 20 percent of the world's population increased their share of the world GNP from 70.2 percent to 82.7 percent. During the same period The countries with the poorest 20 percent of the world's population saw their share of global GNP fall from 2.3 percent to 1.4 percent.

These disparities are further amplified by uneven distributions of wealth within individual countries. Although not one of the world's very poor countries, Brazil in South America provides a worrying example of this kind of inequality. In Brazil, the richest 20 percent of the population receives a joint income 26 times as great as the income of the poorest 20 percent of the Brazilian population. Given that poor Brazilians typically suffer a lack of access to education and healthcare (and sometimes human and civil rights), it is not surprising that Brazil stands 37th in the World Bank's league table of countries based on per capita incomes, but only 59th in the Human Development Index league table designed by the UNDP.

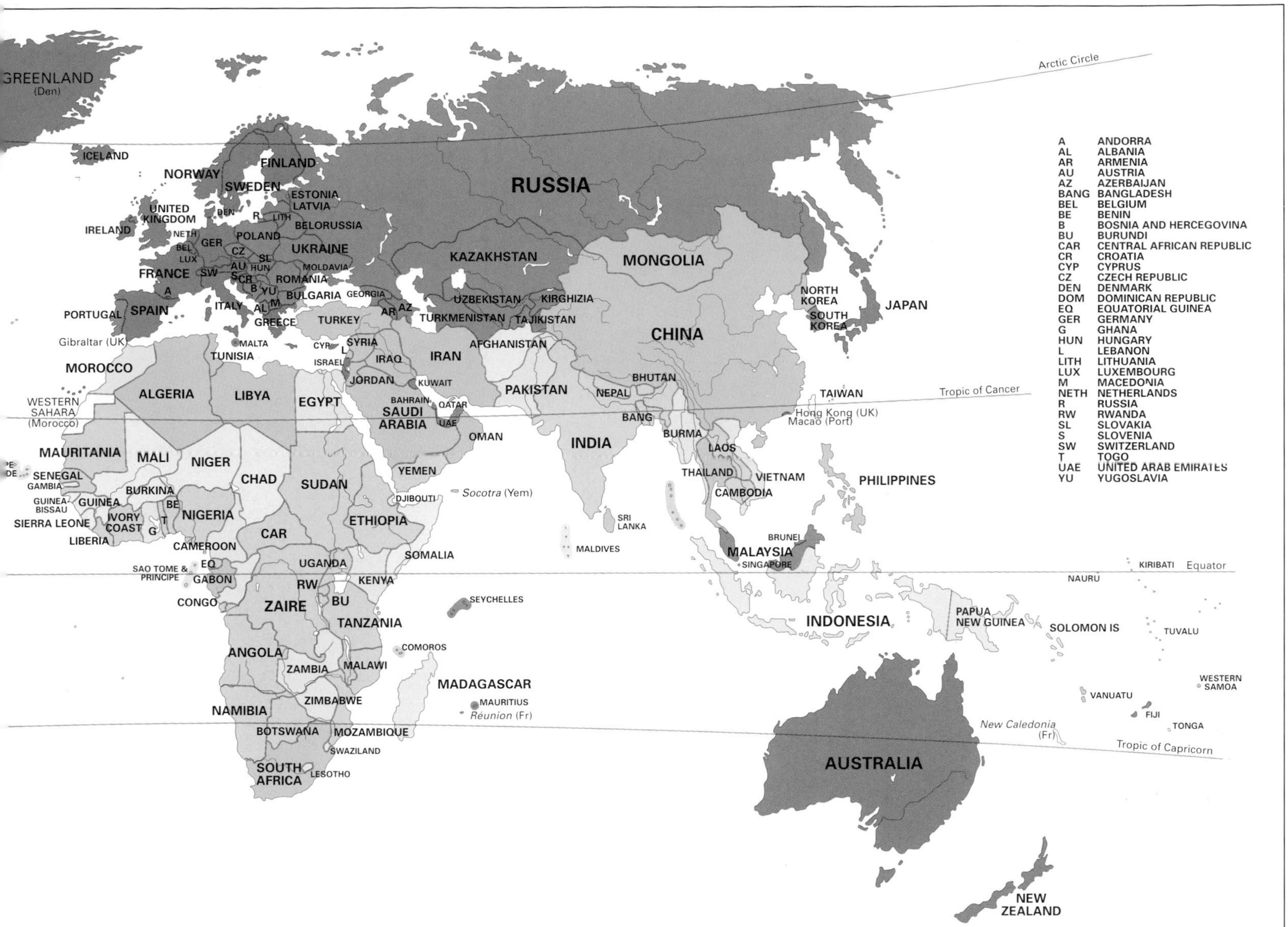

GREENLAND (Den)
Arctic Circle
ICELAND
NORWAY
FINLAND
SWEDEN
RUSSIA
ESTONIA
LATVIA
UNITED KINGDOM
DEN
LITH
BELORUSSIA
IRELAND
NETH
GER
POLAND
BEL
LUX
CZ
SL
UKRAINE
KAZAKHSTAN
MONGOLIA
FRANCE
SW
AU
HUN
MOLDAVIA
ROMANIA
A
SCR
B
YU
BULGARIA
GEORGIA
PORTUGAL
SPAIN
ITALY
AL
M
AR
AZ
UZBEKISTAN
KIRGHIZIA
NORTH KOREA
JAPAN
GREECE
TURKEY
TURKMENISTAN
TAJIKISTAN
SOUTH KOREA
CHINA
Gibraltar (UK)
MALTA
CYP
L
SYRIA
IRAQ
IRAN
AFGHANISTAN
TUNISIA
ISRAEL
MOROCCO
JORDAN
KUWAIT
BHUTAN
ALGERIA
LIBYA
EGYPT
BAHRAIN
QATAR
PAKISTAN
NEPAL
TAIWAN
Tropic of Cancer
WESTERN SAHARA (Morocco)
SAUDI ARABIA
UAE
BANG
Hong Kong (UK)
Macao (Port)
OMAN
INDIA
BURMA
MAURITANIA
MALI
NIGER
LAOS
SENEGAL
GAMBIA
CHAD
SUDAN
YEMEN
THAILAND
VIETNAM
PHILIPPINES
GUINEA-BISSAU
GUINEA
BURKINA
BE
NIGERIA
DJIBOUTI
Socotra (Yem)
CAMBODIA
SIERRA LEONE
IVORY COAST
G
T
ETHIOPIA
SRI LANKA
LIBERIA
CAR
CAMEROON
SOMALIA
MALDIVES
BRUNEI
MALAYSIA
SINGAPORE
SAO TOME & PRINCIPE
EQ
GABON
UGANDA
KENYA
KIRIBATI
Equator
NAURU
CONGO
RW
BU
ZAIRE
SEYCHELLES
TANZANIA
INDONESIA
PAPUA NEW GUINEA
SOLOMON IS
TUVALU
ANGOLA
COMOROS
ZAMBIA
MALAWI
MADAGASCAR
WESTERN SAMOA
VANUATU
NAMIBIA
ZIMBABWE
MAURITIUS
Réunion (Fr)
FIJI
BOTSWANA
MOZAMBIQUE
New Caledonia (Fr)
TONGA
Tropic of Capricorn
SWAZILAND
AUSTRALIA
SOUTH AFRICA
LESOTHO
NEW ZEALAND
A ANDORRA
AL ALBANIA
AR ARMENIA
AU AUSTRIA
AZ AZERBAIJAN
BANG BANGLADESH
BEL BELGIUM
BE BENIN
B BOSNIA AND HERCEGOVINA
BU BURUNDI
CAR CENTRAL AFRICAN REPUBLIC
CR CROATIA
CYP CYPRUS
CZ CZECH REPUBLIC
DEN DENMARK
DOM DOMINICAN REPUBLIC
EQ EQUATORIAL GUINEA
GER GERMANY
G GHANA
HUN HUNGARY
L LEBANON
LITH LITHUANIA
LUX LUXEMBOURG
M MACEDONIA
NETH NETHERLANDS
R RUSSIA
RW RWANDA
SL SLOVAKIA
S SLOVENIA
SW SWITZERLAND
T TOGO
UAE UNITED ARAB EMIRATES
YU YUGOSLAVIA

Health and Social Services

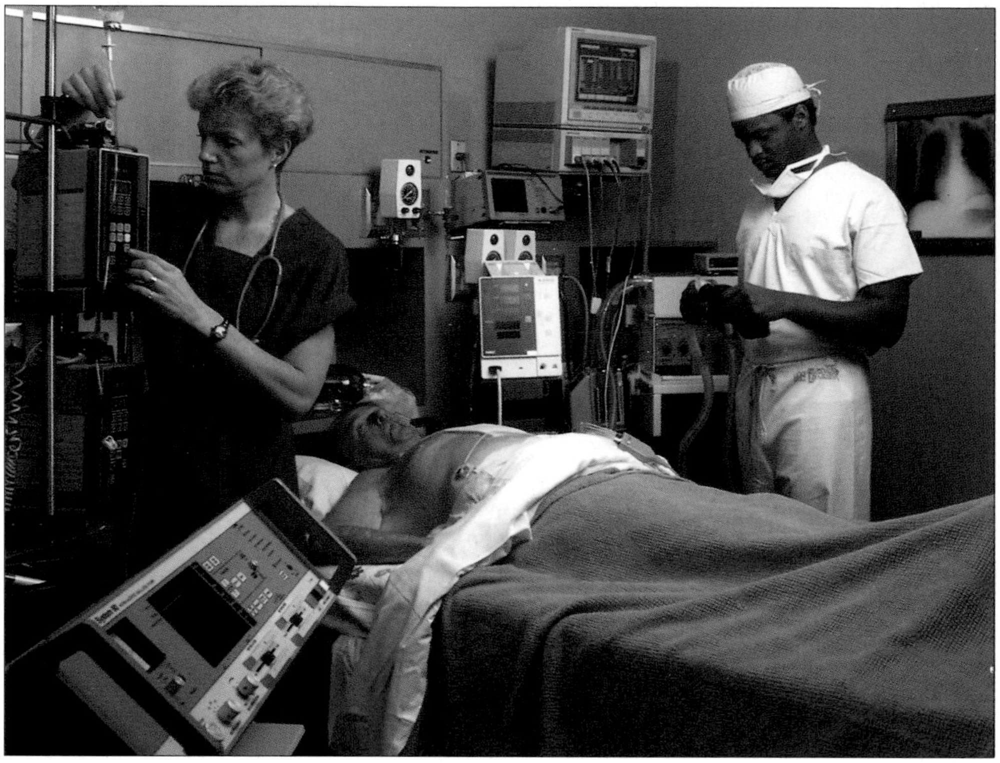

The cost of care *(above)* Western healthcare relies on sophisticated equipment and highly skilled staff. The rising costs of providing these services are usually met by the taxpayer, except in countries such as the United States, which has a mainly private system funded by health insurance.

Bare necessities *(right)* Health workers distribute food, medicine and clothing to flood victims in Bangladesh. The scant welfare resources in developing countries are often supplemented by charitable organizations.

THE WELFARE OF A COUNTRY'S POPULATION is not only determined by the state of its economy. It is also affected by the systems through which healthcare, education and other social services are made available. Such systems vary widely from country to country and may offer strikingly different opportunities to social groups on the basis of income, age, sex, race or religion.

Welfare systems are in place in all the industrialized countries, though the range of benefits varies. In some countries, such as Germany, there is extensive provision for job retraining for the unemployed, whereas in others this is weakly developed. There are also significant differences in the provision of welfare and social security payments.

Sweden is widely regarded as having one of the best welfare systems in the world. After World War II, Swedish governments increased their revenues – mainly by levying high taxes – in order to fund a greatly expanded welfare program of state-provided healthcare, education and generous payments for pensioners and the unemployed. Swedish governments also invested in industry to help create employment. Britain pursued a similar policy in the postwar decades; its National Health Service – which provides free healthcare to all – is still seen as the flagship of its welfare policies.

Rates of direct taxation in the United States are low by European standards. Consequently, there is less government money to spend on welfare provision. Healthcare is not provided by the state for most people, who generally have to rely on personal insurance policies to cover the high costs of private medicine. Those who fall through the insurance net rely on the government-funded system of Medicare (for the elderly) and Medicaid (for recipients of public welfare). Unemployment benefits are also less generous than in most European countries and are available for a shorter period of time after redundancy. Childcare facilities are excellent for those who can afford them, but they are not widely available for those on middle or low incomes. This creates problems for some working women, though there is a system of maternity leave and benefits similar to those in most western European countries.

Meeting basic needs

Welfare priorities are very different in the developing world. Infections, parasitic diseases and respiratory illnesses constitute the main threat to life, so healthcare is oriented primarily to disease prevention rather than cure. Even so, most countries also have showcase hospitals equipped with the latest technology. The most pressing needs are for

safe water, improved sanitation and immunization programs. Many developing countries have set up primary healthcare systems designed to meet these needs, often with assistance from international agencies such as the World Health Organization or the Red Cross. In all developing countries, however, unexpected illness can place families under severe financial strain as social security systems are either not in place or are inadequately funded.

Educational opportunities in the developed world are highly variable. India, for example, has a system of free and compulsory education for all children, excellent publicly funded universities and a well-respected intelligentsia. However, in practice many children are not able to attend school because their parents rely on them to work for the family.

Political systems in developing countries frequently dictate that the welfare system is drawn up with the needs of the economically important middle classes in mind, rather than the underprivileged. The absence of social security and unemployment benefits in most developing countries is an indication of this, though it is also due to shortage of government funds. The extent to which governments should be involved in the provision of welfare services is also a controversial issue in many developed countries. For example, while lobbyists in the United States press for better public provision of healthcare, in Britain there are pressures to make the National Health Service more efficient by means of market-led reforms and internal healthcare markets. Each country has to strike its own balance within the constraints of its facilities and economic resources.

The Socialist World Economy

SINCE THE RUSSIAN REVOLUTION OF 1917 THE world economy has been divided between capitalist and socialist systems. By 1980 almost two people in every five lived and worked in socialist or communist societies; these included the Soviet Union and Eastern Europe, China, Cuba and Nicaragua in Latin America, Angola and Tanzania in Africa and Vietnam and Cambodia in Southeast Asia. The Soviet Union was long regarded as the archetypal socialist economy: collective farms supplied subsidized food to workers in state-sponsored and planned industries. In the 1960s and 1970s the People's Republic of China offered a different version of socialism by emphasizing rural (instead of urban) development and satisfying basic human needs.

The socialist model of economic development was in some disarray in the early 1990s. The Soviet Union had ceased to exist, and the costs of Soviet-style socialism were evident in the shattered economies of the whole of the former Soviet bloc. Poor efficiency and consumer shortages in the state-run shops had made a grim joke of Nikita Khrushchev's promise that the Soviet Union would outproduce the United States. Pollution, too, was a major problem, notwithstanding official declarations that environmental pollution, like prostitution, was a product of the debauched West.

The recent public failures of socialist

Yesterday's socialist *(above)* A peeling poster of President Brezhnev flanked by icons of Soviet society proclaims the unity of the Communist party and the people. By 1991 the entire Soviet empire had been torn apart by nationalist aspirations and economic crisis.

The next generation? *(left)* Red, the color of communism, dominates school assembly in Chengdu, Sichuan Province, China. These children will be growing up in a society more committed to the politics of communism than to its economics.

БАМ
ОБЛАДАЕТ БЕСЦЕННЫМ ПОЛИТИЧЕСКИМ КАПИТАЛОМ –
ПАРТИИ, ЕДИНСТВОМ ПАРТИИ И НАРОДА.
Л.И.БРЕЖНЕВ

economies should be considered along with their successes. For example, at the end of World War II, India and China were in a similar economic position. Both were large countries with rich resources yet with low levels of per capita income, literacy and life expectancy. China became a communist state in 1949; India became independent from Britain in 1947. Between 1950 and 1990, both countries performed similarly in rates of growth of per capita income and manufacturing production. But the communist government in China ensured that all inhabitants were guaranteed employment and access to housing, healthcare and education. On the other hand, the Indian people were guaranteed the right to vote in a political democracy.

Socialist economies have generally performed well in terms of provision of healthcare and education; reducing social and regional inequalities in income; and producing high short-term gains in productivity. Nicaragua and Cuba are good examples of such socialist achievements. However, in 1958–61 an estimated 30 million Chinese people died of famine caused in large part by administrative inefficiencies at a time of low food production, whereas famines of this scale have been unknown in India since Independence. Furthermore, from 1975 India began to close the gap on China in terms of life expectancy.

Socialist ideology tends to place collective goals above the rights of individuals. This may be one reason why socialist countries generally have such a poor record on human rights. However, other political systems can equally give rise to human rights abuses, as the recent history of several capitalist countries including Argentina, Chile, South Africa and Pakistan demonstrates.

Sustainable socialism?

Most of the world's socialist economies achieved high rates of growth in their formative decades by sweeping away obsolete social and institutional practices, though they often failed to sustain their economic performance in the longer term. There are several possible explanations for this. There is little incentive for individuals to be productive and innovative; this and the lack of competition can lead to economic stagnation. Inefficiency can also be introduced into the system because state-run enterprises are not easily penalized or closed down. Corruption, too, can develop, especially when economic decisions are filtered through a bureaucracy rather than through free market mechanisms.

If socialism is to have a future it is most likely to be in the form of democratic socialism. The most interesting question for the 1990s is not whether states are better than markets, or whether capitalism is more efficient than socialism, but how can markets and states be combined most effectively? What matters for economic success is not the quantity of state intervention, but its quality.

Future Prospects

FIVE CENTURIES AGO, MOST ECONOMIC activities were locally based. Although international trade existed, it was of minor significance when compared with the extent of trade today. On the other hand, natural resources were more important in the development of medieval economies than they are today. Japan has few natural resources yet its economy is the most vibrant in the modern world. It buys in all the resources it lacks, and Japanese firms are active in the resource-rich areas of other countries. The world economy has become highly interdependent, with countries being bound together by flows of money, capital, people, commodities, services and information.

The rate of change in the world economy is becoming so rapid that it is difficult to predict its future with any certainty. As the lifestyles of the West are beginning to filter through to poorer and former socialist countries, some proclaim that free markets will shape a future economy in which there is greater leisure time, more consumer choice, and greater international trade. Others believe that environmental considerations will play a more important role in economic decision-making. The only certain thing we can say about the future economy is that it will not be the same as at present.

ECONOMIC AND SOCIAL JUSTICE

The debate over how wealth should be distributed within societies and throughout the world centers on different interpretations of the concept of justice. The "entitlement" theory of justice maintains that each person earns a living according to his or her merits. For example, if a person has studied hard to gain the skills necessary to become a doctor, they are entitled to a salary of, for example, $100,000 a year. The skills of a garbage collector, on the other hand, may entitle them to only $25,000 a year. On this view, justice has prevailed in the distribution of rewards, and it would be an injustice to tax the doctor heavily to give it to the garbage collector.

"Social contract" theories of justice take a very different view. They argue that we are not only the product of skills and hard work but also of circumstance. Someone born into an affluent household in Beverly Hills, California, is almost certain to earn more money than someone born to a family of landless laborers in Bangladesh, regardless of skills or hard work. If this is the case, it is only just to take from the rich and give to the poor. If inhabitants of wealthy countries are not prepared to do without a minimum wage, food, shelter and education; then inhabitants of poor countries should expect no less. This theory of justice is one of the most powerful arguments for progressive taxation, international economic reforms and the donation of foreign aid.

Change also brings uncertainty. Workers in Moscow or Madras, Dortmund or Detroit, have reason to be fearful of the future as well as hopeful of the rewards it could bring. Business is more free than ever before to roam our shrinking world in search of new markets and new locations, bringing unexpected opportunities and problems to the people living there. However, it can pull out of an area just as quickly, causing unemployment and financial hardship to local communities. Many of the old industrial heartlands of North America and western Europe are now blighted by largescale closures of coal mines and factories. In such places, the mobility of capital has harsh consequences for local people who are tied by family or financial commitments to a particular location.

Global challenges

The world economy in the early 21st century is likely to be one of unprecedented prosperity for some nations. Yet it will also bring widening income gaps and increased debt, famine and environmental destruction. Most people in Africa today live in an era of underdevelopment, not development. What is to be done by and on behalf of these people? Socialist systems no longer seem to be the answer, but if capitalist systems replace them, what incentives will there be for the wealthy and powerful to meet the needs of the less privileged? How should developing countries reform their own economies, and to what extent – if at all – should rich countries give aid to poorer ones? How can continued economic development be combined with greater environmental protection, and how should international trading and monetary systems be reformed? These are the economic issues of today and tomorrow.

A bright future? A neon billboard in Hong Kong, one of the most dynamic growth centers in the modern world economy, and ready in the 1990s to show China how to adapt and thrive in the capitalist system.

Hi-Fi & Video
A VERY GOOD SHOP
NIKON
JVC
SONY
SANYO
CANON
YAMAHA
NATIONAL
LEICA
MINOLTA
AIWA
PENTAX
OLYMPUS
PANASONIC AKAI
PIONEER SHARP
DENON TECHNICS
HITACHI LUXMAN
TAX FREE
TAX FREE
TAX FREE
& AUDIO SUPPLIES
VIDEOHIFI CD

REGIONS OF THE WORLD

CANADA AND THE ARCTIC
Canada, Greenland

THE UNITED STATES
United States of America

CENTRAL AMERICA AND THE CARIBBEAN
Antigua and Barbuda, Bahamas, Barbados, Belize, Costa Rica, Cuba, Dominica, Dominican Republic, El Salvador, Grenada, Guatemala, Haiti, Honduras, Jamaica, Mexico, Nicaragua, Panama, St Kitts-Nevis, St Lucia, St Vincent and the Grenadines, Trinidad and Tobago

SOUTH AMERICA
Argentina, Bolivia, Brazil, Chile, Colombia, Ecuador, Guyana, Paraguay, Peru, Uruguay, Surinam, Venezuela

THE NORDIC COUNTRIES
Denmark, Finland, Iceland, Norway, Sweden

THE BRITISH ISLES
Ireland, United Kingdom

FRANCE AND ITS NEIGHBORS
Andorra, France, Monaco

THE LOW COUNTRIES
Belgium, Luxembourg, Netherlands

SPAIN AND PORTUGAL
Portugal, Spain

ITALY AND GREECE
Cyprus, Greece, Italy, Malta, San Marino, Vatican City

CENTRAL EUROPE
Austria, Germany, Liechtenstein, Switzerland

EASTERN EUROPE
Albania, Bosnia and Hercegovina, Bulgaria, Croatia, Czech Republic, Hungary, Macedonia, Poland, Romania, Slovakia, Slovenia, Yugoslavia (Serbia and Montenegro)

NORTHERN EURASIA
Armenia, Azerbaijan, Belorussia, Estonia, Georgia, Kazakhstan, Kirghizia, Latvia, Lithuania, Moldavia, Mongolia, Russia, Tajikistan, Turkmenistan, Ukraine, Uzbekistan

THE MIDDLE EAST
Afghanistan, Bahrain, Iran, Iraq, Israel, Jordan, Kuwait, Lebanon, Oman, Qatar, Saudi Arabia, Syria, Turkey, United Arab Emirates, Yemen

NORTHERN AFRICA
Algeria, Chad, Djibouti, Egypt, Ethiopia, Libya, Mali, Mauritania, Morocco, Niger, Somalia, Sudan, Tunisia

CENTRAL AFRICA
Benin, Burkina, Burundi, Cameroon, Cape Verde, Central African Republic, Congo, Equatorial Guinea, Gabon, Gambia, Ghana, Guinea, Guinea-Bissau, Ivory Coast, Kenya, Liberia, Nigeria, Rwanda, São Tomé and Príncipe, Senegal, Seychelles, Sierra Leone, Tanzania, Togo, Uganda, Zaire

SOUTHERN AFRICA
Angola, Botswana, Comoros, Lesotho, Madagascar, Malawi, Mauritius, Mozambique, Namibia, South Africa, Swaziland, Zambia, Zimbabwe

THE INDIAN SUBCONTINENT
Bangladesh, Bhutan, India, Maldives, Nepal, Pakistan, Sri Lanka

CHINA AND ITS NEIGHBORS
China, Taiwan

SOUTHEAST ASIA
Brunei, Burma, Cambodia, Indonesia, Laos, Malaysia, Philippines, Singapore, Thailand, Vietnam

JAPAN AND KOREA
Japan, North Korea, South Korea

AUSTRALASIA, OCEANIA AND ANTARCTICA
Antarctica, Australia, Fiji, Kiribati, Nauru, New Zealand, Papua New Guinea, Solomon Islands, Tonga, Tuvalu, Vanuatu, Western Samoa

North America

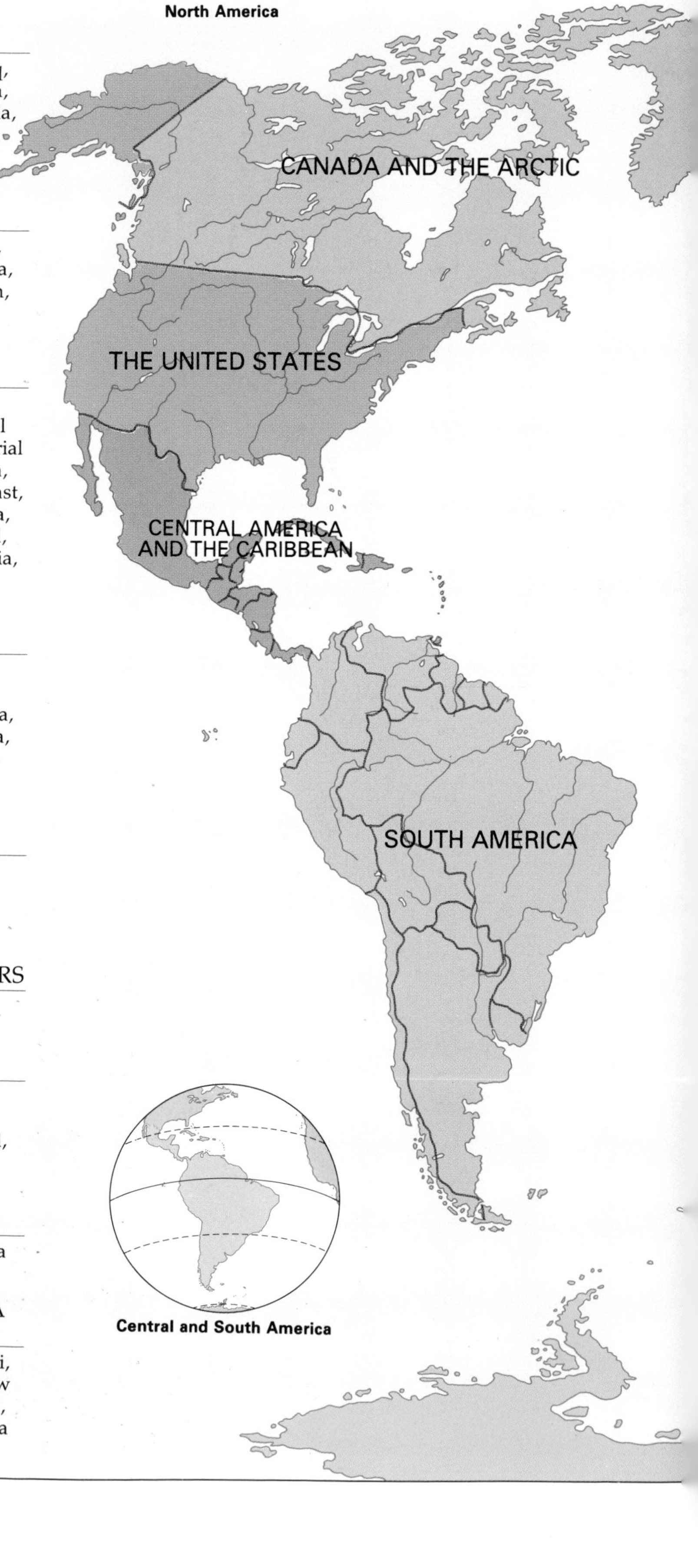

Central and South America

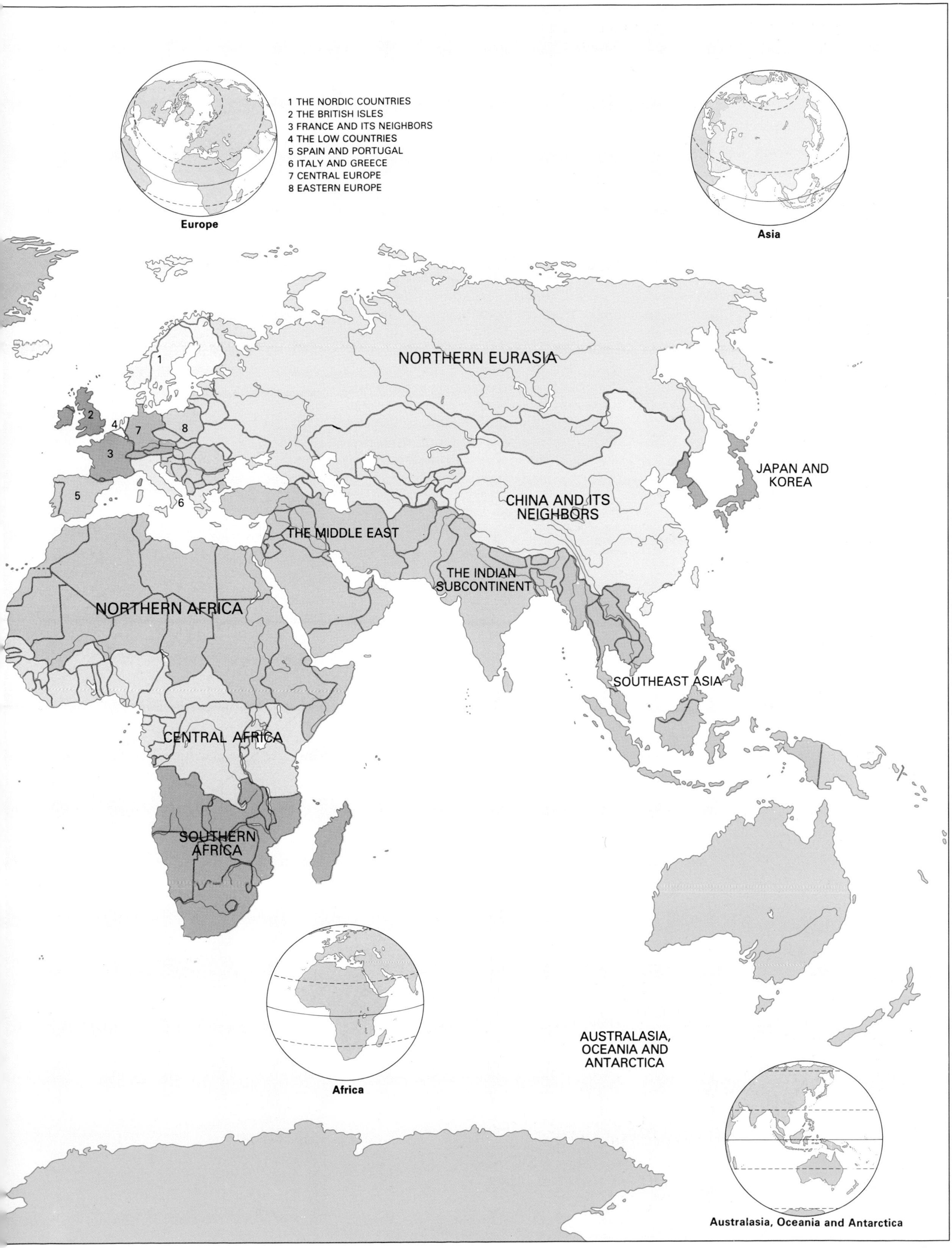

Europe
1 THE NORDIC COUNTRIES
2 THE BRITISH ISLES
3 FRANCE AND ITS NEIGHBORS
4 THE LOW COUNTRIES
5 SPAIN AND PORTUGAL
6 ITALY AND GREECE
7 CENTRAL EUROPE
8 EASTERN EUROPE
Asia
NORTHERN EURASIA
JAPAN AND KOREA
CHINA AND ITS NEIGHBORS
THE MIDDLE EAST
THE INDIAN SUBCONTINENT
NORTHERN AFRICA
SOUTHEAST ASIA
CENTRAL AFRICA
SOUTHERN AFRICA
Africa
AUSTRALASIA, OCEANIA AND ANTARCTICA
Australasia, Oceania and Antarctica

A WEALTH OF RESOURCES

CREATING AN INDEPENDENT ECONOMY · BREAKING THE BOOM-BUST CYCLE · A NATION OF CONTRASTS

The Canadian economy has grown and diversified considerably over the last hundred years, and Canadians now have one of the highest standards of living in the world. This has been achieved despite the potential handicaps of a limited population, regional political pressures and a harsh northern climate. Much of Canada's success springs from the profitable exploitation of natural resources. In the past, an insatiable world appetite for raw materials and primary products allowed Canada to compete effectively in the global marketplace and develop robust manufacturing and service sectors. However, in recent years it has become clear that controlling unprocessed resources can no longer guarantee prosperity. Canada must diversify its economy and seek new markets to maintain its enviable record of growth.

COUNTRIES IN THE REGION

Canada

ECONOMIC INDICATORS: 1990	HIE* Canada
GDP (US$ billions)	570.15
GNP per capita (US$)	20,470
Annual rate of growth of GDP, 1980–1990 (%)	3.4
Manufacturing as % of GDP	13
Central government spending as % of GNP	23
Merchandise exports (US$ billions)	133.5
Merchandise imports (US$ billions)	126.5
% of GNP donated as development aid	0.44

WELFARE INDICATORS	
Infant mortality rate (per 1,000 live births)	
1965	24
1990	7
Daily food supply available (calories per capita, 1989)	3,482
Population per physician (1984)	510
Teacher–pupil ratio (primary school, 1989)	1 : 16

Note: The Gross Domestic Product (GDP) is the total value of all goods and services domestically produced. The Gross National Product (GNP) is the GDP plus net income from abroad.

** HIE (High Income Economy) – GNP per capita above $7,620 in 1990.*

CREATING AN INDEPENDENT ECONOMY

During the 18th and early 19th centuries Canada, then a British colony, supplied raw materials (fur, fish, wheat, and timber) to Britain and the United States. In turn Canadians bought manufactured goods from their trading partners, but had little or no domestic industry. After Confederation in 1867 the government attempted to strengthen the country's economic base and develop a manufacturing sector. A national railroad was created, encouraging settlement and development to spread westward, and protective trade restrictions were introduced to promote local manufacturing.

The industrial base

By 1900, with improved transport and communications and rising domestic production, the Canadian economy was ripe for expansion. Important mineral finds in areas such as the Klondike fueled growth, followed by a massive boom in wheat production as Britain's demand for grain grew and the prairies were opened to cultivation by immigrant farmers. The manufacturing sectors of Ontario and Quebec in the southeast also expanded in order to supply the increasingly prosperous population to the west with both consumer goods and heavy engineering. On the eve of World War I, Canada was on the verge of becoming a mature industrial economy.

Economic slump followed the war years and the demand for many key Canadian products declined. Exports did not return to their wartime levels until 1926. As wheat prices fell and the nation's foreign policy became increasingly independent of Britain, the Canadian economy became more closely linked to the United States. By the mid 1920s many large United States' firms had established branch plants over the border in Canada and their level of investment continued to rise even during the Great Depression of the 1930s. By the 1940s Canada was incorporated into a global trading economy very much dominated by the United States.

Rich neighbors

Following World War II, the Canadian economy experienced another period of sustained economic growth. This was stimulated by increased demand from major trading partners and the investment of almost $1 billion in industry by the federal government. The United States made unprecedented direct investment in the Canadian economy as its manufacturing companies sought a stable supply of raw materials and entry into Commonwealth markets. Production increased dramatically, unemployment fell and workers' wages in Canada rose faster than in the United States. Nevertheless, some Canadians were already expressing fears about the extent of control exercised

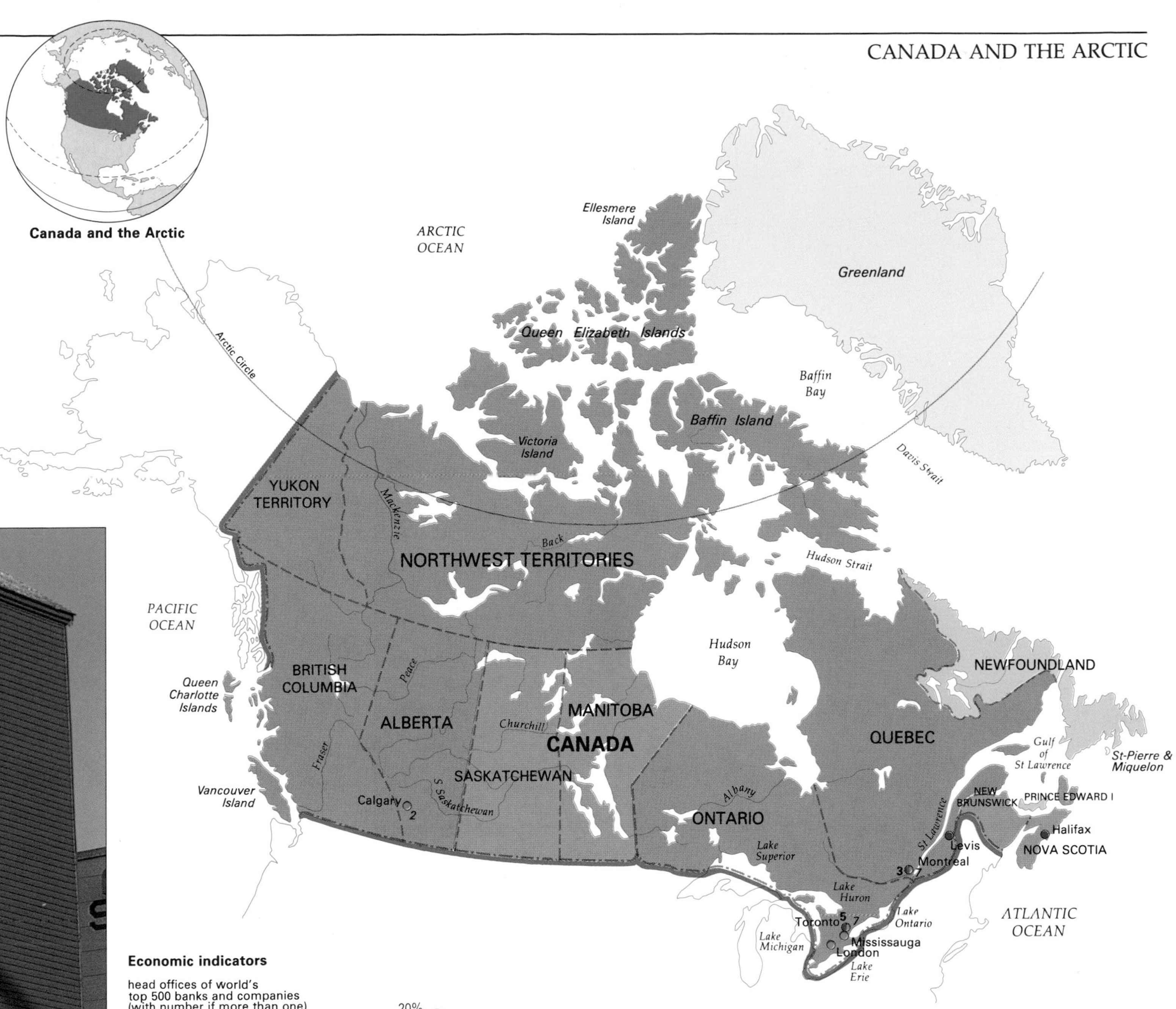

Map of GDP per capita *(above)* Canada's wealth of resources and relatively small population combine to produce one of the highest rates of GDP per capita in the world: an average of $20,470 in 1990. The average annual growth rate of GDP of 3.4 percent (1980–90) was bettered only by Japan among the world's top seven economic powers.

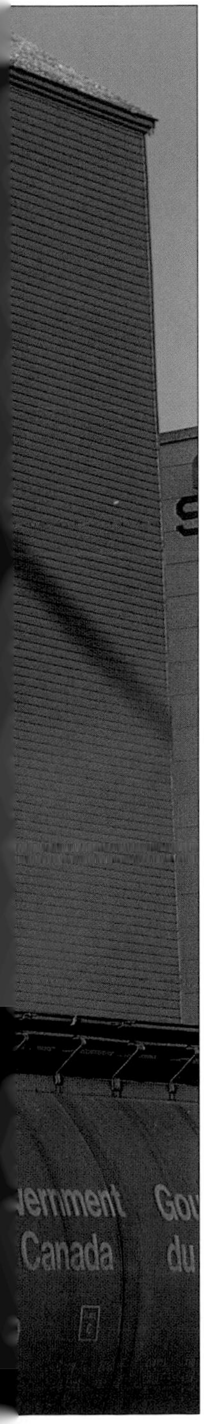

A vast grain elevator *(left)* stores Canadian wheat before shipping to countries all over the world. Wheat is one of the country's principal agricultural exports. In the late 19th and early 20th centuries, revenues from wheat and other farming and forestry industries helped to fund the rapid growth of Canada's manufacturing sector.

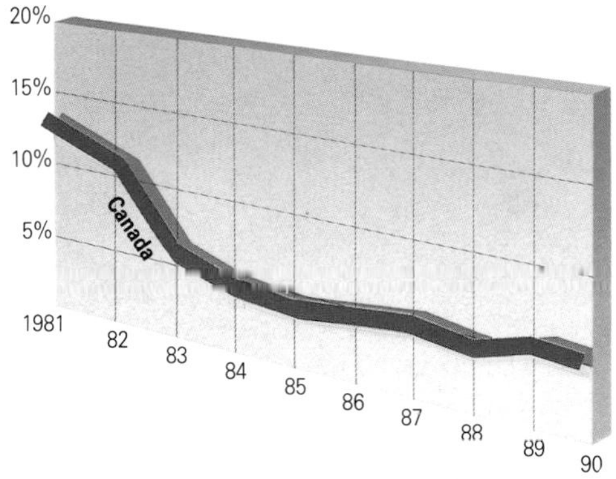

Profile of inflation *(above)* The annual rate of inflation in Canada hit a high of nearly 13 percent in 1981. In response, the government's tight monetary policies brought inflation down to a fairly steady 5 percent from 1983 onward.

by the United States. By the 1970s, almost 60 percent of all financial assets in mining and smelting were owned by United States firms, and the same proportions in the oil and gas industry. In all, United States' companies controlled over half the value of Canadian manufacturing output.

The oil price shock of 1973–74 brought the long Canadian boom to an end. Like other oil-independent industrialized countries, Canada went into deep recession. Commodity exports declined by 1.5 percent in real terms during 1974, and the foreign trade deficit rose from $785 million in 1973 to nearly $2.5 billion a year later. After a brief respite, Canadians entered the most severe of a series of recessions in 1981–82. During 1982 real gross domestic product (GDP) declined by 3.2 percent and the national rate of unemployment peaked at 12.7 percent.

The rapid shifts in Canada's economic fortunes throughout its history displayed the classic "boom-bust" pattern of a resource-based economy. Although the Canadian economy was far more diversified in 1980 than a century earlier, it was still at the mercy of rapid fluctuations in commodity prices. In addition, recessionary pressures in the United States' market still had a major impact on the Canadian economy.

Loading timber *(above)* on a Canadian quayside. Products from Canada's vast forests (including pulp and paper) make up the country's most valuable commodity group. New legislation is forcing forestry companies to invest in more sustainable forestry techniques.

BREAKING THE BOOM–BUST CYCLE

Following the 1981–82 recession, Canada experienced nearly a decade of sustained growth. While the impetus for much of this growth came from traditional sectors such as forestry, mining, agriculture and heavy industry, the economy continued to diversify. High-technology sectors such as telecommunications grew rapidly as did many areas of the service sector. By the end of the decade over 70 percent of Canadian workers were employed in service occupations.

The 1980s also witnessed shifts in trading patterns. Over 30 percent of Canada's income derives from trade, with export businesses providing over three million jobs. The United States' market dominates, accounting for about 75 percent of Canadian exports and 65 percent of imports. While the role of the United States has been strengthened by the 1989 Free Trade Agreement, Canada has also expanded trading relations with Pacific Rim nations such as Japan and South Korea and aims to gain a stronger foothold in Europe.

Gearing up for competition

Canada faces a number of economic challenges in the 1990s. It is competing in an increasingly global marketplace and recent political events have changed the shape and nature of many of its major markets. The liberalization of Eastern Europe, European economic integration through the European Community (EC) and the inclusion of Mexico in a North American Free Trade Agreement (NAFTA) create potential obstacles for Canadian industries. Manufacturers will have to produce high-quality goods efficiently and cheaply as well as investing heavily in new technologies and in research and development if they are to remain competitive. The resource-based sectors must

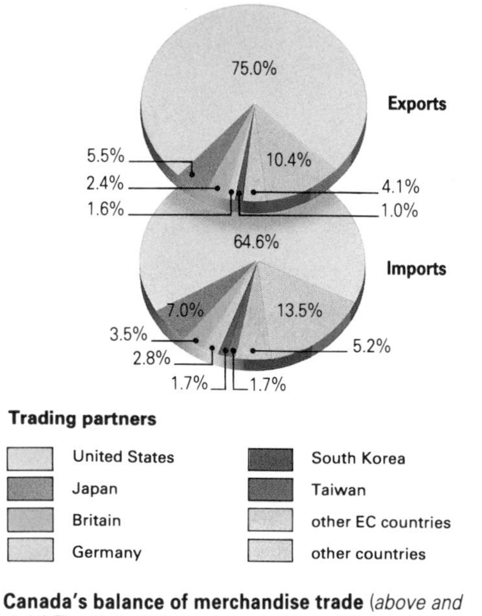

Canada's balance of merchandise trade *(above and right)* The United States is by far Canada's most important trading partner, receiving a massive 75 percent of Canadian exports and supplying almost 65 percent of the country's imports. Exploitation of natural resources contributes a substantial amount to export earnings, especially energy (oil, natural gas, coal and hydroelectricity) processed metals and forest products including paper. Imports are dominated by machinery and industrial equipment.

THE COST OF ENVIRONMENTAL PROTECTION

In recent years the environment has emerged as an important public policy issue throughout the developed world. Canada is committed to spending $6 billion on its ambitious Green Plan, which will result in more stringent environmental regulations. Pressure from consumer concern is forcing many Canadian companies to produce environmentally friendly products and to invest heavily in pollution-control technologies. Such protective measures are extremely costly and companies fear a decrease in profits as they are obliged to make investments in expensive environmental protection programs.

The Canadian pulp and paper industry, for example, employs over 120,000 Canadians and accounts for 9 percent of the nation's manufacturing shipments. It is estimated that Canadian companies will have to spend $5 billion by the mid 1990s to comply with new environmental legislation. The public is increasingly aware of the depletion of Canada's vast woodlands, and forestry companies are being forced to develop improved logging techniques as well as investing more heavily in replanting schemes. But the cost of failing to protect the environment is equally high: Canadian farmers experience annual production losses of $500–900 million due to erosion through environmentally unfriendly farming methods. Several power generating authorities in the United States have begun to reevaluate contracts to buy electricity from Quebec in view of the environmental damage caused by the construction of hydroelectric dams. The state of Maine canceled its $9 billion contract in 1992, and the future of other important contracts is under review. In another market sector, Canadian newsprint producers fear that stringent United States' recycling legislation providing for greater use of recycled paper will restrict their access to a traditionally lucrative market.

add greater value to their raw materials by processing them or using them in manufacturing before trading. Most will have to improve productivity if they are to escape the worst effects of further boom–bust cycles.

To prepare for the challenges ahead, the federal government has adopted a series of free-market policies designed to make the economy more competitive. In particular, direct government participation in the economy has been minimized through the reduction of tariffs, the deregulation of a series of sectors including energy and financial services, and the privatization of a range of publicly owned operations.

Quebec as an economic issue

Meanwhile, economic growth is threatened by political instability and cultural clashes between various ethnic groups.

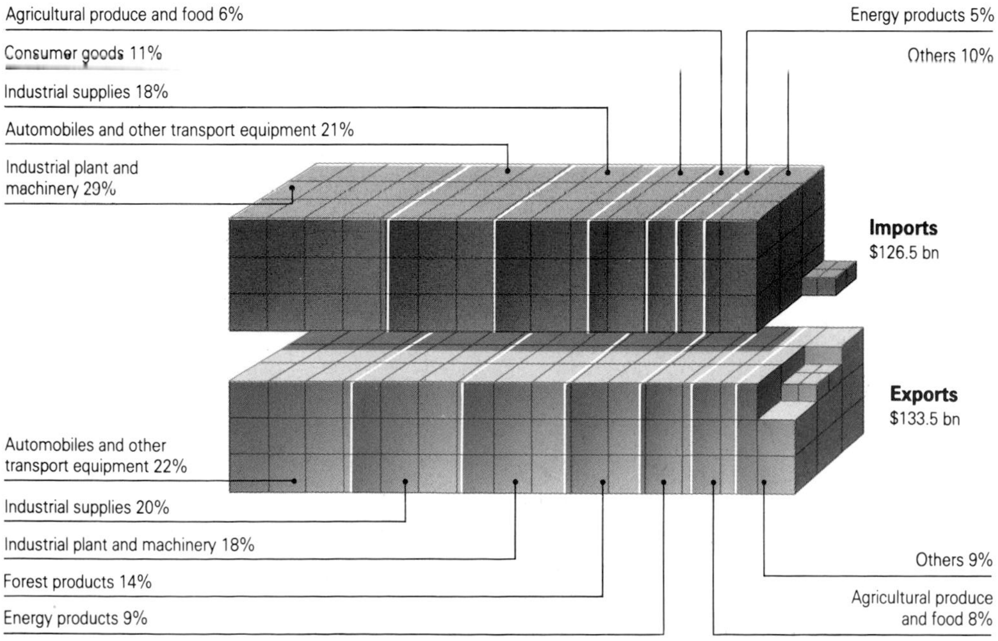

One of the most damaging conflicts is the issue of Quebec's separation from the rest of Canada. French Canadians supporting independence for Quebec want political sovereignty while retaining an economic association with Canada (including a customs and monetary union).

Many commentators feel that such a separation would have dire economic consequences, not only for Quebec, but also for Canada as a whole. The political reorganization of Canada into two sovereign states might tempt the United States to reopen, or reinterpret, existing trade agreements. Also, while a sovereign Quebec would be rich by international standards, it would be distinctly poorer than its neighbors. It would have to shoulder its share of the national deficit, but would no longer receive the federal aid that has, so far, contributed to many of Quebec's social programs. With its existing high taxation, it is not clear how Quebec would raise extra tax revenues and at the same time maintain the competitiveness of its economy.

Debt and taxes

Increasing levels of debt also threaten Canada's economic future. In March 1990 the net federal debt (the money borrowed by the government to cover successive budget deficits) stood at $379,565 million or nearly $15,000 per person. The debt shows little sign of diminishing. Consumer debt, or the money owed by individuals to banks and other institutions, more than doubled during the 1980s to reach $101,500 million in 1990. This is equivalent to 21.5 percent of the average Canadian's after-tax personal income. Such high levels of debt pose serious questions for the future since Canadians will be paying interest on the national debt, much of it to foreign institutions, for many years to come. This in turn prevents reinvestment in the Canadian economy and raises levels of international dependence.

In response, the federal government has cut domestic expenditure, reduced levels of overseas aid and increased tax revenue through a goods and services tax levied on most consumer purchases. While these policies may eventually improve the economy's competitive stance and reduce budget problems, many fear that a shift away from a welfare economy may lead to growing social and economic inequalities within the nation.

A NATION OF CONTRASTS

The average standard of living in Canada ranks among the highest in the world, but members of some ethnic groups and the inhabitants of certain regions fare much worse than others. Unemployment rates and the potential for improving conditions for the inhabitants vary greatly between the provinces. Earlier in the nation's history the Atlantic provinces (Prince Edward Island, New Brunswick, Nova Scotia and Newfoundland) and prairie provinces (Saskatchewan and Manitoba) grew rapidly as a result of resource-based booms. In recent decades, however, they have had to fight hard against low levels of economic growth. Newfoundland in particular has suffered from a decline in its fisheries and some small towns in the region register unemployment rates above 30 percent.

Since World War II the provinces with the most vibrant economies have been British Columbia, Alberta and Ontario. While the average unemployment rate for Newfoundland during the 1980s ranged between 15 and 20 percent, these three regions were characterized by rates of only half this level. Quebec remains something of a special case. While it has a great deal of industrial potential and remains, after Ontario, the second largest producer of manufactured goods, political uncertainty and a dependence on declining sectors such as clothing and textiles have affected its performance in recent years. Montreal now has the highest urban unemployment rate in the nation. Canada has attempted to overcome these inequalities through a system of transfer or equalization payments. These redirect federal tax money from the wealthier to the poorer provinces.

Evening the odds

Canada has long prided itself on its relatively fair system of welfare support. As in the United States, the way government-funded education is organized varies from province to province. In particular, the federal government takes responsibility for education in the Yukon

Vive la difference! (*below*) French Canadians campaigning for separatism. Quebec's declining economy has been assisted by federal resource transfer schemes recently, and experts doubt that an independent Quebec could survive economically.

A day at the lake (*left*) City-dwellers taking a relaxing break on the shores of Lake Ontario. The highly urbanized Canadian population enjoys one of the highest standards of living in the world, including ample time and money to spend on leisure pursuits. Affluent city-dwellers frequently own a second home in the countryside. By comparison, the standards of living of inhabitants of some isolated rural areas, particularly the indigenous peoples of the northwest, are low.

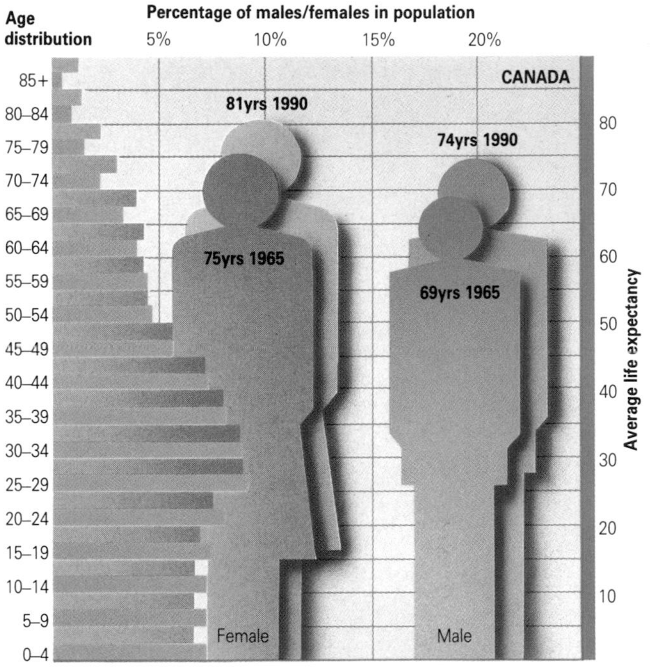

Life expectancy and age distribution (*right*) In common with other developed countries, life expectancy in Canada is high – the average female life expectancy (81 years) is second only to Japan's. Among the indigenous Inuit population, however, the average life span is shorter, even though access to healthcare and other social services is relatively equitably distributed. Since the 1960s' baby boom, birthrates have dropped steadily.

and Northwest territories where the majority of schools cater specifically for Canada's indigenous peoples including the Inuit and native Indians. The Federal Government also contributes to the higher education budget of each province. Most Canadian children go to elementary school at the age of six, and spend eight years there. Virtually all students go on to secondary school at 14, and spend five or six years there (depending on the province). Bilingual or French-language instruction is increasingly common in English-speaking areas.

The government also provides health and welfare services, through universally funded taxation programs. Nevertheless, inequalities appear to be growing as the economy enters the 1990s and the international political trend moves away from the welfare state. Canada has begun to cut transfer payments and there has been some discussion about the possibility of partly privatizing the healthcare system. It is estimated that 3.5 million Canadians (over 10 percent of the population) live below the poverty line.

THE INUIT: MAKING A LIVING

Approximately 35,000 Canadian Inuit live in small, isolated villages spread throughout the Northwest Territories and the Yukon. In these government-built communities, incomes are well below the national average and unemployment rates are generally high. Social welfare assistance is a fact of everyday life. This state of affairs is mostly the result of long-standing problems: the disadvantage of the remote location coupled with high transportation costs; low levels of education leading to poorly skilled workers; the sheer lack of people to sustain large-scale ventures; and a limited range of occupations and business activities.

Hunting, fishing and trapping remain important occupations among the Inuit, providing food that would otherwise have to be imported and raw material for clothing. While these traditional forms of economic activity also provide some cash income, the market for seal and other furs has been cut drastically as a result of international bans on fur trading and changing consumer demand. In consequence, traditional economic activities are no longer sufficiently profitable in the modern economy. Inuit communities have to rely heavily on handicrafts, especially carving, as a source of income. The main chance for future economic development is seen to lie with tourism, bringing with it the risk of cultural and environmental damage.

Conditions for the disadvantaged

Some ethnic and cultural groups can be identified as being more impoverished than others. In the 1960s restrictions that had effectively encouraged only European immigration were relaxed and more immigrants began to arrive from developing countries, particularly from Asia. As this flow of new workers and their families has continued, they have tended to settle in the inner cities and a number of related problems have arisen.

A lack of training has restricted migrants to jobs in the nonskilled sector, which has become substantially reduced as industries have modernized and relocated to hightech offices in outer city areas. While the federal and provincial governments have introduced a variety of assimilation and training schemes, several ethnic groups continue to experience unemployment rates that are well above the national average. Racial prejudice is becoming a growing problem in some parts of the country.

Perhaps the most pressing issue, however, is the relatively low standard of living of Canada's indigenous peoples. In the north and on native Indian reservations across the country, unemployment rates often exceed 40 percent and average life expectancy is much lower than for the nation as a whole. In most of these areas, harsh climatic conditions and limited resource bases reduce the potential for future economic development and create a cycle of poverty that is difficult to break.

The free-trade debate

The Free-Trade Agreement (FTA) between Canada and the United States is the most significant economic treaty ever signed by Canada. It took effect in January 1989 and, according to the original terms, virtually all goods produced in the two countries will be traded without restriction by 1998. Predictably, the FTA has fueled a great deal of political and economic debate on both sides on the potential benefits and damaging side effects of freer trade.

Opponents of the agreement believe that Canada still requires some form of protection for its economy if it is not to be overwhelmed by its larger neighbor. They argue that by 1991 over 200,000 jobs had already been lost as a result of the FTA. This has happened mostly because Canadian firms moved south of the border into the United States to preserve their competitiveness by taking advantage of lower labor costs there. Political opponents of the agreement also argue that the United States is already in economic decline and that Canada has tied itself to the wrong economic partner if it wishes to improve its competitive position in the global economy.

Supporters of the agreement argue that any firms that have closed would have been forced to rationalize their operations regardless of the agreement. They point out that 75 percent of all trade between the two countries was already free of barriers before 1989. Proponents believe that while free trade will increase competition at home, it will also provide secure access to a market of some 275 million consumers. They are confident that the market will be large enough to offer Canadian industry the possibility to obtain economies of scale and improve productivity. In this way the FTA will actually assist Canada in becoming more competitive in the global marketplace.

North America, Inc.

Supporters of the FTA believe that only by extending the nation's trading links can Canadians continue to enjoy the standard of living achieved by the end of the 1980s. It is this thinking that led the country into negotiations with both the United States and Mexico for the establishment of a North American Free-Trade Agreement (known as NAFTA).

New trade links between Canada and Mexico amounted to C$2.3 billion in 1989, of which imports from Mexico accounted for C$1.7 billion. When compared with the Canada–United States' trading figure of C$185.8 billion for the same year, the partnership with Mexico does not appear to be significant. However, Mexico is Canada's leading trading partner in Latin America. Canada's imports from Mexico are mainly manufactured products (principally transportation equipment and parts for machinery) while its exports to Mexico are largely agricultural products and some transportation equipment.

The NAFTA treaty was signed in Texas in 1992, but it was not ratified by the Canadian government. There are still important issues to be discussed before

Left out in the cold *(right)* Trade union members protest against the Free Trade Agreement. Representatives of selected industries voiced widespread opposition to the agreement in 1988 on the grounds that free trade with the United States would cause substantial job losses and damage the economy.

Steeled for change *(below)* Workers in steel manufacturing and the related automobile industry are likely to be hit hard by redundancies as a result of factory relocation to the United States or Mexico where wages are lower.

Canada can agree to abide by its stipulations. Mexico is at a far lower level of development than Canada. The large differences in wage levels and productivity that exist between Canadian and Mexican manufacturing plants mean that free trade with Mexico will have to be introduced gradually. An agreement that quickly removed tariffs on most trade with Mexico could make it difficult for Canadian producers to compete with cheaper Mexican goods. Many unions are already strongly opposed to the NAFTA treaty, believing that it may encourage manufacturers of certain goods to shift their operations to Mexico in order to take advantage of cheap labor and lax environmental regulations.

Supporters of NAFTA think that consideration must be given to Mexico's potential for growth. They argue that labor costs are only one of the elements to take into account, and that factors such as the overall efficiency of the economy, the skills of the workforce, the quality of management and the cost of capital will provide Canada with a competitive advantage. For example, as Mexico modernizes, it will have to invest heavily in transportation and communications. With its expertise in these areas, Canada would be well positioned to take advantage of free trade. Proponents also believe that only by participating in NAFTA can Canada influence the flow of future trade and investment in the region.

THE MIGHTY DOLLAR

GROWTH OF A GIANT · A GLOBAL ECONOMIC LEADER · THE PRICE OF LEADERSHIP
POST-INDUSTRIAL AMERICA? · HEALTH, WEALTH AND WORK · HOUSING, EDUCATION AND WELFARE

Since the late 19th century the United States has grown to become the world's most powerful economy. Traditionally, its economic strength has been founded on free enterprise, but with generous help from federal and state governments. Following rapid industrialization between 1870 and 1910, the United States rose to new prominence, achieving international economic leadership by the end of World War II. The 1950s and 1960s were decades of unprecedented economic growth and saw vast improvements in living standards for most Americans. Since 1970, however, the economy has been in a period of relative decline. The rewards of economic growth are divided unequally and there are signs that welfare provision is in crisis, particularly in the inner cities and among certain ethnic minorities.

COUNTRIES IN THE REGION

United States of America

ECONOMIC INDICATORS: 1990

	HIE* USA
GDP (US$ billions)	5,392
GNP per capita (US$)	21,790
Annual rate of growth of GDP, 1980–1990 (%)	3.4
Manufacturing as % of GDP	17
Central government spending as % of GNP	24
Merchandise exports (US$ billions)	393.0
Merchandise imports (US$ billions)	495.3
% of GNP donated as development aid	0.21

WELFARE INDICATORS

Infant mortality rate (per 1,000 live births)	
1965	25
1990	9
Daily food supply available (calories per capita, 1989)	3,671
Population per physician (1984)	470
Teacher–pupil ratio (primary school, 1989)	1 : 21

Note: The Gross Domestic Product (GDP) is the total value of all goods and services domestically produced. The Gross National Product (GNP) is the GDP plus net income from abroad.

** HIE (High Income Economy) – GNP per capita above $7,620 in 1990.*

GROWTH OF A GIANT

The American economy is so often associated with technological prowess that it is easy to forget its humble origins as a colony providing raw materials. Just 400 years ago the region was home to numerous Native American communities and was largely unknown to Europeans, who settled there in the early 17th century. By the late 18th century the British dominated Native Americans and other European settlers alike through sheer force of numbers and a powerful navy. Virginia in the south became the hub of a tobacco trade with Britain and Continental Europe, while New England in the northeast began to specialize in shipbuilding and shipping services. Agricultural produce was the mainstay of the economy in this early period since there was little manufacturing until the mid 19th century. In the north, food was produced on small family farms mainly for local consumption. The spirit of individualism did not take hold in the south in the same way that it did in the north. In the southern states, large plantations and estates (growing tobacco and later cotton) were the norm, serviced by slave labor.

Expanding autonomy

After the colonies won independence from Britain in 1783, a system of federal government was adopted in 1789. The new Constitution spoke up for the rights of individual citizens, but also accepted collective responsibility to develop the nation's economy. These dual strands of individual and collective responsibility have been a consistent theme in American economic and political life ever since.

Between 1800 and 1850 the land area of the future United States increased threefold. In part, this was a matter of chance. In 1803, for example, Louisiana (then a much larger territory than the modern state) was purchased from the cash-strapped Emperor Napoleon (1769–1821). More often, expansion was made possible by imports of capital and technology from

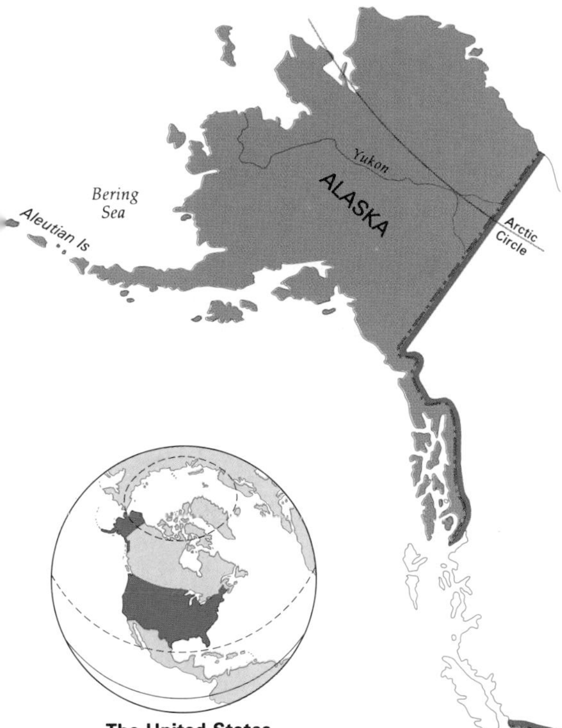

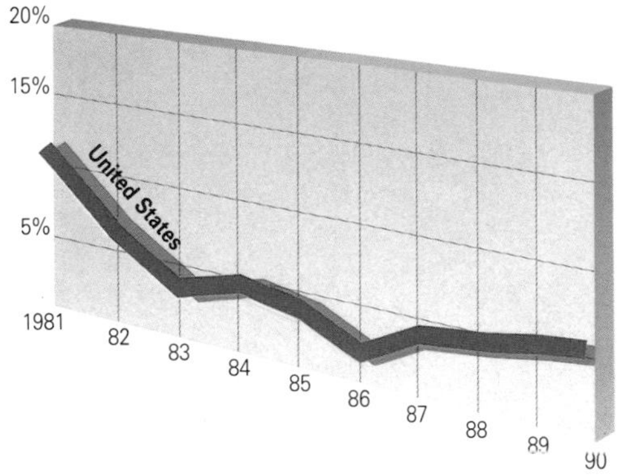

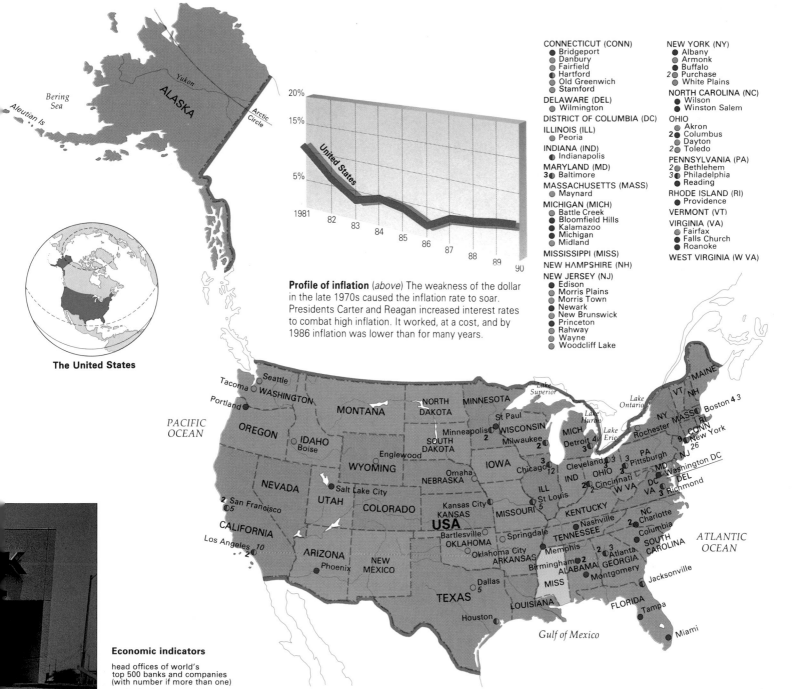

Profile of inflation *(above)* The weakness of the dollar in the late 1970s caused the inflation rate to soar. Presidents Carter and Reagan increased interest rates to combat high inflation. It worked, at a cost, and by 1986 inflation was lower than for many years.

CONNECTICUT (CONN)
Bridgeport
Danbury
Fairfield
Hartford
Old Greenwich
Stamford
DELAWARE (DEL)
Wilmington
DISTRICT OF COLUMBIA (DC)
ILLINOIS (ILL)
Peoria
INDIANA (IND)
Indianapolis
MARYLAND (MD)
3 Baltimore
MASSACHUSETTS (MASS)
Maynard
MICHIGAN (MICH)
Battle Creek
Bloomfield Hills
Kalamazoo
Michigan
Midland
MISSISSIPPI (MISS)
NEW HAMPSHIRE (NH)
NEW JERSEY (NJ)
Edison
Morris Plains
Morris Town
Newark
New Brunswick
Princeton
Rahway
Wayne
Woodcliff Lake
NEW YORK (NY)
Albany
Armonk
Buffalo
2 Purchase
White Plains
NORTH CAROLINA (NC)
Wilson
Winston Salem
OHIO
Akron
2 Columbus
Dayton
2 Toledo
PENNSYLVANIA (PA)
2 Bethlehem
3 Philadelphia
Reading
RHODE ISLAND (RI)
Providence
VERMONT (VT)
VIRGINIA (VA)
Fairfax
Falls Church
Roanoke
WEST VIRGINIA (W VA)

The United States

Economic indicators

head offices of world's top 500 banks and companies (with number if more than one)

- 2 bank
- 2 company

(underlined name indicates a capital city)

GDP per capita (US$)

- over 20 000
- 15 000–20 000
- 10 000–14 999

Map of GDP per capita *(above)* Despite an uneven spread of income and business across the country, the United States is one of the most uniformly prosperous nations in the world. Most of the world's top 500 banks and companies are based here, with a particular concentration along the east coast.

Making a quick get-away *(left)* Two of America's popular status symbols – money and automobiles – merge at the drive-in bank. Years of continued growth have given Americans large disposable incomes to spend on comfort and convenience.

abroad. When Britain entered a recession in the 1820s and 1830s, British capital flowed eagerly to North America to exploit new business opportunities, especially in the railroads, where it was encouraged by government land grants and tax concessions. The expansion of the railroads fostered a sense of unity among the states, and shaped them into an economic unit. Special interests also began to emerge among the regions. The northeast, boosted by tariffs introduced against some European imports in 1816, consolidated its position as a center of shipbuilding and manufacturing. It also became a major source of technological innovation, especially in New England, as local manufacturers tried to reduce the country's dependence on imported machinery. Meantime, the south continued to rely on slave labor and remained dependent on British customers, particularly as a market for its cotton crop.

Power in the north

Regional economic conflicts are now recognized as a major factor leading to the American Civil War (1860–65). When the South was defeated, the United States' government put its might firmly behind the industrial North. By 1890 a new industrial core had emerged in the northeast and in the Great Lakes regions, centered on the city economies of New York and Chicago. The rest of the country provided food and natural resources to this core. The power of urban–industrial America was consolidated at the end of the century by a massive new wave of immigrants from southern and eastern Europe who provided cheap and willing labor to power further economic growth.

A GLOBAL ECONOMIC LEADER

By the turn of the 20th century the United States was a central player in the world economy. Its rapid industrial evolution between 1870 and 1910 enabled it to challenge Britain's strong position in the international marketplace. Ascendancy was confirmed in 1918 when World War I left Britain and Germany in debt and disrepair. American businesses consolidated both at home and abroad during this period. Despite a national ideology of individual endeavor, giant American industrial houses such as Standard Oil and the Carnegie Company began to increase in size and strength. By 1905 about two-fifths of United States' manufacturing capital was controlled by just 300 corporations.

American business leaders continued to expand into new world markets by various means, both subtle and aggressive. In 1898 the United States went to war with Spain for control of the Philippines, having already secured control of most of its central and South American "backyard". In the early 20th century American firms invested in sugar plantations in Cuba and banana plantations in Costa Rica. Latin American governments were encouraged to support United States' business interests in the region in return for protection and financial loans. By 1929 the United States was a major creditor country across its spheres of influence and spoke up in international politics for a new vision of post-imperialism – a democracy of the marketplace. The world was to be opened up not for American settlers, but for American goods and services.

Roosevelt's New Deal

Although the Great Depression of 1929–33 temporarily put an end to expansionist economic policies, America kept its vision for the future alive during the darker days of the early 1930s. In the 1920s production had run ahead of consumption as new forms of mass production were introduced by Henry Ford and other entrepreneurs. After the mid 1930s this balance was corrected as a result of President Franklin D. Roosevelt's New Deal, which boosted business confidence by supporting private and public-sector spending and increased employment.

The federal government and state

Smaller markets for bigger automobiles *(right)* Cheap gasoline and high disposable incomes meant that until the mid 1970s American automobiles were large "gas-guzzlers" like these. The oil price rises in the 1970s increased energy awareness and, with the new 55 mile-per-hour speed limit, prompted Americans to buy smaller models.

The capitol of capitalism *(left)* The New York Stock Exchange is the center of the American – and global – financial system. The stock exchange also acts as an economic and social thermometer for the United States. Stock prices rise and fall according to good or bad news in the country.

THE GREAT DEPRESSION

The stock market crash on New York's Wall Street on 24 October 1929 – Black Thursday – is popularly seen as the start of the Great Depression. The sudden drop in share prices is said to have eroded American business confidence and caused an investment strike, which led to decreased production and massive unemployment. The stock market, however, had been in decline since August 1929 and the crash was by no means confined to the equities market. This was also a period of record bank failures. Some 352 institutions closed in December 1930 alone, one of the most important being the Bank of United States, on 11 December. Between 1929 and 1933 the dollar income of the United States was halved, total output fell by a third and unemployment affected a quarter of the workforce.

With hindsight, some modern monetarists assert that the Great Depression was caused not by the stock market collapse, but by the Federal Reserve Bank's failure to increase the nation's money supply in 1929 and 1930. People could not buy goods and services (they argue) and so restore business confidence, because the government was taking currency out of circulation. The Depression began to lift with the inauguration of Franklin D. Roosevelt as president in 1933 and the start of his New Deal. "Big Government" (increased welfare spending) in the United States dates from this time.

authorities such as New York and Georgia funded increased spending on highways and house building. They also introduced price support for agricultural produce and new social insurance benefits for pensioners and the unemployed. The New Deal also revitalized America's longstanding tradition of economic and political decentralization. For example, it funded the establishment of the Tennessee Valley Authority, which developed projects to encourage industrial expansion within the Tennessee river basin.

Postwar economic cooperation

The American economy was boosted again by World War II. Toward the end of the war, at the Bretton Woods Conference in 1944, the United States' government mapped out its vision for a postwar world economy based on expanded free trade and a strong US dollar. In order to encourage international economic cooperation and to end currency instability, the United States undertook to convert foreign holdings of dollars into gold at a fixed price and to pump dollars abroad. This was how the dollar became the capitalist world's principal reserve currency. In the late 1940s and for most of the 1950s Americans made huge investments in Europe and Japan in an attempt to ensure that markets would be available for their new powerhouse economy. There was a political motive too. Expanding the United States' sphere of economic influence helped to prevent the spread of communism in Europe and Asia.

The United States now acted as a benevolent despot in world affairs. It set the rules of the postwar international economic system, but it allowed some countries to break these rules in order to rebuild their domestic economies. For example, tariff restrictions against American goods were not uncommon in friendly countries during this period. At home, the 1950s and 1960s were decades of unprecedented prosperity for most Americans. Average real incomes went up by 70 percent between 1950 and 1970. Most Americans came to own their own homes and automobiles and any number of consumer durables. Increased spending power among young Americans sustained a teenage market and a new youth culture emerged.

Dark shadows were cast across the "American Dream" of rising standards of living in the 1960s – not least by the war in Vietnam and the conflict surrounding it at home. Nevertheless, the financial rewards from "marketplace imperialism" seemed secure. In 1970, few Americans doubted that the United States was the chosen land. Most would not have believed that within 20 years its unquestioned economic might would be challenged by Germany and Japan, and that inflation, unemployment and debt would undermine prosperity.

Black Tuesday *(right)* Stock markets around the world came near to total collapse in October, 1987. The Wall Street market had its worst day ever, falling 508 points and wiping 22.5% off share values. Black Tuesday marked the end of a five year bull market in which share prices quadrupled.

THE PRICE OF LEADERSHIP

The American economy since the late 1960s has experienced shifts in industrial and regional prosperity as well as relative international decline. This slowing down was, in some respects, inevitable. The American economy was so dominant at the end of World War II that it was forced to protect its own markets by promoting the rapid economic growth of its former allies and enemies. As Europe and Japan regained strength, they came into competition with the United States once more. Nevertheless, the speed of economic decline in the United States came as something of a shock. By 1990 the Gross Domestic Product (GDP) of the United States was still nearly twice that of Japan, but its overall rate of growth was substantially slower than that of either Germany or Japan. In particular, the United States lagged behind in export growth and productivity increases. In 1990 it was running a substantial trade deficit with its major economic rivals. The economic rise of Germany and Japan, and America's relative decline in prosperity, were closely linked.

The reasons for this sudden reversal in fortune were partly that business in the United States had begun to look outward rather than inward. In the 1950s and 1960s American companies began to invest overseas, especially in Europe after the formation of the European Community (EC) in 1957. Exploiting new communications technologies, many companies expanded and became multinational corporations. Banks based in the United States also began to internationalize, and this enabled American companies to borrow dollars in offshore (non-American) financial markets. This, in turn, allowed United States' companies abroad to escape the restrictions on direct lending to foreigners imposed in the mid 1960s. The result was that many United States' businesses flourished abroad but their activity brought very little benefit to the domestic economy.

On the international political stage, too, the United States' economy began to wilt under the pressure of discharging its responsibilities as a superpower. Defense spending escalated sharply in the 1960s with the country's growing commitment to the war in Vietnam and taxes also

Trump Tower (*right*) One of the most spectacular successes – and failures – of the 1980s was Donald Trump – the personification of the boom-bust culture. He built up huge personal wealth on the back of property developments, such as this one in Manhattan, but the collapse of the property market in the late 80s reduced him to near bankruptcy.

Undetectable costs (*below*) The radar-evading Stealth bomber was one of several high profile – and high cost – defense programs initiated during the 1980s' economic boom. These programs were partly responsible for the highest American defense budgets in peacetime history (around 25 percent of GDP) and they put a further strain on the nation's deficit.

increased markedly. By 1970 the federal government was taking about 19 percent of the nation's wealth in the form of taxes; in 1950 the taxable proportion had been just 15 percent.

Dollar depreciation

In the 1970s the signs of imperial wear and tear on the United States' economy became increasingly evident. Gold began to drain from the country's reserves as many countries, including France, began to mistrust American intentions to maintain the gold-value of the dollar. This mistrust was vindicated in August 1971 when Richard Nixon (president 1969–74) broke America's undertaking at Bretton Woods to maintain a fixed exchange rate between gold and the US dollar. He sought instead to rebuild the international economic competitiveness of the United States on the back of a depreciating dollar.

Nixon's strategy was initially successful, but it could not conceal the underlying weaknesses of the economy: relatively high labor costs, low rates of productivity increase and poor investment in capital stock. By 1979 the dollar had been driven down so far that it could not safely fall further. Inflation was stalking the economy and non-United States' enterprises were threatening to exchange their dollars for more stable currencies.

From July 1979 Jimmy Carter (president 1977–81) forced up the value of the dollar by reducing its supply. He also tackled domestic inflation by raising interest rates to unprecedented postwar highs. Inflation duly declined – from 14 percent in the second quarter of 1979 to less than 4 percent in 1983. However, high interest rates choked business investment and checked consumer spending. Between 1979 and 1982, America, along with the rest of the world, fell into deep recession, and President Carter lost office to the conservative Republican Ronald Reagan (president 1981–89).

Reaganomics and its aftermath

The 1980s came to be known as the decade of Reaganomics. In the Economic Recovery Tax Act budget of 1981, Reagan attempted to cut the rate of tax that most Americans paid while maintaining the total amount of taxes (and spending) available to the federal government. The logic was that tax cuts would create incentives to work hard and hard work would bring rewards for individuals and governments alike in terms of higher incomes (bringing more tax revenue) and full employment. This was a form of supply-side economics.

So began the Reagan boom years. Unemployment fell to just 6 percent in 1986 and consumerism became the watchword of modern America. However, the boom was unsustainable. Military spending increased as America sought to redefine its political role in world affairs. As total tax yields failed to increase in line with expectations, spending was financed by borrowed money, and the United States moved into debt.

In the meantime, American multinational corporations continued to sever some links with the homeland. By the early 1990s they were doing as well as ever on the world stage. However, this was of little comfort to the United States' government whose problem was that, increasingly, American businesses were setting up plants and offices abroad. United States' capital was creating more and more jobs – but these were often overseas and for non-American workers.

AMERICA: FROM BOOM TO BUST

The Reagan years saw a dramatic reversal in the financial fortunes of the United States and in the nation's balance-of-payments position. The gap between spending on imports and revenue from exports widened rapidly for the worse, as did the gap between federal tax revenue and expenditure. In order to finance a high level of spending, borrowing soared. Between 1982 and 1986 a historic buildup of net assets abroad worth $141 billion was transformed into a net foreign debt of $112 billion. At the beginning of the 1990s the net external debt of the United States was close to $1,000 billion, and the country was the largest debtor nation in the world.

The repercussions were, and still are, immense. Although America is not party to the international debt crisis (no one doubts its ability to meet interest payments on its debt) the world economy will have to adjust for some years to come if America services its debts by expanding its export trade. If the United States is to run a balance-of-payments surplus, Germany and Japan may have to begin to run balance-of-payments deficits.

The selling of the United States

As late as 1970, the United States' economy was one of the most self-reliant in the advanced industrial world. In 1969 its total imports were worth a tenth of the value of goods (GDP) produced within the country. In western Europe during the same period the average figure was a quarter of GDP. In the following two decades American imports increased massively. By 1989 the country was importing merchandise worth nearly $500 billion – more than the total imports of Germany and Japan combined.

An increase in imports would not usually be a matter of political concern, but the decades between 1970 and 1990 coincided with a period of relative decline in the United States. During the same period there were growing fears that the nation's economy was becoming dependent on the funds and activities of foreigners. The growing national debt is one index of this dependency. Another index is what some describe as the "buying of America", or the extent of foreign ownership of United States' assets. By 1990 an estimated 20 percent of the American gross national debt was owned by foreigners, with Japanese investors alone holding close to $400 billion.

More visible than foreign investment in United States' debt has been the increasing purchase of United States' companies and real estate by non-United States' citizens since the mid 1970s. In terms of country of origin, the British are probably the largest investors in the United States – this has been the case since the 18th century. The British are now closely followed by the Japanese, and significant shares in United States' wealth are also owned by the Dutch, Canadians, Germans, Swiss, French and South Koreans. In the 1980s the Japanese electronics company Sony bought the American record company CBS, and the Japanese bank Sumitomo bought a $500 million equity stake in the famous Wall Street firm of Goldman Sachs. Another prominent firm, Wertheim and Co., fell to the British merchant bank Schroders plc, and the financial giant First Boston Inc. saw more than 20 percent of its equity bought by Credit Suisse of Switzerland. British investors own close to a billion dollars of real estate in Washington DC, where property prices increased rapidly in the 1980s. Real estate in the Pacific-rim cities of Los Angeles, San Francisco and Seattle also suffered inflation, partly through investment from east and southeast Asia, including Hong Kong. A quarter of all property finance in California is now controlled by Japanese banks, as is a third of the state's corporate lending.

Home away from home (*above*) Since the 1970s, foreigners have been buying into the American Dream. Japanese car manufacturers, Mazda, have bought out existing American companies or have set up their own production lines in the United States to avoid expensive import tariffs and quotas.

Just say no (*right*) The extent of foreign ownership of United States' wealth combined with perceived unfair trading practices has provoked a patriotic backlash among many Americans who believe that buying foreign goods jeopardizes American jobs and wealth.

The pessimistic view

Whether or not United States' citizens should be worried by all this activity is an

open question. Many agree with the maxim "once they own your assets, they own you", and there are good reasons to fear the consequences of being dependent on external decision-makers and the agendas of foreign businesses. For example, America might want to rebuild its industrial competitiveness by devaluing the dollar. Such an intention, however, might run counter to the interests of foreign investors who own large amounts of United States' debt (in dollars). These investors could threaten to withdraw their funds, causing a stock market crash. Other critics bemoan the loss of control over research and design, which might accompany a foreign takeover of corporate America.

By contrast, Ronald Reagan declared that "there are only winners, no losers" from greater participation in international economic exchanges. He might also have noted that the ratio of American imports to GDP remains low, at around 10 percent. For economic internationalists, foreign investment in the United States is no different from United States' investment overseas. Both forms of investment are supportive of enterprise and generate much needed jobs. United States' workers at Toyota's plant at Georgetown, Kentucky, can be expected to support this point of view (even if some redundant car-manufacturing workers in Detroit might see it otherwise). In the short term, at least, foreign investment in America allows United States' residents to live beyond what otherwise might be their means. Economic dependency can be a boon as well as a burden, as many countries dependent on United States' investment have long since discovered.

POST–INDUSTRIAL AMERICA?

The 1970s and 1980s were years of post-industrialism in the United States, characterized by a decline in manufacturing industry and explosive growth in the service sector. The change of emphasis was accompanied by a marked drift of economic power from the north and northeast to the south and west, and a tentative shift to new, flexible production systems within the workplace.

As early as 1973 commentators were talking of the coming of a postindustrial America but the change since then has been quite gradual. In 1990, for example, the United States was still the world's most powerful industrial nation. Manufacturing industry still accounted for 29 percent of GDP, though the proportion of GDP accounted for by service industries had risen to 69 percent. A continued decline of traditional manufacturing in the United States seems both inevitable and, in some ways, to be welcomed. Many Americans now expect their supplies of shoes and textiles, and even iron and steel, to come from abroad (often the Pacific basin). In return for these items they also expect to supply the rest of the world with services and with the high-tech goods in which the United States has a comparative advantage.

Alarm bells in the north

Nevertheless, the relative decline of manufacturing jobs since the 1960s has caused concern. Between 1962 and 1978 many United States' export markets shrank by more than half. In chemicals, steelmaking, agricultural machinery and particularly in the automotive trade, America was at a growing disadvantage in world markets. The Reagan years did little to change this. Manufacturers also faced competition at home, as imports increased massively through the 1970s and 1980s. United States' industries lost about a quarter of their share of world export markets in these two decades in spite of a general devaluation of the dollar during the period.

This loss of market share badly affected the traditional manufacturing states, particularly Massachusetts, Connecticut, Pennsylvania, New York, New Jersey, Ohio, Michigan, Illinois and Indiana (all in the north and northeast). Detroit, the Michigan automobile capital, lost more

A ship in every port (*right*) Almost every country in the world sells some American goods. The westcoast port of Seattle in Washington State services the fast-growing trade routes between Japan, the Far East and the United States.

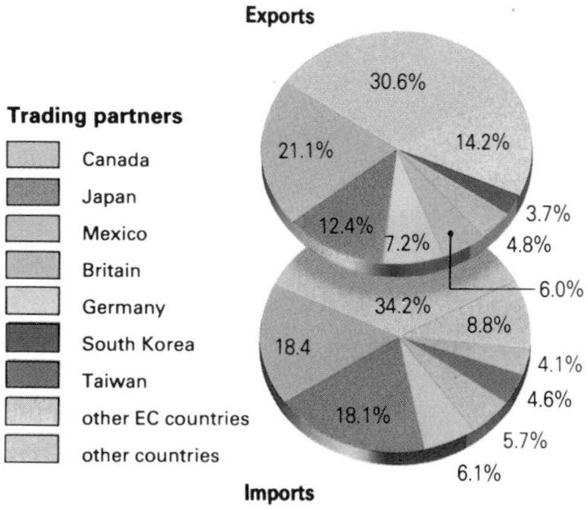

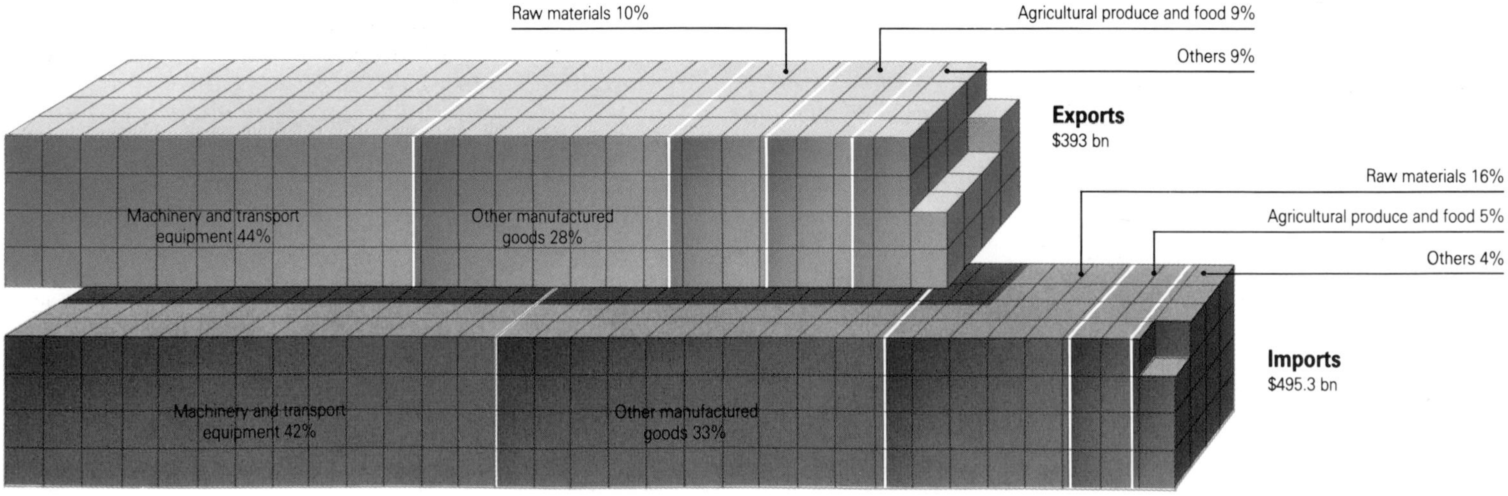

United States' balance of merchandise trade (*above and below*) The United States has a huge visible trade deficit; in 1990 it imported over $100 billion worth of goods more than it exported. Despite the decline in industry over the past two decades, manufactured goods are over half of American exports. The EC is the largest customer, followed by Canada and Japan.

MIAMI VICE

Miami Vice – a popular television program in the 1980s – featured designer suits, fast automobiles, rock music and boat chases around the drug-ridden waterways of Miami and Miami Beach. But drugs were not the only vice that shaped Miami and its environs. The city was transformed in the 1980s by speculative investments, often involving money of suspicious origin. Some banks in Miami had longstanding reputations for being repositories for the wealth of gangsters. Others benefited from capital in flight from Latin America in the wake of the 1980s' debt crisis there. Miami's skyline is now dominated by the banking industry – only New York surpasses it as a financial center in the United States. Brickell Avenue is the banking capital of Hispanic America. More than 100 banks from 25 countries have their headquarters or important branch operations in Miami. More than 100 non-banking multinational corporations also have their Latin American headquarters in the Miami area. These cater to a city where the population is nearly 50 percent Hispanic and to investors who live far beyond Miami.

than 70 percent of its manufacturing jobs between 1960 and 1985, and the city's population declined by 27 percent.

By the end of the 1980s more than one in three workers in the manufacturing city of Detroit was unemployed and in receipt of some form of public assistance. In spite of a boom in automobile sales during the Reagan years, many Americans had become reluctant to buy American vehicles, and favored more compact fuel-efficient Japanese models. Even some ostensibly "American" automobiles such as the Chevrolet Spectrum are Japanese by origin and made under license in the United States.

New regions of prosperity

Not all of America was hit by recession and hard times. The 1970s and 1980s were boom years for the economies of many of the southern states and those west of the Rockies. Although not previously noted for its manufacturing industries, California was home to more manufacturing jobs in 1985 than any other state. Meanwhile, service jobs were being created throughout the United States, particularly in New York where financial services were flourishing.

The drift of old and new industries to the south and west has been made possible by several recent developments. Communications have played a significant part: the building of the interstate highway system in the postwar years opened up these areas; as did the growth of air traffic in southern "hub" cities such as Atlanta, Georgia and Houston, Texas. Industry was also attracted by lower than average land costs in the south and by an abundance of available office space and greenfield sites. The absence of strongly unionized workforces was also a factor, as was the growth of cheap immigrant labor forces in southern states such as Florida, Texas and California.

Finally, the drift southward and westward was aided by the relative decline of mass-production technologies and products. The new industrial centers were able to introduce more flexible production systems and to take advantage of the trend toward specialist marketing and customization. Innovations included computerization, particularly in sophisticated stock control systems, and part-time working days. Improved communications technology and transport systems allowed a much wider choice of location. Instead of being limited to an expensive inner-city area, new businesses could set up an equally efficient plant on the outskirts of a city. The workforce would benefit, on the one hand from the educational and cultural facilities offered by the city, and on the other hand from better housing on the outskirts, open spaces and excellent leisure facilities. In the modern United States' economy, work and leisure more than ever go hand in hand. In the 1950s the Ford Motor Company was the icon of American business; the icons for the 1990s are service industries such as Columbia Records (owned by the Japanese conglomerate Sony) or the sportswear company Nike.

HEALTH, WEALTH AND WORK

The conditions governing employment and welfare benefits in the United States are based on a philosophy of individualism that is not often found in the social democracies of Western Europe. This philosophy is both a blessing and a burden for United States' citizens. In most of the country, economic vitality has long assured them of low unemployment, low inflation and high standards of living. The United States' economy is vibrant because individual firms are encouraged to be innovative, and floundering businesses are allowed to fail (but without fear of harsh punishment for bankruptcy). Yet unemployment pay in most states is low and (at least by European standards) offered only for a limited period. Labor is expected to be mobile and self-supporting, continuously on the lookout for better opportunities. On average, middle-class Americans change jobs and homes once every three years. Wages are sufficiently high to allow the majority of families in regular employment to own a house and automobile and a wide range of consumer goods.

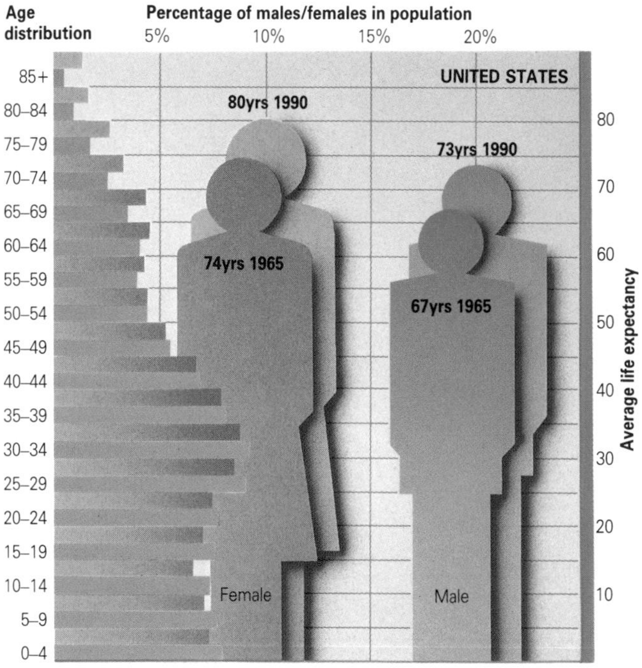

Life expectancy and age distribution *(left)* Like most developed countries, the United States has a large proportion of older people. In 1990 women could expect to outlive men by an average of seven years. Life expectancy is still rising, and retirement-aged citizens have begun to outnumber the total number of workers. This has caused cash-flow problems in Social Security (state pension) payments as more people are taking out of the system than are putting in.

Getting what you pay for *(right)* The United States is alone among the major developed countries in that it does not offer a comprehensive healthcare system for all its citizens. Private healthcare in America is the best in the world, but it is very expensive. Workers for caring companies can afford to be sick, but a major illness can quickly wipe out an uninsured family's savings and increase its debt.

The poverty trap

The problem is that not all families are average families. American society is divided by income, region, education, gender and ethnic background. In the early 1990s the richest 10 percent of United States' households received 25 percent of after-tax incomes; the poorest 20 percent of households received just 4.5 percent. Typically the poorest section of society lacks good quality healthcare and education and lives in more threatening neighborhoods. An estimated 30 percent of the population falls below the official poverty line, and this disadvantaged group is made up disproportionately of blacks and lone women with children. Black households headed by women are

Sport as business accessory *(above)* Not only do sporting events, such as professional football and baseball games, attract huge amounts of sponsorship money, they also provide an opportunity to do business. Hospitality suites, owned or rented by large companies, are common at stadia and other sporting venues. Here businessmen can wine and dine their clients while watching the game in comfort.

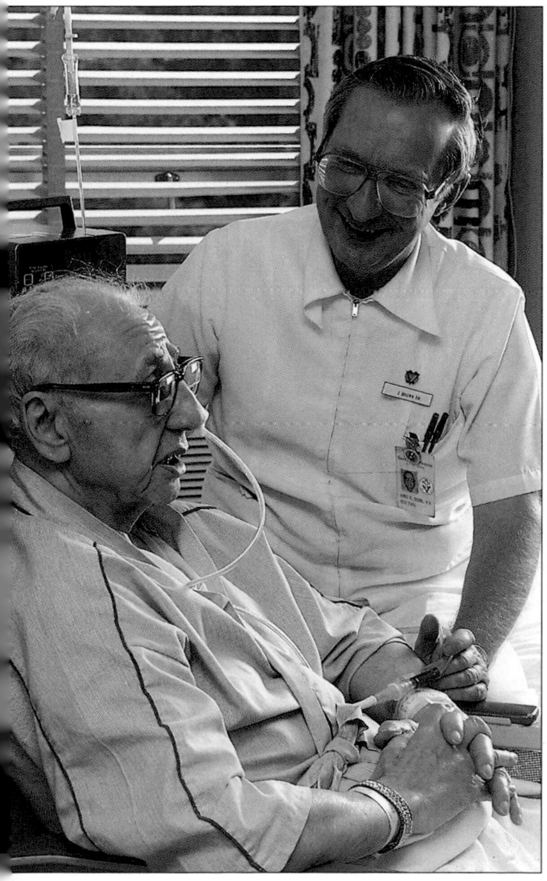

THE SPORTING LIFE

Many people associate the American economy with automobiles (Ford and General Motors), iron and steel (US Steel), or computer technology (IBM). These are (or were) the high-profile industrial goods and corporations of the country. In the United States in the 1990s, however, most people are employed in the service sector. This is a broad banding that includes leisure, entertainment and the sports industry – itself one of the fastest growing elements in the "new" economy. Sports are big business not just because of the clothing, and equipment needed, but also because of sponsorship, television rights and the power to draw income to wherever sports are played.

The financial stakes are now so high that cities compete to host the big teams that make up the National Football League, the National Basketball Association, and the American and National Baseball Leagues. Sold-out games generate cash incomes for the franchise holders, local hoteliers, concessionaires, retailers, restaurateurs and car-lot owners. Even some universities are chasing this money. Syracuse University in New York State opened its spectacular Carrier Dome in the early 1980s. The Dome, and other venues like it, vie with each other to feature rock concerts and state or national sporting events, all major revenue earners for the stadium and surrounding area.

at a particular disadvantage. In 1960 20.6 percent of American black children were being raised by their mothers alone; in 1985 the figure exceeded 50 percent.

The soaring cost of healthcare

Some typical difficulties facing poorer Americans are apparent in their access to medical care. The majority of Americans buy healthcare through medical insurance. Those in well-paid jobs expect their employer to cover most of the bill, and, for them, the standard of care is probably as good as anywhere in the world. However, there are significant administrative problems with this system. Not least, it is a huge drain on the national purse. Expenditure is unpredictable as medical insurance is based on retrospective payments for work performed.

Some critics see this as a recipe for overspending by the medical and drugs communities at the expense of the purchaser (including the government). In 1950 just over 4.4 percent of GNP in the United States was spent on healthcare; by the mid 1980s spending had soared to more than 10 percent. Meanwhile, insurance is too expensive for many individuals and families not covered by employers, and they sometimes fail to receive the treatment they need.

In recent years healthcare provision in the United States has been partially reformed. The federal government is now heavily involved through the Veterans Administration system, through environmental health legislation, and through the Medicaid and Medicare programs. Medicaid and Medicare were created in 1965 to provide health insurance for public welfare recipients and the elderly, respectively. They confirm that present American practice is to access care by means of private insurance, with only "target" groups being eligible for public subsidy. In the 1970s and 1980s the system changed again with the introduction of prepaid health plans. These allow healthcare to be purchased by fixed monthly premiums paid in advance of need (and even where there is no need of service). The scheme was intended to encourage contracted medical practitioners to buy healthcare services more efficiently. Their incentive is to keep health costs down rather than to bill for "unnecessary" treatments. By 1990, however, only about 7 percent of Americans were covered by prepaid health plans.

HOUSING, EDUCATION AND WELFARE

A major element in the American philosophy of life is that individuals should achieve what they want by their own endeavors. In spite of this deep-seated belief, there has been a gradual increase in federal and state intervention on behalf of the less well off throughout the 20th century. This happened particularly after the Great Depression (1929–33) and again during the 1960s after the Great Society programs of Lyndon Johnson (1908–73, president 1963–69).

Regional development (bringing jobs and services to disadvantaged areas) and public housing are among the most prominent areas where government has intervened. Regional development in the United States exists mainly in an indirect form. Industries are not generally coerced to locate in one part of the country rather than another, but government spending on defense and welfare can have a significant impact on particular regional economies. The states in the Great Lakes area and the Middle Atlantic states have been the main "losers" in terms of new patterns of spending by federal government since 1970. The main beneficiaries of federal spending since then have been the Pacific states (especially California and Washington) and the south–central region or Sunbelt states, particularly Florida and Texas.

The cost of home ownership

Home ownership came within the reach of most Americans after World War II. Mortgages at comparatively low interest rates were available from savings and loan associations and banks, and homeowners routinely claim tax relief on their mortgages. In spite of the economic boom of the last two decades, house prices are generally low by European standards. This is especially true where land is not expensive (most of the southeast, for example). Florida, with its beach resorts, is a notable exception in this otherwise inexpensive area. Land and house prices vary dramatically across the country between highly developed and less developed locations, with California at the top of the scale. Higher costs of living offset higher salaries in major metropolitan areas. Salaries and overheads tend to be lower in rural areas. State and local taxes also vary widely.

As the traditional northern manufacturing cities declined, the need for public assistance to lower-income families there has risen accordingly. Finding housing is generally up to the individual, but the government has increasingly found it necessary to intervene on behalf of some low-income groups. Chief among these are the large numbers of urban poor in the inner-city areas of New York City, Washington DC, Los Angeles and Chicago (among others). People below a certain income level are eligible for assistance from the federal government and are usually placed in public-sector housing. Such housing is typically associated with low levels of service provision and with high levels of violence. At the same time, the number of homeless people is increasing, and temporary shelter as well as long-term housing is becoming a national issue. Rural poverty persists in the Mississippi Delta and remote areas of the Deep South, where household income is often half the national average.

Living by the roadside off Route 66 *(above)* Running from Chicago to Los Angeles, Route 66 was for years a means of escape to a better life out west. However, this traveller has settled for a semi-permanent home by the highway.

The most expensive street in the world *(left)* The Giorgio department store is just one of the many exclusive and expensive shops on Beverly Hill's Rodeo Drive. The division between haves and havenots is very evident in Los Angeles.

Public and private education

Standards of education vary greatly within the United States. The vast majority of American children attend neighborhood public schools financed mainly out of local taxation. The quality of these schools varies enormously in terms of the maintenance of buildings, student-teacher ratios, standardized test scores and the number of students who go on to higher education. In some metropolitan areas, public schools have come to be associated with crime and violence as much as with education. As many people died in Los Angeles school playgrounds in 1988 as were killed in the whole of London, England in the same year. Alongside the public schools there is also a system of private schools.

About half of all American students continue their education beyond high school, and the majority of middle-class teenagers go on to college or university. Most students attend state universities, where typical annual fees in the early 1990s averaged $5,000. These fees are generally financed by student loans, though some students pay their way through university with part-time jobs. Still others are on partial or full scholarships, and a few have all expenses paid by their families. A minority of American students attend private universities, such as Harvard, Yale and Princeton. Typical fees at these Ivy League schools in the early 1990s were $18,000–$22,000 per year. The total cost of a four-year undergraduate degree at these rates can exceed $100,000 per student. Short of buying a house in a very expensive area, such as a coastal metropolitan city, this is probably the single largest expense that will face an upper-middle income American family. Higher education has become big business in the United States.

CALIFORNIA DREAMING

New York City remains the largest metropolitan center in the United States, but Chicago – traditionally at the heart of North America's communications – is no longer the nation's second city. That honor now belongs to Los Angeles, whose continuing growth signals an important change in the economy since the 1960s. As workers moved away from the declining manufacturing industries of the north and northeast and toward expanding service and manufacturing industries in the south and west, the economic center of the United States has moved from the Atlantic to the Pacific coast.

By the 1970s, California was the dominant state in America, the power generated by its newly acquired manufacturing capacity (particularly in high-technology industries) being clustered in and around Silicon Valley and Los Angeles. California returns more representatives to Congress than any other state, and wields considerable economic and political power. So vibrant is the modern Californian economy that, if it were a country in its own right, it would rank fifth among the world's economic giants. Even the Greater Los Angeles region would feature in a list of the world's 15 major economies. There is clearly more to California than Disneyland, Hollywood, sunworshiping and good wines. Los Angeles is the nation's most important port, and California may prove to be the key to the United States in the 21st – or Pacific – century. California is America's new heartland, and the "new Americans" are the legal and illegal Latinos who make up so much of the population of the southwest.

Violence and death in black urban America

The riots in south–central Los Angeles in April 1992 seemed to confirm the worst fears of many white Americans. Following the acquittal of four Los Angeles Police Department officers for the alleged beating of a black motorist, Rodney King, angry crowds of black Angelenos began to loot local stores and to set fire to large parts of the neighborhoods of south–central Los Angeles.

The Korean community suffered especially badly at the hands of these black activists, not least because the two communities have experienced considerable friction since a well publicized local court case. (In March 1991 a 15-year-old black girl, Latisha Harlins, was killed by a Korean shopowner over a disputed $1.79 bottle of orange juice; the shopowner was convicted, but sentenced only to community service and a $500 fine.) The so-called black underclass, featured in the films of Spike Lee and others, appeared to be standing up to the affluent white and Asian communities which surrounded the black community to the west and the north. Not for the first time, law and order had to be restored in black urban America by means of an occupying National Guard and night-time curfews.

Fears of rebellion in black urban America have prompted a spate of defensive architecture in west coast cities including San Francisco and Los Angeles. Transients (or homeless people) are discouraged from sleeping rough in more affluent areas by parks which are locked and patrolled at night, and by new "bump-proof" benches which can be sat upon but not slept upon. Meanwhile, some shops have installed small water-cannons in their doorways. These "sprinkler systems" are programmed to switch on at various times during the night, drenching anybody who might happen to be sleeping outside the shop's premises. Other defense systems include sophisticated security alarms in private apartment blocks and even the use of private bodyguards by members of the upper middle class. A siege mentality is apparent in some parts of Los Angeles and New York City.

A spiral of destruction

Notwithstanding these efforts and fears, the risks faced by middle-class white Americans are small, both in regard to property and person. The main victims of violence in urban America are the black and immigrant communities. This is true in two main ways. It is apparent, first, in the violence of poverty and neglect. In New York City, black Americans are disadvantaged from the time of their birth. City Health Department data from New York reveal that infant mortality rates in large parts of the largely white and prosperous boroughs of Queens and Staten Island are now less than 8.3 per 1,000 live births. In the predominantly non-white neighborhoods of Harlem, the south Bronx and central Brooklyn, infant mortality rates in 1990 were in excess of 14.4 per 1,000 live births. In some parts of black and Hispanic New York infant mortality rates are still in excess of those found in Jamaica and Chile; two of the world's relatively undeveloped countries.

A Bronx Yankee in Harlem *(above)* Although this part of Harlem might be mistaken for almost any inner city area in the United States, the level of danger threatening this young man on the streets is as high as it was on the battlefields of Vietnam during the height of the fighting there.

Down and out on Third St, New York *(right)* Homelessness is a major problem in most American cities. A lack of affordable housing has forced many onto the streets or to soup kitchens and shelters.

Black households also face violence of a more direct sort. In the Los Angeles riots of 1992 it was mainly black businesses that were looted or set ablaze. It was mainly blacks, too, who died in the riots, sometimes in exchanges with members of the Los Angeles Police Department.

From the ashes (*below*) The Los Angeles riots in 1992 may have finally galvanized public and governmental opinion that urban areas need immediate help and support. In the aftermath of the riots, President Bush announced a package of aid that was designed to help foster localized economies in Los Angeles and other inner city areas. These programs were also intended to provide jobs, housing and support services to urban areas and to improve the quality of life for urban dwellers.

Blacks also comprise a disproportionate element of the prison population, prompting some to inquire whether black offenders are treated too harshly by the criminal justice system. Finally, it is a startling fact that a black male in his twenties is more likely to be murdered in New York City than to die in any other way. The streets of some American cities are as dangerous for male black citizens as were the battlefields of Vietnam in the late 1960s and early 1970s.

The passport to a well-paid job?

Since World War II it has become something of a truism in American life that a college education is a passport to a well-paid job. In fact, this does not always follow. It would be more accurate to suggest that access to well-rewarded employment in the United States is difficult for those men and women who have not invested heavily in a postschool education. America's major employers compete to attract new recruits from the country's top colleges and universities: from private Ivy League schools such as Harvard, Yale and Princeton; from small liberal arts colleges such as Colgate and William and Mary; and from prestigious public-sector institutions such as the University of California at Berkeley and Los Angeles, and the University of Illinois at Champaign-Urbana.

The cost of a college education in the United States varies widely. In the fall of 1992 a student could register at the public two-year College of the Mainland in Texas City for a mere $321 a year. By contrast, a four-year degree course at the private Sarah Lawrence College in New York would cost a "freshman" student $24,380 in the same year. Average tuition costs at private four-year institutions in 1992–93 were $10,498. Average costs in the public sector are often half this amount. Student loans now provide 50 percent of total student financial aid. In the mid 1970s just 17 percent of student financial aid came in this form, with far more coming from parents directly, from student grants and awards and from the wages of students in part-time employment. Most student loans are taken out over a 10-year period or longer, and rates of interest vary from as low as 3 percent to 8 percent and more.

Graduation ceremony at the University of Notre Dame, Indiana, 1988.

I NEED

DEBT AND DEPENDENCE

THE TRADING LINK WITH EUROPE · FRAGILE INSTABILITY · POVERTY AND PREJUDICE

Drawn into the international economy as colonies of European powers, Central America and the Caribbean islands have traditionally been producers of raw materials (silver, coffee, bananas, sugar, bauxite and oil) for Western markets. Apart from Mexico, where manufacturing and the oil industry are thriving, the economies of the region remain undeveloped. Most are linked closely to the fortunes of a single export sector and are dangerously dependent on their largest trading partner, the United States. Since the 1960s, economic cooperation has been promoted through several organizations – the Caribbean Community (CARICOM) is the most recent. These have foundered due to competition instead of cooperation, and Mexico is seeking new allies through the North American Free Trade Agreement (NAFTA).

COUNTRIES IN THE REGION

Antigua and Barbuda, Bahamas, Barbados, Belize, Costa Rica, Cuba, Dominica, Dominican Republic, El Salvador, Grenada, Guatemala, Haiti, Honduras, Jamaica, Mexico, Nicaragua, Panama, St Kitts-Nevis, St Lucia, St Vincent and the Grenadines, Trinidad and Tobago

ECONOMIC INDICATORS: 1990

	UMIE* Mexico	LMIE* Jamaica	LIE* Honduras
GDP (US$ billions)	237.75	3.97	2.36
GNP per capita (US$)	2,490	1,500	590
Annual rate of growth of GDP, 1980–1990 (%)	1.0	1.6	2.3
Manufacturing as % of GDP	23	20	16
Central government spending as % of GNP	18	n/a	n/a
Merchandise exports (US$ billions)	26.8	1.35	0.92
Merchandise imports (US$ billions)	29.8	1.69	1.03
% of GNP received as development aid	0.1	7.1	16.4
Total external debt as a % of GNP	42.1	132.0	140.9

WELFARE INDICATORS

Infant mortality rate (per 1,000 live births)			
1965	82	49	128
1990	39	16	64
Daily food supply available (calories per capita, 1989)	3,052	2,609	2,247
Population per physician (1984)	1,242	2,040	1,510
Teacher–pupil ratio (primary school, 1989)	1 : 31	1 : 34	1 : 39

Note: The Gross Domestic Product (GDP) is the total value of all goods and services domestically produced. The Gross National Product (GNP) is the GDP plus net income from abroad.

** UMIE (Upper Middle Income Economy) – GNP per capita between $2,465 and $7,620 in 1990. LMIE (Lower Middle Income Economy) – between $610 and $2,465. LIE (Low Income Economy) – below $610.*

THE TRADING LINK WITH EUROPE

The 33 countries of the region first encountered international trading when European explorers and merchants established colonies after Columbus's voyage to the region in 1492. During the colonial period, trading in each country was dominated by its European mother country. Spain held sway over the mainland while Britain, France and Spain each controlled several Caribbean islands. During the late 17th century, the British established a trading network linking Europe (supplying manufactured goods), Africa (slaves), the colonies in the Caribbean (sugar), North America (wood and provisions) and the Spanish Main. Throughout Central America, production depended on forced labor. Central American Indians worked for the Spanish government in return for "protection" (*encomienda*) and black Africans were imported throughout European and American territories to work as slaves.

Independence and free trade

Following the withdrawal of Spanish colonial power in 1821 and the emancipation of British slaves beginning in 1834, free trade was established in the region. The British immediately began to trade with the countries of the mainland, where the United States became their chief rival. The building of the railroads, made it possible to open up land in the interior to grow coffee and bananas, newly introduced as cash crops. Several American corporations took advantage of the improved infrastructure to establish their own banana plantations, while the coffee growers of El Salvador set up locally controlled rural ventures. In the Caribbean, sugar plantations flourished in Cuba and the Dominican Republic, and the crops fetched good prices on the open market. After Spain's defeat in the Spanish American war of 1898 United States' involvement in sugar growing and processing, in the former Spanish islands of Cuba and Puerto Rico, grew substantially. In contrast, sugar plantations in the former British and French Caribbean territories declined or stagnated after 1900 and the loss of trade was only partly offset by banana exporting (particularly in Jamaica), controlled by an emerging class of peasant farmers, the descendants of former slaves. The economy continued to develop along these lines until the Great Depression of 1929, when the progress made in previous years was swept away and recession set in during the 1930s.

The agriculture-based economies of the Caribbean have suffered from France's and then Britain's membership of the European Community (EC). Various supply agreements have been set up to try to maintain the region's trade in bananas, sugar and rum (distilled from fermented sugar cane). However, the Caribbean is a high-cost producer, making their exports uncompetitive in a market that is shrinking anyway as Western nations reduce their sugar consumption. The countries of Central America have diversified away from bananas and coffee into cotton,

sorghum (used for cattle fodder and processed into a sweet syrup) and cattle farming. However, these largescale enterprises benefit the large multinational corporations, with little being passed on to the impoverished rural population.

The need to diversify

In recent years several parts of the region have followed policies of diversification into modern manufacturing and service industries. This has proved most successful in Mexico and the surrounding countries where American firms are prominent. Various tax incentives have also

Borderline economy *(above)* Mexican workers ending their shift at a Chrysler automobile plant. Manufacturing industry in Mexico is heavily dependent on this and other United States' multinationals who have moved south to take advantage of lower labor costs.

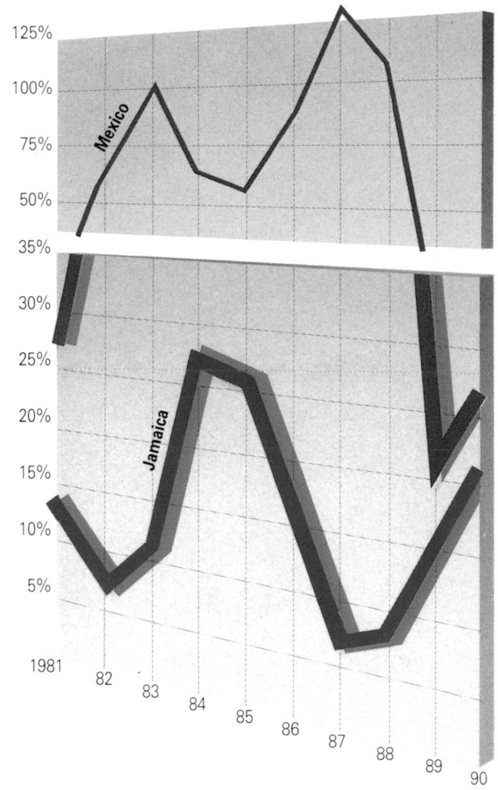

Profile of inflation *(above)* Linked to the international debt crisis, inflation in Mexico rose and fell sharply in the 1980s. Even at its peak, over 125 percent, Mexico's figure was far from the region's highest. Foreign debt drove Jamaica's inflation to a peak in 1984.

Map of GDP per capita *(below)* The Cayman Islands and Bahamas, due to offshore banking, have by far the region's highest GDP per capita. Mexico City, the region's only major international business center, houses the largest banks and commercial offices.

encouraged diversification in the Caribbean, but growth is still relatively slow. Jamaica, Guyana and Haiti export unprocessed bauxite and alumina (the semi-refined state) for aluminum production but have been slow to undertake the processing themselves because of the high amount of energy used in refining. Mexico and Trinidad and Tobago export oil, particularly to their northern neighbors. Jamaica, Barbados, Cuba, Puerto Rico and the Windward and Leeward Islands have developed tourist enclaves on their white sandy beaches, and for many islands this is their main economic activity. However, civil war and worldwide recession have restricted the development of tourism in Central America, with the exception of Mexico.

The economy in Cuba represents a major deviation from the pattern in the rest of the region. Following the Castro revolution in 1959, a socialist economy was constructed around sugar exports to the former Soviet Union, and Cuba later joined the communist trading alliance. The former Soviet Union subsidized Cuba through cheap supplies of oil, and by buying Cuban sugar at above-market prices. Cuban dependence on the Soviet Union became as complete as its previous reliance on the United States. At the end of 1991 Cuba's whole trading network was threatened as Soviet unity collapsed.

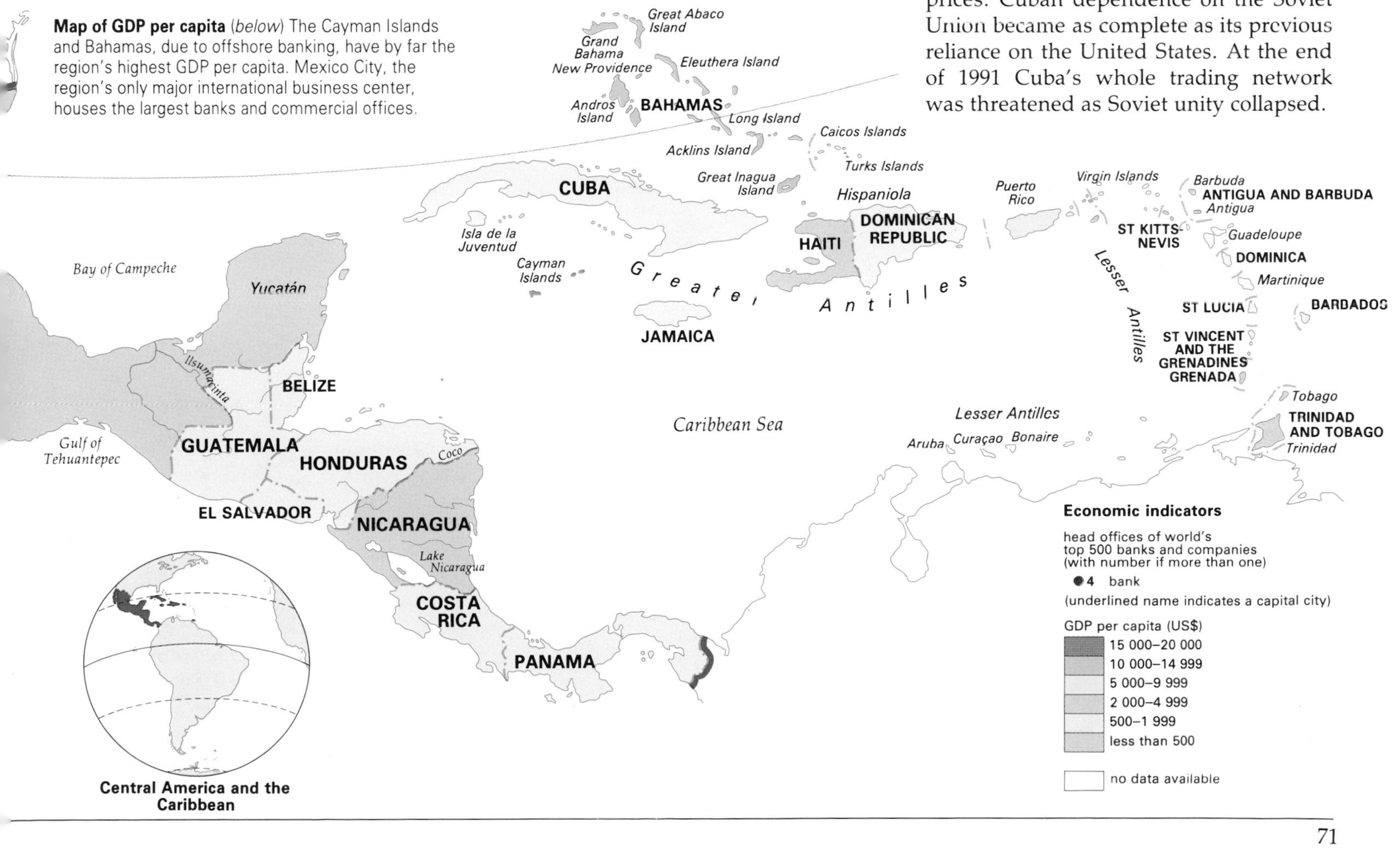

FRAGILE INSTABILITY

In the early 1990s the economies of Central America and the Caribbean were still predominately dependent on aid and borrowed money. Exports were mostly raw agricultural products or mineral resources, and imports were manufactured goods or fuel for energy – so the terms of trade remained weighted against the countries of the region. During the world recession of the 1980s, the prices of commodities dropped in the world market and dependence on the United States deepened. Only a near monopoly of a vital commodity could empower any country to maintain high prices, and no part of the region has ever achieved that. Japanese purchases of Jamaican Blue Mountain coffee have greatly stimulated coffee production, but at the expense of renewed soil erosion. In Central America only the Mexican oil industry controls a primary product vital to the United States in all political and economic climates.

Sporadic warfare also devastated several Central American and Caribbean economies during the recession years of the 1980s. The invasion of Grenada by the United States in 1983 turned its minuscule economy upside down, only for the redemocratized government to have financial support from the United States withdrawn in the late 1980s. During a period of guerrilla warfare, El Salvador received vast amounts of United States' aid and support for its disintegrating economy, but it still fears being abandoned in the way that Grenada was. Perhaps the most extraordinary economic developments have been in Nicaragua, where the United States funded a low-intensity war against the left-wing Sandinista government, consuming half the tiny country's budget. The Chomorro government's victory in 1990 established some degree of stability. Nicaragua's economy was subsequently shored up by the World Bank and the International Monetary Fund (IMF), though the bulk of the population remained unemployed.

Mexico's balance of merchandise trade *(below)* Trade with the United States dominates imports and exports. Mexico is one of the world's largest exporters of energy, ahead of Kuwait and Libya; oil provided more than 35 percent of export revenues in the 1980s. Its exports account for nearly 1 percent of world trade.

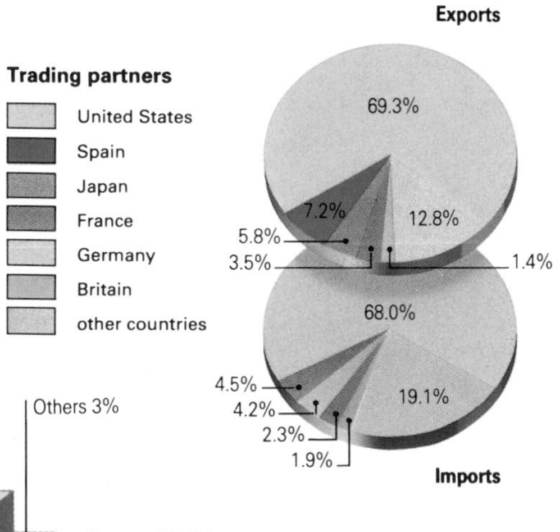

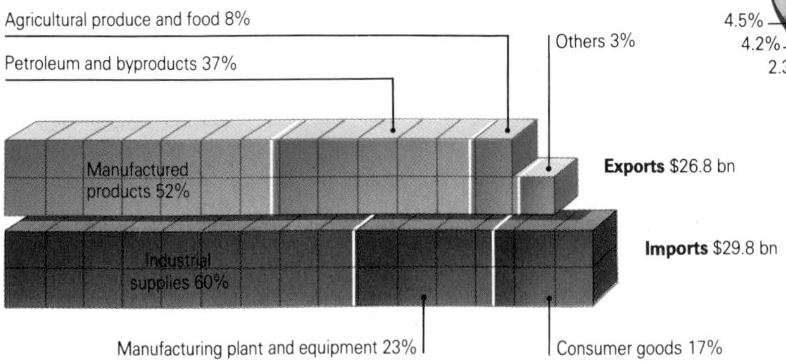

Rescue packages

Efforts to rebuild economic confidence in the region have had limited success. Political volatility has frightened off new investors and made existing investors anxious to move their money elsewhere. In a bid to create stability, Jamaica's right-wing government led by Edward Seaga has established a policy of friendship with the United States as the main platform of its reforms in the early 1980s;

Gateway to trade *(left)* A loaded ship passes through the Panama Canal, opened in 1914 to create direct access between the Atlantic and Pacific oceans. Trade is crucial to Panama's economy, equivalent to 80 percent of GDP in 1992.

Small business in Jamaica *(right)* Washing car windows on a street in Kingston, this boy joins the ranks of Jamaica's thriving informal economy. Jobs in the formal sector are scarce, providing employment for only 37.5 percent of the population in 1990.

but American financiers and manufacturers could still not be persuaded that investment in Jamaica was a good risk.

The United States has also made attempts to improve the situation. As early as 1982, President Reagan's Caribbean Basin Initiative was intended to stimulate United States' investment and open the American market to Caribbean products. However, the United States' sugar and textile lobbies (protecting their own interest) limited the impact of the initiative and much of the aid money involved went to trusted antisocialist regimes in El Salvador, Costa Rica, Jamaica and other countries of the Commonwealth Caribbean. As a result, Costa Rica, Jamaica and the Dominican Republic, all with democratic regimes and skilled labor forces, have benefited from the Caribbean Basin Initiative but the rewards have not been shared out more widely.

In Mexico, government efforts to regenerate growth in the economy using the revenues from vast new oil discoveries in the late 1970s failed miserably. By 1982 inflation and the balance of payments deficit created by collapse in the world price of oil had become an intolerable strain on the whole economic structure. In the same year Mexico gave the world a new term – "debt crisis" – when it admitted that it could no longer service its debt of more than $100 billion. Opening up the Mexican economy to capitalist forces and expanding the geographical extent of its duty-free export zone seem to be bringing Mexico out of recession, but the smaller economies of the Caribbean appear not to be responding to similar initiatives. Jamaica and Trinidad and Tobago are both in the hands of the IMF, but they are struggling to meet its stringent financial targets. Their already fragile economic structures have been damaged by falls in the world prices of oil and bauxite.

Finding new directions

Establishing new forms of dependency seem to be the only solutions currently being pursued to solve the region's economic problems. Mexico is on the brink of entering the North American Free Trade Association (NAFTA), a move that is likely to increase its dependence on the United States' economy. Some politicians and businessmen were hopeful that the creation of a single European market in 1992 would bring about new trading opportunities, but others feared it would marginalize the region still further as new global trading blocs emerged. However, attempts to challenge age-old dependency in Central America and the Caribbean have come to very little. It is extremely difficult for small countries, such as Jamaica, Grenada, Nicaragua and Cuba to isolate themselves from their traditional trading partners or to renegotiate new trading terms with them. The world's largest capitalist nation, the United States, can exert powerful commercial and military leverage against smaller countries. Only Cuba was comparatively successful in confronting capitalist dependency in recent years by shifting into the socialist camp. It is difficult to predict how the Cuban economy will fare as its moral and economic support crumbles in the aftermath of Soviet dissolution.

CARIBBEAN OFFSHORE BANKING

Almost devoid of natural resources to trade, several Caribbean islands have legislation that allows offshore banking. Most activity is concentrated in the Cayman Islands, the British Virgin Islands, Anguilla, the Turks and Caicos Islands, the Bahamas, and the Netherlands Antilles, all of which have unsavory associations with laundering drug money. The Bahamas have been independent of Britain for over 20 years, but the Caymans, British Virgin Islands, Anguilla, and the Turks and Caicos are still dependent, leaving Britain with the responsibility of maintaining some degree of economic supervision.

The key factor in the development of offshore banking has been proximity to the United States. The islands provide tax havens for American investors and for those trafficking in drugs into the United States, generating profits that must be handled clandestinely. Anguilla had 42 banks by the late 1980s; the Cayman Islands recorded 520 banks and trust companies; and the Bahamas boasted 380 banks, only half of which had more than a name plate and a numbered post box.

Acapulco, Mexico's most luxurious city *(above)* is the center of the country's tourist trade. Most tourists come from the United States, swelling an industry that generated revenue of $5 billion in 1991, creating 650,000 jobs in construction and service industries.

POVERTY AND PREJUDICE

In almost all the countries of Central America and the Caribbean, wealth is highly concentrated in the hands of the few. The majority of societies continue the pattern of privilege established during the colonial era when Europeans formed an exclusive elite. Subsequent government policies have tried to redistribute prosperity more widely but with little success. In the early 1990s most inhabitants of the region still lacked access to even basic healthcare, social services or education.

Class, race and hierarchy

Everywhere, the class hierarchy remains steeply graded, particularly in unreformed societies (such as El Salvador) where the rural working classes live in hovels on the verges of the roads. In the Caribbean, the class hierarchy has been partly broken down by the welfare policies of colonial and postcolonial governments (especially in the British and French Caribbean) but the quality of life for the majority of the population is still very poor.

Up to two-thirds of the urban labor force in the region work as domestic servants, yard boys, shoe shine boys, market traders or unskilled repairmen. Some survive through a range of quasi-legal or illegal activities. The bulk of the higher-grade and better paid jobs in government, financial services, public services, manufacturing or port-side activities are also concentrated in the cities, and those fortunate enough to hold them have access to cheap domestic servants.

The class hierarchy is reinforced by race, color or ethnic and cultural distinctions. In the British and French Caribbean, the white, brown and black populations generally correspond with the elite, middle class and the working class respectively. Peasants and manual workers are black or East Indian; white-collar workers are normally brown or mulatto; planters and influential businessmen are white. Decolonization, however, has brought black people into political prominence. Central America has similar correlations between color and class: elite groups are typically European in appearance, though the middle and lower classes may be of mixed race. At the bottom of the scale is the vast class of impoverished landless peasants, which in some countries (notably Mexico and Guatemala) is predominantly Amerindian.

Small exceptions

In this web of privilege and prejudice only Cuba and Costa Rica have made significant headway in providing a more equal quality of life for all of their citizens. During the 1960s and 1970s Soviet aid helped to fund welfare programs in Cuba providing education and healthcare to the mass of the population. It was also the government's declared intention to stamp out the racial inequality so prevalent throughout the rest of the region, albeit without much success. During the 1980s the Gorbachev regime severely cut back aid to Cuba, and its economy reached a crisis with the dissolution of the Soviet Union in 1991.

Costa Rica, an oasis of democracy and stability since 1920, is unique in Central America because it has a social security system. Its health service and old-age pension schemes are far superior to anything else available in the region. In 1992 about 27 percent of the national budget was allocated to healthcare, distributed through community hospitals. As a result, life expectancy at birth is as good as in the United States and infant mortality is the lowest in Latin America. Government agencies cooperate to bring health services and preventive medicine

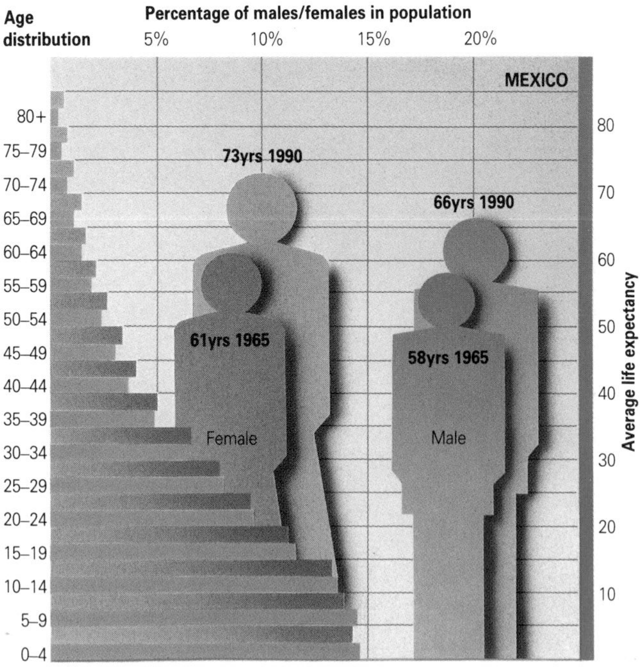

Lessons in hardship *(right)* A young Nicaraguan girl carries her chair home at the end of the school day in one of the poor neighborhoods of the capital, Managua. Seven years' free compulsory education is offered by the government, but the severe shortage of facilities means that it is not unusual for children to bring their own materials and furniture. Trained staff are also in short supply, and only about half of the school-age children can be provided for. Of these, fewer still receive secondary education.

Life expectancy and age distribution *(left)* Mexican women now live an average of 12 years longer than they did in 1965, while men have gained an average of only 8 years. The average number of children per mother in Mexico is 3, contributing to a relatively large segment (37 percent) of the population that is under 15 and a low percentage of over 65s (3.8%).

to the poor, especially in dispersed rural communities. Two meals a day are served to all preschool and primary school children as well as to expectant and nursing mothers. Costa Rica also has a good education system from primary through to tertiary level and the highest literacy rate (93 percent) in Central America.

If the vast majority of the inhabitants of Central America and the Caribbean are underprivileged, this is even more true of women than of men. Middle-class women are now prominent in the professions, supported by a huge underclass of female servants. Women of the working class, whether peasants or members of the urban poor, are forced to supplement household income by work as seamstresses or craft producers; or work outside the home as servants, factory workers or market stallholders. Women are noticeably absent from the public arena of politics. They are "invisible" even in small administrative units in rural Mexico, where, otherwise, a strong sense of democratic involvement exists.

LEARNING TO READ AND WRITE IN NICARAGUA

The left-wing Sandinista revolutionaries who seized power in Nicaragua in 1979 inherited a society that was 40 percent illiterate. In rural areas, the figure rose to 70 percent. Provision of schooling was at the root of the problem – in rural areas only 5 percent of children finished primary education, compared with 44 percent in urban areas. In 1980, a literacy crusade was launched, funded by foreign governments and nongovernmental organizations. The crusade involved some 100,000 teachers, many of them foreign volunteers, and in just 6 months they cut illiteracy drastically.

The Sandinistas proposed to introduce work-study programs at all levels from kindergarten to university. By the mid 1980s, a seven-fold increase in children enrolled in preschool and special education had been recorded, but only at the expense of engaging untrained teachers. All these achievements were to be engulfed by the low-intensity warfare unleashed by the United States-backed Contras. As early as 1985, about 800 schools had been closed in response to fighting and almost 30 had been totally destroyed. By the time the Sandinistas were defeated in the 1990 election, Nicaragua was desperate for peace at any price.

The informal economy in Mexico

Two factors favor a thriving informal economy in Mexico: the lack of an effective political opposition to challenge the long-incumbent ruling party, the PRI (Institutional Revolutionary Party), and the chronic shortage of formal-sector employment in the urban areas. This shortage has been made even worse by the debt crisis that has overtaken Mexico since 1982. In some cities more than 60 percent of the labor force is employed "off the record" and avoids paying taxes on earnings. Many simply describe themselves as self-employed; others form shifting work crews, are paid irregular wages and lack any formal job security. The majority of the tasks carried out in this way are, in a strict sense, illegal: stallholders do not hold licenses, food sellers disregard public health requirements and construction workers are unprotected by safety regulations.

Even more blatantly illegal transactions are common. Begging, stealing, prostitution, extortion and drug smuggling are rife in the more dangerous sections of Mexico's towns and cities. In view of the general poverty in urban areas and the comparatively vast sums of money that can be made by these illegal activities, it is not surprising that the organizers of crime often act under political protection; or that law enforcement is frustrated by political insiders, if not by the police.

Spreading the rot

Corruption extends into many walks of Mexican life, from bribing traffic policemen to ignoring real-estate developers who make illegal sub-divisions in new property. The degrees of illegality involved in the informal housing market are legion. The plots of land for building may not even be owned by the developer; and even if the land tenure is legal, the development may contravene planning, public health or building-structure requirements. In outright squatter settlements, the main organizer may demand protection money from the squatters, and later use the money raised to buy electoral votes. Local political leaders have been known to impede legalization and slow down the provision of services to maintain their control over the poor. The politically ambitious have no economic leverage over people without needs.

In Mexico City, the world's largest metropolis, almost half the inhabitants in the last two decades have been housed in self-built neighborhoods, all illegal in one sense or another. The PRI-government has presided over the creation of this state of affairs and controlled every kind of state intervention and regulation, including the recent social welfare program

Skilled workers (*below*) advertising their availability for work in Mexico City. Only 36 percent of Mexicans were active in the formal economy in 1992, reflecting the extreme shortage of jobs. Corrupt officials often sell jobs – hiring workers in return for cash payments.

Single-party domination (*right*) The PRI has controlled the Mexican economy since 1929. New administrations announce anticorruption measures, but officials continue to line their own pockets as insurance against losing office.

known as Solidarity. In this way, the government has been able to retain considerable control over the urban poor without making a vast outlay in state funds to subsidize formal housing. Most urban Mexicans cannot avoid some element of illegality and corruption in their daily lives, either in the informal labor market or through informal housing.

The PRI has been put under great pressure, particularly from the United States, to permit fair elections and stop vote rigging, leading to a genuinely plural political democracy that would bring about much-needed financial reform. However, the police and state officials who might be expected to implement change are themselves under suspicion of offering protection to Mexican drug dealers and other forms of racketeering.

The situation continues to cause grave concern among those Mexicans who campaign for a fairer society. Corruption and illegality may appear to offer opportunities to disadvantaged groups, but they perpetuate the inequality that leads to worsening poverty. Increasing numbers of Mexicans recognize that corruption may intensify existing exploitation, while blocking calls for radical change.

STRUGGLING TOWARD SOLVENCY

A LAND OF PRECIOUS METALS · BORROWED SUCCESS · EVENING THE ODDS

South America is often classified as part of the Third World, a view that reflects the extreme poverty in parts of the region, but fails to take account of sophistication and wealth elsewhere. Certainly conditions in Bolivia, Peru or northeastern Brazil resemble the standard of living in developing countries. But the region also contains advanced urban industrial economies that produce the majority of their own manufactured goods. South America makes most of its own cars, most of its population watches television, most can read and write. The first three-quarters of the 20th century was a period of rapid growth in many parts fueled by extensive international borrowing. Only since 1980 have rising interest rates caused loan repayments to soar, and decline to set in throughout all but 3 of the region's 12 countries.

COUNTRIES IN THE REGION

Argentina, Bolivia, Brazil, Chile, Colombia, Ecuador, Guyana, Paraguay, Peru, Surinam, Uruguay, Venezuela

ECONOMIC INDICATORS: 1990

	UMIE* Brazil	LMIE* Colombia	LIE* Bolivia
GDP (US$ billions)	414.06	41.12	4.48
GNP per capita (US$)	2,680	1,260	630
Annual rate of growth of GDP, 1980–1990 (%)	2.7	3.7	−0.1
Manufacturing as % of GDP	26	21	13
Central government spending as % of GNP	36	15	19
Merchandise exports (US$ billions)	31.4	7.1	0.92
Merchandise imports (US$ billions)	20.4	5.6	0.72
% of GNP received as development aid	0.0	0.2	10.9
Total external debt as a % of GNP	25.1	44.5	100.9

WELFARE INDICATORS

Infant mortality rate (per 1,000 live births)			
1965	104	86	160
1990	57	37	92
Daily food supply available (calories per capita, 1989)	2,751	2,179	1,916
Population per physician (1984)	1,080	2,598	1,530
Teacher–pupil ratio (primary school, 1989)	1 : 23	1 : 30	1 : 25

Note: The Gross Domestic Product (GDP) is the total value of all goods and services domestically produced. The Gross National Product (GNP) is the GDP plus net income from abroad.

** UMIE (Upper Middle Income Economy) – GNP per capita between $2,465 and $7,620 in 1990. LMIE (Lower Middle Income Economy) – GNP per capita between $610 and $2,465. LIE (Low Income Economy) – GNP per capita below $610.*

A LAND OF PRECIOUS METALS

South America's position in the current world economy has been carved out by its colonial past. From the 15th century, the whole area was conquered by European powers – the west by the Spanish, Brazil by the Portuguese, Guyana by the British, and modern Surinam by the Dutch and French. The new colonies were exploited to produce wealth for the colonizers. Spain, for example, taxed its colonies heavily, levying one-fifth of the wealth of Venezuela, Colombia, Ecuador, Peru, Bolivia, Chile, Paraguay, Uruguay and Argentina, mainly in the form of gold and silver. In Brazil, cotton and sugar were the principal exports to Portugal, though gold also became important in the 18th century. In return, European countries supplied the colonies with manufactured products, a pattern of trade that was to dominate even after most of the region became independent during the 1820s.

Independent exporting

Britain helped the fledgling republics gain their independence from Spain and Portugal because it wanted to trade directly with the new nations. By the end of the 19th century, South America was well integrated into the world economy. It exported agricultural produce and unrefined minerals and imported most of its manufactured goods, the majority from Britain, which was then the world's major industrial power.

During the 20th century South America developed a wider range of exports. In addition to the established commodity trade in gold and silver, the region began to export iron ore, tin, bauxite and copper. Different kinds of agricultural products were also developed for international markets: wheat from Argentina, lamb and beef from Argentina and Uruguay, coffee from Brazil and Colombia, and fruit from Chile. Most important of all, oil was discovered in Venezuela in the 1920s, and in several other republics in subsequent years.

Expanding trade created considerable new wealth, but it was concentrated in the hands of a few. By 1914, Argentina and Uruguay were close to being among the world's richest countries and their economies were expanding very rapidly. Southern Brazil was also booming, stimulated by massive exports of coffee. Venezuela, an economic backwater until oil was discovered, became the world's largest exporter of petroleum and profited accordingly.

Industrial economies

The export boom began to fund industrialization in parts of the region – by the 1920s, Argentina and Brazil, who led the way, had developed into important manufacturing nations. Ironically, the process of industrialization was hastened by the world recession of the 1930s: faced with shrinking revenues from a greatly reduced export market, local economies were forced to produce manufactured goods that they had previously been able to afford to import. This process – known as import substitution – was encouraged by governments during and after World War II through a combination of import restrictions and incentives for local and foreign investors. This policy led to the rapid expansion of industry in South America between 1940 and 1980. By 1980, most of the region's cars, steel, refrigerators and textiles were made locally.

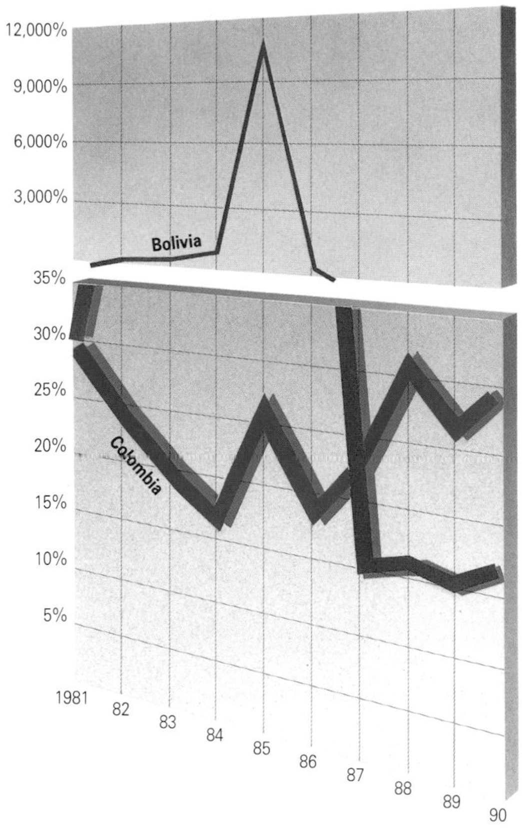

Profile of inflation *(above)* Inflation in South America spiraled out of control in some countries during the 1980s as a result of huge budget deficits related to the debt crisis. In 1985, Bolivia's inflation reached a staggering 11,752 percent.

Map of GDP per capita *(above)* The region encompasses wide variations in wealth and poverty. Even within Brazil, which had the highest average GDP per capita in 1990, there are stark contrasts between the relatively affluent urban areas and the countryside. Per capita incomes in Bolivia, Ecuador and Peru are among the lowest in Latin America.

Made in Brazil *(left)* Hundreds of Fiats ready for export from the docks at Rio de Janeiro. High investment by foreign corporations has boosted rapid expansion of the region's manufacturing industry since World War II, particularly in Brazil.

Although agriculture continued to be a major employer, its contribution to the economy of the region shrank relative to industry throughout the postwar period. Despite rapid population growth, which averaged about 2.5 percent during this period, most countries were much more prosperous in 1980 than they had been in 1940. The new affluence was, however, spread unevenly: living standards in Venezuela, Argentina and southern Brazil were comparable with those in Italy or Spain; while Bolivia, Ecuador and Peru had per capita incomes little higher than many African countries.

BORROWED SUCCESS

By the 1980s South American industry had grown to the extent that the region was nearly self-sufficient in manufactured goods. The number of jobs had risen dramatically in this sector and industrial wages had increased, but employment opportunities could not keep pace with the region's high population growth. Many South Americans were forced to eke out a living in the informal sector. Street trades, smallscale manufacturing and domestic service employed large numbers at very low incomes.

In the rural areas, many export producers were discovering that it was no longer profitable to produce for the world market. Government taxes and distorted exchange rates were reducing the incentive to export. Largescale agricultural exporters such as Argentina and Uruguay were seeing their share of world trade fall rapidly. At the same time, the rate of industrial growth had also begun to slow; once manufacturing output could satisfy the domestic market, opportunities for new growth were limited.

Paying the piper

This situation might have continued unchanged for a number of years. Conditions were worrying but not catastrophic. However, the development of South America in the 1970s had been based on extensive borrowing. Transnational companies had invested heavily to develop manufacturing plants and to open up new mineral reserves. Foreign banks had been eager to lend large sums to local governments in an attempt to recycle the savings of Middle Eastern oil producers. Additional loans, from multinational institutions such as the World Bank and the Inter-American Development Bank, had been used to build up urban infrastructure. When exports failed to keep up with imports, many countries began borrowing again to finance the deficits on their balance of payments. After a sharp rise in worldwide interest rates in the late 1970s, few of the region's economies could service their overseas debts.

Since 1980, most South American countries have been forced to ask the International Monetary Fund (IMF) for additional time to repay their debts. In return, the IMF has stipulated that they restructure their economies by raising taxes, cutting public expenditure and balancing their national budgets. Governments have been encouraged to sell off their unprofitable enterprises, such as state airlines, railroads, banks and electricity companies. Local currencies have been devalued to make exports more competitive and imports more expensive. As a result, exports (particularly manufactured goods) increased, sometimes dramatically, and imports fell greatly in volume. Finally, governments have been required to reduce subsidies and other forms of intervention in the market. Countries that did not comply with the IMF's requests risked having future help and funds withheld.

The price of reform

There can be little doubt that some of the recommended changes were necessary. Exchange rates were unrealistic, political

Aluminum products (*right*) at a processing plant in Surinam. Both Surinam and Guyana have large deposits of bauxite – the ore from which aluminum is made. More and more of the region's raw materials are now processed before export as protection against fluctuating commodity prices.

The drug war (*left*) Soldiers set fire to an illegal cocaine-making laboratory in rural Bolivia, where many poor communities rely on coca cultivation as their main source of income. The powerful drug barons, who make millions from the region's massive drugs industry, are often beyond the reach of the law.

corruption was endemic and governments were operating many of their enterprises inefficiently. Under the new regime many inefficient state enterprises have been liquidated, saving tax-payers large sums of money.

However, the cost of restructuring has been steep, and standards of living have dropped accordingly. During the 1980s only Chile, Colombia and Paraguay were able to increase their per capita incomes, while all of the rest experienced decline. Sometimes the declines were dramatic: between 1981 and 1990, per capita incomes fell 30 percent in Peru, 28 percent in Guyana, 24 percent in Argentina, 23 percent in Bolivia and 20 percent in Venezuela. Inflation achieved spectacular rates: over 11,000 percent in Bolivia in 1985; almost 5,000 percent in Argentina in 1989; and over 8,000 percent in Peru in 1990.

Most of the urban population – middle class and poor alike – suffered badly. Real wages fell in 10 years in Peru to two-fifths of their earlier value. Years of progress were wiped out as nutrition levels declined and living standards fell to levels typical of the 1960s. By the early 1990s, confidence in government performance throughout the region was low.

The wealthy elite are less affected by these problems. In Brazil and elsewhere, many moved their capital out of local banks and deposited it in more stable financial institutions abroad. Among the wealthiest of all are the Colombian drug barons. Operating out of Colombia's second city, Medellín, and increasingly out of its third city, Cali, they have developed a global industry in less than a decade. Their web of influence now stretches from local agriculture (farmers growing coca, from which cocaine is refined) into the higher realms of international banking. Profits are so great that it is difficult to find adequate outlets for laundering the money through outwardly respectable channels. The domestic and foreign pressure to stop the drugs trade is deeply unpopular with the poor farmers of Bolivia, Peru and Colombia, who have depended for generations on the production of coca.

DEBT AND HYPERINFLATION IN BOLIVIA

Landlocked mountainous Bolivia, always one of the poorest countries in the region, had a GDP per capita of less than $400 in the mid 1970s, and a national unemployment rate of 15 percent. In the mid 1980s Bolivia's economy was further undermined by its foreign debt: the total amount of interest due on the country's external debt amounted to half of its revenue from exports in 1984. To make matters worse, per capita incomes were falling and inflation reached 11,752 percent in 1985 – the highest in South America.

The new president in 1985, Dr Victor Paz Esterssoro, implemented a package of radical measures to deal with the crisis. Devaluing the currency and removing much of the protectionist duties on imports forced Bolivian industry to improve its efficiency in order to compete in the international market. The first steps were taken to privatize COMIBOL, the state mining corporation, and some of its largest mines were closed – the number of miners working for COMIBOL fell from 28,000 to 5,000 by the mid 1980s. Wages were frozen and, because of rapid inflation, their purchasing value fell by two-thirds between 1985 and 1986.

These drastic measures caused a turnaround in Bolivia's economic fortunes. In 1987, inflation fell rapidly, dropping to around 14 percent, the lowest figure that decade. After six successive years of economic decline, the economy grew consistently after 1987. Export revenues started to increase and foreign capital began to flow into the country again. Whether or not economic growth can be sustained is uncertain, but unless economic progress is maintained the desperate poverty of so many Bolivians will continue unabated.

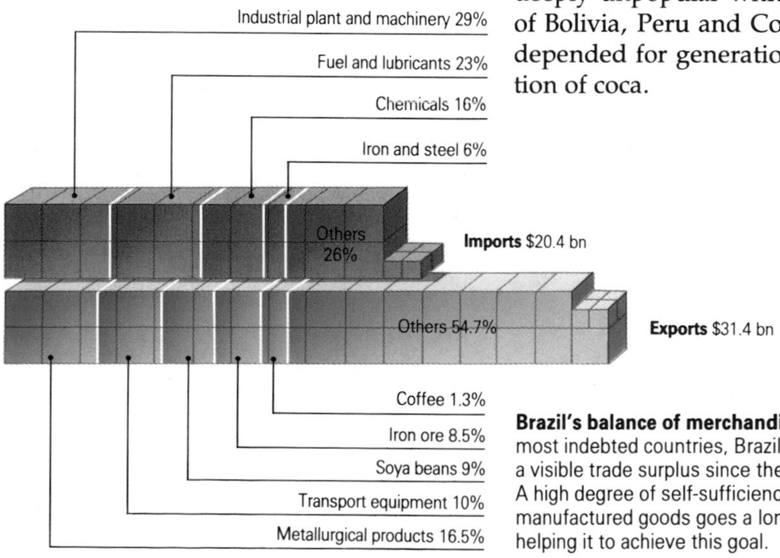

Brazil's balance of merchandise trade Like most indebted countries, Brazil has had to run a visible trade surplus since the mid 1980s. A high degree of self-sufficiency in manufactured goods goes a long way toward helping it to achieve this goal.

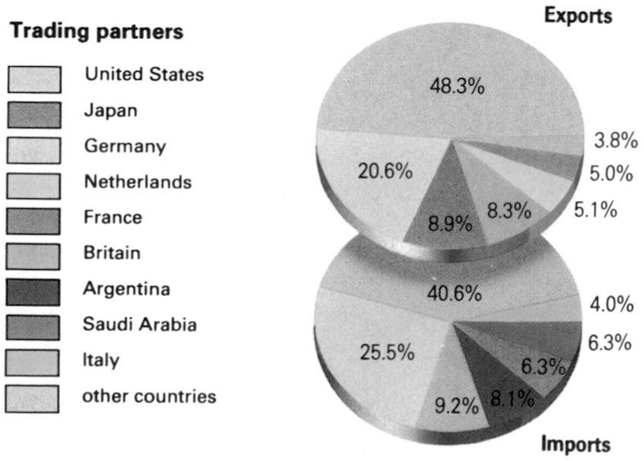

EVENING THE ODDS

In Latin America the gap between rich and poor is wider than almost anywhere else in the world, and is further complicated by racial differences. In Brazil the richest 20 percent of households (usually with the lightest complexions) have incomes 33 times higher than the poorest (and darkest) 20 percent. The size of this gap means that substantial economic growth is necessary if the poor are to experience any real improvements to their standards of living. Those who live in the countryside are the most exploited, especially the indigenous peoples. It is only in recent years that they have begun to organize themselves to petition and fight for land and welfare rights.

Land ownership has much to do with the unequal distribution of wealth. Since the Spanish and Portuguese arrived, the ownership of land has been concentrated in relatively few hands, with vast estates coexisting with large numbers of tiny, peasant-run farms. This pattern of ownership was deliberately set up to create a cheap labor force. Many indigenous people were enslaved; others had too little land to support their families and were forced to work for the major landowners for very low wages. It is only since industrial development in the 1940s that any alternative way of life has been possible for the rural and urban poor.

Escape to the cities

During the 1960s and 1970s urban life offered many poor families a route out of absolute poverty. On the whole it was the young and better educated who migrated, leaving behind the aging and less able to eke out an existence on tiny plots of land subject to soil erosion and overcropping. Migration has often been a forced choice as people sought to escape starvation or rural violence. But generally the movement of people from rural to urban areas reflected the desperately low standards of living in the countryside. Although an urban shanty town was hardly an ideal neighborhood, incomes, even from casual labor, were higher than in the countryside, and there was always the prospect of finding the security of work and a comparatively high wage in the industrial sector. Basic services such as water, electricity, schooling and healthcare were much more accessible, though still deficient in the shanty towns.

Industrialization created the revenue needed to improve welfare provision in the region, which varies greatly from country to country. Healthcare and education services are well established in Argentina, Chile and Uruguay, and this is reflected in the high life expectancy and

HOLDING DESPERATION AT BAY IN PERU

Peru began to experience a serious foreign debt crisis in 1976. The 1980s were characterized by "stagflation" (a stagnant economy and crippling inflation). A brief recovery from 1985 to 1987 occurred under the administration of President Alán García, which defaulted on Peru's loan repayments. The banks responded by refusing to extend credit when it was desperately needed in 1988 and 1989. By the time President Alberto Fujimori took office in 1990, hyperinflation had returned, and GDP had fallen to the levels of the 1950s.

Fujimori's austerity measures, introduced to allow foreign debt repayments to resume, coincided with a recession. The number of people living in poverty has nearly doubled, from 7 million to 12 million – more than half the total population. In Lima, the capital, where one-third of all Peruvians live, it is estimated that 90 percent of residents are without steady employment. The price of staple foods such as milk and bread doubled overnight with the announcement of the austerity measures.

A variety of urban grass-roots organizations, mostly run by local women, are striving to keep desperation at bay. Neighborhood coordinators distribute free milk and operate public kitchens in Lima's many shantytowns. With some foreign aid and much independent fundraising, the groups have managed to keep operating through even the worst months of crisis. In 1991, healthcare volunteers went door to door in one district to warn about a cholera epidemic, saving the lives of all but two of 40,000 residents. Although independent of the government, which offers no financial support, some of the neighborhood groups have been targeted by the terrorist group Shining Path. In February 1992 the terrorists murdered Maria Elena Moyano, the founder of a local women's federation, while she attended a barbecue to raise funds for the free milk program.

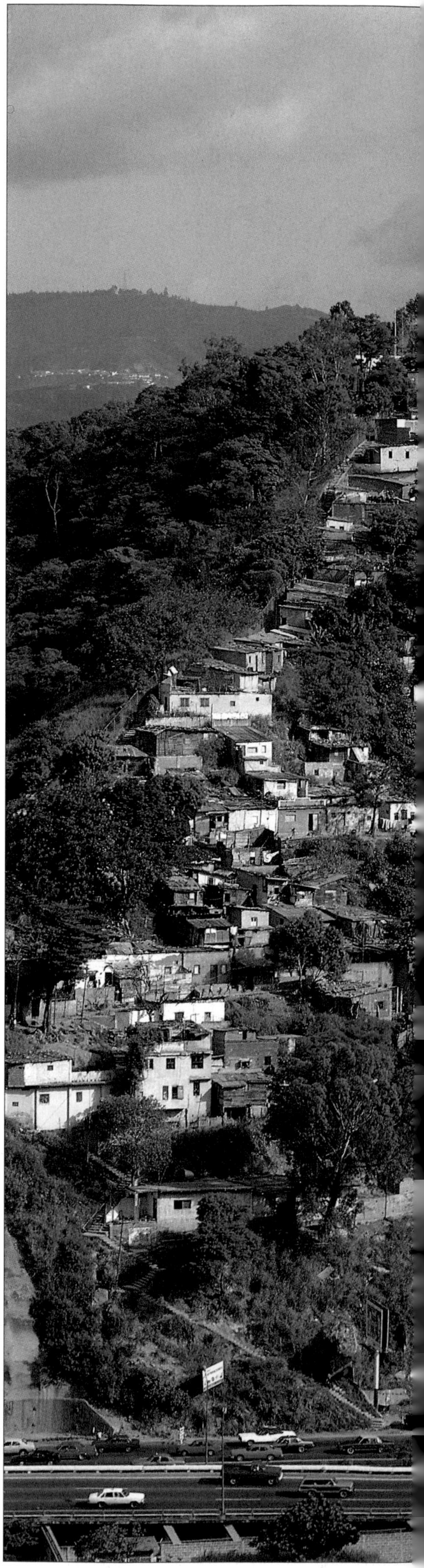

Room on the top *(above)* In Esmeraldas, Ecuador, women and children occupy the safer lower deck of a "lanchero" – an old truck converted into a bus – while men take the precarious seats on the roof. Cutbacks in state-run services have encouraged private lancheros.

Two sides of the track *(left)* Extremes of wealth and poverty are highly visible in oil-rich Venezuela. Only the thin strip of a freeway separates an oil company's prestigious headquarters from the shanty town straggling down the hillside.

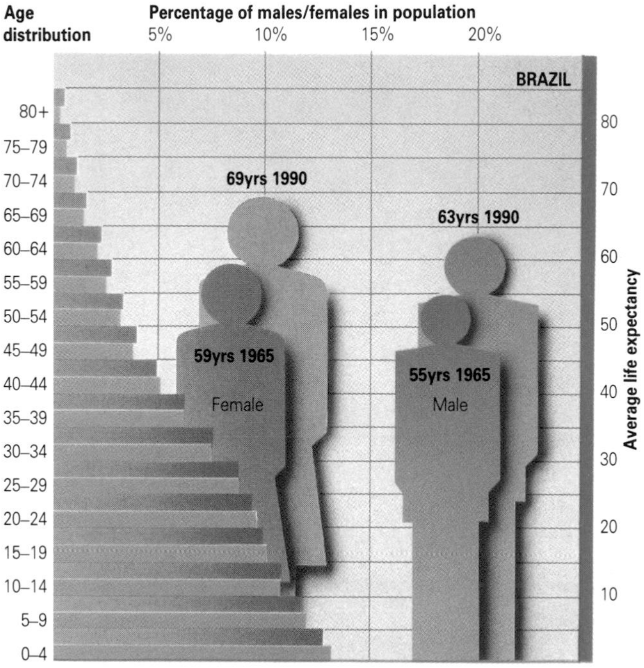

Life expectancy and age distribution *(right)* At 69, the average life expectancy of a Brazilian woman is six years higher than a man's. High birthrates and limited numbers of over 65s create the steeply tapering profile of age distribution associated with a developing country. Uruguay and Argentina have higher life expectancies (an average of 72).

low level of illiteracy in these countries. Peru and Bolivia have few financial resources and correspondingly few services.

State provision of education and healthcare is extremely variable across the region. Primary education is generally provided by the state; at the secondary level, private education becomes more important. Throughout South America, the middle and upper classes send their children to private schools and universities. The region has an extensive network of private hospitals, which only people with private means or employees covered by social security can afford to use; the public health system is accessible to everyone, but all too often lacks the staff, beds, drugs, and other resources needed to provide adequate care.

Tightening the belt

The debt crisis of the 1980s hit the urban poor hardest of all. The long-standing prosperity gap between urban and rural lifestyles narrowed as a result, but the crisis reduced inequality in the wrong way – by cutting living standards in the urban areas without raising them in the countryside. The economic reforms instituted throughout the region have improved the national economies – controlled by the very rich – at the expense of the poorest members of society.

Governments have cut back on food subsidies and bus and railroad fares have risen markedly. Healthcare, the provision of water and protection of the environment have all suffered neglect. Incomes have fallen relative to prices and in some cities the standard of living has declined to levels more typical of the 1950s. Malnutrition, never far away, has become common as household budgets have been cut. Schooling has suffered as education budgets have been cut and more families have been forced to push older children onto the labor market. More mothers are now going out to work; they earn little, just enough to make the difference between survival and starvation.

Chile's economic miracle?

In 1970, just before the debt crisis began to slow down South America's booming export trade, Chile elected its first socialist government to power. Led by Salvador Allende (1908–73), it introduced several radical economic reforms, redistributing rural land and nationalizing the foreign-owned copper industry. Within a few years, however, the economy was in trouble. Inflation was rising rapidly, the deficit on the balance of payments was growing and confidence in the country's economy was at a low ebb. Opposing political parties blamed each other, and in September 1973 the socialist government was removed by a military coup in which President Allende was killed. The regime that ruled for the next 16 years was led by General Augusto Pinochet. His government was characterized by an authoritarian style and scant respect for human rights. But his dictatorship became a vehicle for the transformation of the Chilean economy.

A copper-funded recovery

For many years the Chilean government had intervened heavily in the economy. It had established many state industries and protected private manufacturing from foreign competition. Revenue from the foreign-owned copper industry supported this structure until the copper companies were nationalized by Allende.

Pinochet's strategy was to open up the Chilean economy to outside competition, reduce the role of government and regulate the economy through the discipline of the market. Most state enterprises were sold – in 1992 only 20 remained in the government's hands. Import tariffs were sharply reduced, forcing the manufacturing sector to become more efficient so that it could compete with imported goods, and the power of the trade unions was curbed. Regular devaluation of the currency lowered the cost of Chile's goods in the international marketplace and encouraged exports.

The initial impact of all these measures was dramatic; the economy declined and unemployment rose. But once the initial

Stacks of copper (*right*) Chile is the world's largest producer of copper and is estimated to have 25 percent of the world's reserves. Although copper is still a major export earner in the 1990s, the opening up of the economy to foreign competition combined with plummeting commodity prices during the 1970s and 1980s have reduced its importance.

Fruits of success (*below*) Freshly picked grapes being sorted and packed. Land redistribution schemes under President Allende's socialist government encouraged the development of commercial farming and laid the foundations for a rapid expansion of agricultural exports during the 1980s.

trauma had been overcome, the economy began to grow, the rate of inflation fell and exports began to increase impressively. The government's long-standing fiscal deficit was reversed and from 1978 to 1989 the overall trend was toward recovery. GDP rose impressively – by 8.3 percent in 1979 and 7.8 percent in 1980 – and GNP nearly doubled over the decade.

However, Chile's overall economic recovery was interrupted by the worldwide recession of 1981 and subsequent internal problems. In 1981 copper prices fell to their lowest point since World War II. In 1982, major mistakes in setting the exchange rate led to a spectacular fall in GDP. Many companies went out of business and unemployment in Santiago rose to more than 30 percent; the national figure for 1983 was nearly 18 percent. As the world's most indebted nation per capita – debt swallowed more than three-quarters of export earnings in 1982 – Chile made an emergency appeal to the IMF and its creditors. This resulted in short-term loans and the rescheduling of another $3.4 billion worth of debt for the following year. By May 1985 austerity measures were announced as part of a deal with Chile's creditors.

The quest for longterm recovery

A major export drive led to impressive growth after 1983. Copper exports remained important but contributed only two-fifths of external revenues in 1987 compared with 73 percent in 1971. New export products were developed in the rural areas, particularly fruit and timber, and new manufactured goods, principally paper and cellulose, fishmeal, fish products and chemicals. It appears that the basis for future growth is solid.

Some of the claims made for the Pinochet economic miracle, however, have been excessive. The overall growth rate between 1973 and 1987 was only 2 percent – substantially undermined by the economically disastrous years of 1975 and 1982–83. And while incomes grew during the 1980s, distribution became very unequal. One estimate suggests that one-fifth of the population now receive 81 percent of the income. In terms of their purchasing power, wages in 1988 were 7 percent lower than they had been eight years earlier. Although infant mortality had not begun to rise yet, there was considerable concern in 1992 that malnutrition was once more on the increase.

QUIET PROSPERITY

FOUNDATIONS OF WEALTH · SECURING THE FUTURE · WELFARE AND WELL-BEING FOR ALL

A skilled workforce, valuable exports and (except in Denmark) well developed energy production have helped to make the Nordic Countries some of the wealthiest regions in the world. Most of the population enjoys a high standard of living, but they pay for sophisticated education, health and welfare systems with high taxes. The region has a tradition of competitive exporting and has been quick to harness new technology. However, its divided approach to the European Community (EC) threatens the future. By 1992, only Denmark had joined and Sweden was negotiating membership. Finland's economy has been particularly affected by the traumatic changes in the former Soviet bloc. All countries will need to diversify their economies and develop new markets if they are to maintain prosperity.

COUNTRIES IN THE REGION

Denmark, Finland, Iceland, Norway, Sweden

ECONOMIC INDICATORS: 1990

	HIE* Denmark	HIE* Norway	HIE* Sweden
GDP (US$ billions)	130.96	105.83	228.11
GNP per capita (US$)	22,080	23,120	23,660
Annual rate of growth of GDP, 1980–1990 (%)	2.4	2.9	2.2
Manufacturing as % of GDP	20	15	24
Central government spending as % of GNP	41	46	42
Merchandise exports (US$ billions)	35.0	33.8	57.5
Merchandise imports (US$ billions)	31.6	27.2	54.7
% of GNP donated as development aid	0.93	1.17	0.90
WELFARE INDICATORS			
Infant mortality rate (per 1,000 live births)			
1965	19	17	13
1990	8	8	6
Daily food supple available (calories per capita, 1989)	3,628	3,326	2,960
Population per physician (1984)	400	450	390
Teacher–pupil ratio (primary school, 1989)	1 : 12	1 : 16	1 : 16

Note: The Gross Domestic Product (GDP) is the total value of all goods and services domestically produced. The Gross National Product (GNP) is the GDP plus net income from abroad.

** HIE (High Income Economy) – GNP per capita above $7,620 in 1990.*

Fueling the economy *(above)* The Norwegian oil industry has helped the country to achieve remarkable prosperity, with a higher per capita GDP than the United States or Germany.

FOUNDATIONS OF WEALTH

Sweden's early wealth derived from its mining industry, which began in the 13th century and dominated Swedish exports for 200 years. Swedish silver, copper and iron figured prominently in trade with the Hanseatic League, the powerful merchants' association of northern Germany. Norway too exported significant amounts of copper and iron, as well as timber and fish, from the mid 16th century. Denmark, like the rest of the region, remained almost exclusively agricultural. Feudal landowning patterns persisted well into the late 18th century, delaying the development of a modern farming industry.

Coping with competition

The 19th century was a period of hardship throughout the region. Economic crisis coincided with increasing competition from North American products, particularly Canadian timber and grain, in British and other European markets. By 1840 the crisis prompted mass emigration, chiefly to the United States and Canada.

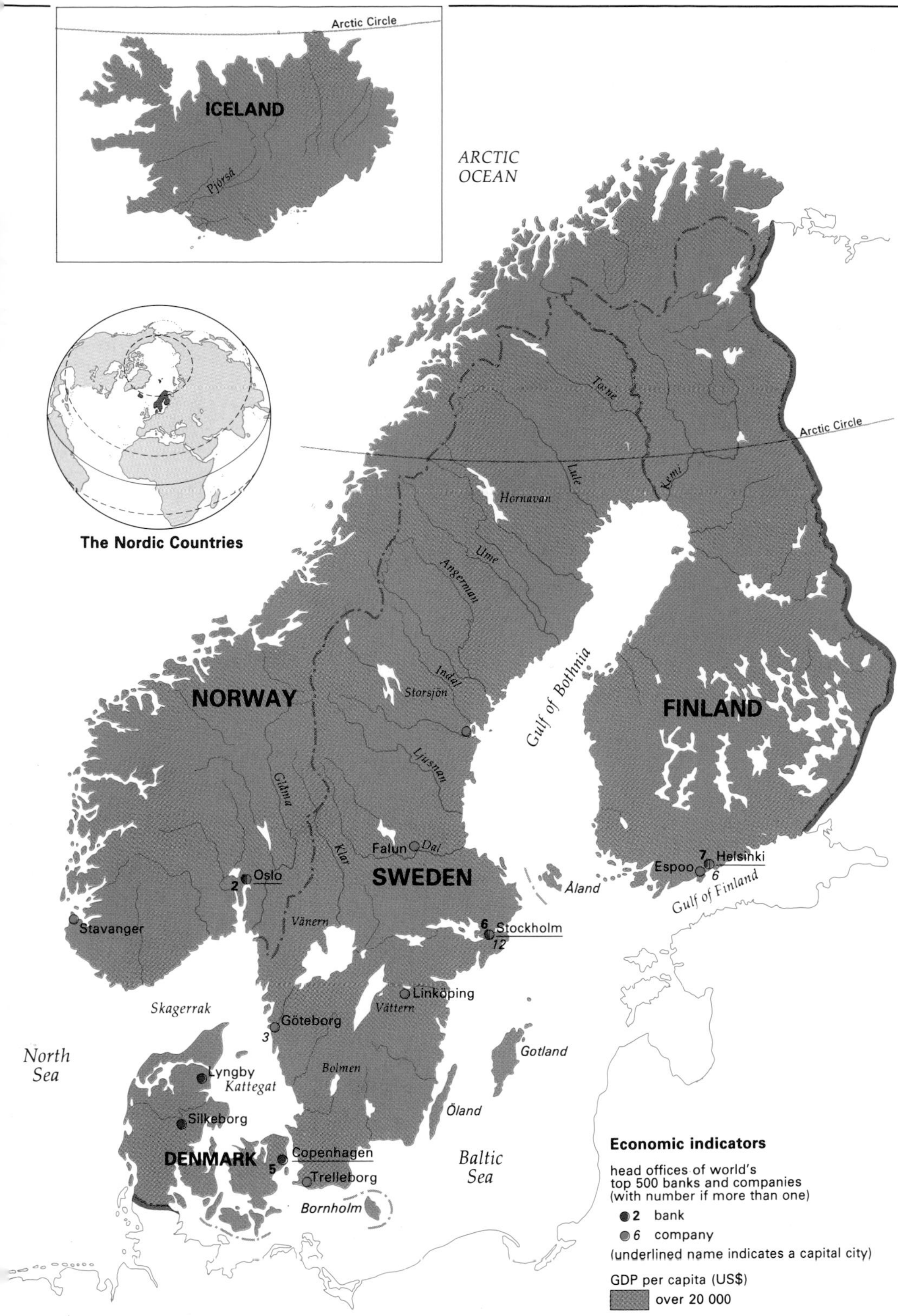

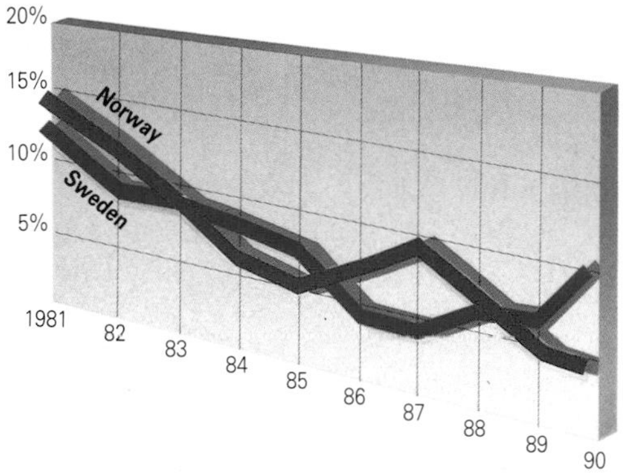

Profile of Inflation (*above*) During the early 1980s Norway and Sweden both experienced falling inflation, but by 1990 Sweden's seemed set to rise again.

Map of GDP per capita (*left*) Finland had the region's highest GDP per capita in 1990, though every country in the region ranks in the world's top 10. Oslo, Copenhagen, Stockholm and Helsinki are the leading commercial centers.

Bad harvests in the late 1860s increased the exodus; by 1920, a total of 2.7 million Scandinavians – 17 percent of the population – had emigrated. In response, governments in the region prompted export-led recovery by developing new technologies for their primary sectors: fishing in Norway, Iceland and the Faroes; dairy-farming and pig-rearing in Denmark; and wood-pulp production in Norway, Sweden and Finland.

Reverberations of war

Economic growth was interrupted by the Great Depression (1929–33), and a decade later the economies of Denmark and Norway suffered under German occupation during World War II. Sweden remained neutral in the war and profited from supplying iron ore and ball bearings to the German war machine. The fishing industries of the Faroe Islands and Iceland profited from the other side by supplying food to the British and American naval bases stationed there. Finland, which had sided with Germany to resist the strategic claims of the Soviet Union, lost territory and resources in the peace settlement following the Red Army's expulsion of Nazi forces. Finnish reparations payments made up four-fifths of the country's exports in the immediate post-war years. While increased demand stimulated the Finnish economy, it also encouraged excessive reliance on the Soviet market.

In 1950 agriculture still employed half of the Finnish male workforce, a third in Norway and Denmark and a quarter in Sweden. An international shift in trade away from primary goods and toward secondary goods soon produced a fresh challenge to the Nordic economies. The region responded by diversifying its economies into increased industrial development. From 1945–1960, industrial growth was greatest in those countries which had suffered most war damage: sixfold growth in Norway and Finland, and fivefold growth in Denmark. Industrial expansion in Sweden also proceeded quite rapidly: output in 1969 was three-and-a-half times its 1945 level, with Swedish cars and engineering in particular claiming new world markets. Finland continued to provide metals and wood pulp to the Soviet Union and its satellite economies.

With the exception of Norway, all the region's economies became very heavily dependent on oil imports during the postwar decades. In 1970 petroleum and related products accounted for over 10 percent of the value of all imports to Denmark, Finland and Iceland. These countries were badly hit by the oil price rises imposed by the Organization of Petroleum Exporting Countries (OPEC) during the 1970s. Norway was protected from the shock by the development of its North Sea oilfields in the late 1970s, which became a significant earner of foreign revenue.

SECURING THE FUTURE

The Nordic Countries are modern, urbanized societies that enjoy high standards of living and economic performance. Oil has been the key to Norway's emergence as one of the world's most prosperous countries. Between 1965 and 1988 Norway's gross national product (GNP) per capita grew by 3.5 percent a year, ranking the country alongside Japan, Switzerland and the United States. Tight economic management by the Soviet-aligned government of Finland produced a similarly healthy growth rate of 3.2 percent over the same period. While economies in other parts of the world grew more slowly, in 1990 Norway, Denmark, Sweden and Finland maintained their position (in terms of GNP per capita) among the top seven most prosperous nations in the world.

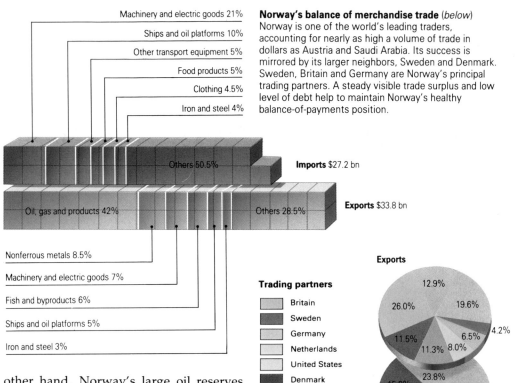

Norway's balance of merchandise trade (*below*)
Norway is one of the world's leading traders, accounting for nearly as high a volume of trade in dollars as Austria and Saudi Arabia. Its success is mirrored by its larger neighbors, Sweden and Denmark. Sweden, Britain and Germany are Norway's principal trading partners. A steady visible trade surplus and low level of debt help to maintain Norway's healthy balance-of-payments position.

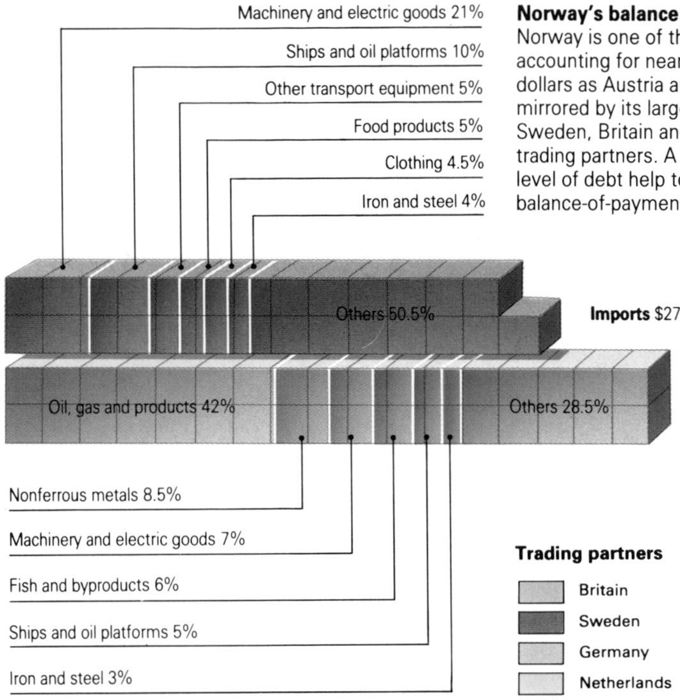

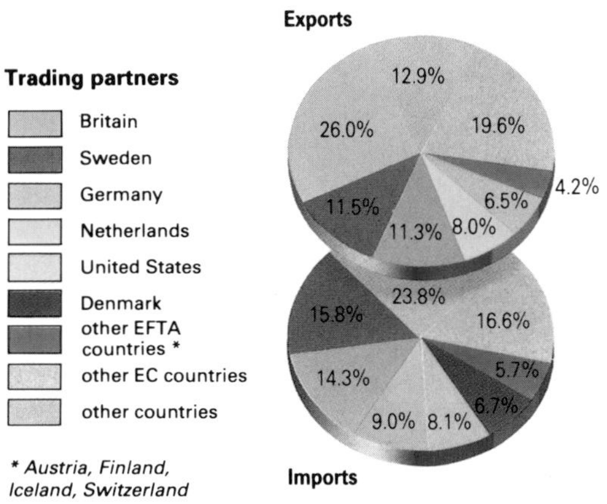

Reaching out to Europe

About 25 percent of all Nordic production is exported to meet the costs of essential imports. The relatively small Nordic economies must continue to diversify and capture new markets if they are to sustain their profitability. Sweden has diversified most successfully: one-seventh of its exports consist of cars and lorries, mostly from the prestigious Volvo factories, and it also exports significant amounts of high-grade iron and steel to Europe. The country has reduced its reliance on imported oil by extending its hydroelectric power capacity. Iceland has also substituted some imported oil with increased geothermal energy production. On the other hand, Norway's large oil reserves may prove to have been a mixed blessing. High oil revenues – which accounted for 40 percent of export earnings until 1986 – allowed diversification to be postponed; after prices fell in 1986, Norway's dependence on oil revenues began to appear increasingly dangerous.

The search for new markets in the 1980s saw a shift in exports from a mainly British to a broader European market. In 1992, all countries were members of the European Free Trade Association (EFTA), though only Denmark was a member of the European Community (EC); Sweden has applied to join in the mid 1990s. The EC now accounts for 30–40 percent of Nordic exports and some analysts consider that it is only a matter of time before all the Nordic Countries apply for EC membership, Britain remains the most important single customer, receiving 26 percent of Norway's exports, 20 percent of Iceland's and just over 10 percent of the other countries' exports. The United States takes about 14 percent of Iceland's exports but is not an important customer for the rest of the region.

In the late 1980s, the collapse of the uncompetitive Soviet market left Finland with outmoded industries and reduced demand from a formerly loyal and undemanding customer. In 1991, the gross domestic product (GDP) of Finland suffered a 6 percent fall as a result of lost Soviet markets. On the other hand, the Nordic Countries are beginning to look toward Eastern Europe as a market with obvious new potential.

The squeeze on social spending

During the 1980s most Nordic governments continued extensive intervention in their economies, as a means of maintaining fullish employment and high standards of living. Unemployment in

THE INS AND OUTS OF TOURISM

Tourism is an increasingly important source of revenue in the region. In 1989, it provided the equivalent of about 2 percent of GDP in Denmark and Iceland, 1.5 percent in Norway and Sweden, and 1 percent in Finland, despite the fact that the Nordic Countries are comparatively expensive places to visit. The number of tourists to Norway, Sweden and Denmark remained fairly constant between 1984 and 1989. By contrast, Finland and Iceland, more unusual destinations for Western tourists, welcomed 80 percent and 50 percent more tourists respectively over the same period. However, the people of the Nordic Countries still spend more money abroad as tourists than their countries earn from visitors.

Holiday travel within the region itself is also popular. Norwegians are the most common tourists in Sweden, Danes in Norway, and Swedes in Finland. Germans are the most numerous visitors to Denmark, accounting for a third of its total number of tourists in 1989. By attracting a wider international tourist base, the region hopes to gain some protection against recession. Americans are now the largest visiting group to Iceland. With the lure of its dramatic scenery, the country is also aiming to capture more of the lucrative Japanese tourist business.

1989 was only 1.6 percent in Sweden and Iceland, 3–4 percent in Finland and Norway, but more than 9 percent in Denmark. The Nordic governments funded generous public spending – which in the early 1990s accounted for half of GDP in Norway and Sweden, and a third in Denmark, Finland and Iceland – by high taxation and government borrowing.

By 1990, the worldwide recession – coupled with lower oil prices and burgeoning public sector growth in Denmark and Sweden in particular – had begun to put the region's economies under pressure. Unemployment in 1991 increased sharply to over 6 percent in Sweden and Norway, and about 13 percent in Finland. For the first time in decades the region's creditworthiness was called into question. In 1990 Swedish debts to foreign lenders totaled the equivalent of one-third of GDP. Although the deficit is lower in the rest of the region – and negligible in Denmark – it is doubtful how long government borrowing can continue to insulate the Nordic economies against world recession. As a result, traditional economic policies, with their expensive emphasis on social welfare, have come under severe scrutiny. In the early 1990s conservative governments in Finland, Norway and Sweden introduced economic reforms designed to reduce the role of the state and modify welfare provision.

Demographic trends are also beginning to alter the balance of the Nordic economies. Uniformly high life expectancy and low birthrates have resulted in rapidly aging populations. Governments will have to consider how to support their old people with customarily generous pensions on the basis of tax revenue from a shrinking labor force. Furthermore, there is a danger that industry will flee abroad in the face of the high wages that inevitably accompany labor shortages, while the use of cheap immigrant labor could threaten the social homogeneity that nourishes the traditional Nordic societies. On the other hand, the well-motivated and highly educated Scandinavian workforce may continue to attract the most advanced manufacturing and service industries, and Scandinavian companies seem fully aware of the possibility of shifting their low-wage sector into Eastern Europe through the sort of partnership arrangements that Volvo, for example, have with Renault.

Cold weather market *(above)* Sheep at a livestock market in Iceland. In the 1970s and 1980s a wool industry grew up around the Icelandic herds, and agriculture developed to the extent that the island became self-sufficient in milk and meat products. However, in spite of prolonged efforts to diversify the economy, fishing remains the main export industry.

On a roll *(right)* Paper products made from wood pulp in Finland's paper mills accounted for $8.3 billion of export revenue in 1992. Forestry is the mainstay of Finland's considerable prosperity, accounting for over 65 percent of the country's land area, and generating enough wood and paper products to make up 40 percent of national exports.

WELFARE AND WELL-BEING FOR ALL

The economic success of the Nordic Countries rests upon a highly skilled workforce, and they have made a large investment in education. Most schools are state run, with the option of subsidized private schools. Where there are fees, financial assistance is available to most students. About one-third of young adults are in higher education, and a strong emphasis is placed on adult training. Free evening and daytime courses run by local authorities are available throughout Sweden; Norway has expanded its higher education facilities in order to accommodate the expected doubling of student numbers by the end of the 20th century; and Denmark has invested heavily in a folk high school for adults which has no entrance requirements or examinations, an unrestricted curriculum and a practical bias.

The national health

While beset by the same budget dilemmas as other rich countries, the healthcare systems of the Nordic Countries deliver a level of service which makes its citizens among the healthiest on earth. Denmark runs a free national health service. Norway and Sweden operate a compulsory health insurance service which reimburses the majority of fees. Family counseling is also available under Norway's plan, while Iceland offers free dental care to children aged 6–15, with 50 percent discounts for younger children and the elderly. Most hospitals are state run and the region is a world leader in

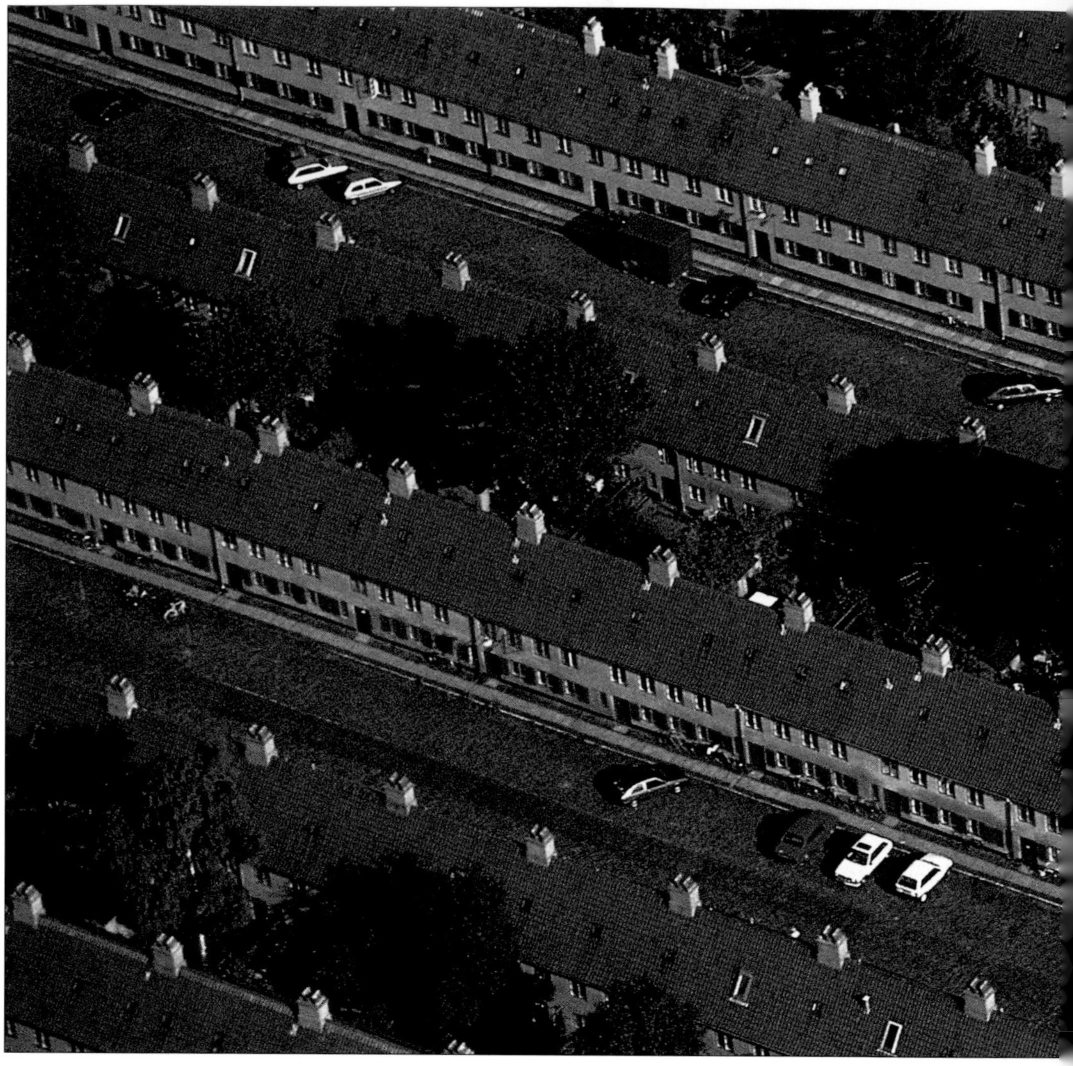

Investing in comfort (*above*) A large housing project in Copenhagen, Denmark. In a city that has one of the world's highest costs of living, the government ensures that, even in crowded conditions, housing is of a uniformly high standard.

A broad-based education (*below*) starts early for children in the Nordic Countries. Most students learn English as well as another regional language and have a solid grasp of national geography and history.

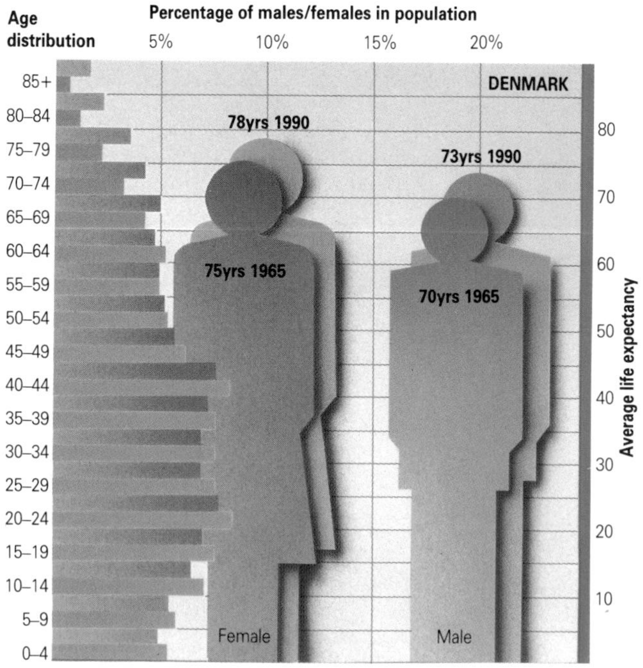

Life expectancy and age distribution (*below*) Denmark, like its neighbors Sweden and Norway, has one of the largest proportions of elderly people in the world, and one of the lowest birthrates.

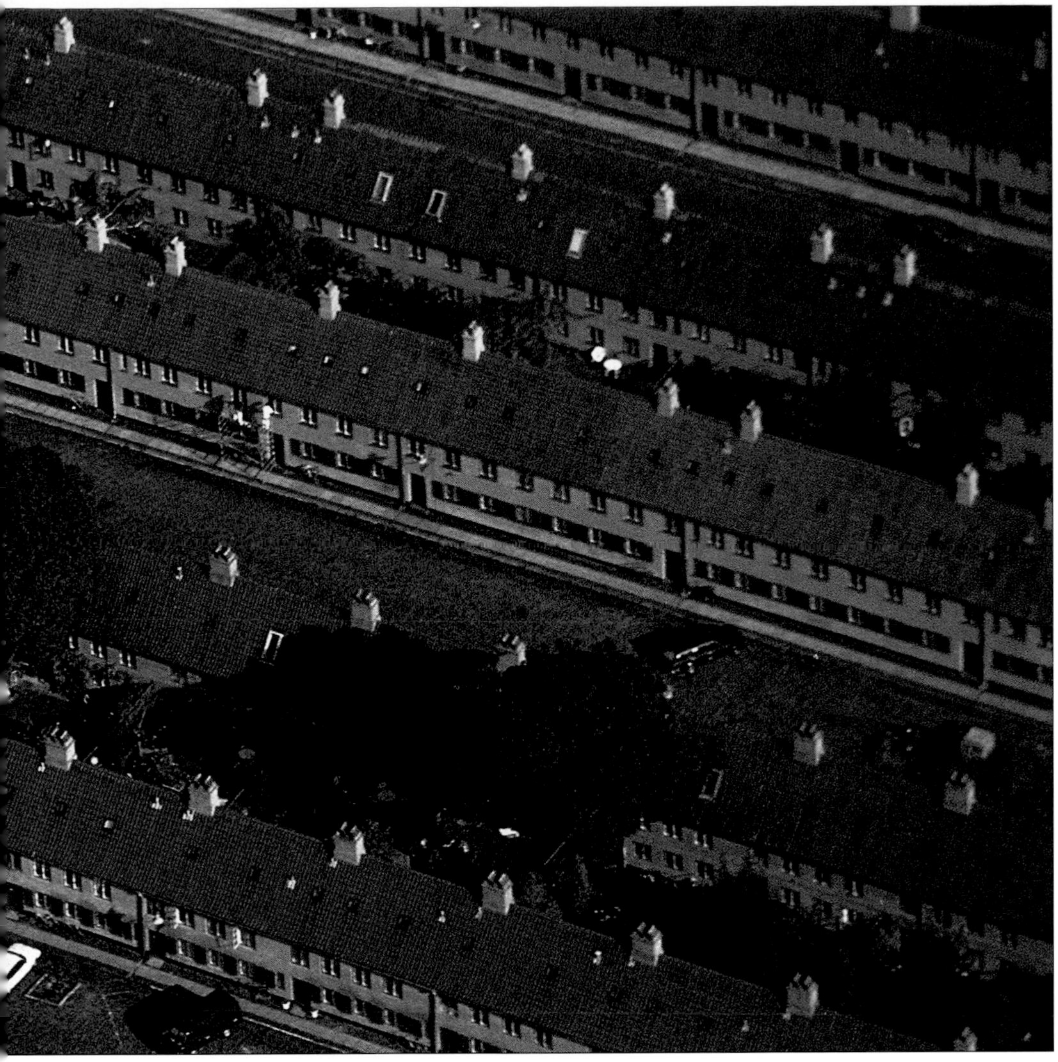

GREEN ECONOMICS

The environmental movement is strong in the Nordic Countries. In 1988 Sweden met 22 percent of its need for glass from recycling and Denmark 27 percent. Although figures for Finland (3 percent) and Norway (6 percent) are significantly lower, a feeling for conservation is reflected in the growing prominence of "green" politics. In a 1980 referendum Sweden voted to phase out all its nuclear power by the year 2010. Following the Chernobyl accident, the Swedish government decided to close two reactors as early as 1995 and 1996. The cost of this plan – an estimated 5 to 10 billion kronor ($0.8–1.6 billion) for every year that the reactors are not in use – indicates Sweden's commitment to environmental safety.

Environmental protection frequently seems incompatible with economic growth. The Nordic Countries may be better prepared than most to reconcile growth with long-term conservation but there are other issues too pulling at the purse strings. Given the aging population and the consequent mushrooming of pensions paid out, welfare expenditure can only grow dramatically in the next few decades.

preventive medicine and research. During 1988 the rate of infant mortality in Sweden and Finland of 6 deaths per 1,000 live births was bettered only by Japan. Denmark and Norway with 8 deaths per 1,000 were equal with the level of the OECD countries as a whole.

Rural populations and the citizens of small remote towns have equal access to public services. Services in towns such as Umeå in northern Sweden are almost entirely the creation of regional policy; even at such a far remove from Stockholm there are not only hospitals but also theaters, universities and opera houses. The real problem is that in a time of recession, private sector jobs are withdrawn first from peripheral areas, reducing incomes of those living away from the major population centers.

Striving for equality

The Nordic Countries have a reputation for promoting legislation on equal rights for women. There is extensive provision of childcare facilities, part-time work rights for both men and women with children, maternity and paternity leave and generous amounts of annual leave. Although expensive, these provisions allow the Nordic economies to offer women the choice of combining formal careers with childrearing. Compared with the EC average proportion of women in the workforce of 40.3 percent, in Norway it is 44.5 percent, Iceland 44.9 percent, Denmark 45.8 percent, Finland 47.2 percent and Sweden 47.9 percent. However, as elsewhere in the world, women's salaries tend to be lower than men's, and rural and working-class communities remain patriarchal. Nonetheless, substantial gains have been made. In Finland, one-fifth of the judges and two-fifths of the lawyers are women. Iceland's President Vigdis Finnbogadottir, the first woman in the region to win a national popular election (1980), was also one of the first single women in Iceland to win a legal battle to become an adoptive mother.

Class differences in Nordic society are growing despite the tradition of solidarity. Differences in income levels between professionals and manual workers have always been narrow, though wider in Denmark; in 1984 a member of the Swedish cabinet earned about twice as much as a factory worker. During the 1980s living standards in Sweden and Norway rose continually due to the welfare state. However, national wage bargaining seems under threat, and the gap between the very rich (usually working for foreign companies) and the growing numbers of unemployed is growing while the ability of the state to retain its own employees and attract new ones is questioned throughout the region.

In spite of the social homogeneity of the Nordic Countries, there are still some ethnic issues. Minorities comprise a very small percentage of the population – often less than 1 percent. First, there are the Sami (or Lapp) peoples, nomadic people who follow the reindeer herds in northern Norway, Sweden and Finland. Their livelihood is threatened by commercial lumbering, mining and other development in the areas they move through. The second source of ethnic difference is immigration. The capital cities of Scandinavia have attracted not only guest workers – from Germany, Italy, Greece, and the former Yugoslavia and also from Finland in the 1960s – but also political refugees. There are substantial Latin American communities in Swedish and Danish cities. Often, despite a highly qualified educational background, the immigrants are unable to find work and find themselves socially and geographically isolated.

High taxation – high protection

Mikhail Gorbachev has said that he would like to see a Swedish-style welfare state replace state socialism in Eastern Europe. He is only the latest in a long line of commentators who have seen in Sweden a unique compromise between capitalism and socialism: an economy based on private property but with a large, redistributive state sector providing generous healthcare, education, unemployment benefits and pensions. Denmark and Norway have similar, though less generous, welfare systems.

A contract against poverty

The distinctiveness of Sweden dates from the 1930s. In response to the Great Depression the Swedish people committed themselves to full employment through state intervention in the economy. The left-wing political parties suspended the struggle for socialism in favor of an alliance with liberal and agrarian parties, ensuring support for ambitious job-creation programs. Outside Scandinavia, no such consensus was built, isolating socialists, undermining democracy and delivering the people into the horrors of mass unemployment and, in the case of Germany and Italy, fascism.

After World War II, many European countries adopted the Swedish strategy of the 1930s, now justified by the demand management philosophy of John Maynard Keynes (1883–1946). Many countries followed Sweden in rationalizing their welfare systems and removing the stigma that had previously been attached to receiving state assistance. But Sweden went further still, raising the level of benefits to about 80 percent of regular pay. This new and very generous support was accompanied by additional benefits for single parents, the disabled and families with children. The Supplementary Pensions legislation of the late 1950s gave manual workers the same pension rights as senior civil servants: a pension based on 60 percent of salary during the 15 best-paid years of work.

Supporting the system

These programs are expensive and the Swedes pay high taxes, but the system has significant ethical and economic supports. A corporatist system of national wage bargaining (over 80 percent of Swedish workers are unionized) rests on the solidarity of skilled workers and professionals with manual laborers. It has produced quite a narrow band of incomes, discouraging both the vandalism of resentment and the consumerism of the upwardly mobile. These national wage agreements allow weaker enterprises to fail and ensure large profits for successful ones, since workers in both will be on about the same wage scale. Workers paying high taxes have the security of knowing that their earnings will suffer only marginally if their ability to work is interrupted. Most of the redistribution of wealth via public assistance is across the life-cycle rather than between classes.

The incorporation of organized labor and organized management into the political process has many advantages. It promotes industrial democracy by ensuring that workers have a formal role in decision making. Counter-cyclical economic management is made possible as the state accumulates investment funds during booms and releases them during slumps, promoting stability. There is a strong incentive for all sides to maintain industrial harmony, as the costs of failure in national wage bargaining would be inconceivable.

Finally, the workforce identifies more strongly with the discipline of international competitiveness, and is less resistant to new technology than is generally the case elsewhere.

Presiding over this corporatist consensus has been the Social Democratic Party, whose failure to insulate Sweden from the world depression of the early 1990s cost it political legitimacy. A government intent on retrenchment is now cutting back some of the branches of the Swedish welfare state – ironically at a time when the collapse of the command economies in Eastern Europe is directing the eyes of the world toward the Swedish model, the middle way. As even the world's wealthiest nations, such as the United States, battle against the latest international depression, with high unemployment and the soaring costs of often inadequate healthcare programs, the Swedish welfare state continues to be very attractive.

Protesting against education cuts. Swedish citizens voice their anger at a clamp down on spending that threatens their local People's High School. This is one in a network of higher education facilities established to provide free education to adults and teenagers alike.

19 92
VÅR KÄRA
FOLKHÖGSKOLA
KLYFTAN
STENSUNDS-
FOLKHÖGSKOLA
LYFTER
VINGARNA
BÄR !!
UTBILDNING
SKA GÄLLA
ALLA!

Santa's package tour

Efforts are being made throughout the Nordic Countries to maximize the invisible earnings brought by foreign tourism, and Lapland is no exception to this. Package tours to visit Santa are unusual, but not unique; Lapland faces competition from sites in Norway and Denmark in offering itself up as the home of Santa Claus. Not only are the children's letters posted all over the world routed to Santa Claus in Lapland, but many children are also now visiting Santa and his helpers "at home" near the North Pole.

However, the Santa Claus industry is not just a seasonal gimmick or a godsend for the under-twelves. Santa's package tours are big business in the Nordic region and exemplify a recent shift in what we mean by industry in some developed countries. Industry does not only refer to the production of consumer goods and machine tools. Almost as important as this conventional economy of imports and exports is the culture industry and what some academics refer to as the commodification – or selling – of pleasure. Christmas is still about jingling bells, but it is also about jingling cash registers. Lapland is cashing in on this general trend.

Sick and underpriviledged children visit Santa Claus in Lapland as a special treat, paid for by charitable organizations.

ORIO

ESCAPING FROM THE PAST

THE LOSS OF WORLD SUPREMACY · A RESTRUCTURED ECONOMY · THE NORTH–SOUTH DIVIDE

During the 19th century Britain was the world's leading financial power and industrial nation. Since then, the country has had to come to terms with the loss of that role, and of most of its overseas territories. Manufacturing has declined sharply and the United Kingdom is now among the world leaders in only a few areas, such as luxury goods, defense equipment and chemical products. Overall, imports consistently outstrip exports creating a longterm balance-of-payments problem. In place of manufacturing, North Sea oil production and service industries (particularly in the financial sector) have become more important. Many services are based in London, which has retained its role as a principal money market. The region as a whole suffers persistent problems of high unemployment.

COUNTRIES IN THE REGION

Ireland, United Kingdom

ECONOMIC INDICATORS: 1990

	HIE* Ireland	HIE* United Kingdom
GDP (US$ billions)	42.5	975.15
GNP per capita (US$)	9,550	16,100
Annual rate of growth of GDP, 1980–1990 (%)	3.1	3.1
Manufacturing as % of GDP	3	20
Central government spending as % of GNP	55	35
Merchandise exports (US$ billions)	23.8	183.6
Merchandise imports (US$ billions)	20.7	222.6
% of GNP donated as development aid	0.16	0.27

WELFARE INDICATORS

Infant mortality rate (per 1,000 live births)		
1965	25	20
1990	7	8
Daily food supply available (calories per capita, 1989)	3,778	3,149
Population per physician (1984)	680	680
Teacher–pupil ratio (primary school, 1989)	1 : 28	1 : 20

Note: The Gross Domestic Product (GDP) is the total value of all goods and services domestically produced. The Gross National Product (GNP) is the GDP plus net income from abroad.

** HIE (High Income Economy) – GNP per capita above $7,620 in 1990.*

THE LOSS OF WORLD SUPREMACY

By the 18th century Britain had emerged as the world's leading trading and colonial power. Industrialization strengthened its position in the 19th century making the region a leading producer of textiles, metals and engineering goods. The growing empire provided both raw materials and a market for British products, which proved so competitive that they dominated the trade of the United States, continental Europe, Latin America and other

The British Isles

Economic indicators

head offices of world's top 500 banks and companies (with number if more than one)

●2 bank

●2 company

(underlined name indicates a capital city)

GDP per capita (US$)

15 000–20 000

10 000–14 999

5 000–9 999

no data available

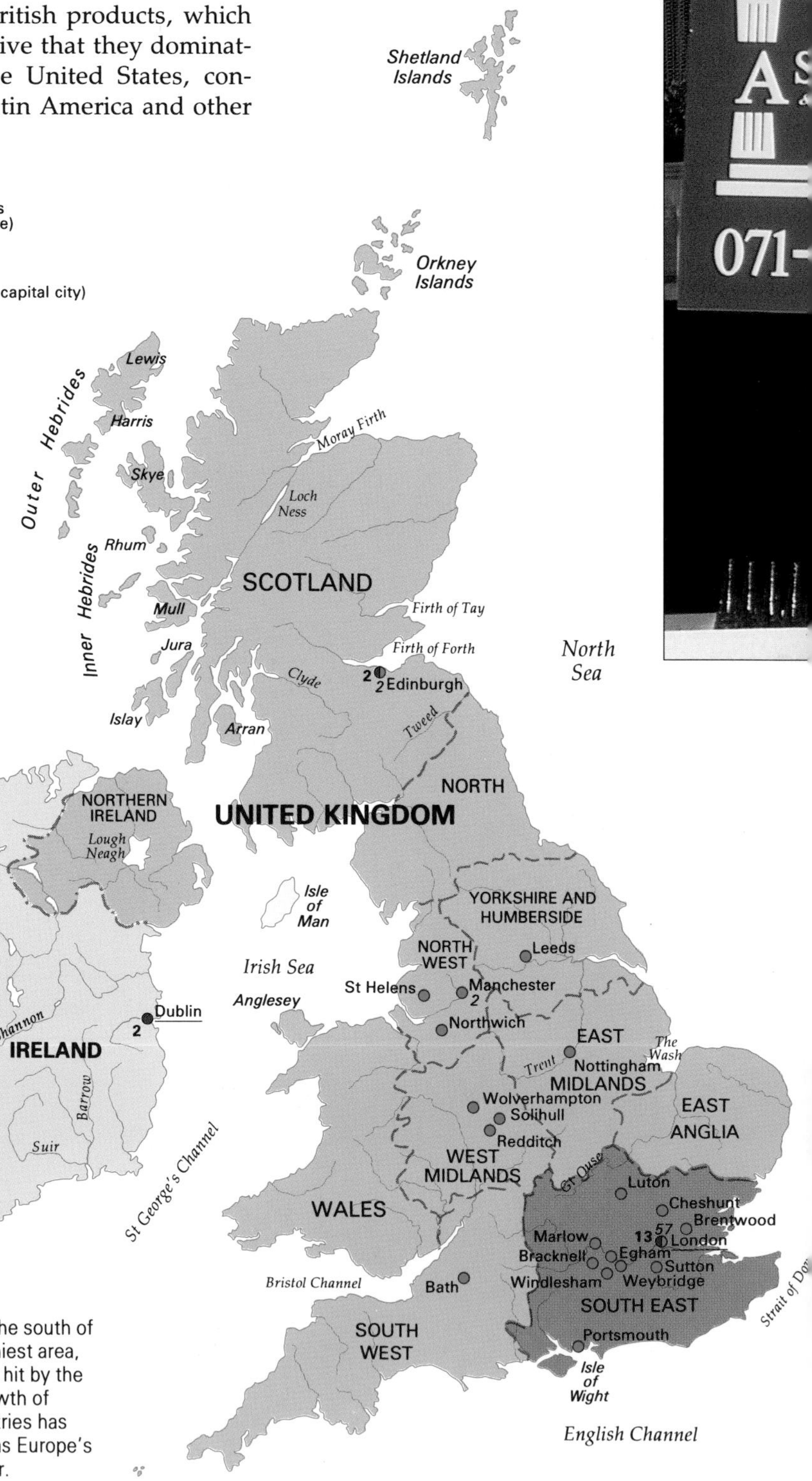

Map of GDP per capita The south of England, by far the wealthiest area, has also been the hardest hit by the 1990s recession. The growth of finance and service industries has confirmed London's role as Europe's leading commercial center.

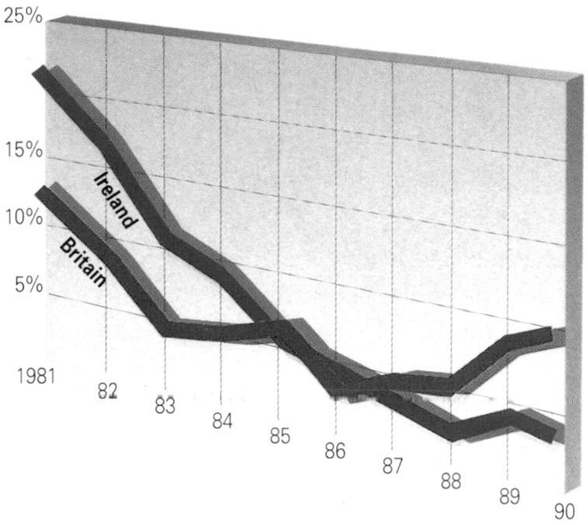

Profile of inflation *(above)* Inflation in both Britain and the Republic of Ireland fell throughout the early and mid 1980s, but after 1988 Ireland's remained steady while Britain's began to rise again in spite of the stated government policy of reducing it to 4 percent.

Britain for sale *(left)* but no one is buying. The property market, the key to consumer spending in the region, reached its peak in 1988 as Britons rushed to buy homes. By 1992 values were falling monthly, leaving many owing far more than they could raise by selling.

areas. By the beginning of the 20th century, however, Britain began to suffer increasing competition in both trade and manufacturing. In particular, the older heavier industries in the north and west were badly affected. New growth was in light industry and automobile manufacturing, particularly in the midlands and the southeast. Overall decline was hastened by the great destruction and expense of the two World Wars, and the breakup of the British Empire.

The era of intervention

In 1945 the Labor government set a course of postwar recovery through greater intervention by the state. Railroads and mines were nationalized and the National Health Service (NHS) was established. During the postwar boom of the 1950s and 1960s there was steady growth, especially in vehicle production, chemicals and electric goods, and unemployment was low. However, Britain failed to keep pace with its international competitors and the country's share of the world market continued to decline. Investment in nuclear energy proved an expensive venture at a time when cheap oil fueled growth in the rest of Europe during the 1960s. Britain's trade surplus in manufactured goods – traditionally the strongest part of the economy – was also sliding, from 10 percent of the country's production in 1950 to only 2 percent in 1973.

The country's problems were only fully revealed during the mid 1970s. As a trading nation, Britain was particularly vulnerable to the worldwide economic crisis. Faced with competition from a shrinking market, it became obvious that British production methods were frequently outdated, that industry was suffering from poor investment and that labor disputes were pushing up costs. Heavy industries such as coal, steel and shipbuilding, which had been so important during the two World Wars, still dominated the peacetime economy and required heavy subsidies. Government spending was high – more than 40 percent of GDP – but it was not generating sufficient growth. Between 1973 and 1979 growth fell to barely 1 percent per year – a third of the level during previous decades – and inflation soared to above 25 percent. For the first time in decades unemployment began to rise rapidly. The manufacturing workforce declined from a peak of 8.7 million in 1966 to 7.1 million in 1979, and unemployment doubled to more than a million. Disparities in wealth between different regions grew wider. The decline that had begun a century earlier continued unchecked.

The Irish economy

Ireland, by contrast, underwent almost no industrialization in the 19th century. A system of large estates and absentee landlords brought agricultural stagnation and poverty, culminating in the potato famine of the 1840s, when a million died and a million emigrated. By the time the southern 26 counties gained independence from the United Kingdom in 1922, the Republic of Ireland remained one of the poorest countries in northern Europe. The following decades saw some development, with a steady growth of towns, especially Dublin. From the 1960s the government Industrial Development Agency attracted increasing foreign investment in manufacturing, much of it from the United States. In spite of these efforts the economy continued to be dogged by problems until the early 1980s.

A RESTRUCTURED ECONOMY

The 1980s saw the most rapid and profound economic upheaval ever to occur in Britain. The country's long-established manufacturing economy was replaced by a new emphasis on services, particularly financial services, and revenue from North Sea oil and gas became a mainstay. World recession undoubtedly played a major part in this reshaping. A second factor was the emergence of new manufacturing methods (particularly in Japan and Southeast Asia) based on information technology and leaving much of British production dangerously outdated. Finally, there was the radical change in government policy that occurred under the governments of Prime Minister Margaret Thatcher (1979–90), which abandoned state intervention in industry in favor of market forces, deregulation and privatization of nationalized companies. The privatization of British Telecom in 1984, for example, generated the largest share issue the world had ever seen.

From manufacturing to services

These changes transformed the structure of the British economy. Manufacturing declined, soon employing only 4.7 million people – no more than in the late 19th century. Large firms with more than 1,000 employees were particularly hard hit: in 1979 these had accounted for 54 percent of all manufacturing jobs, but by 1989 they employed only 25 percent of the manufacturing workforce. In three decades the country moved from being the most intensively industrialized of the developed nations to one of the least industrialized. As manufacturing shrank, services expanded, employing 13.3 million in 1979 and 15.2 million in 1991. A key growth sector was financial services, which created one million jobs during the 1980s and by the early 1990s employed about one-eighth of the working population.

The longterm effects of this restructuring are not easy to evaluate. There are encouraging signs that the surviving part of British manufacturing is now more competitive. During the 1980s the annual rate of growth in manufacturing – 4 percent per annum – was among the highest in the developed world, and second only to Japan. In the early 1990s some experts speculated that the country's share of world trade had finally ceased to decline:

THE CAMBRIDGE PHENOMENON

In 1972 Trinity College, Cambridge, established a science park. Within a few years this had attracted a growing number of high-technology enterprises, both within and outside the science park itself. These were mostly small, independent and locally based companies that were closely linked with the university and focused on exportable products. The overall development, which became known as the Cambridge Phenomenon, was hailed by academics and politicians as Britain's investment in a high-technology future while retaining the advantages of local economic growth, rather than growth in response to foreign capital investment.

By the early 1990s there were no fewer than 300 companies within a 12-mile radius of Cambridge, employing some 13,000 staff. The Cambridge Phenomenon has become a role model for other clusters of high-technology companies across the country. Most of these grew up around the 40 or 50 university science parks established since Trinity's success. However, many of the companies around Cambridge have proved vulnerable to recession and takeover. Of those located in the Science Park, as many as half are now subsidiaries of large corporations; of these, half again are owned by foreign multinationals. Locally based independence has proved hard to sustain.

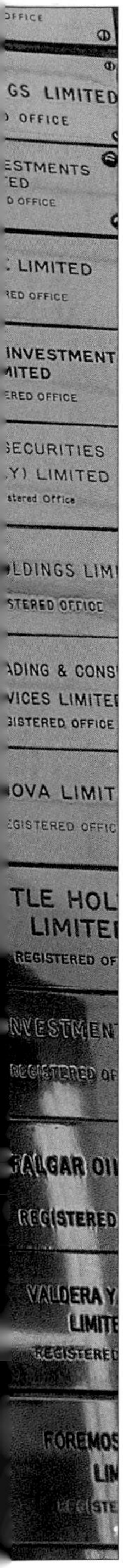

An impressive front *(left)* Nameplates of businesses based in the Channel Islands off the British coast, where many companies register to evade taxes that apply on the mainland. Most do not even keep an office here – a postal address is sufficient. Offshore banking has become one of the islands' economic mainstays.

Last of the mining communities *(below)* A mother and child near Easington colliery in the north of England. Miners and their families were devastated when British Coal proposed the closure of 31 pits like this one in 1992. The action threatened 30,000 jobs during the worst of the recession when the prospects for reemployment were bleakest.

British exports of manufactured goods seemed to have stabilized at around 6 percent of the global total. On the other hand, for the first time in British history, exports were consistently outstripped by imports. Britain was a net importer of manufactured goods in its trade with all important regions of the world except the oil-producing nations. This deterioration has caused the country to become increasingly dependent on earnings from three main activities: exports of North Sea oil; profits from overseas investments; and British service industries earning foreign currency. Income from all of these sources peaked in the mid 1980s. Since then the country has suffered persistent problems with its balance of payments, finding it impossible to earn enough through exports to balance spending on imports.

Building an international economy

In the 1980s British firms invested more than £30 billion (approximately $50 billion) outside the United Kingdom, especially in western Europe and the United States. Relative to its size, the country possesses substantially greater foreign assets than any other developed nation. Foreign money has flowed into the country from abroad – particularly from Japan – in greater quantities than in any other European country. More than a third of all Japanese direct investment in Europe in the 1980s has been in Britain. This may help Britain to keep abreast of new technological and financial developments. However, the public sector – chiefly the defense industry – continues to monopolize resources for research and development, causing Britain to lag ever further behind its rivals in commercial applications of technological innovation.

Important changes also occurred in the economy of the Republic of Ireland. The most positive development was in the country's balance of trade. Historically Ireland has imported more industrial and agricultural goods than it exports, but during the 1980s – in marked contrast with Britain – this situation began to improve, and by the end of the decade the country enjoyed a healthy trade surplus. Other changes were less encouraging. In Dublin and the more developed east of the country older manufacturing industries, such as textile production, have declined. There has been a growth in service industries, as well as electronic and instrument engineering – much of it in the rural west – but this has proved insufficient to balance the jobs and loss of revenue caused by factory closures. Consequently, unemployment has soared, increasing by as much as 155 percent from 1979 to 1991. Investment by the European Community (EC), which Britain and Ireland joined in 1972, has failed to overcome this problem. At the same time there has been a worrying increase in government indebtedness. By the mid 1980s as much as one-quarter of government spending was on interest and repayments on borrowing.

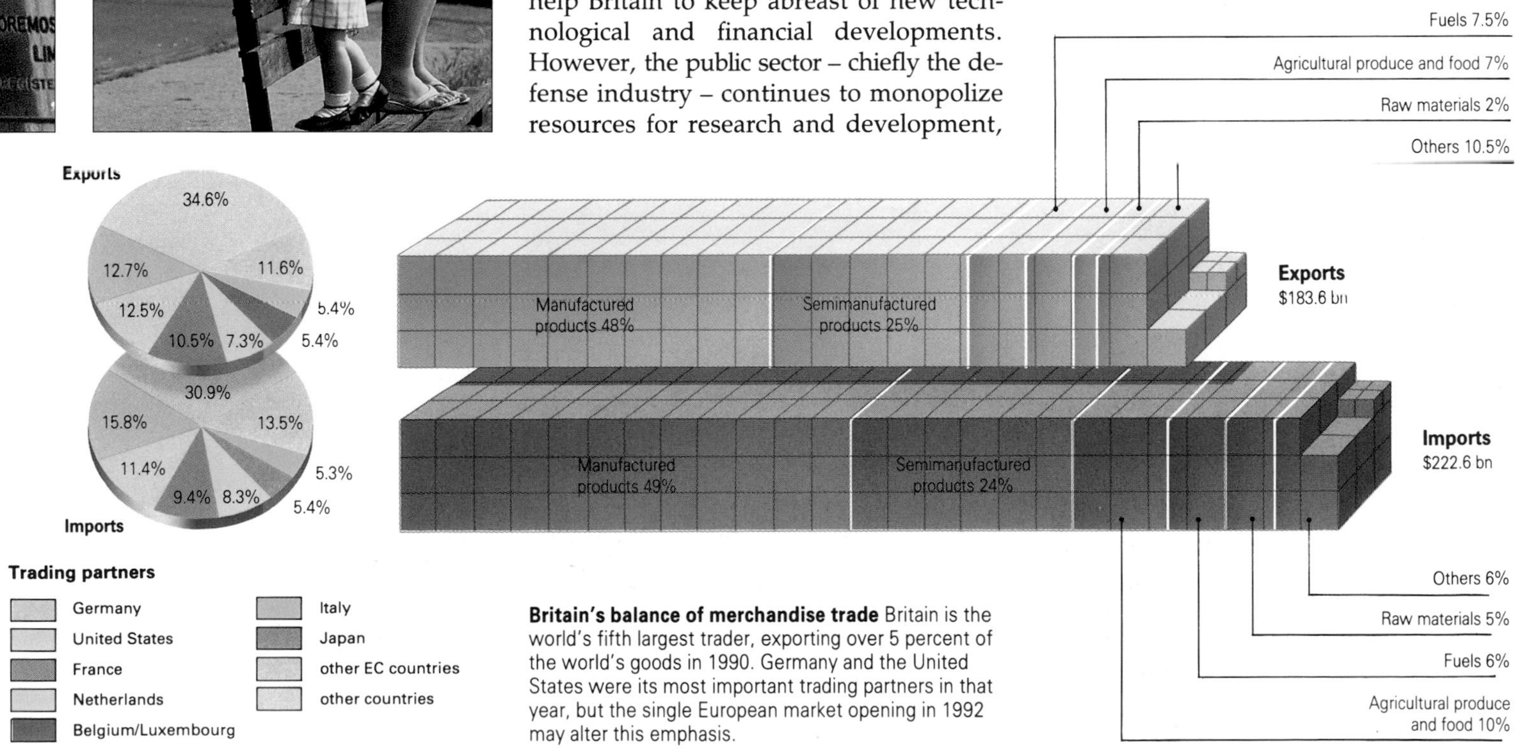

Britain's balance of merchandise trade Britain is the world's fifth largest trader, exporting over 5 percent of the world's goods in 1990. Germany and the United States were its most important trading partners in that year, but the single European market opening in 1992 may alter this emphasis.

THE NORTH–SOUTH DIVIDE

The 1980s also saw the emergence of a north–south divide, particularly between a low-unemployment, high-income southeast, and a high-unemployment, low-income northwest. Areas with low incomes and high unemployment have often been dependent on coal mining or older forms of manufacturing. Internal strife in Northern Ireland has discouraged investment. Only southeast England has grown steadily wealthier, even experiencing economic "overheating" in the late 1980s, which led to high inflation in wages and property values. The recession that began in 1990 has hit wealthy areas hardest, but the gap remains striking.

A second divide can be found all across the country in large cities: the contrast between affluent suburbs and depressed inner-city areas. Since the early 1970s many inner-city districts have experienced growing problems of poverty, unemployment, poor housing, drug abuse and crime. Widespread urban riots in the early 1980s forced the government to expand its urban aid and redevelopment programs. More recent disturbances indicate the problem is by no means solved.

On the job, on the dole

The size of the workforce has risen steadily as women and the postwar generation sought work. Between 1973 and 1991 women's participation in the workforce increased from 39 percent to 48 percent. Many women, however, are in part-time employment, often in the newly developed service industries. In 1973 only 17 percent of the workforce was part-time while today the proportion has grown to 30 percent. Union membership, which peaked at more than 13.3 million (58 percent of the workforce) in 1979, had fallen to 10.2 million (45 percent) by 1990.

A second major change, closely linked to the growth of the workforce, has been the rise of unemployment – from an average of 1 million during the 1970s to 2.5 million by the late 1980s. This has been caused by the economy's failure to expand quickly enough to keep up with labor supply, while increased automation in manufacturing and other industries has reduced the number of employees in some sectors. Overall, however, the number of full-time jobs available has remained steady. Part-time work has substantially increased, as has self-employment, which has almost doubled since 1973 to 3.3 million.

Out of the gloom *(below)* A new airport at Knock, in the Irish Republic's western county of Mayo, has brought jobs to the area and boosted tourism in the least developed part of the country, away from the urban center of Dublin.

The Republic of Ireland also has a regional disparity in wealth, but here it is an east–west gap. The eastern area, particularly around Dublin, is significantly more prosperous, urbanized and industrially developed than the rest of the country. During the 1980s this east–west gap has narrowed as new engineering and service industries have developed in the west and midwest. Overall, however, the loss of manufacturing jobs (down 17 percent from 1979 to 1991) has proved especially difficult to overcome. Unemployment in 1991 was two and a half times higher than in 1979, even though some 200,000 workers emigrated during the 1980s. Many of those were well qualified; between 1980 and 1988 the proportion of Irish graduates emigrating increased from 8 to 29 percent.

The rich get richer

From the late 1940s the share of private property owned by the wealthiest 10 percent of the British population fell from one-third to one-quarter. Since 1979, however, ownership by the richest 10 percent of the people has risen again to 30 percent. The bulk of the workforce has also seen a rise in real incomes during the last 10 years. By the 1990s some two-thirds of households owned their homes, compared with only half in the 1970s. Of these, the vast majority are skilled workers, professionals or managers. Among unskilled workers the picture is bleaker. Over 60 percent are tenants of public-sector (council) housing, and two-thirds of these are dependent on welfare. Added to universal high taxes, Margaret Thatcher's "poll tax" of the late 1980s – a municipal tax that did not exempt low-income groups such as the unemployed or the elderly – provoked mass protests.

The education muddle

Education has been called the most socially divisive aspect of Britain, and the struggle to provide more equal opportunities for all children continues. In the past state-supported schools were run by local and regional authorities throughout the United Kingdom, though in the early 1990s they were given the choice to opt out of this system and manage their own

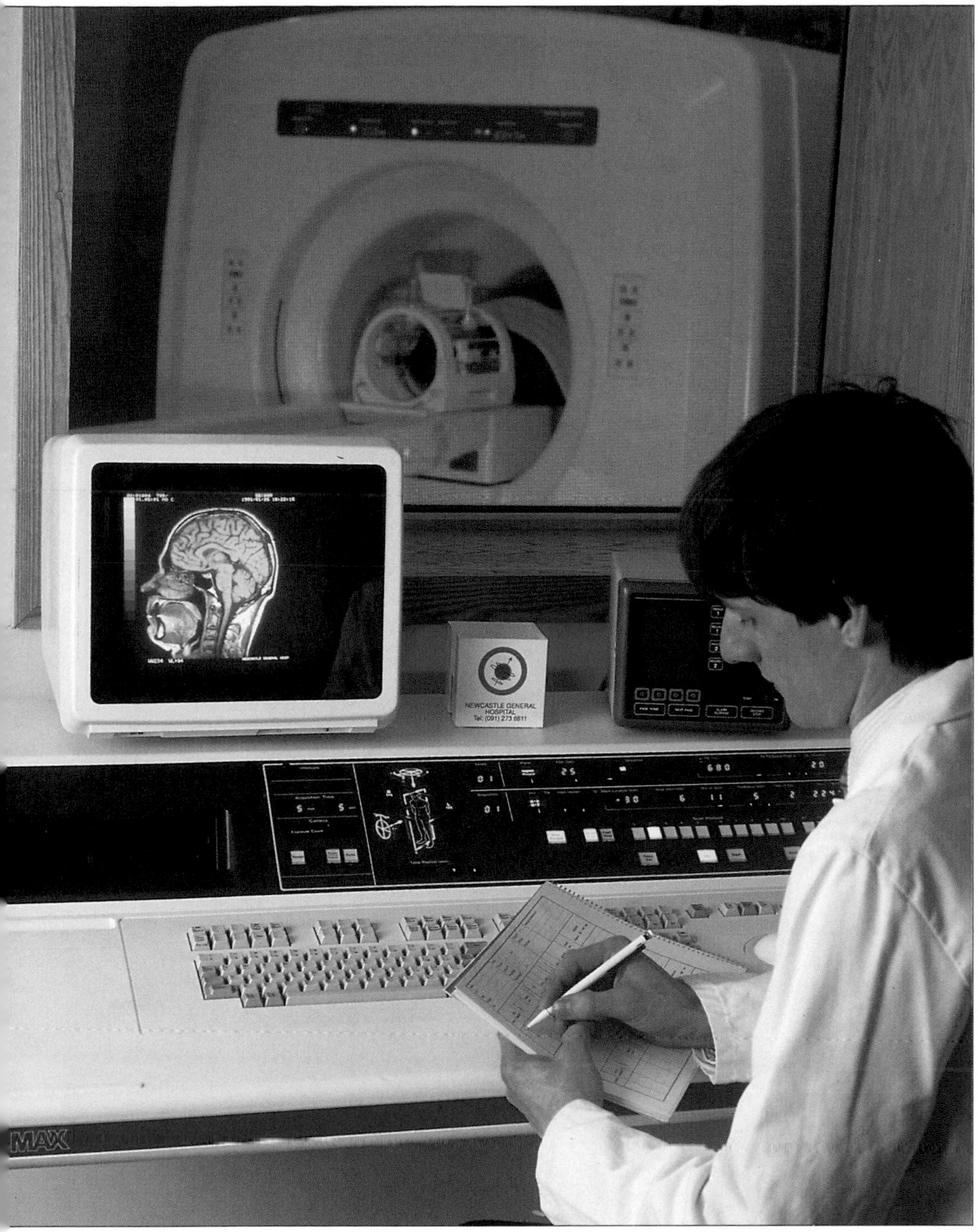

THE GEOGRAPHY OF HEALTH AND DISEASE

The state-run National Health Service (NHS) has existed in Britain since 1948, making healthcare available to the whole population, rich or poor. Despite recent problems of morale and funding it is probably the most efficient program in the developed world, and has helped raise standards of healthcare throughout the United Kingdom.

However, it has not promoted equally high life expectancy across the country. The mortality rate among male manual workers in the north of England and Scotland is 40 percent higher than in the south; among nonmanual workers the discrepancy is 20 percent. Death rates from both cancer and heart disease are higher in northern England and Scotland, and levels of heart disease in Northern Ireland are among the highest in the world. A similar north–south divide emerges in the pattern of health and care among women.

Certainly, the standard of healthcare is not the only issue at stake and other factors cloud the issue. Lifestyle (diet, exercise, and stress) as well as genetic inheritance make a tremendous difference to life expectancy. Smoking and heavy drinking are more prevalent in some northern areas, and environmental factors – climate and industrial pollution – also contribute. Nevertheless, it seems more than coincidence that the pattern of the country's ill health closely matches the pattern of the country's poverty.

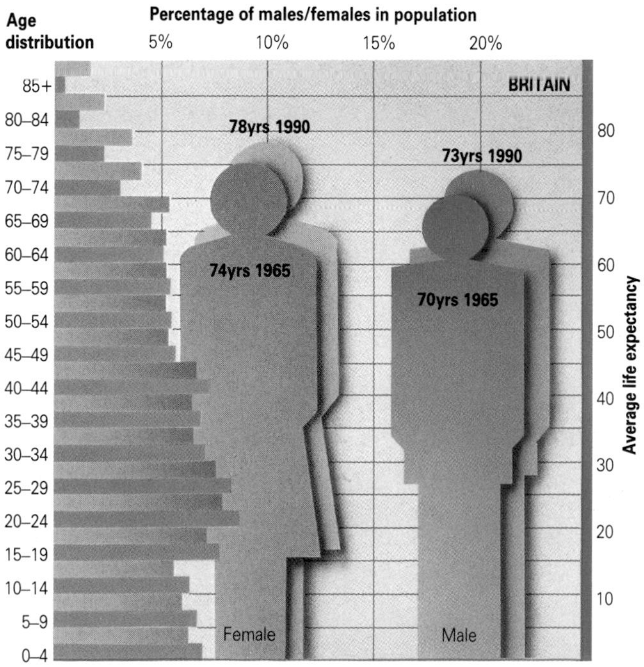

State-of-the-art treatment (*above*) is generally available through the National Health Service as well as through Britain's growing private healthcare industry. At Newcastle General Hospital in the north of England, for example, a radiographer administers an MRI (magnetic resonance imaging) brain scan to an NHS patient. Long waiting lists exist for many of the more common procedures. How quickly patients are seen is frequently fuel for national political debate.

Life expectancy and age distribution (*left*) Though life expectancy has improved in Britain since 1965, the country has lost ground compared with the rest of western Europe; only people in Ireland, Luxembourg and Portugal have a lower average lifespan. Birth rates are slightly higher than average for Europe but have fallen since 1950. By 1992 over 15 percent of the population was over 65 – one of the highest proportions in the world.

budgets. A national curriculum has recently been introduced to promote uniform standards throughout the country. Independent (public) schools charging fees continue to attract the children of the wealthy, though they are less prevalent in Scotland. Public-school students go on to make up nearly half the students at Oxford and Cambridge, still the most prestigious British universities. University places are available to only 12 percent of students who compete for them by national examination. The government pays university fees and makes a contribution toward living expenses according to means. Polytechnics and vocational colleges (many of which acquired university status in the 1990s) are numerous, promoting vocational training. Continuing education for adults is increasingly popular through the Open University, and other forms of distance learning.

The City – a global financial center

For more than 300 years London has been one of the world's leading financial centers. The City, or the "Square Mile" as the main financial district is familiarly known, is centered on slightly more than one square mile in the heart of London. Its rise to importance can be traced back to the 16th century, when London first emerged as a hub of Europe's merchant trading. By the late 17th century London and Amsterdam were competing for world financial leadership, and it was at this time that many of London's major financial institutions were established, including Lloyd's shipping insurance (1687–88), the Bank of England (1694), and an embryonic stock exchange (1670s). During the 18th century British colonial conquests in Asia and the Americas – together with a booming Atlantic trade – secured London's preeminence as a city of international trading, and the City's merchants became the wealthiest in Europe. During the 19th century this advantage was strengthened by the industrial revolution. As the British Empire grew, sterling became more widely used as an international currency and the City's activities became focused on overseas trading. This international trading role has become increasingly important as British industrial production has waned.

Adapting to change

During the 20th century London's money markets struggled hard to maintain their international position, though the British financial sector during this period had a great deal more success than most other sectors of the economy. By the 1950s, the strain of two world wars had taken their financial toll, as had the loss of the empire; these combined factors greatly reduced sterling's status as a leading world currency. In response, the City was forced to adapt. The growth of offshore banking and Euromarkets helped to secure London's place as a global financial center. For example, the value of trade in the Eurodollar market rose dramatically from about $10 billion in the early 1960s

Showing the right colors Traders on the floor of the London International Financial Futures Exchange (LIFFE), one of the City of London's fastest-growing institutions in the 1980s, identify themselves by color. Each jacket signifies a different profession: blue jackets are LIFFE officials; orange jackets (known as "yellow jackets") are worn by trainee traders and clerical or administrative staff; red jackets belong to independent traders, known as "locals." Additional styles and colors are worn by traders from other member companies.

to as much as $2,500 billion in the mid 1980s, with this trade being dominated throughout by London. The City is currently a leading center for trade in international equities, with a turnover in foreign equities that is almost half as much again as New York and 10 times as much as Tokyo. London remains the largest market for foreign exchange as well as a major center for international insurance. It also has the greatest concentration of foreign owned banks of any financial center.

Another significant development in the City of London has been the growth of a specialist market in financial futures and options. These offer some protection against changes in interest rates and stock market conditions – valuable in the increasingly complex and swift-moving international financial world. The London International Financial Futures Exchange, founded in 1982, has grown from a million contracts written in its first year to processing 38 million in 1991.

Sharing the wealth

The wealth generated in the City has had a profound effect on the whole south-eastern part of the country. It is one of Britain's leading sources of employment, both through its institutions and through the many services they require. More than 1.86 million square metres (20 million square feet) of office space has been built since the mid 1960s as the City has spread beyond the old frontiers of the "Square Mile". Office rentals soared in the 1980s, making it the world's most expensive downtown site after central Tokyo. The City played a leading role in the transformation of the British economy in the 1980s, by financing growth in new market sectors, and by funding the Conservative government's privatization program.

Despite its recent good fortune, London's status as a financial center is by no means guaranteed. The loosening of financial regulations worldwide has added to the danger of business being transferred to other locations, as has the growing foreign ownership of London's banking business. By the late 1980s, the City had lost its primacy in international banking to Tokyo, while Frankfurt had overtaken it in terms of equity business. Within the region, Edinburgh is becoming a leading financial center in its own right, specializing in investment trusts, particularly in North America.

Empty office space at Canary Wharf

The London Docklands development, to the east of the Square Mile (London's financial center) was intended to be a symbol of Britain's economic regeneration since 1980. A large area of former docklands, industrial land and low-income housing was razed in the late 1980s and early 1990s to make way for a shining new complex of office blocks, shops, leisure centers and waterside apartments. Thousands of jobs were created in the construction industry as this new enterprise zone took shape, and the expectation was that thousands more workers would be attracted to Docklands as London consolidated its position as Europe's leading financial center. Towering over Docklands is the Canary Wharf building, Britain's tallest structure and the provider of a projected 1.4 million square metres (15 million square feet) of commercial property. Canary Wharf was developed by the private, Toronto-based property company, Olympia and York.

By the early 1990s, the Docklands development had not yet fulfilled its potential. When Olympia and York signed an agreement with the London Docklands Development Corporation in 1987 it did so at a time when property prices in London were at a postwar high. It hoped to let Canary Wharf to international financial businesses such as Merrill Lynch, Credit Suisse-First Boston and Morgan Stanley. By 1992 commercial property prices in London had collapsed by between 50 percent and 90 percent and the supply of commercial property far exceeded demand. Olympia and York, moreover, had borrowed heavily in the boom years to finance its developments in London and New York and by 1992 it was unable to meet all of the interest payments due on its debt. The completion of Canary Wharf was postponed as a consequence.

Canary Wharf, the tall building to the right, dominates the skyline in Docklands, London. The development is approached by the Docklands Light Railway.

AN OLD ACTOR IN A NEW ECONOMY

COLONIAL POWER TO INDUSTRIAL NATION · A HARD ACT TO FOLLOW · THE PROSPERITY GAP

Before World War II France was a major colonial power. However, much of its infrastructure was destroyed during the Nazi occupation, and after 1945 France underwent profound social and economic change. As most of its empire broke up, France's international role became tied to the construction of a united Europe. State-led modernization made the country the world's fourth most important industrial nation, and living standards increased more than fourfold in the 30 years up to 1975. Over that period the economic balance of the region altered dramatically: from approximate equilibrium between agriculture, industry and services, to an economy dominated by service industries. After 1973 growth slowed down, with recession in the 1980s contributing to social polarization and racial and political tension.

COUNTRIES IN THE REGION

Andorra, France, Monaco

ECONOMIC INDICATORS: 1990

	HIE* France
GDP (US$ billions)	1,190.78
GNP per capita (US$)	19,490
Annual rate of growth of GDP, 1980–1990 (%)	2.2
Manufacturing as % of GDP	21
Central government spending as % of GNP	43
Merchandise exports (US$ billions)	215.8
Merchandise imports (US$ billions)	233.8
% of GNP donated as development aid	0.79

WELFARE INDICATORS

Infant mortality rate (per 1,000 live births)	
1965	22
1990	7
Daily food supply available (calories per capita, 1989)	3,465
Population per physician (1984)	320
Teacher–pupil ratio (primary school, 1989)	1 : 16

Note: The Gross Domestic Product (GDP) is the total value of all goods and services domestically produced. The Gross National Product (GNP) is the GDP plus net income from abroad.

** HIE (High Income Economy) – GNP per capita above $7,620 in 1990.*

COLONIAL POWER TO INDUSTRIAL NATION

In the 19th century France established colonies in North Africa and Southeast Asia. Made up of some 3.5 million square miles of land, French overseas territories were second in extent only to the British empire. Given this wide access to raw materials and extensive trading networks, France became one of a core group of advanced capitalist countries whose dominance was built on expanding productivity and steadily rising income. In 1820, for example, France's gross domestic product (GDP) per capita was surpassed only by Britain, the Netherlands and Australia. After the development of modern industries in the mid and late 19th century (textiles, leather, transport, metals, coal, railways and engineering) its rate of economic growth lagged behind growth in other developed economies. In the period 1820 to 1950 France's GDP per capita increased 3.9 times compared with an average of 4.7 for the world's 16 most developed economies.

Until the rise of Germany as an industrial force in the 20th century, France was the leading industrial power in continental Europe. Development was concentrated in the northern coalfields, along the northeastern frontier with Belgium and Germany and in Rhône-Alpes; while the newer industries of the second industrial revolution developed around Lyon and Paris, France's commercial and financial center. On the eve of World War II, over one-third of employment was in indus-

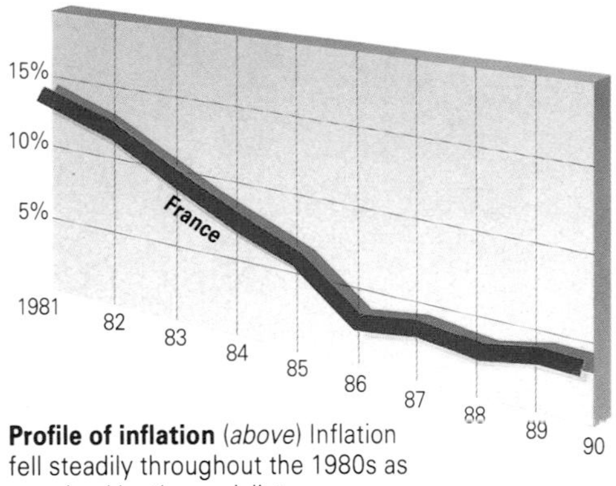

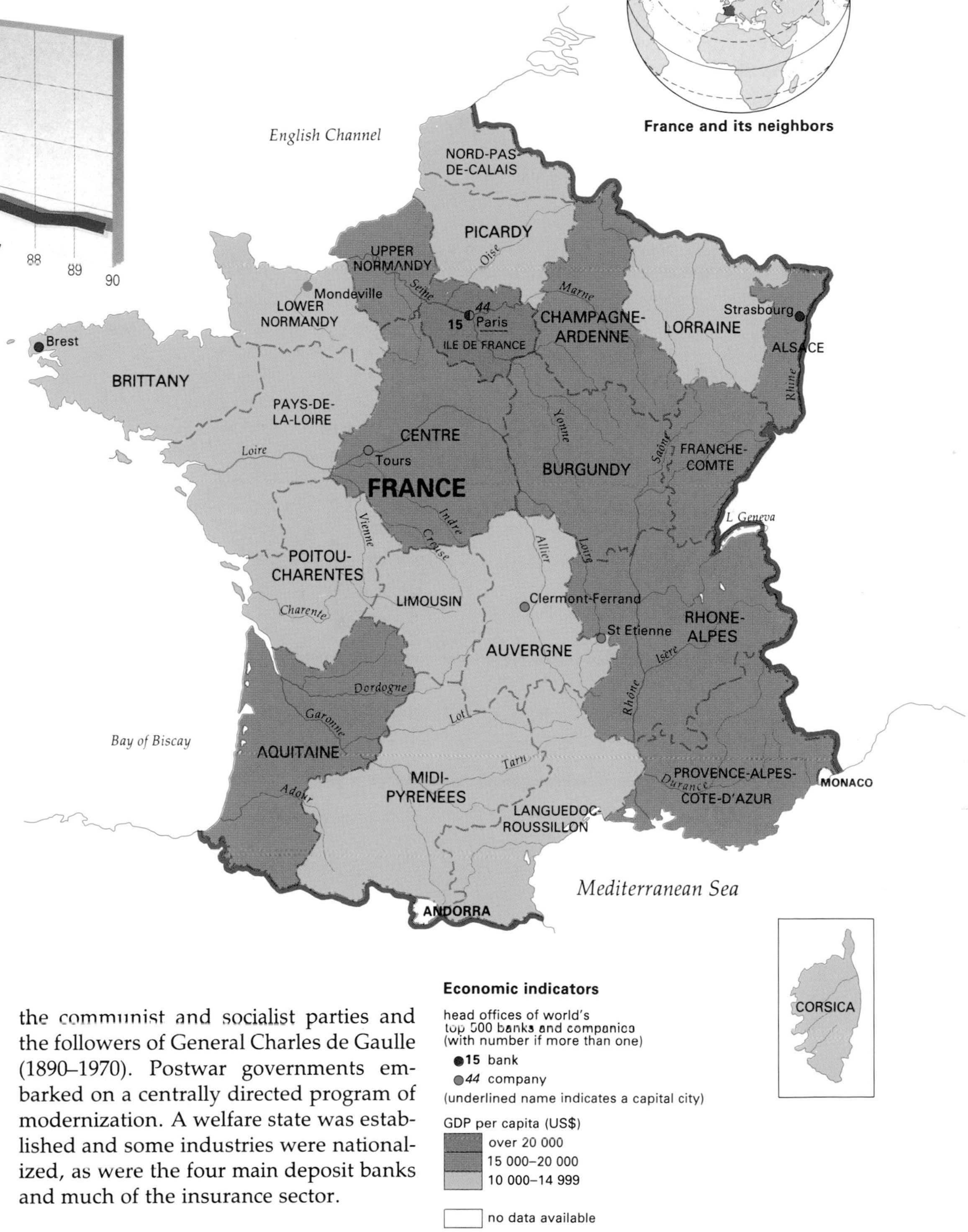

Profile of inflation (*above*) Inflation fell steadily throughout the 1980s as promised by the socialist government of Francois Mitterrand elected in 1981. By 1990 inflation was the second lowest in Europe (slightly higher than Denmark). However, this controversial success was achieved alongside a rising trade deficit and high unemployment.

Map of GDP per capita (*right*) The concentration of industry in northern France has established the area as the most prosperous in the country. Paris is the unrivaled financial and commercial heart of the country, with an increasing number of foreign companies opening offices there. Revenue-generating activity is particularly high in the northeast.

Business and pleasure at La Défense (*left*) 3 km (1.86 mi) from the Arc de Triomphe in Paris, a new World Trade Center has been opened. The complex at La Défense is filling up rapidly with the offices of French and European companies. Shops, restaurants and other amenities draw businesses away from the crowded center of Paris; there are also hotels and apartments among the many high-rise buildings.

try, almost one-third in agriculture and just less than one-third in services.

Devastation and reconstruction

France's failure to modernize its industrial system as fast as Germany was one of the reasons for its dramatic defeat in 1940. By 1944 the economy was devastated – any surviving plant or infrastructure was antiquated due to a lack of pre-war investment, and there was a chronic housing shortage. The workforce too was sadly reduced. Over 600,000 people had been killed or were missing and another half million were in German prison camps. Industrial output fell to below its 1938 level, and France lost its pre-war status as a major economic power. During the 1950s political forces determined to promote renewal came to power, including the communist and socialist parties and the followers of General Charles de Gaulle (1890–1970). Postwar governments embarked on a centrally directed program of modernization. A welfare state was established and some industries were nationalized, as were the four main deposit banks and much of the insurance sector.

Les Trentes Glorieuses

Thirty glorious years of spectacular and unprecedented growth followed (1946–75) in which productivity grew at 5 percent per year. They encompassed France's entry to the European Community (EC) as a founder member in 1957, and the breakup of the French empire (1954–62) leaving only a scattering of dependencies. The period 1962–73 saw very rapid growth as the postwar generation came into the labor market, women joined the workforce in larger numbers, and the immigrant population mushroomed. However, adjusting to a new position in the world economy still proved difficult. In particular France could not easily come to terms with United States' world economic domination and with the spectacular economic recovery and rearmament of West Germany.

A HARD ACT TO FOLLOW

The 30 glorious years set expectations of economic growth that were impossible to match in the years that followed. The 1980s and early 1990s were years of economic crisis in France. The immediate cause of this reversal of fortunes was the quadrupling of oil prices in 1974 when, in spite of a healthy exporting position, the cost of imported energy caused a trade deficit. France is dependent on imported fuel; its 1990 energy deficit (FF 94 billion, approximately $17 billion) was twice its overall trade deficit. The underlying cause was a production slowdown and the globalization of the French economy.

Throughout the 1970s and 1980s international trading became increasingly important to the French economy. Exports and imports increased from 14 percent of GDP in 1973 to 27 percent in 1990. By that year France was exporting one-third of its industrial output, making it responsible for 6.2 percent of world exports and the fourth largest international exporter after Germany, the United States and Japan. Inevitably, the pattern of whom France traded with and why also changed significantly in the 20-year period between 1970 and 1990. The most important factors were the loss of protected French colonial markets and the development of the EC. By the early 1990s, 60 percent of trade was with other EC countries, and trade with countries not in the Organization for Economic Cooperation and Development (OECD), including former overseas territories, had fallen to 15 percent.

Domestic deficits

In spite of this widespread trading network, France still suffered from current account deficits (FF 41 billion, approximately $7.5 billion in 1990) which constrained its economic development. The deterioration in its balance of trade position led the first socialist government in 1981–82 to switch to a strategy that reduced inflation but at the cost of high unemployment. Deficits caused by energy imports have been a constant problem since 1973. Since the mid 1980s France has also had deficits in industrial goods, importing more than it exports due to low investment in domestic industry. On the positive side, France is the world's second most important exporter of food products. Invisible earnings from tourism and services also make significant contributions to France's current account.

During this period of readjustment in France's trading position, the ownership structure of international industry was also changing. Many French companies were acquired or funded by foreign multinationals, and, in turn, a higher proportion of French capital was invested abroad instead of at home. Since 1986 there has been a remarkable increase in

Unwanted at home, well received abroad (*above*), crates of Beaujolais Nouveau await export. Although most French wines for export are of higher grades, there is also a demand for the latest season's yield, which the French consider too new and raw to drink.

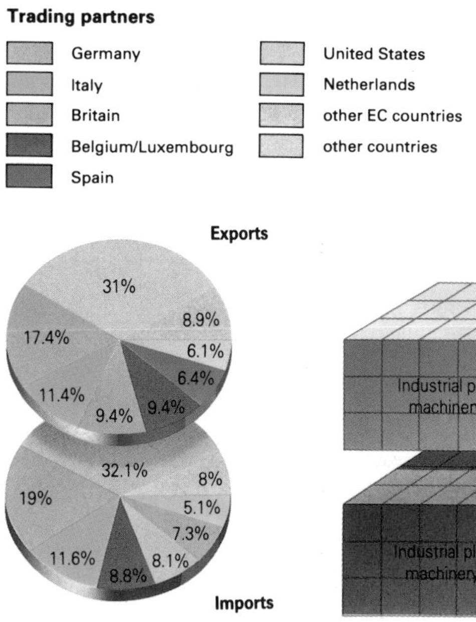

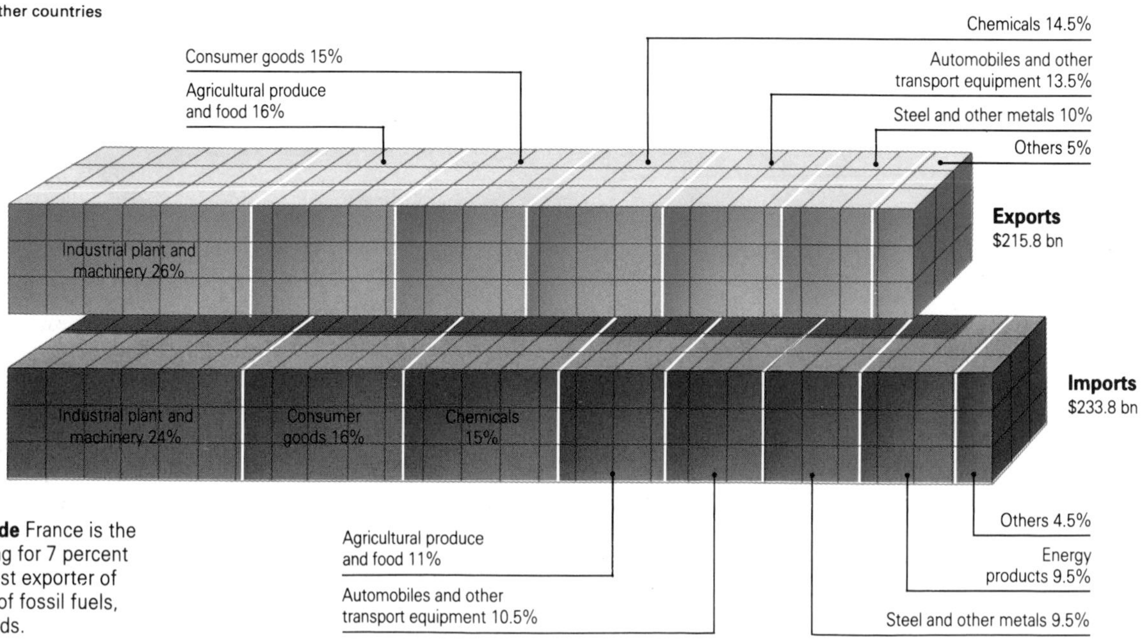

France's balance of merchandise trade France is the world's fourth largest trader (accounting for 7 percent of global exports) and the second largest exporter of agricultural products. Poor in deposits of fossil fuels, France imports much of its energy needs.

Wheel of fortune *(above)* The state-run casino at Monaco is a cornerstone of the economy, drawing affluent tourists. Citizens of Monaco – who comprise a mere 15 percent of the population – are prohibited from gambling but are also exempt from income tax.

French investment overseas, with public-sector companies such as Rhône-Poulenc, Elf Aquitaine, Credit Lyonnais and Péchiney playing a leading role. In 1988–90 alone two-thirds of their investments were in other EC countries. The combination of a current account deficit and of high levels of French investment overseas created a significant increase in French indebtedness. To attract and retain investment at home, the French government pursued rigorous monetary policies, protecting the franc and keeping interest rates at levels that made French assets attractive for foreign investors.

Economic restructuring

Despite government efforts, falling profits and major technological change (leaving French industry behind) contributed to the economic crisis as a process of de-industrialization set in. The number of industrial jobs in France fell from 8.3 million in 1974 to 6.5 million in 1990, with the greatest decline occurring in the north and east. Meanwhile the service sector boomed. Office jobs increased by 175,000 jobs per year, doubling the number of clerical staff from the 1960s. The number of executive and professional staff increased by two and a half times. In 1990, about 65 percent of the workforce – approximately 75 percent of women and 50 percent of men – worked in services. Of these, 45 percent were in market services (finance, catering, retailing, publishing, clerical work and personal services such as hairdressing) and 20 percent worked in government-run services and public administration.

PROFIT BY THE VINE

Wine, food and other agricultural products are among the chief exports of the French economy. Since the 1970s the average yearly output of wine is about 70 million hectoliters (over 1.84 billion gallons), but output has fluctuated from the record 1979 figure to a disappointing low in 1981. Vine production in the 1990s is far less extensive than in previous decades, with vines being grown on less than 1 million hectares in almost every department except those near the north coast, Vosges in the northeast and Creuse in the center. The reduced acreage is partly a result of EC grants to growers to pull up their vines in order to limit overproduction and the build-up of stocks. The EC also requires the distillation of excess production at half the guide price or less.

However, there is still a strong concentration of vineyards in a small number of wine-producing areas, and these are at the heart of France's lucrative wine-exporting industry. The Midi extending along the Mediterranean coast from the eastern Pyrenees to Var (the extreme southeast province of France) has extensive vineyards. The other well established major wine-producing areas are Charente, the Rhône valley, the Pays de la Loire, Burgundy, Champagne and Alsace.

All the wines produced in these regions face acute competition from Italian and Spanish wines in the world market. The strain has begun to tell: in 1987 fewer than 600,000 wine producers declared a harvest compared with 1 million in 1970; 45 percent of them produced solely for their own use. Of the wine that reached the market in 1987, there were 20 million hectoliters of *Vins de qualité produits dans des régions déterminiés* (VQPRD), 11 million hectoliters from the production of alcohol for cognac and armagnac, and some 40 million hectoliters of *Vins de consommation courante* (VCC – *Vins de pays* and *Vins de table*). Of the VCC wines about two-thirds came from Languedoc-Roussillon in southwest central France.

THE PROSPERITY GAP

With economic growth in postwar France came increasing purchasing power and rises in standards of living. The rise of urban industrialization, bringing with it higher incomes, encouraged the demand for home ownership, consumer goods and urban services. During the period 1949–88 the purchasing power of French households increased fivefold with the fastest growth from 1959–73. The share of household budgets devoted to items other than food, clothing and fuel fell, and from 1959 to 1988 the number of French workers owning cars, televisions, refrigerators and washing machines increased from less than 20 percent to more than 90 percent.

At the root of these changes were alterations in the average household structure. The model of a married couple with children was still the norm, but single parent households were becoming more common, and there were significant changes in the earning power of women. By the early 1990s almost 75 percent of French women aged 25 to 39 were economically active; as were 70 percent in the same age group with two children.

Haves and have-nots

This new prosperity generated during the boom years was not evenly distributed through the population. In the 1950s and early 1960s the groups to suffer most were farmers, artisans and small shopkeepers whose incomes grew slowly and who were damaged by the drive to modernize. Rising numbers in the school-age population and shortages of resources in rapidly growing urban areas contributed to social unrest. In May 1968 at Nanterre in the north, and Nantes in the west, students, manual workers and professionals started to protest against the lack of school places, hospital facilities, and accommodation. After the economic crisis of the mid 1970s, there was a marked increase in unemployment, industrial dereliction, urban decay and social polarization. The main victims this time were unskilled workers, unqualified young people, and second-generation immigrants. In 1986 the poorest 10 percent of households had less than FF 32,000 per year ($4,600) while the richest 10 percent had more than FF 200,000 ($29,000). In that same year almost one in five households were living below the poverty line (defined as having less than half the median income). One child in four lived in these families – the poor were no longer a marginal group.

More education, fewer jobs?

French students are spending longer in full-time education than their parents did, and the proportion of them pursuing higher qualifications has increased. The share of 5 to 24 year-olds in full-time education is high: in 1986–87 it stood at 83 percent compared with 62 percent in neighboring Britain. About one-fifth of French students attend private (Catholic) schools; the rest attend state schools. School is compulsory until age 16, but technical specialization may begin at 14. In 1959 just 9.7 percent of young people received a baccalauréate, the passport into higher education; by 1981 the

Disenchanted *(above)* Arab immigrants in France often live below the poverty line in urban ghettos. Most are young unskilled males who work for low wages if they can find jobs at all. Racism is a growing social problem.

A privileged education *(left)* A lecture room in the Sorbonne, now the core of the University of Paris. Since 1968 higher education in France has been governed by autonomous multidisciplinary universities who establish their own teaching programs and means of assessment.

Life expectancy and age distribution *(right)* Life expectancy has increased since 1965, particularly for French women who are now among the longest lived in the world. The 1930s saw new legislation to increase the population, producing a baby boom that ended in the 1960s. This accounts for the large numbers in their 30s and 40s.

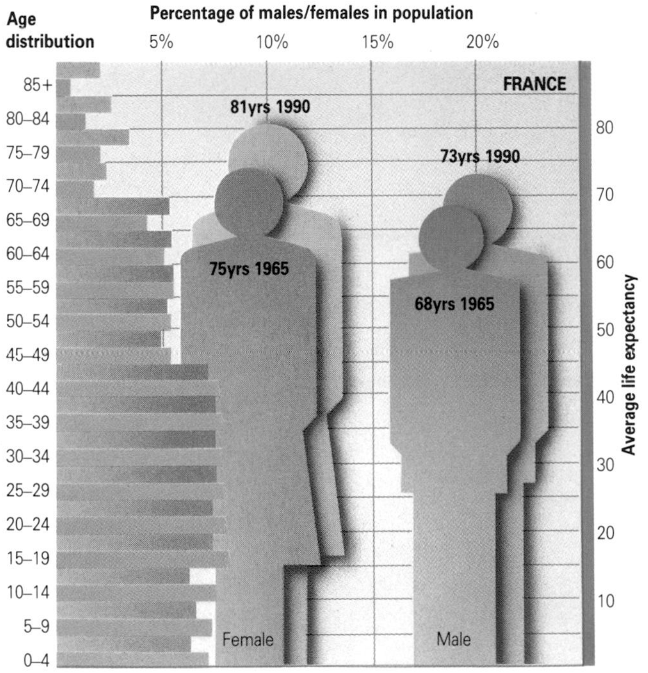

EURODISNEY: OF MICE AND MEN

In April 1992 the first stage of the EuroDisney amusement park outside Paris opened to visitors. Attractions included a replica of the skating rink at the Rockefeller Center in New York and an imaginary turn-of-the-century small-town main street. There is also space for Autopia, sponsored by Renault, with its dream cars of the future. There are 5,200 rooms in thematic hotels; 22,000 square meters of shops and restaurants; a camp site for 500 people; 570 homes; and a golf course.

The American Disney corporation signed the contract for the development in 1987 under very attractive terms, acquiring the 2,300 hectare site at the bargain price of FF11 ($1.8) per square meter. The state-owned Caissee des Depots et Consignations provided a loan of FF4.4 billion ($732 million) at a preferential interest rate, and the French government put up an extra FF45 ($7.5) billion to extend and develop transportation facilities, and reduced the tax on entrance tickets. In return, France expects to receive an investment of FF22 ($3.7) billion and 12,000 new jobs. To make a profit, EuroDisney will have to attract 11 million visitors a year, or 30,000 daily. On summer days it will undoubtedly attract capacity crowds, but the northern climate is variable and winters severe. EuroDisney organizers are confident of success and are planning a second stage of development with facilities for an additional 10 million visitors. Only time will tell whether the venture will have been worth the large investment the French government has made in it.

percentage was 26.4. It is the declared goal of the French government that 80 percent of 18 year-olds should receive an academic or technical baccalauréate by the year 2000.

However, even very highly educated workers face an increasingly uncertain future. In the job market there are relatively fewer secure lifetime jobs and the expansion of the wage-earning class has slowed down. In particular, it has become harder for young people to get their first job. In 1988 the average figure for French unemployment stood at 9.6 percent but among young adults it was 20.5 percent, and 24.8 percent for men without diplomas. Geography makes a significant difference – the center north (Ardennes, Somme and Nord-Pas-de-Calais) near the Belgian border and the Mediterranean coast around Marseille are traditionally the worst affected areas with unemployment rates rising to 12 and 14 percent. Fixed-term contracts, temporary work, government-assisted jobs, working freelance from home, part-time employment, and self-employment are all becoming more common. In 1982–88 fixed-term and temporary jobs increased two-fold, and in 1988 2.2 million jobs (occupying 12 percent of the workforce) were part-time. In 1980–85 self-employment was one-third higher than in 1965–70.

The paradox of advanced countries such as France is the existence of two economic climates within the same economy. In one, a large minority of the population suffers from high unemployment, low incomes, and discrimination against them in the areas of healthcare, housing and education. Those who suffer most are the unskilled, the elderly, the young unemployed, single parents and immigrants. There was a clear increase in the size of these marginalized groups during the 1980s. In the other climate technological and scientific progress takes place with dramatic speed, a large section of the population increases its professional skills and is rewarded by rising incomes and higher standards of living. The consequence is a split society where areas of remarkable growth coexist with poverty and homelessness.

France and the new European railroad age

During the 1980s the French government continued to intervene directly in economic development with strategic plans for key national industries including nuclear energy, telecommunications and aerospace (Ariane and Airbus). Their investment in high-speed locomotives, the *Train à Grande Vitesse* (TGV), was part of this pattern of state-led initiatives to promote growth.

The most attractive feature of the TGV is that it provides rapid mass transport while retaining the conventional advantages of rail travel – safety, environmental protection and energy conservation. Trains are one hundred times safer than automobiles, and use two to three times less space than road transport. In addition to its energy efficiency, electric power is less polluting than the internal combustion engine. The TGV uses two to three times less energy per passenger kilometer (or mile) than the most economical large capacity aircraft or cars, and is not dependent on oil which accounts for such a large part of France's trade deficit. It offers high-speed travel into city centers – for long-distance travelers this eliminates an additional journey to and from out-of-town airports.

A "Plane On Rails"

High-speed railroads are particularly well suited to travel across Europe, where the population is concentrated in cities between 200 and 1,000 km (125 and 621 mi) away from each other. Over these distances the TGV journey times are up to 4 hours from city center to city center.

At present there are two lines in service: TGV Sud-Est, which was developed to solve the congestion on the Paris–Lyon line; and the newer TGV Atlantique running to west coast destinations. On the newer line trains run at 300 kilometers per hour (186 mph) instead of 270 (168 mph). The TGV Sud-Est demonstrates clearly the value of inter-city services in Europe. Covering the 427 kilometers (265 mi) from Paris (with 9 million inhabitants) from Lyon (with over 1 million) in two hours, it attracted 18 million passengers in 1989. In 1980–88 the annual number of passengers traveling between Paris and the southeast went up from 12.2 million to 22.1 million. The line has proved to be a great commercial success, all the loans should be repaid within 10 years of the start of the service.

Paris to London

Now under construction are the TGV Nord, the Eastern Interconnection (Ligne d'Interconnection Est) in Ile-de-France, and the TGV Rhône-Alpes which extends the TGV Sud-Est to Valence via the station of Lyon-Satolas. New projects have been identified, and there are plans for an entire network with some 4,500 kilometers (2,790 mi) of new infrastructures. Final decisions as to whether and when the new lines will be developed remain to be made. The government's required rate of return is 10 percent, which only one of the proposed new lines (TGV Provence–Côte d'Azur) meets.

With the completion of these projects, France's major cities will have much improved connections with other EC cities including high-speed routes to Britain, Belgium, Germany, Italy and the Mediterranean. Journey times to almost all parts of mainland Europe will fall sharply: the journey to Barcelona from Paris will be halved and, if a high-speed line is built through the Channel Tunnel, it will be possible to make the journey from Paris to London in 2 hours 45 minutes. The prospect opens up a wealth of new possibilities for European trade and business development.

Indeed there are plans to develop passenger platforms that combine airports, TGV stations and motorways. Examples include the area northeast of Paris and the Satolas L'Isle d'Abeau near Lyon. The newly-achieved accessibility of these towns is stimulating a wave of major industrial investment there.

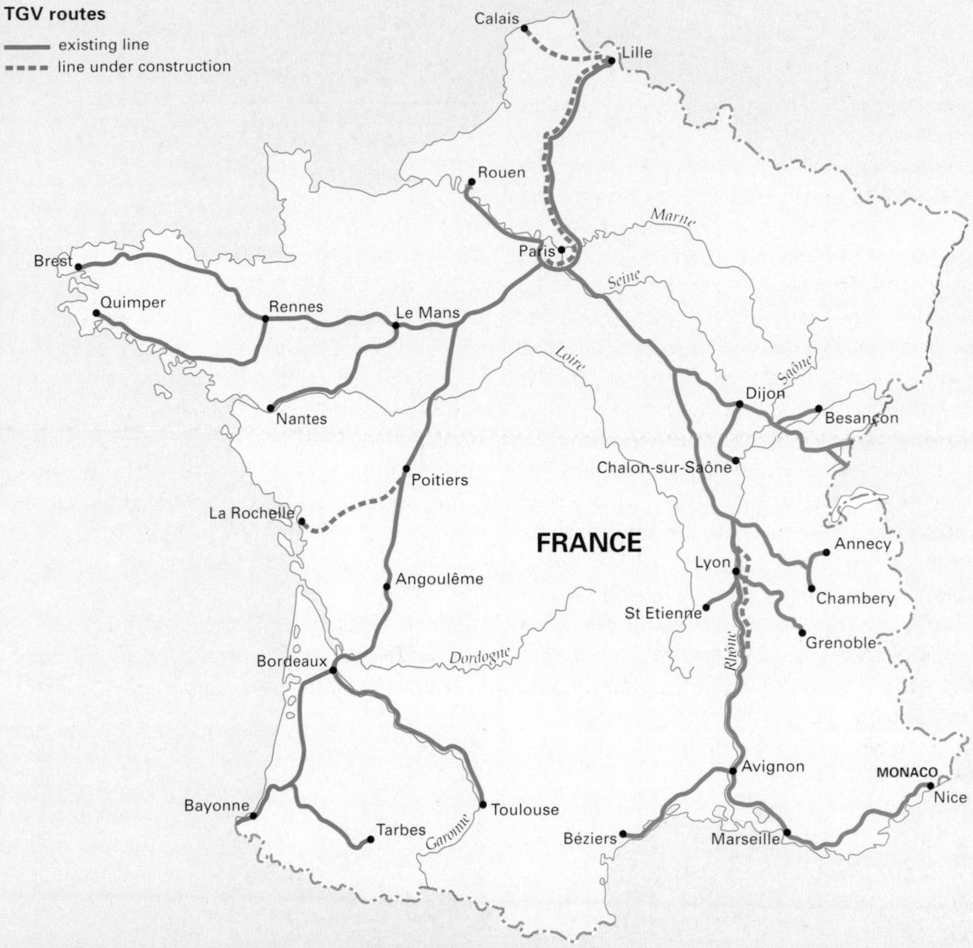

Standard, express or TGV services (*above*) are listed on the departures board at Gare Montparnasse, Paris. Shortened journey times between major European cities make rail travel cheaper than flying and more efficient than going by road.

Extending the routes (*right*) A further investment of FF 187 billion ($36 million) is planned in the TGV system in the mid 1990s. The proposed new infrastructure will add a further 400 km (240 mi) of track to the existing network and extend the service to several new areas.

A pause in flight (*below*) a high-speed train comes to a halt in one of France's most modern stations built to accommodate the huge volume of TGV traffic on the Paris–Lyon line.

EUROPE'S MAJOR TRADING CENTERS

TRADE, DOMINANCE AND DECLINE · OLD AND NEW SOURCES OF PROSPERITY · SPREADING PROSPERITY

International trading has been the main economic activity of the Low Countries for centuries. The Netherlands was the world's leading colonial and trading power in the 17th century, but by 1700 its supremacy had faded. During the 19th century Belgium and Luxembourg became manufacturers and exporters of steel. After 1950 deposits of coal began to run out and these industries declined. Once again, the region became a trading center, exploiting its location astride the main routes between the industrial and financial centers of France, Germany and Britain. In the late 20th century, Belgium and the Netherlands developed successful light manufacturing and service industries, while banking thrived in Luxembourg. All three countries have benefited from the European Community (EC), and are among Europe's richest states.

COUNTRIES IN THE REGION		
Belgium, Luxembourg, Netherlands		
ECONOMIC INDICATORS: 1990		
	HIE* Belgium	**HIE* Netherlands**
GDP (US$ billions)	192.39	279.15
GNP per capita (US$)	15,540	17,320
Annual rate of growth of GDP, 1980–1990 (%)	2.0	1.9
Manufacturing as % of GDP	23	20
Central government spending as % of GNP	49	53
Merchandise exports (US$ billions)	118.1	131.4
Merchandise imports (US$ billions)	119.8	125.9
% of GNP donated as development aid	0.45	0.94
WELFARE INDICATORS		
Infant mortality rate (per 1,000 live births)		
1965	24	14
1990	8	7
Daily food supply available (calories per capita, 1989)	3,679	3,151
Population per physician (1984)	330	450
Teacher–pupil ratio (primary school, 1989)	1 : 10	1 : 17

Note: The Gross Domestic Product (GDP) is the total value of all goods and services domestically produced. The Gross National Product (GNP) is the GDP plus net income from abroad.

** HIE (High Income Economy) – GNP per capita above $7,620 in 1990.*

TRADE, DOMINANCE AND DECLINE

From the late 16th century the United Provinces (now the Netherlands) began to supplant Spain and Portugal as the world's leading colonial powers. By the 1650s Dutch trading bases had been established all across the globe, from the Americas in the west to Java in the east. Amsterdam was a leading financial center and Dutch ships dominated the most lucrative cargo routes, particularly in the spice trade (dominated by the Dutch East India Company) and along trading routes to the Baltic.

From 1700 Dutch trade was increasingly challenged by European rivals. During the 19th century the country's economic development was mostly fueled by exports from the newly industrialized Ruhr area of Germany passing through the port of Rotterdam. In spite of growth in the finance and shipbuilding sectors, this was a period of overall decline for the Netherlands. By contrast, the southernmost part of the region entered a period of dynamic economic expansion. From 1800 Wallonia (now southern Belgium) became the first part of continental Europe to undergo an industrial revolution, emerging as a leading exporter of iron, coal and textiles. This development was encouraged by the occupying French (1795–1814)

The growing industry (*below*) Customers are confronted with a bewildering choice of flower bulbs at a large horticultural market in the Netherlands. Cut flowers and bulbs from the region are also exported all over the world.

and assisted by the long Napoleonic wars, which blocked exports from England. After Belgium's independence in 1830 Wallonia developed as a thriving steel-making area while the huge European railroad projects of that time created an expanded export market. Neighboring Luxembourg, which gained its independence from the Netherlands after 1867, also developed a steel industry.

Postwar integration and prosperity

World Wars I and II encouraged greater economic integration in Belgium, Luxembourg and the Netherlands, with their exiled governments forming the Benelux economic union in 1944. However, this organization – a precursor of the EC – did little to offset the harshness of the immediate postwar years, especially in the Netherlands. The country lost its main colony, Indonesia, and much Dutch manufacturing had been destroyed in the war. Ironically, this last problem proved an advantage. The new production lines that were built in the 1950s – with American financial help offered under the Marshall plan – proved internationally competitive. The Netherlands became a successful trading nation once more, and the port of Rotterdam flourished again. At the same time, Belgian Wallonia's heavy industry, which had survived World War II largely intact, began to decline, suffering from the depletion of the area's coal mines. The same was true of Luxembourg's steel industry. Northern Flanders, began to develop light industry, and took over as Belgium's principal growth area, with Antwerp emerging as a major international port.

During the postwar decades the governments of both Belgium and the Netherlands played an important role in shaping economic growth, especially in planning and controlling industrial relations. Both were committed to full employment, although the economic institutions they guided were mostly privately owned. From the 1950s the EC also began to play a part in influencing economic development, and the period 1950–80 was one of growth throughout the region. However, by the 1970s the rate of development had slowed, an indication that new problems were emerging.

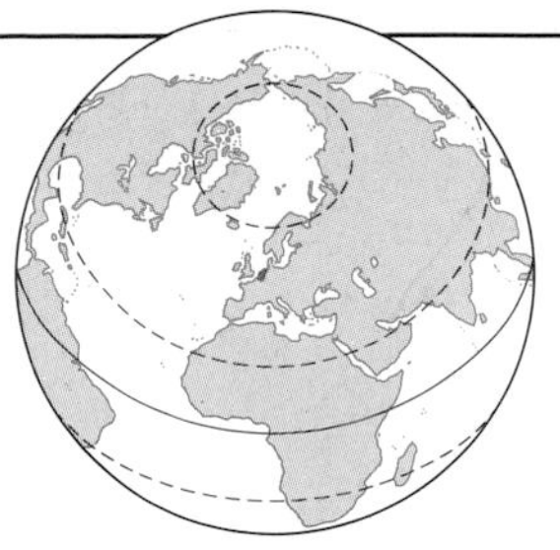

The Low Countries

Map of GDP per capita *(right)* Brussels is the wealthiest part of the region, its prominence as an administrative center of the EC attracting major companies and banks to establish head offices there. Tax advantages in Luxembourg also attract major international business investment.

Economic indicators

head offices of world's top 500 banks and companies (with number if more than one)

- **2** bank
- *2* company

(underlined name indicates a capital city)

GDP per capita (US$)

- over 20 000
- 15 000–20 000
- 10 000–14 999

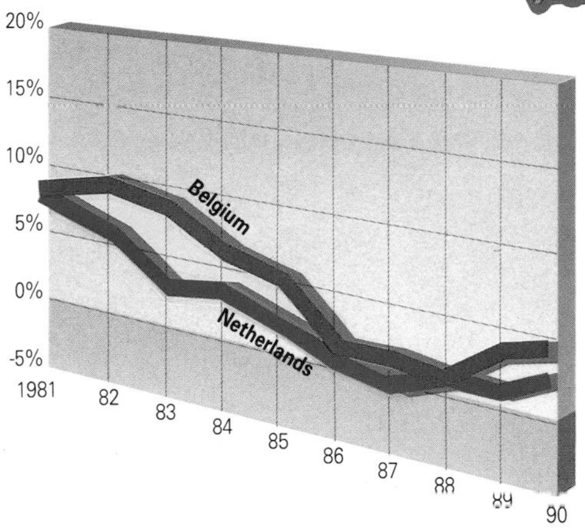

Profile of inflation *(above)* The inflationary spiral of the 1970s was brought under control during the 1980s by a move away from established economic policies. During this decade the Netherlands generally maintained a lower rate of inflation than Belgium.

OLD AND NEW SOURCES OF PROSPERITY

Trade remained the mainstay of the region's economy through the 1980s and early 1990s. In the Netherlands imports and exports were equivalent to almost half of the country's gross domestic product (GDP) in 1990, while in Belgium the figure was even higher at more than two-thirds. Rotterdam in the Netherlands is now the world's busiest port and handles the greater part of continental Europe's sea trade, while Antwerp in Belgium is also a fast-growing port and ranks as Europe's third busiest. This reliance on trade makes the region vulnerable to recession. In the long term, however, it is likely to maintain the three countries' considerable prosperity. In recent decades trade has been sufficiently profitable to allow the region to play an important role in offering assistance to developing countries. One percent of the GDP of the Netherlands is given as foreign aid, making it one of the world's most generous donor nations.

Inflation and the public sector

By 1980 two economic problems were afflicting the region. First, inflation was a growing threat, particularly in the Netherlands. The country's new wealth as a producer of North Sea gas in the late 1970s caused the Dutch guilder to soar in value, reducing the cost of imports and beginning an inflationary spiral that became known as the "Dutch disease". Secondly, a growing public-service deficit was becoming a problem both in Belgium and in the Netherlands. During the 1960s and 1970s the governments of both countries had created extensive and growing systems of public services. Public-sector employees usually had their incomes index-linked to local inflation rates and, not surprisingly, income rises tended to run ahead of increases in productivity. To pay for the rising costs of public services, higher taxes had to be levied, putting a strain on the private sector. Only in Luxembourg did the government adopt a less interventionist role.

During the 1980s both Belgium and the Netherlands took steps to deal with these problems. Government policies moved away from the corporatism of previous decades and some state enterprises were privatized, such as the Dutch postal service. At the same time, public expenditure was scrutinized to find ways to save money. In order to soften the blow of unemployment caused by restructuring

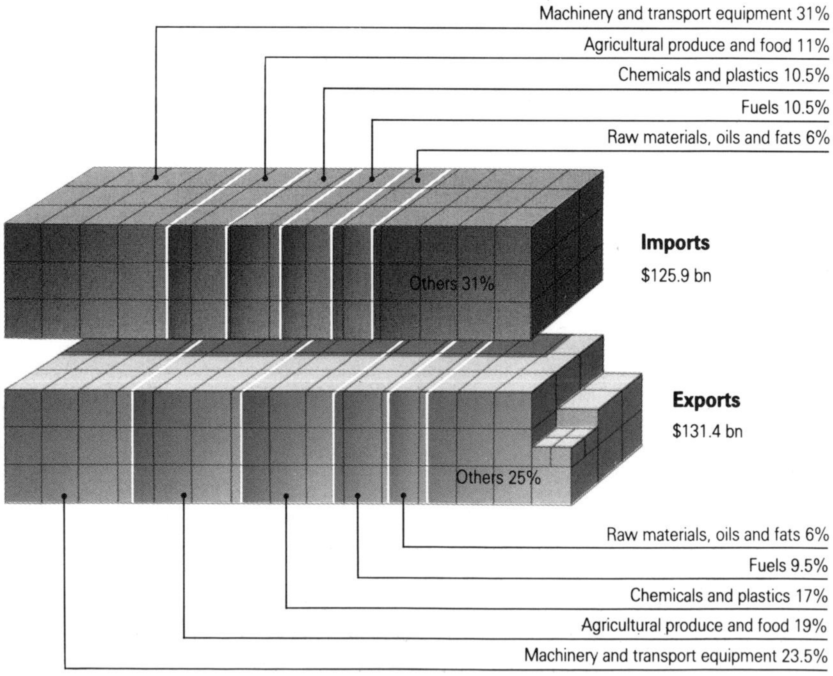

The beer boom (*left*) Light beers – especially "designer beers" – brewed in the Low Countries are becoming increasingly popular in the European export market.

The Netherlands' balance of merchandise trade (*above*) The Netherlands thrives as an entrepôt, importing raw materials for processing and exporting the products to European buyers. The country is also Europe's leading producer and exporter of natural gas.

Diamonds are forever *(above)* Tourists ponder over the price of cut diamonds in Amsterdam. The city has been a world center for the diamond industry since the 16th century, when Jewish refugees from Antwerp settled there.

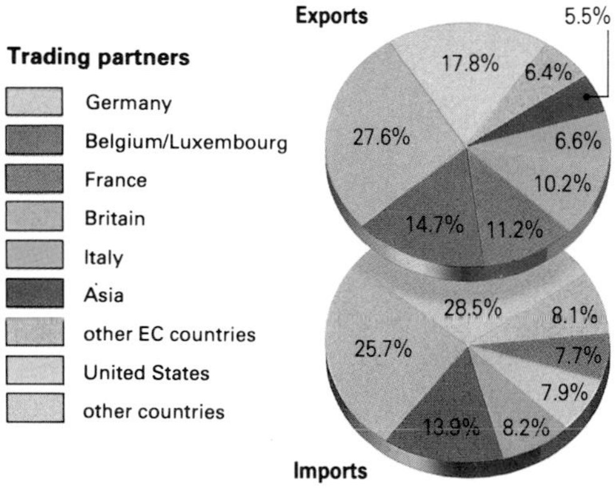

the government set up schemes to retrain workers for new jobs in the private sector. However, unemployment still increased significantly, with the figure rising to 10 percent of the workforce in Belgium in the early to mid 1980s. Overall, government policies had a mixed result. Inflation was brought under control but curbing public expenditure proved more difficult. This was especially true of the Netherlands, where public opinion remained largely opposed to radical spending cuts.

Alongside restructuring, important changes were also taking place within the private sector during the 1980s. The decline of Wallonia's heavy industry was followed by decay in other largescale manufacturing, such as Dutch shipbuilding. Growth was mainly in areas of light manufacturing, much of it export-based, such as engineering, biotechnology, microelectronics and chemical products. Belgium's main export market for these products in the 1990s is France, closely followed by Germany; while the Netherlands sells its goods chiefly to Germany. The main area of growth in the region, however, has been in service industries, which now employ as much as 60 percent of the workforce in both Belgium and the Netherlands. Financial services and banking have spearheaded rapid growth in this sector, especially in the Grand Duchy of Luxembourg, where financial houses have established a leading role in the Eurocurrency markets.

LUXEMBOURG'S FINANCIAL SECTOR

In recent decades Luxembourg has emerged as one of Europe's leading financial centers. The country has a multilingual tradition and is well located to attract international clients, midway between the economic heartlands of France, Germany and the Low Countries. Political leaders have capitalized on these advantages by introducing financial legislation to attract foreign companies to the area. Luxembourg offers Swiss-style banking confidentiality while funds belonging to foreigners are exempt from income, inheritance or capital-gains taxes.

These policies proved effective, and by 1989 the country contained no fewer than 120 banks, 7,000 holding companies and increasing numbers of investment companies. Financial services had become the greatest single source of employment and provided 20 percent of government revenue. As Luxembourg became a recognized tax haven within the EC, office space in the capital fell into short supply and some institutions began setting up their headquarters outside the city center. Soon the very scale of this success caused problems, as some EC countries resented the drain of funds across their borders. In 1989, Luxembourg had to fight to defeat an attempt to require all EC members to charge a withholding tax (levied on payments made to overseas investors), which would have greatly reduced its ability to attract foreign capital.

Growing with the EC

The expansion of the EC also brought important changes during the 1980s, as the community located many of its most important political and administrative institutions in the region, boosting employment and creating new potential for growth. Luxembourg houses both the European Court of Justice and the European Investment Bank, while the International Court meets at the Hague in the Netherlands. Brussels has benefited even more, emerging as a virtual capital city of the EC. The town is the seat of the European Commission and is a part-time base for the European Parliament. Many of the EC's "Eurocrats" live in and around Brussels where they have brought a discernible rise in property prices. By 1990 an estimated 27 percent of Brussels citizens were foreigners, a clear indication of the cosmopolitan flavor of the city.

SPREADING PROSPERITY

The Low Countries are among the most prosperous countries in Europe, and their wealth is relatively evenly distributed when compared with the United States, Britain and other developed Western countries. In 1980, when the last survey was conducted, the richest 20 percent of Belgian households received 36 percent of the country's income and the poorest received 7.9 percent. In the Netherlands in 1980 the figures were only slightly more polarized, with the richest 20 percent receiving 38.3 percent and the poorest 6.9 percent.

Regional variations in wealth

Within this general prosperity, there are still significant variations from one area to another. Wallonia in southern Belgium has seen its share of GDP fall significantly between 1960 and 1980, from 33 to 28 percent, and unemployment is now highest in this part of the region. Flanders, in the north, has enjoyed growing prosperity as industry and trading facilities have developed around Antwerp and the canals of Ghent, keeping unemployment comparatively low. The attitude of the workforce has also played a shaping role in regional development, as Wallonia has experienced some labor militancy while Flanders has not.

In the Netherlands the greatest disparities in standards of living occur within the urban areas of the Randstad, which contains all of the country's leading cities, including Amsterdam, Utrecht, Haarlem to the north, and Rotterdam and The Hague to the south. The country has some inner-city areas of considerable deprivation, often housing immigrants, or the descendants of immigrants from Dutch colonies. One example is the Bijlmermeer district of Amsterdam, the scene of a tragic aircrash in October 1992, which has a high proportion of inhabitants of Surinamese origin.

Winding down the welfare state

The Low Countries are generally well provided with social welfare facilities, though Dutch and Belgian citizens are shifting away from longstanding dependence on state welfare services. In the 1980s and early 1990s healthcare in both Belgium and the Netherlands was paid for by a system of public insurance (*Ziekensfonds*), with richer citizens paying higher premiums than those whose earnings are below the average wage. In the Netherlands, higher-income families are also expected to take out private health insurance. Private insurance requirements were extended in the 1990s, with all citizens expected to take out cover through a variety of packages at varying costs.

Throughout the Netherlands, healthcare is provided through both public and private institutions, though most of the country's private hospitals are run by the Protestant or Catholic churches and are nonprofit-making. All private health facilities are closely monitored by the central government and local authorities, with regular inspections. The central government also regulates the level of premiums charged, to ensure they do not

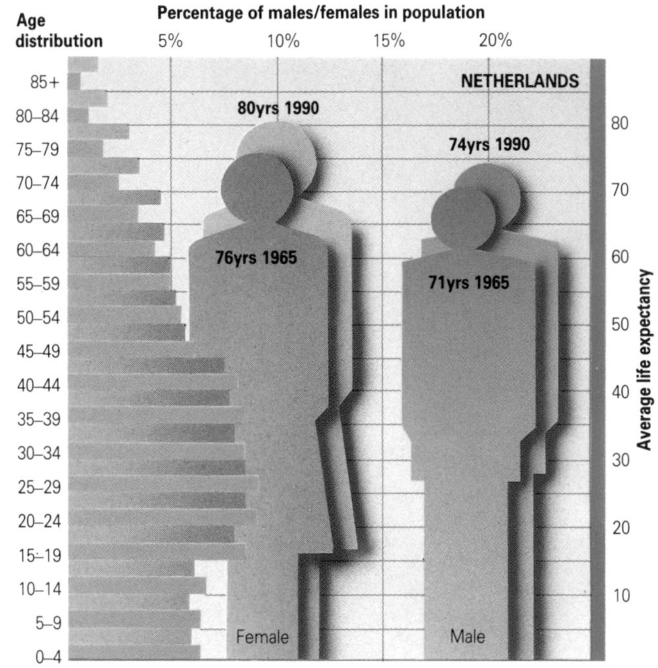

Aspects of affluence (*right*) Members of Amsterdam's immigrant community return home with their day's shopping. The region's economic boom years of the 1960s and 1970s attracted large numbers of immigrants and guest workers from former colonies, North Africa, and poorer European countries. Many of these became well established, but continued immigration in the 1980s coupled with rising unemployment consigned large sections of the immigrant community to poverty in deprived inner-city areas.

Life expectancy and age distribution (*left*) Excellent healthcare in the Netherlands ensures a healthy population, with low infant mortality rates and high life expectancy for both men and women. Birthrates are low across the region. The populations of Belgium and Luxembourg are expected to become stationary by the turn of the century.

become too high, as well as setting the minimum standards of care available to everyone. In terms of infant mortality and life expectancy, the Dutch are the healthiest nation in Europe. Rates of absence from work due to sickness in the Netherlands are western Europe's highest, connected with the intense work pressure that is common in the country, linked to its impressive levels of productivity.

Some other forms of social welfare are provided, not through premiums or insurance, but directly from local taxes. Throughout the region employees contribute to funds for sickness pay and unemployment benefit. In the Netherlands most of these payments are made by male employees, as the country's women make up an unusually small part of the labor force, at least by western European standards: only 18 percent of Dutch married women are employed. In Belgium the proportion is nearer the 50 percent found in Denmark and Britain.

Public and private education

Education levels are generally high throughout the region. Compulsory schooling lasts until 15 in Luxembourg, 16 in the Netherlands and 18 in Belgium. Schools are provided by the state and also by private nonprofit-making religious foundations, receiving state subsidies in the Netherlands alongside the state schools. Educational standards are equally high in state and private schools. More than 20 percent of secondary school students continue into higher education, including the universities.

Economic interchange (*left*) International travelers while away the time buying luxury goods in the duty-free shop at Amsterdam's Schipol airport, one of the largest duty-free shops in the world. The region's ports and airports are major links in European trade and international business networks.

ROTTERDAM: A HUB OF EXPORTING

Since 1962, when it surpassed New York, Rotterdam has been the world's largest port. It handles over half of all Europe's sea trade – some 291.8 million tonnes of cargo in 1991. The site confers particular advantages, especially since a channel was cut through the Hook of Holland to deeper coastal waters in 1872. The New Waterway, as this route was called, allowed larger vessels to reach the harbor and opened up areas of flat land for new port facilities.

Rotterdam also has excellent access to Germany and Central Europe, since it lies near the mouths of the rivers Lek and Maas leading back to the Rhine. By the late 19th century the Rhine had become one of Europe's top internal trade routes, with waterways linking the river to many fast-growing centers of manufacturing in Germany, France and Belgium. New canals completed in the 1990s link the Rhine and the Danube, placing Rotterdam at the ocean-end of a vast trans-European waterway. The port has capitalized on these advantages by adopting new technologies to match changing economic circumstances. After 1945 it became a center for oil imports and related petrochemical industries, and later built facilities to handle giant supertankers – 300,000 tonne vessels may berth there. In the 1960s it added container handling activities and opened the Europort complex. With such facilities, Rotterdam seems set to remain at the forefront of European trade.

Belgium's European challenge

The Belgian economy has expanded and flourished within the EC, but since the late 1980s the possibilities of further growth are constrained by local limiting factors. These include the country's smallness, its openness to world trade and its concentrated pattern of ownership among major banks and companies.

The limiting factors

Belgium's GDP is about one-sixth that of France and domestic demand is often too small to support many large industries. The economy, therefore, depends heavily on trade, with exports and imports amounting to 70 percent of GDP. As a result, Belgium seeks stable currency, stable exchange rates, competitive wage costs and opposes trade protectionism. To achieve these aims it supports economic and monetary union within the EC. Since 1960 it has also supported the Benelux Economic Union, an agreement between Belgium, Luxembourg and the Netherlands with the objective of bringing about total economic integraion and pursuing a common policy on foreign trading.

Belgian exports are mainly manufactured goods, and it benefits from Germany's demand for metals and chemicals; three-quarters of its chemicals production goes abroad. However, this dependence on foreign trade means that Belgium's economy is highly sensitive to fluctuations in the world economy, for example high oil prices produced a trade deficit in 1990. The particular importance of Germany as a market means that Belgium's progress in meeting the criteria for a single EC currency (the reduction of public debt and the budget deficit) depends critically upon German policy decisions.

Consolidated interests

Another feature of Belgium's economy, and one that may limit its future growth, is the unusually high concentration of ownership and control in an elaborate system of holding companies, which play a major role in almost every sector of industry, trade and finance. The largest are Société Générale de Belgique (SGB) and Groupe Bruxelles Lambert. Founded in 1822, SGB alone controls 1,200 companies in 67 countries, and its holdings represent about one-third of Belgium's economy. Traditionally associated with the French-speaking elite, by 1980 two-thirds of its interests were in Flanders. But SGB's remaining investment in the smokestack industries of Walonia meant that it was underutilizing its assets and had developed a reputation for conservative management, making it ripe for takeover. This came in 1988 when Italian entrepreneur Carlo de Benedetti launched a hostile bid as part of his plan to create the first pan-European holding company. Benedetti was opposed by the government, which did not want such an important company falling into foreign hands. The battle left half of SGB's shares with the Italian and 32 percent with the French financial services company Suez, regarded as a friendly foreigner.

After this affair the government passed new laws to check similar acquisitions, but foreign takeovers were increasing rapidly in the 1980s. By 1992, foreign firms controlled one-third of the largest 3,100 companies, produced 43.5 percent of their total added value and employed 37.5 percent of their workers. They are often more profitable and invest more in research and development than Belgian-owned concerns, which tend to be locked into low-value-added activities. Foreign companies are particularly significant in science-based sectors – such as engineering, metals and electronics.

Few Belgian companies are large enough to buy their competitors. An exception is the chemicals giant, Solvay, which bought the United States Tenneco Minerals Corporation in 1991. An alternative to foreign takeover is domestic merger, but this often flouts EC rules against monopoly; Solvay itself was fined for operating a soda-ash cartel with British based Imperial Chemical Industries (ICI). State aid to small, failing companies is also vetted; Sabena, the national airline, was investigated in the early 1990s for excessive government support.

One positive side effect of the wave of EC-wide mergers may be that Brussels is chosen as the site of new company headquarters. In the meantime, the Belgian government is trying to maintain economic growth and redress regional imbalances while key sectors of the economy are passing into foreign hands. This makes regulation of economic activity at EC level, where the government can have some input, an attractive proposition.

Losers from free trade (*right*) Belgian farmers in 1992 demonstrating against the General Agreement on Tariffs and Trade (GATT) after the European Community agreed to cut agricultural subsidies in response to a threatened trade war with the United States.

s refusons d'être
du au GATT

IBERIA'S INVESTMENT BOOM

COLONIAL POWERS TURNED TOURIST HAVENS · RESTRUCTURING CLOSELY LINKED ECONOMIES
PATCHWORK PENINSULA

During much of the 20th century the economies of Spain and Portugal have been in the shadow of their affluent northern neighbors, yet 400 years ago both countries were prosperous imperial powers. Industrialization occurred relatively late on the Iberian Peninsula, but by the 1960s Spain (helped by American investment) had become Europe's fastest-growing economy. The return of democracy followed by integration into the European Community (EC) in 1986 led to another investment boom in both countries. Nevertheless, significant problems remain. Economic structures need further modernization to make products competitive in the international marketplace. At home, wealth and prosperity are unevenly distributed – isolated rural areas in particular still suffer longterm economic decline.

COUNTRIES IN THE REGION

Spain, Portugal

ECONOMIC INDICATORS: 1990

	HIE* Spain	*UMIE Portugal
GDP (US$ billions)	421.24	56.82
GNP per capita (US$)	11,020	4,900
Annual rate of growth of GDP, 1980–1990 (%)	3.1	2.7
Manufacturing as % of GDP	18	9
Central government spending as % of GNP	34	43
Merchandise exports (US$ billions)	56.3	16.3
Merchandise imports (US$ billions)	89.0	23.0
% of GNP donated as development aid	n/a	–

WELFARE INDICATORS

Infant mortality rate (per 1,000 live births)		
1965	38	65
1990	8	12
Daily food supply available (calories per capita, 1989)	3,572	3,495
Population per physician (1984)	320	140
Teacher–pupil ratio (primary school, 1989)	1 : 25	1 : 17

Note: The Gross Domestic Product (GDP) is the total value of all goods and services domestically produced. The Gross National Product (GNP) is the GDP plus net income from abroad.

** HIE (High Income Economy) – GNP per capita above $7,620 in 1990. UMIE (Upper Middle Economy) – GNP per capita between $2,465 and $7,620 in 1990.*

COLONIAL POWERS TURNED TOURIST HAVENS

Both Spain and Portugal were world economic powers in the 16th century, sustained by the wealth of their extensive empires. Imports of gold and silver from South America filled the Spanish treasury, while much of Portugal's prosperity was derived from trade in slaves and spices. However, these riches were squandered on a succession of religious and colonial wars, and by the turn of the 20th century most of their territories overseas had won independence or had been taken over by political rivals. Spain's loss of Cuba, the Philippines and Puerto Rico in 1896 plunged the country into a prolonged recession. Portugal, meanwhile, had suffered severe economic decline following the loss of its Brazilian colony in the early 19th century, but held on to possessions in Africa and Southeast Asia. Its richest colony – Angola – continued to fill Portuguese coffers well into the 20th century. Eventually the cost of retaining these other colonies became prohibitive, especially after fullscale colonial wars in the 1960s and 1970s.

Civil war and fascism

The Spanish Civil War (1936–39) was followed by a major economic crisis, which deepened as Europe plunged into World War II. In addition, both Spain and Portugal found themselves politically isolated as a result of their dictatorial regimes. The United Nations (UN) imposed a trade and investment blockade on Spain, which had openly supported Adolf Hitler (1889–1945) during World War II.

In response to these sanctions, General Franco adopted a policy of national self-sufficiency, producing essential goods in

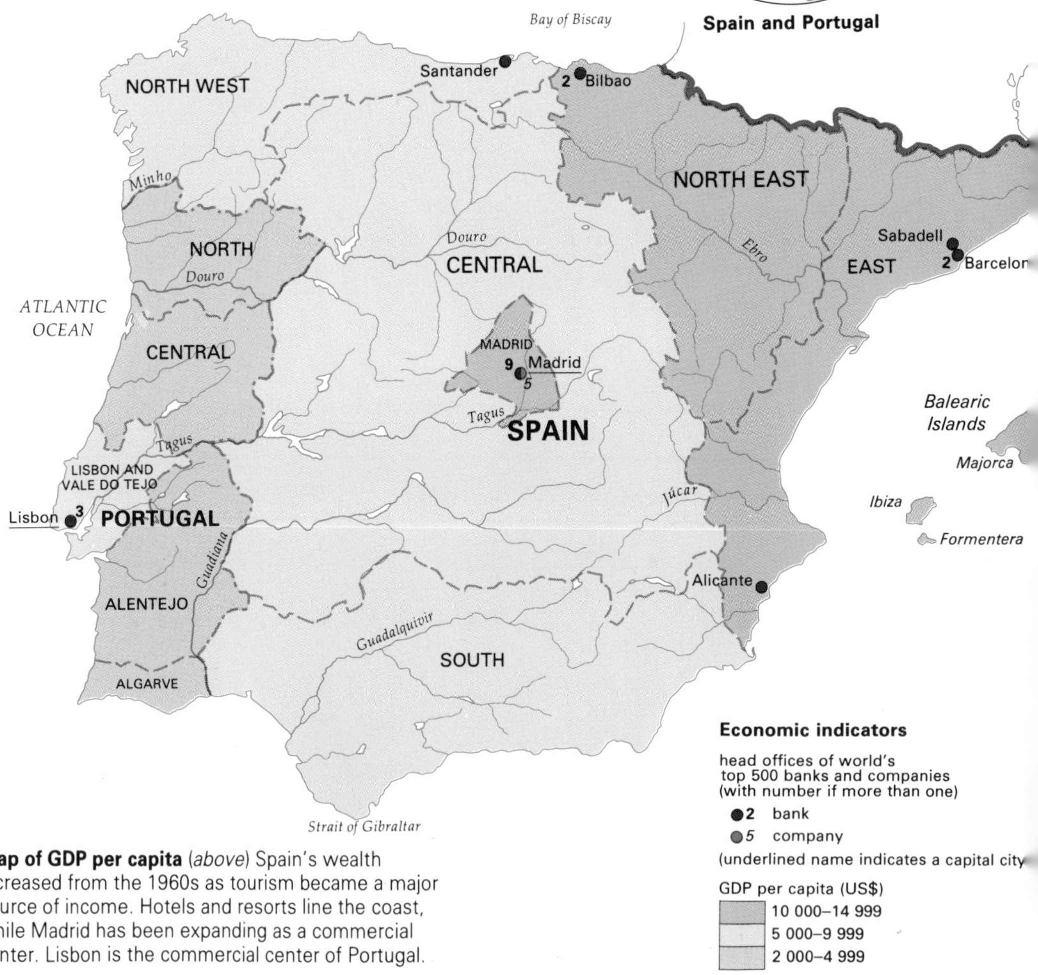

Map of GDP per capita (*above*) Spain's wealth increased from the 1960s as tourism became a major source of income. Hotels and resorts line the coast, while Madrid has been expanding as a commercial center. Lisbon is the commercial center of Portugal.

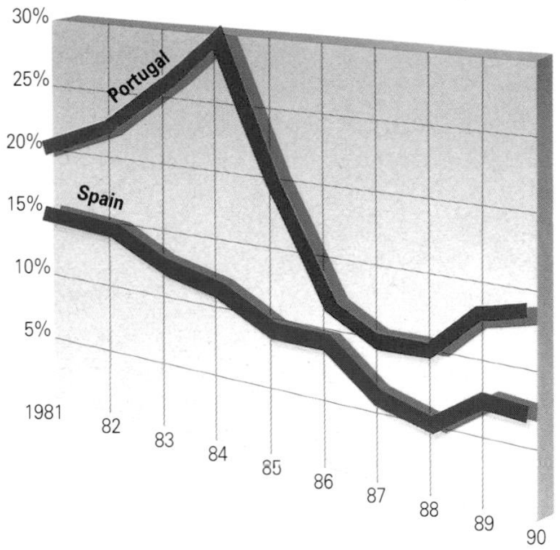

Profile of inflation *(above)* High inflation in Portugal during the early 1980s reflected political and economic crisis after 1974. From 1983, reforms led to Portugal's acceptance into the EC. Spain, politically more stable, has been able to keep inflation much lower.

High-speed spending *(left)* Seville spent more than US $10 billion over 4 years to stage and support Expo 92, an international trade exhibition. The new airport, high-speed rail link to Madrid and other facilities will be of long-standing benefit to the area.

Spain instead of importing them, regardless of the cost. Economic barriers were erected against trading abroad, and central control was exercised over major industries through a state holding company, the Instituto Nacional de Industria (INI). The government also implemented a system to enforce strict regulation over the labor force through state-controlled "syndicates".

Franco's policies mirrored a system already established in Portugal by the prime minister and creator of the "New State" Antonio de Oliveira Salazar (1899–1970), who had gained power in the 1920s and was to preside over his rigorously authoritarian regime until 1968. In both Spain and Portugal, however, economic performance was poor in the postwar period, and negative growth rates were recorded in some years.

Openness and growth

In 1953 the UN lifted its economic boycott on Spain after the United States (seeking anticommunist allies) made substantial loans in return for the use of military bases. These changes coincided with a gradual opening up of both Spain and Portugal to world trade. Contrary to previous policy, imports were allowed to outstrip exports, but damage to the balance of trade was redressed by large inflows of money from foreign investors attracted to the region by low wages and rigid control of trade unions. Money also flowed into both countries through foreign exchange earnings from the massively expanding tourist industry. Remittances from migrant workers and Spanish and Portuguese workers living abroad were another important source of foreign currency (it is estimated that 300,000 people left Spain alone immediately after the Civil War).

These factors, combined with a general boom in the world economy, produced unprecedented economic growth during the 1960s, particularly in Spain. From 1961–73, the Spanish "economic miracle" produced an average annual growth rate of 7.5 percent of Gross Domestic Product (GDP). Among the member countries of the Organization for Economic Cooperation and Development (OECD), this performance was exceeded only by Japan. During the early 1970s Iberia, along with the rest of Europe, was badly affected by oil price rises. Both countries were in deep recession by the end of the decade. Furthermore, Portugal's economy was crippled by the high cost of war to maintain its African territories (roughly 45 percent of GDP). Economic and political pressures prompted a left-wing military coup in 1974. The new government introduced sweeping measures such as nationalization of land, heavy industries, banks and insurance companies. These put Portugal into economic turmoil and caused a flight of foreign capital.

The installation of democratic governments in Spain in 1975 and Portugal in 1976 opened the door to greater European integration. When the two countries eventually became members of the EC in 1986, the move was keenly supported as a means of strengthening both economies and safeguarding democracy.

RESTRUCTURING CLOSELY LINKED ECONOMIES

Despite progress in the 1960s and early 1970s, Spain and Portugal entered the 1980s still relatively underdeveloped, with poor infrastructures, large inefficient agricultural sectors and slow economic growth. After joining the EC in 1986, however, both countries enjoyed average annual growth of GDP of between 4 and 5 percent – a rate well above their European partners and on a par with Japan. Spain, in particular, has experienced a tremendous surge of economic optimism and energy. By the early 1990s it had become a substantial industrial power, raising its international profile with events such as the 1992 Olympic Games in Barcelona (in the northeast) and Expo 92 in Seville (in the southwest). Portugal lagged behind its larger neighbor and was still classified as an upper-middle-income country by the World Bank in 1990. Its GDP was less than 50 percent of the EC average compared with 80 percent for Spain – a figure that probably does not represent Spain's true prosperity, which is boosted by a thriving unofficial economy.

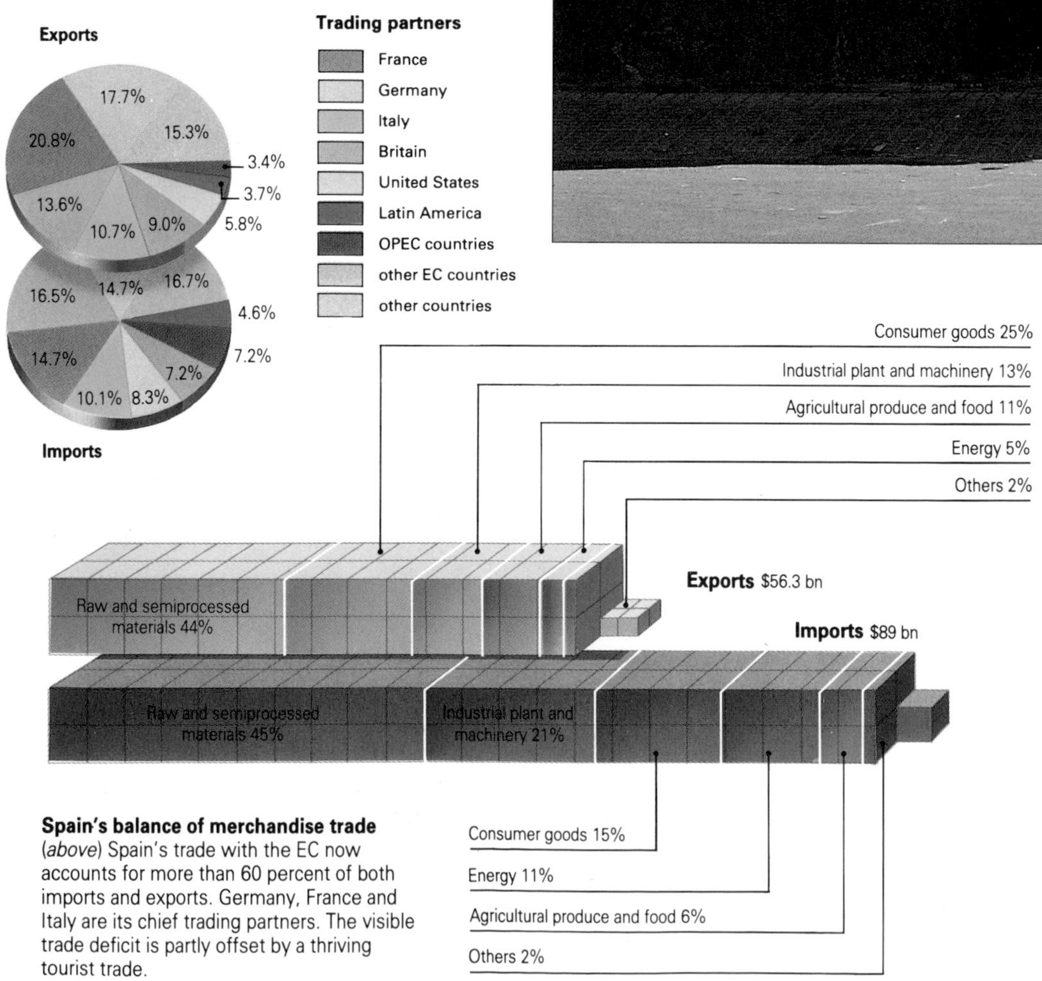

Spain's balance of merchandise trade (*above*) Spain's trade with the EC now accounts for more than 60 percent of both imports and exports. Germany, France and Italy are its chief trading partners. The visible trade deficit is partly offset by a thriving tourist trade.

The push for greater industrialization and modernization across the region has been reflected in changes in the job market. For example, agriculture in Spain in 1989 employed only 13 percent of the working population, compared with 22 percent in 1975. Employment in manufacturing, and the manufacturing sector's contribution to GDP, has remained relatively stable since 1980. The service sector, on the other hand, is booming. Of a total growth in the employment market of over 1.3 million jobs between 1985 and 1989, almost 85 percent was in the service sector. From 1986–91, foreigners invested almost $80 billion in Spain, with over half of this being in the service sector, particularly financial services. Preparations for the 1992 Olympics in Barcelona attracted major new funding, and foreign

HOMAGE TO CATALONIA

With 44 percent of its working population employed in industry, the northeastern province of Catalonia is Spain's leading industrialized area and one of the most dynamic economies in Europe. It industrialized relatively early in the 19th century (notably in textiles) and has a history of strong commercial links with the rest of Europe. Contributing more than 20 percent of Spain's industrial production in 1990, the area still specializes in textiles, though the chemical, metal and paper industries are also important.

With such a large industrial sector, Catalonia inevitably suffered in the world recession of the 1980s. In 1985 its unemployment rate was more than 20 percent, but restructuring and new enterprise brought the figure down to under 10 percent by 1990. This was the largest fall in unemployment anywhere in Spain, and has been sustained since, despite continued rural migration to the cities. Although Catalonia's old urban core is still being affected by industrial decline, new growth, particularly in high technology and fashion textiles, is providing attractive employment opportunities in other parts of the province.

Since 1988, Catalonia has consistently outperformed both the rest of Spain and the EC as a whole in terms of growth of GDP. The level of GDP per employee is also well above the European average. Growth was boosted still further in 1988, when the decision was taken to hold the 1992 Olympic Games in Catalonia's capital city, Barcelona. This encouraged substantial investment in new and improved sporting and transportation facilities, allowing the construction industry and a host of related services to enjoy sudden and spectacular growth.

Importing America *(above)* James Dean and Mae West advertise a well-known American cigarette on a billboard in Majorca. American products and culture, kept out by the socially conservative Franco regime (1939–75), are now visible everywhere in Spain.

High rise, high rent *(right)* The Picasso Tower is one of the prestigious facilities built during Madrid's 1980s construction boom. Luxury offices, apartments and hotels contribute to a new high-rise skyline – and to the soaring cost of metropolitan living.

investment has continued in the manufacturing and mining sectors, leading to domination by multinational corporations.

New trading patterns

Membership of the European Community has caused a dramatic change in trading patterns across the region and brought new partners to the fore. Since the 1980s, both Spain and Portugal have substantially increased imports from and exports to other member countries and the rest of Europe. In addition, trade between Spain and Portugal more than doubled between 1986 and 1992. Overall, the value of Portugal's exports rose by almost 50 percent between 1985 and 1989, while Spain's rose by more than 20 percent over the same period. However, spending on imports has grown much faster than revenue from exports, moving both countries into substantial trade deficits.

The shift of emphasis has inevitably meant that trade has declined with non-OECD countries, notably those within the Organization of Petroleum Exporting Countries (OPEC). For example, as late as 1983, almost a quarter of Spain's imports came from OPEC countries, but by 1989 this trade had almost halved in value and had been reduced to just 7 percent of the total import bill. Portugal, however, remains heavily dependent on oil imports from OPEC.

Removing old barriers

Iberian governments have traditionally exercised strong control over their economies through protective measures such as import tariffs and state subsidies. This has been particularly true for major industries such as automobiles, coal and steel. In Spain the state owns most of the major public services including telecommunications, radio, television and the railroads. The government, through the INI, is also a major shareholder in hundreds of industrial companies. Since joining the EC in 1986, both the socialist government in Spain, and the Social Democratic government in Portugal have been committed to privatizing some of the state-owned industries that they inherited from the older regimes. At the same time, measures have been introduced by both governments for financial and labor-market reforms in line with EC policy.

PATCHWORK PENINSULA

Not everyone in Portugal and Spain benefited from the economic boom of the late 1980s. In Spain, there are marked concentrations of wealth in core regions such as Madrid, the Basque Country, Catalonia, and major tourist areas. The Balearic Islands, including Majorca, have become the richest of Spain's 17 autonomous provinces on the basis of tourist revenue. By contrast, there are large areas of Spain that are still underdeveloped, mostly in the south and northwest. The poorest region, Extremadura in west-central Spain, has a GDP per capita of under half the European average, and almost a quarter of the working-age population is officially unemployed. During much of the 1980s, unemployment in Spain exceeded 20 percent, though this had fallen to 15 percent by 1991. In 1990 the EC published figures showing unemployment in member countries broken down by area. Of the 13 worst affected areas, 7 were in Spain, all with rates of more than double the EC average.

Employment opportunities and welfare

Portugal maintained near full employment in the late 1980s – largely because many people still lived and worked on small family farms. In spite of the fact that the majority of people were in employment, there were (and still are) significant differences between the north and the more affluent south, and between the two main cities (Lisbon and Oporto) and the rest of the country.

Recent action to create job opportunities in both countries has focused on retraining programs, many supported by EC grants. In 1988, government schemes created more than half of all new employment opportunities in Spain. Meanwhile, the workforce itself is expanding. In particular, changes in cultural values are making it easier for women to work outside the home. The proportion of working women aged between 25 and 54 in Spain rose from 32 percent in 1982 to 48 percent in 1991.

Welfare provision in both Spain and Portugal was seriously inadequate until the 1980s when central government expenditure was greatly increased. Even in the early 1990s benefits were less than those offered in most other European countries. Of the Spanish unemployed, those who have recently been in work receive 70 percent of their salary for up to two years. Only those who have family responsibilities continue to receive an allowance after that, and the amount is much reduced. Those who have not worked receive nothing – this particularly affects young people who have not been able to find a job after leaving school or university. Although the situation is changing all the time, the onus continues to fall on the family unit, rather than the state, to look after its members. Many families support their elderly relatives unaided, and prospects are bleak for those with no such support. Older women are particularly vulnerable in a system where pension provision is limited. In 1988, for example, there were over 400,000 elderly people in Spain receiving no form of state pension.

The elderly population has also been swelled by northern Europeans seeking retirement homes in the Costa del Sol in southern Spain and the Algarve in south-

Tourist trap (*above*) Luxury villas at Marbella, on the southern coast of Spain attract visitors from all over the world. In the 1960s the low value of the peseta allowed middle-class foreigners to holiday in luxury. Recently local authorities have invested considerably to maintain the resort's image.

In search of prosperity (*left*) African immigrants from Cape Verde (formerly a Portuguese colony) cook outside their temporary shelter in Lisbon. More people are now emigrating to Portugal (sometimes illegally) in search of work than are leaving the country for better jobs.

Life expectancy and age distribution (*right*) Improved nutrition and medical care in Portugal have raised life expectancy to a level comparable with other European countries. Birthrates, as elsewhere in Europe, are lower in recent years with most of the population aged between 15 and 50.

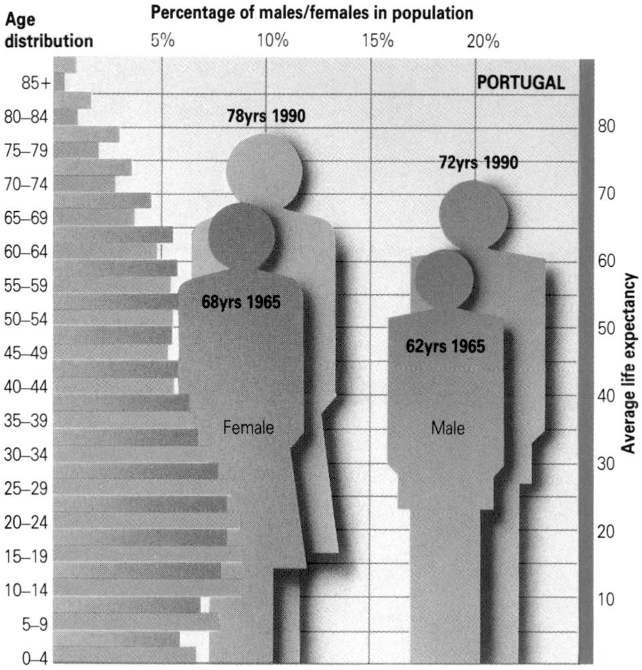

PORTUGAL'S MIGRANT WORKERS

For several decades after World War II, migration was the only way that people from rural areas in southern Europe could hope to improve their standard of living. Between the mid 1950s and 1974, over 1 million Portuguese workers – mainly from the center and north – took this option. They left rural areas where employment opportunities and political freedom were severely restricted, to work (often illegally) in the factories and cities of northern Europe and North America. Since the political changes of 1974–76, however, many have returned, often to their home villages, with greatly improved wealth and increased local prestige.

Remittances from migrants became a mainstay of the Portuguese economy, especially during the 1960s and early 1970s. Cash earned abroad has been reinvested in rural areas, creating local business development, a boom in the construction industry and mechanization on some farms. This more recent turn of events is not without its disadvantages. Some economists argue that the inflow of capital from returned migrants has contributed to Portugal's high inflation rate.

Those who do return are the lucky few. For every migrant who could choose to go home again, there were many others who were unable or unwilling to return to their birthplace. The less fortunate ones generally work long hours in difficult circumstances while at the same time suffering economic and social marginalization and limited rights of employment in a foreign country.

ern Portugal. This influx of people to relatively affluent areas has given quite a substantial boost to economic growth there, widening the gap between wealthier and poorer provinces. However, they have also increased pressure on local healthcare systems.

Two-tier health and education

In spite of moves to introduce a national state health service, the Spanish healthcare system still retains features of the Franco era, such as church and charity hospitals. The private sector remains an important option for those wishing to avoid the delays and relatively poor quality of care associated with the state service. Staffing is not the problem; Spain is well provided with doctors (20 percent more than the EC average), but this reflects duplication within the system rather than better service. Portugal also has public and private healthcare with a free national health service existing, at least in theory, since 1979. However, the service is patchy, and it is estimated that in practice patients pay on average 30–40 percent of costs directly.

All Portuguese and Spanish children receive compulsory primary education. Although this is provided free by the state, some parents (about a third in Spain) send their children to private schools. There are two kinds of private school in the region: those run by religious orders, usually offering high standards of teaching and charging high fees; and those run by individuals, frequently as family concerns.

After primary education, Spanish children aged 14 to 16 may study for their baccalaureate, followed by a preuniversity course; or may attend two-year sessions of professional training. A minority of this second group attends university afterward. A similar system of higher education exists in Portugal. Opportunities to study for degrees and professional qualifications have been improved across the region by increased financial aid in the form of scholarships, loans and other subsidies. Nevertheless, many students continue to rely on their families – or their own efforts – to support them through higher education. In Spain, over half of all students in higher education are now women.

Economic unity with Europe

The full impact of Spain and Portugal's membership of the European Community will not be felt until after 1996, when the transitional arrangements made to ease the countries' integration into the EC come to an end. Nevertheless, economic unity has already had noticeable effects on the Iberian Peninsula. Spain has had to remove substantial import barriers, both within and outside the EC, where these exceeded rates laid down by the Common External Tariff. Portugal has long been more open to the world economy. Since the 1970s, trade with the EC (measured as a percentage of GDP) has been running at more than twice the Spanish level. Even so, the industries of both countries (particularly steel and textiles) are being exposed to more intense competition than ever before. Pressure comes not only from Europe but also from the newly industrializing countries of the Third World, where labor costs are low. Competition is helping to make Iberian industry more efficient and better able to survive in the world economy in the long term; in the short term, however, company closures and redundancies have been inevitable, particularly in the industrial area of the northeast.

Intensive cultivation of strawberries (*above*) in Andalusia, southern Spain. Export crops like this one are high-revenue earners for Spain in the tariff-free European market.

New infrastructure in Portugal (*right*) A freeway bridge spans the Douro river in the seaport of Oporto in northwest Portugal. EC money has been invested in several high-speed road and rail links to connect major Portuguese cities including Oporto and Lisbon with other member countries.

Massive restructuring is also required in the agricultural sector, particularly in Portugal, before it can compete on equal terms with its European counterparts. The EC has implemented many investment programs to assist this process, though the longterm prospects look bleak for the small traditional mixed farms of the center and north of the peninsula. On the other hand, intensive cultivation of fruit, vegetables and flowers in the Algarve region of southern Portugal and along the southern and eastern coasts of Spain, is feeding a thriving market in the expanded European Community.

In June 1989 Spain joined the Exchange Rate Mechanism (ERM), an agreement that binds member countries to maintain their currency exchange rates between established upper and lower limits. One

of the aims of the ERM is to control inflation, but Spain's inflation rate of 6.8 percent in 1991 was still high by EC standards. Portugal's rate of 9.6 percent in 1991 was the second highest in the EC, mainly due to the country's continued dependence on imported oil. Such a high rate of inflation prevented Portugal's entry into the ERM in the early 1990s. Deregulation of the financial sector as part of the provisions of the Single Europe Act of 1987 has also contributed to inflation through an increase in personal borrowing, much of it from foreign sources. On the other hand, deregulation has encouraged investment, prompting economic growth, in both countries.

Grants and subsidies

The EC has used a number of policies to help Spain and Portugal to catch up with the economic development of their European partners. Since 1987, both countries have received more in grants and other financial assistance than they have contributed to central funds. Between 1986 and 1992 grants to Spain have been worth over $3 billion each year, with 58 percent coming from the European Agricultural Guidance and Guarantee Fund.

The European Regional Development Fund allocates investment money for productive schemes in underdeveloped or "assisted" areas – for which virtually the entire Iberian Peninsula qualifies. However, two major problems have prevented Spain and Portugal from making full use of the available development funding. The first is the issue of "additionality", the need for the government receiving an EC grant for a particular project to fund a proportion of the scheme itself; the second is the lack of entrepreneurs in the region with suitable investment proposals to put forward.

EC funds for improving transportation and comunication in the region have, on the whole, been used more effectively. Both countries are at an initial disadvantage by being on the physical periphery of Europe, and they are still trying to overcome the problems this presents. Since 1989, substantial sums have been invested in overhauling telecommunications systems, upgrading railroad lines and building new expressways. This should make it easier for Spain and Portugal to export goods to the rest of Europe – though it will also help competitors to exploit Iberian markets.

A place in the sun

The demand for housing in Spain and Portugal does not come only from the local populations. Increasing numbers of men and women are coming from northwest Europe to set up second homes or retirement villas in the warmer climates of the Algarve, Costa del Sol and other Mediterranean regions. This is especially true of elderly people who have retired from work in countries such as Germany and the United Kingdom.

Once in the sun belt such people are bound to contribute to the local economy, both as purchasers of local commodities and as consumers of services. The coastal economies of Spain and Portugal benefit from expatriate spending in these "homes from homes", though there is concern that the newcomers are driving up the price of housing in such regions to a level where local people are excluded from the housing market.

From the point of view of the settlers, healthcare provision and social services become a major source of concern as they get older. Some northwestern Europeans will be used to much higher standards of healthcare than the facilities available to EC citizens in Spain and Portugal. In Spain, particularly, other family members are expected to bear much of the burden of care of the elderly, but few expatriates will be able to rely on their families to nurse them if they are taken into hospital. For many who leave northern climates behind to make a new beginning, life in the sun does not always turn out as they imagined it would.

Elderly people on apartment balconies on the Costa del Sol, Spain.

A MEDITERRANEAN MOSAIC

CHANGES OF FORTUNE · THE WIDENING GAP · REDISTRIBUTING PROSPERITY

The economies of Greece and Italy, stifled by centuries of foreign domination, had by the 19th century fallen far behind the industrializing countries of northwestern Europe. Independence and political unification (achieved in 1830 in Greece and 1870 in Italy) marked a turning point in the fortunes of each, though the region's lack of natural resources and its protectionist policies restricted economic growth in the longer term. Since World War II, Italy's industrial expansion into consumer goods for international markets has transformed its economy into the fifth largest in the world. Greece, however, lags behind and is the poorest member of the European Community (EC). Economic growth in both countries is threatened by foreign competition, rising import bills and high levels of government debt.

COUNTRIES IN THE REGION

Cyprus, Greece, Italy, Malta, San Marino, Vatican City

ECONOMIC INDICATORS: 1990

	*UMIE Greece	*HIE Italy
GDP (US$ billions)	57.9	1,090.75
GNP per capita (US$)	5,990	16,830
Annual rate of growth of GDP, 1980–1990 (%)	1.8	2.4
Manufacturing as % of GDP	14	23
Central government spending as % of GNP	36	49
Merchandise exports (US$ billions)	6.4	182.2
Merchandise imports (US$ billions)	18.7	193.6
% of GNP donated as development aid	–	0.32

WELFARE INDICATORS

Infant mortality rate (per 1,000 live births)		
1965	34	36
1990	11	9
Daily food supply available (calories per capita, 1989)	3,825	3,216
Population per physician (1984)	350	230
Teacher–pupil ratio (primary school, 1989)	1 : 22	1 : 12

Note: The Gross Domestic Product (GDP) is the total value of all goods and services domestially produced. The Gross National Product (GNP) is the GDP plus net income from abroad.

** UMIE (Upper Middle Economy) – GNP per capita between $2,465 and $7,620 in 1990. HIE (High Income Economy) – GNP per capita above $7,620 in 1990.*

CHANGES OF FORTUNE

During the 14th century, the wealthy city-states of northern and central Italy became international leaders in trade, finance and craftsmanship. From the late 15th century, however, political fragmentation and domination by the competing powers of Austria, France and Spain smothered economic growth. Greece stagnated after becoming an occupied province of the Turkish empire in the mid 15th century. Both countries were peripheral to the developing world economy until the late 19th century.

Economic growth was slow to begin even after Greek independence in 1830 and Italian political unification in 1870. The Italian fascist regime (1924–43) made a concerted effort to catch up with the major industrial powers. Despite some initial success, by 1938 real incomes were only slightly higher than in 1925. Increased military spending after 1935 failed to stimulate industrial expansion, which remained dominated by a few large firms such as FIAT and Olivetti.

On the eve of World War II, Italy and Greece were still predominantly agrarian economies. Italy, however, had begun to build up a transport infrastructure and modern services across the nation. By comparison, Greece and the British colonies of Malta and Cyprus remained undeveloped. In Greece, foreign companies extracted mineral resources for export, and the colonial economies were dependent on revenue and employment generated by British military bases.

The postwar boom

Both Italy and Greece emerged from World War II on the edge of mass starvation and with their economic infrastructure devastated by war. In 1945 total production from industries that were damaged, obsolete and inefficient had fallen to the abysmal levels of 1900. Foreign aid – especially as part of the United States' Marshall Plan in the late 1940s and early 1950s – laid the foundations for impressive postwar recovery and growth. Low labor costs, monetary stability and low (often unenforced) rates of business taxation also stimulated economic growth. Italy made more progress during this period of recovery than Greece did. The giant public holding companies IRI (Institute of Industrial Reconstruction) and ENI (the state-owned Italian energy group founded in 1953) were important in rebuilding major steel, petrochemical and energy industries.

From 1951 to 1958, the Gross Domestic Product (GDP) of Italy grew at an average 5.5 percent a year, due largely to increased domestic demand. From 1958 to 1963, growth in GDP reached 6.3 percent. Much of this success was achieved through the expansion of exports. When Italy joined the EC as a founding member in 1957, exports to other EC countries increased from 23 percent in 1955 to over 40 percent in 1965.

Since World War II, the basis of the region's economy has shifted sharply from agriculture to industry. Between 1951 and 1981, agriculture's share of GDP declined from 28 percent to under 9 percent in Italy, and from 35 percent of GDP to 18 percent in Greece. Over the same period, service-sector employment grew rapidly, accounting for over half of GDP in both countries by 1981.

Crisis and renewal

High growth rates were sustained in the 1960s, but declined sharply in the 1970s and early 1980s. Inflation and the oil crisis damaged all European economies alike, but Italy and Greece suffered a greater setback than their European neighbors. In Italy the economic slump resulted in labor unrest and political volatility, which in turn reduced the profitability of the larger companies. In addition, struggling industries suffered from underfunding, with limited access to a conservative,

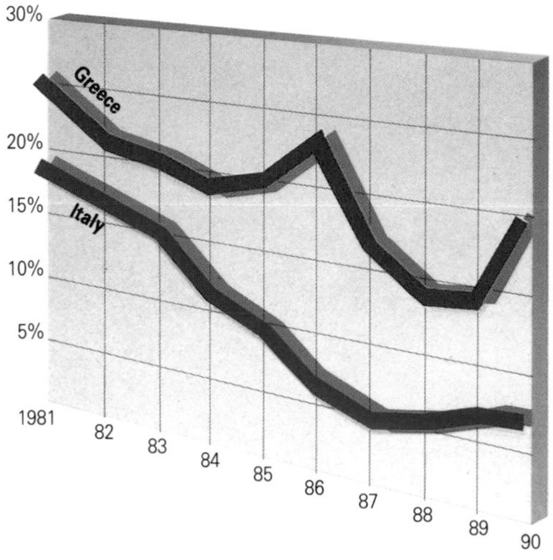

Profile of inflation *(above)* Inflation in Italy fell steadily throughout the 1980s amid growing economic prosperity. Greece continued to struggle with relatively high inflation even after joining the European Community in 1981.

High profile export *(above)* A billboard advertising Benetton knitwear towers over a street vendor's stall in Naples. Textiles have become one of Italy's great export stengths: by 1992 Italy was the world's third largest producer of textiles and clothing.

Map of GDP per capita *(below)* Wealth in Italy is concentrated in the northern industrial cities, though some international companies have offices in Rome. Athens is the commercial heart of Greece.

government-dominated banking system and minimal stockmarket capitalization. The domination of family groups in the Italian private sector has limited the growth of independent financial institutions.

The growth of small businesses in Italy compensated to some extent for the crisis in larger companies by reducing the power of the unions and by creating a more flexible labor market. By the late 1980s the large private-sector firms had reestablished their relative efficiency, extended their borrowing capacity, and begun to expand internationally. Widespread exploitation of family labor and massive tax evasion made smaller firms more competitive in foreign markets against newly industrializing countries such as Taiwan and South Korea.

In Greece, military rule (1967–74) undermined the country's trading potential abroad. In particular, Greece was ostracized by the EC nations, and did not achieve membership until 1981, a delay that severely hampered its economic growth. During the period of dictatorship expatriate Greeks no longer invested significantly in the country's manufacturing industries or sent remittances home. Greece continued to be out-performed by Italy, chiefly because it failed to build up a strong industrial sector with an international customer base. Membership of the EC, when it did come, began to stimulate new economic growth, particularly through the availability of regional development funds. However, political unrest and unwieldy state bureaucracy remain huge obstacles in the way ahead.

THE WIDENING GAP

Italy and Greece occupy very different positions within the world economy. At the beginning of the 1990s, Italy was the third largest economy in the EC after Germany and France; Greece was the EC's poorest country with a recent record of serious economic stagnation. Italy's strength is based on high labor productivity, increased levels of foreign investment, government subsidies to small businesses and lax tax collection. Its major weaknesses are a very high level of public debt, and longterm unemployment (especially in the south). In 1990 Italy's unemployment rate was the second highest among all countries in the Organization of Economic Cooperation and Development (OECD). This economic fragility has reduced Italy's influence in the councils of the EC.

Greek isolationism

While other EC countries made preparations for the single market of 1992, Greece continued to follow independent economic policies. It still does not have open trade or banking, the Greek government controls its own currency, and maintains barriers to other European investors. A significant proportion of the development funds received from the EC (totalling $9 billion for 1989–93) was channeled into

Keeping the island economy afloat *(above)* One of Greece's huge number of commercial ships delivers food and other supplies to one of the country's many islands where the main economic activities are tourism and fishing.

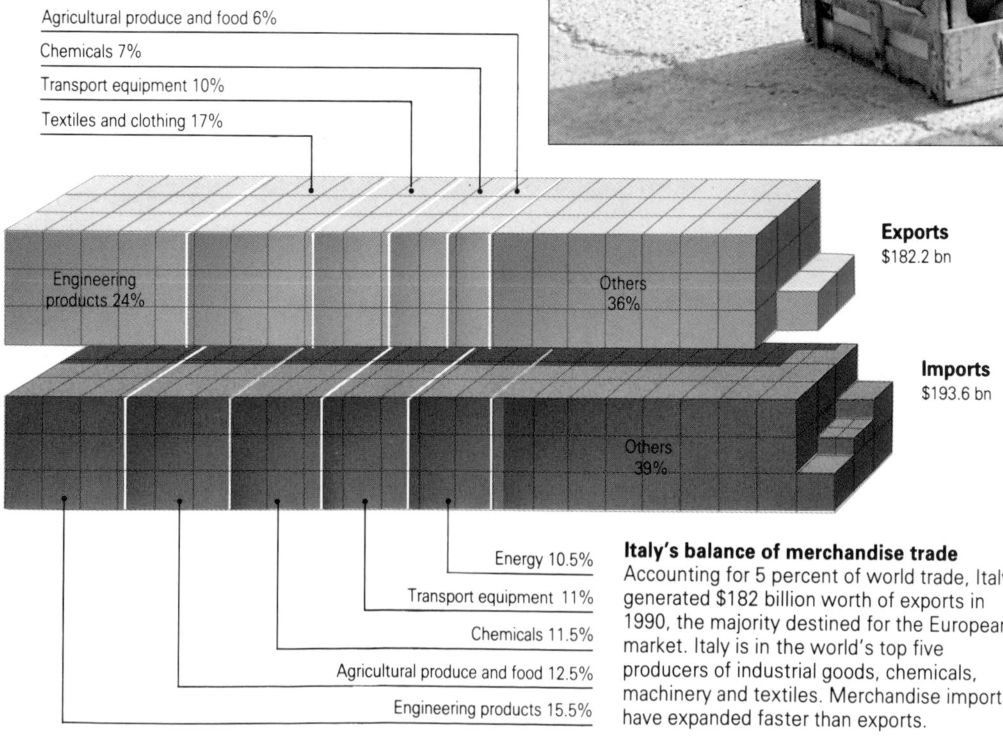

Italy's balance of merchandise trade Accounting for 5 percent of world trade, Italy generated $182 billion worth of exports in 1990, the majority destined for the European market. Italy is in the world's top five producers of industrial goods, chemicals, machinery and textiles. Merchandise imports have expanded faster than exports.

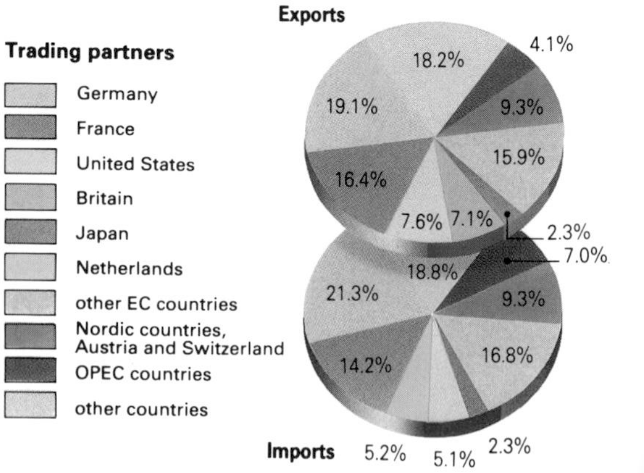

Corridor of wealth *(left)* Businessmen congregate in the streets of Milan, a major European center of industry, fashion and banking. The Italian rubber and tire giant, Pirelli, is based here. So are the financial houses that have funded industrial growth since World War II. The concentration of power here has promoted affluence far beyond the national average.

political "featherbedding" and buying votes rather than into industrial development or improving Greece's educational, transportation and communications systems. In 1990, Greece had the highest rates of inflation and government debt of all EC countries, and the lowest growth rates and GDP per capita. Improvement is slow and painful – GDP per capita fell from 52 percent of the EC average in 1983 to 48 percent in 1988. As in Italy, the extremely high public sector debt, due in large part to increased welfare spending without a corresponding growth in revenue, is a serious threat to the longterm health of the economy.

The development of manufacturing and business enterprise in Greece trails a long way behind other EC countries. Most of its industries are connected with food processing or building and construction. Its limited consumer goods industries are dominated by foreign companies and located almost exclusively in the Athens metropolitan area.

Trading status

Italy, on the other hand, has a relatively well-developed mix of heavy industries and consumer-goods manufacturing, largely under domestic control, and significant foreign investment in other sectors such as pharmaceuticals. Italian businesses received nearly $13 billion in government subsidies to manufacturing in 1988 – twice the EC average. Manufactured goods – particularly machinery and metal goods, textiles, clothing, footwear and transportation equipment – are the country's most valuable exports. Nevertheless, Italy still had a slight trade deficit in 1990 due to large imports of energy products, chemicals and foodstuffs. The vast majority of Italian trade is with other EC countries, particularly Germany and France; the largest individual trade surpluses are with the United States and Britain. However, as a group, the other Mediterranean EC members (particularly Spain) provide Italy with its largest consistent trade surplus. At the same time Italy runs huge trade deficits with developing countries such as Algeria and Libya, due to extensive high-cost imports of oil and natural gas.

Greece, by comparison, appears to be specializing in the wrong kinds of goods for success in the international market of the 1990s. World demand for the resource-based and labor-intensive products it exports has declined in recent years. About three-quarters of Greek exports are textiles, clothing, footwear, cement, aluminum (refined from deposits of bauxite), iron and steel. In the EC and other markets where Greece trades, Asian exporters such as South Korea and Hong Kong have emerged as major competitors since the 1970s. At the same time, Greece's membership of the EC has led to significant increases in its imports of manufactured goods due to the lowering of tariff barriers and a failure to invest in domestic production of these goods. In the past, trade deficits were offset by tourism, shipping and emigrant remittances, but since the mid 1980s (mainly because a high percentage of these revenues was in the declining US dollar) trade deficits have also plunged further into the red.

TOURISM AND THE GREEK ISLANDS

Picturesque beaches, a warm sunny climate and a rich classical heritage make the Greek islands popular destinations for international. More than 7 million tourists visited Greece each year during the mid 1980s – most of them bound for Corfu or the many islands of the Aegean. In 1989–90 fear of terrorism reduced the number of visitors, but the industry has since recovered. Most tourists come from the other EC countries, the United States, Austria and Sweden. In addition to the established island resorts, Cyprus, divided since 1974 into Greek and Turkish zones, and Malta have also shared in the region's tourist boom.

Successive Greek governments have fixed upon tourism as a major national and regional development strategy, and have even devalued the drachma in foreign exchange markets to stimulate the industry. The local economies of many of the Greek islands have become almost exclusively dependent on tourism. In Rhodes in the summer months tourists outnumber the local population by four to one, and in Corfu by two to one. The Greek construction industry has been one of the major beneficiaries of the tourist boom as the need for new hotels and resorts to cater for the influx of visitors has steadily increased since the 1970s.

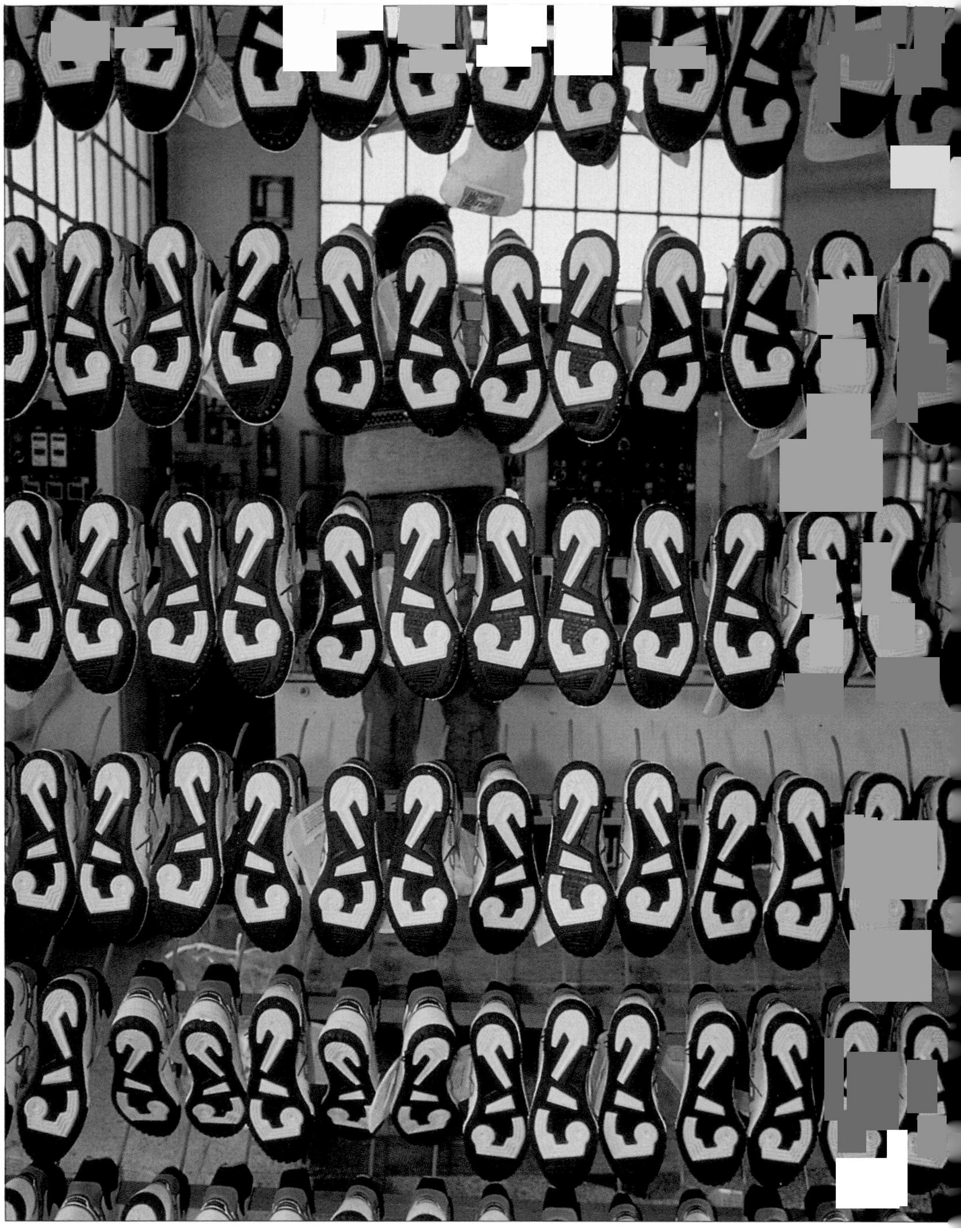

REDISTRIBUTING PROSPERITY

In both countries there are sharply defined areas of relative wealth and poverty. In Greece, the greatest contrast is between the industrialized Greater Athens and Salonika areas and the rest of the country. Italy is also divided economically between the advanced and prosperous north and center and the underdeveloped south known as the *Mezzogiorno*. In 1987–88, for example, there was 20 percent unemployment in the south compared with 7 percent in the north and 9 percent in the center. Industrial and manufacturing output per capita in the south was only 55 percent of that in the north of Italy.

The severity of Italy's north–south divide can obscure local differences. For example, in the south there are dynamic nodes of smallscale industry along the Adriatic coast of Abruzzi and Apulia. On the other hand, not all areas of the north and center have shared in recent economic growth. Parts of Piedmont, Liguria and the port of Genoa in particular, are all suffering from decline in their traditional industries.

Subsidizing the *Mezzogiorno*

During the 1950s and 1960s massive migration from the *Mezzogiorno* took place, mainly to northern Italy and other European countries. This, together with the government's decision to transfer resources to the south from the rest of Italy, helped to prevent even greater economic discrepancies between north and south. From 1950 to the late 1970s the Southern Development Fund (*Cassa per il Mezzogiorno*) encouraged land reform and infrastructure development. The state holding companies also invested massively in projects such as steel mills and petrochemical plants. These, however, generated few jobs and were particularly vulnerable to external influences such as the oil price increases of the 1970s.

More recent government policy for the south has concentrated on welfare subsidies rather than stimulating employment. This, and the abolition of regional wage differentials in 1969, reduced the level of migration from the south during the 1970s and 1980s. Despite the growth of "antisoutherner" sentiment in the north, figures for 1988–91 suggest that migration to the south is beginning to

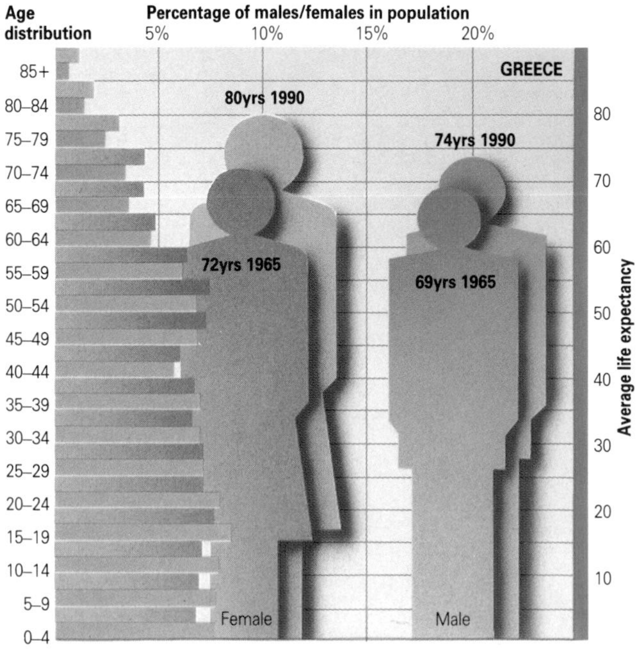

Running to catch up (*above*) Racks of shoes produced by a new factory in southern Italy are evidence of a government program to promote economic growth in the *Mezzogiorno*.

The intimidation racket (*right*) A bomb attack by the Mafia reminds local shopkeepers of what will happen if they fail to pay "protection money". In the early 1990s a legal crackdown on Mafia activities was followed by the assassination of several outspoken Italian judges.

Life expectancy and age distribution (*left*) Improved healthcare in Greece has increased average life expectancy to figures comparable with the rest of Europe. The life expectancy of Greek men may be affected by the fact that they smoke more than any other national group in the world. Birthrates are among Europe's lowest, and both Greece and Italy have high numbers of people over 65.

increase. Improved educational opportunities coupled with poor employment opportunities mean that the *Mezzogiorno* now has a surplus of high school and university graduates at precisely the time that major shortages of labor are occurring in the expanding northern service sectors such as banking and finance.

In fact, banking has become big business in recent years. Across the region, maintaining a high standard of living, especially in Italy, has become increasingly dependent on income from investments – such as government bonds or property – rather than on salaries. In 1987 Italians contributed more to GDP through savings than did the Japanese (23 percent compared to 18 percent). Lower-income households dependent on salaries or welfare payments alone are increasingly being left behind those with accumulating assets. This situation has been intensified by smaller wage increases as a result of declining union power and the abolition of inflation-indexed pay increases. In addition, recession and unemployment have meant that the opportunities for "moonlighting" (multiple job-holding, an established way of boosting income) are now far fewer than they were in the 1970s and early 1980s.

Building welfare states

Although 64 percent of Italian families own their own homes, there is also a relatively high incidence of extreme poverty (defined as income that is half the national average or less). Almost 22 percent of Italian families fall within this category, compared with 14.6 percent in France and 6 percent in Britain and Germany. The concept of a "welfare state" is relatively new in both Italy and Greece. Most facilities were only put in place during the 1960s and are less developed than those in northern Europe, though the absolute poverty epitomized by the barefoot children of pre-war days has all but disappeared. Both countries have placed greater emphasis on financial subsidies to individuals and families than on public provision of facilities such as daycare, clinics and social work. Unemployment benefits in both Italy and Greece are available to all those who are unemployed or who have never worked.

Welfare policies have encouraged striking improvements to healthcare in both countries over recent decades. For example, female life expectancy in Italy rose from 73 years in 1970 to 80 in 1988, and from 72 years to 79 in Greece over the same period. In Italy, particularly in the south, private hospitals are generally of a better standard, more highly regarded and more widely used than public hospitals, with the exception of a few outstanding public hospitals such as those in Bologna in the central region.

Conversely, there is little prestige attached to private education in either country and private universities are actually banned by the Greek constitution. Free compulsory state education is established in Italy and Greece, and in both countries the official school leaving age has recently been extended from 14 to 16 years old. Higher education has expanded enormously since the 1960s, and by the early 1990s 25 percent of all students in both countries continued their education beyond the compulsory period. However, tertiary students receive little state support and often drop out without completing their degrees. Many universities are overcrowded and do not offer vocational training for professional employment.

THE MAFIA ECONOMY

Although the Mafia is usually associated with parts of the Italian south, particularly western Sicily, Calabria and Campania, its influence penetrates deep into the peninsula. Behind the basic activity of "selling" protection lies a vast enterprise of illicit activities including prostitution, gambling, drug dealing, kidnapping, political manipulation and union racketeering. There is a good deal of controversy over why the Mafia has such a strong grip. Lack of faith in the institutions of government and the legal system is one obvious contributing factor.

The Mafia economy depends on exacting tribute in return for favors and protection – a system that is hardly unique to southern Italy. However, in Italy this crude way of accumulating power and wealth has persisted in the long term and increased in importance. Some political parties, especially the Christian Democrats and Socialists, have used Mafia connections to mobilize electoral support in parts of the south. There is also evidence that the Sicilian Mafia in particular is engaged in "joint ventures" with legitimate businesses outside the south and that it is gaining direct political power by infiltrating political and administrative appointments. In the 1990s the lines between politics, the underground economy, and Mafia activity are becoming increasingly blurred.

Mafia extortion costs Italian shopkeepers an estimated 800 billion lire ($650 million) a year. An average of 10 percent of all businesses are affected, rising from less than 5 percent in the north to 25 percent in the south. Mafia made 256 attempts on business people's lives in 1983 alone. Its ready recourse to violence and intimidation is now directed toward destabilizing state institutions, such as the law courts, that refuse to accept its new economic and political power.

The Third Italy

Until the second half of the 20th century, the basic economic contrast in Italy was between the industrial northwest and the rest of the country. In the 1950s, however, a new economy began to develop in the center and northeast around Verona, Modena and Florence. The area has since become known as the "Third Italy".

Italy's economic boom in the years after World War II was concentrated in the "Industrial Triangle" of the northwest between Turin, Milan and Genoa. In particular, the state-backed steel industry grew in parallel with the private sector (its biggest customer) making domestic appliances and consumer durables. The partnership between the two stimulated the growth of a large number of small firms that supplied components to the assembly plants of the big private firms. This particular pattern of success has not been copied outside the northwest. Attempts to reproduce similar economic development in the *Mezzogiorno* largely failed, not least because economic planners did not stimulate the growth of a network of small firms that were so important in the northwest.

After the formation of the EC in the 1950s, tariffs were removed from goods such as textiles, clothing, leather, jewelry and ceramics. Italy has a strong manufacturing tradition in all these products, and producers, particularly in the center and northeast, who had previously concentrated on domestic markets, began to search out and capture international markets. They quickly began to achieve remarkable success through competitive pricing and the flair for design that is associated with Italian workmanship throughout the world.

Small-business boom

Despite their new prominence, typical Third Italy firms retained their links with small-business practices. Usually they had fewer than 100 employees (often they had less than ten) and most grew up around family-owned businesses using traditional artisan skills. Many subcontract work to even smaller workshops and to home workers, a practice reminiscent of the early Industrial Revolution in England. Another typical feature is that these smallscale businesses are frequently allied with local agriculture – for example they may use wool and leather as raw materials. This allows for a wide variety of industrial development scattered throughout the countryside.

Small is beautiful A craftsman works on the carved wooden frame for a sofa at a small furniture-making workshop. Natural materials, high quality workmanship and specialist production are the hallmarks of small businesses in the "Third Italy".

Hat rack (*above*) Stylish hats made from local wool are checked for quality before leaving the workshop. This factory, like other textile, clothing and leather manufacturers in the area, still maintains close links with local agricultural suppliers.

On the whole, businesses in the Third Italy cooperate as well as compete with one another. They may contract work out to rivals with spare capacity, or pool resources for marketing and advertising. Specialized production with strong family and cooperative connections has emerged in a few areas, such as Prato in Tuscany making woolen textiles, Sassuolo in Emilia-Romagna making ceramic tiles and Recanati in the Marches making musical instruments. During the 1960s and 1970s "unofficial" employment was common, generating extra profits tax-free for the companies and enabling them to compete internationally with firms paying low wages. This gave labor-intensive firms an important advantage. Though it robbed the government of the funds, the practice did result in small clothing and shoe businesses flourishing and providing employment in traditionally agricultural areas such as the Marches. The success of small firms has also been allied to their ability to respond quickly to shifts in fashion in industries such as clothing, footwear and jewelry.

Some specialist areas have more conventional ownership–employee relations, but most of the Third Italy is characterized by businesses rooted in the local community. Capital-intensive sectors, such as the machinery and metal processing plants Bologna and Modena in Emilia-Romagna, are more closely tied to the large firms of the northwest.

Economic growth in the Third Italy slowed down during the 1980s due to a combination of circumstances producing a less favorable business climate. Many of the goods from labor-intensive sectors became less competitive internationally compared with similar goods from newly industrializing countries, particularly in Asia. The pressure may cause the Third Italy to begin to lose the characteristics that are the cornerstones of its success. The increased need to hire nonfamily workers as local birthrates decline may erode the cooperative way of life that has made business in the region so successful. On top of all this, high levels of pollution and the lack of investment in infrastructure such as telecommunications and electricity distribution have all begun to take their toll as the global climate for selling becomes more difficult.

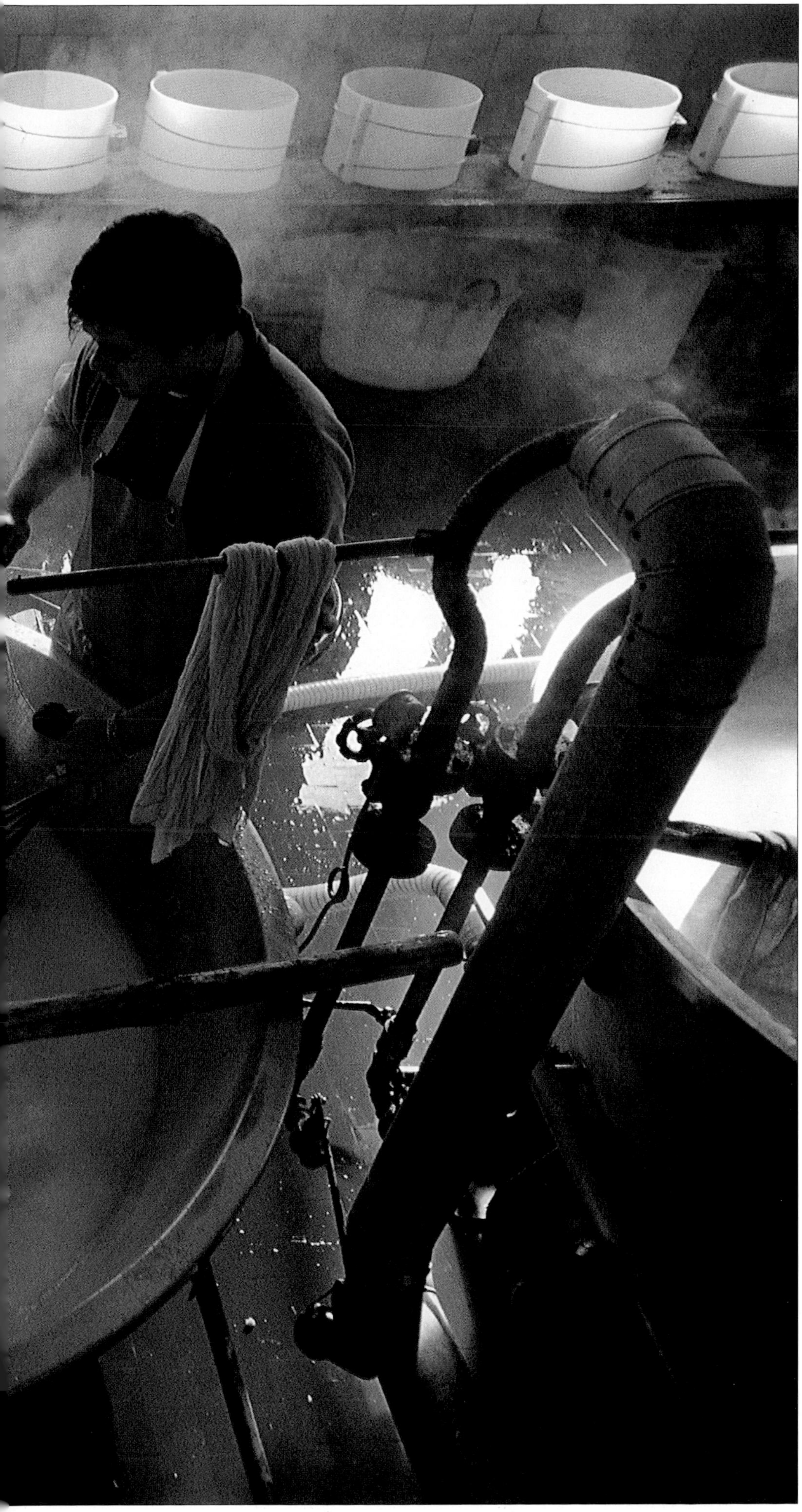

Profitable produce

The Parmesan cheese industry, based in the Po valley of northern Italy is one of Europe's most successful businesses in the food producing sector. Parmesan is sold in most major outlets throughout Europe and the United States, and a wide range of Italian dishes, popular throughout the Western world, now rely on this distinctive cheese for their flavor.

The industry is a fine illustration of the importance of niche marketing combined with an excellent distribution network, and its success is in sharp contrast to the fortunes of many other agricultural products and producers in modern Greece and Italy. Given the enormous range of dairy and other food produce on the international market, the manufacturer has to back up high-quality production with market research, and a high-profile advertising campaign.

In addition to the existing pressure of competition, Greek and Italian farmers, like their colleagues all over Europe, are coming under fierce pressure as the European Community (EC) is being forced to change its rules for the subsidization of European agriculture. The Common Agricultural Policy has met its main aim of ensuring that Europe is not dependent on other countries for its basic food supplies, but the costs of the policy are now being challenged by more efficient agricultural countries such as Britain and the United States. Indeed, the United States threatened a full-scale trade war against Europe in 1992 if the EC did not agree to move toward what America calls a "level playing field" in the global food market.

European agricultural practices and policies have been at the heart of the sixth round of the General Agreement on Tariffs and Trade (GATT) negotiations started in 1986, and their prospective reforms emphasize the need for European farmers to diversify their product ranges and to market their goods carefully. In this respect, Europe's farmers might learn something from the cheese manufacturers of the Parma region in Italy.

Lifting cheese out of the vat ready for pressing and maturing in a Parmesan cheese factory, Italy.

ECONOMIC BIRTH AND REBIRTH

PERFORMING AN ECONOMIC MIRACLE · RESTRUCTURING AND REORGANIZATION · THE ADVANTAGES OF AFFLUENCE

The postwar reconstruction of the German economy, particularly in former West Germany, has been hailed as a 20th-century miracle. Before unification in 1990, West Germany was the third largest economy in the world, depending for much of its success on highly profitable exporting. Austria, Switzerland and Liechtenstein have also made impressive postwar recoveries, but their industrial production and exports are less important than in Germany. The socialist economy of East Germany grew less quickly after World War II than the economies of other countries in the region, though it provided basic goods and services such as education and housing. A reunited German economy is widely expected to form the cornerstone of an expanded European Community (EC) at the end of the century.

COUNTRIES IN THE REGION

Austria, Germany, Liechtenstein, Switzerland

ECONOMIC INDICATORS: 1990

	HIE* Austria	HIE* Germany†	HIE* Switzerland
GDP (US$ billions)	157.38	1,488.21	224.85
GNP per capita (US$)	17,000	22,320	32,680
Annual rate of growth of GDP, 1980–1990 (%)	2.1	2.1	2.2
Manufacturing as % of GDP	27	31	n/a
Central government spending as % of GNP	39	29	16
Merchandise exports (US$ billions)	41.1	396.7	63.5
Merchandise imports (US$ billions)	49.0	339.9	69.5
% of GNP donated as development aid	0.25	0.42	0.31

WELFARE INDICATORS

Infant mortality rate (per 1,000 live births)			
1965	28	24	18
1990	8	7	7
Daily food supply available (calories per capita, 1989)	3,495	3,443	3,562
Population per physician (1984)	390	380	700
Teacher–pupil ratio (primary school, 1989)	1 : 11	1 : 18	n/a

Note: The Gross Domestic Product (GDP) is the total value of all goods and services domestically produced. The Gross National Product (GNP) is the GDP plus net income from abroad.

** HIE (High Income Economy) – GNP per capita above $7,620 in 1990.*

† West Germany, before unification.

The road to prosperity *(above)* runs through breathtaking Alpine scenery in the Tyrol region of southern Austria and extends into neighboring Germany. The economies of Central Europe are as closely linked together as their highly developed and well engineered road networks.

PERFORMING AN ECONOMIC MIRACLE

The economic origins of modern Central Europe date back as far as the Congress of Vienna in 1815, which established a German Confederation (*Deutscher Bund*) in place of the Holy Roman Empire. The Confederation was a loose alliance of monarchies and free cities until the unification of a smaller Germany in 1871, and the establishment of other self-governing states. Prussia (with Berlin as its capital) emerged as the strongest of the Confederation states, made economically powerful by the "marriage of iron and rye". This referred to the dual strength of Prussian industrial combines and large agricultural estates, controlled by the Junker class of provincial landowners.

Rebuilding from the ruins

In 1914 German imperial ambitions came into conflict with those of Britain and France, prompting World War I, which ended with political and economic defeat for Germany and Austria. Austria was particularly badly affected since it lacked Germany's means of recovery – the industrial base built up before the war. The war debts imposed on Germany in 1921 contributed to the destabilization of the German economy during the time of the Weimar Republic (1918–32). Although the German economy made a significant recovery, it was largely dependent on short-term loans from the United States. Following the Wall Street Crash in 1929 these loans were recalled and the German economy fell into a deep and enduring recession. By 1933 one in three of the working population was unemployed.

It was against this background that Adolf Hitler seized power, promising to put Germans back to work again. By 1938 German industry was running at full capacity as its military machine prepared

Map of GDP per capita (*left*) Switzerland's banking industry and tiny population gave it the world's largest GDP per capita in 1990. The chief business center is Frankfurt, Germany, and several of the world's top 500 banks and companies are found the region.

to annex Austria, Czechoslovakia and Poland. World War II put an end to Germany's new crusade, and by 1945 the country was in ruins again. About 40 percent of Germany's industrial capacity was destroyed or severely damaged by the war and the country had fallen under the divided supervision of the allied powers. Britain, France and the United States occupied the west and south, while the Soviet Union occupied the east, partitioned off as a separate country within the communist bloc. The allies also occupied Austria until 1955 and made considerable investment in the region.

The second revival

The economic recovery of Central Europe post-1945 was remarkable. Much of it was financed by the United States who feared that poverty and unemployment would encourage the spread of communism. In 1947 George Marshall, the former United States Army chief of staff during World War II, proposed a European Recovery Program that became known as the Marshall Plan. It was designed to rehabilitate the economies broken by war in order to preserve stability and democracy. Only East Germany pursued a program of recovery along socialist lines. There the state owned almost all the means of production – capital, land, even labor. Its controllers "planned" which sectors of the economy should be most favored by government funding and where particular factories should be located. The leading sector of the East German economy quickly became and remained heavy industrial goods, supplemented by a collectivized system of agriculture. So-called luxury goods were discouraged by high sales taxes, while basic consumer goods were heavily subsidized by the state. A constant problem throughout this period of recovery was that East Germany suffered from a lack of skilled workers and professionals. The Berlin Wall was erected in 1961 partly to stop the hemorrhage of such workers to the West.

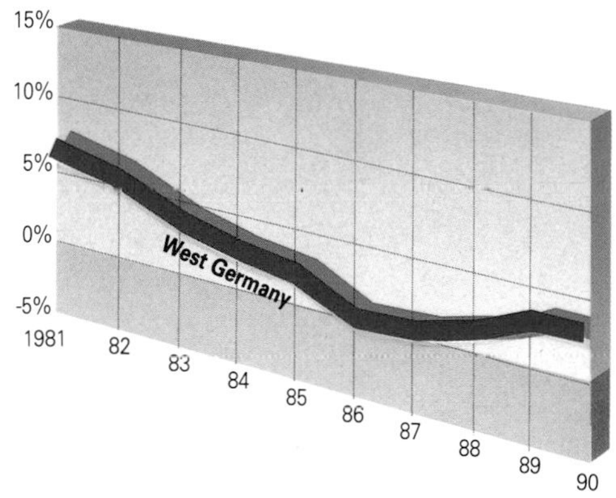

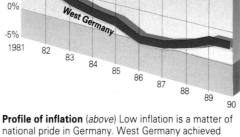

Profile of inflation (*above*) Low inflation is a matter of national pride in Germany. West Germany achieved zero inflation in 1986, and since reunification in 1990 the government has been heavily involved in maintaining low rates against the odds.

The West German economy doubled its output in the 1950s, and it increased by a further 70 percent and 50 percent in the 1960s and 1970s respectively. In the 1950s and 1960s the undervalued deutschmark gave West German exporters an artificial price advantage in international markets. The Austrian economy also prospered in the postwar, with precision machinery, chemicals and banking leading the way in a classic mixed economy, combining privately owned and nationalized businesses. Liechtenstein and Switzerland, too, enjoyed economic growth with the most significant advances in the banking and finance sector. The absolute secrecy surrounding their banking systems, combined with remarkable political stability, have made them leading international financial centers, while the registration of foreign companies, particularly in Liechtenstein, provides a significant source of tax income.

RESTRUCTURING AND REORGANIZATION

In the 1980s East Germany's rate of growth slowed down as some of the economy's more evident inefficiencies made themselves felt. One such inefficiency was the lack of technological innovation in industry and the engineering sectors compared with its western neighbor. Gradually the socialist state became heavily reliant on the expertise of West Germany with whom it maintained a system of more or less free trade. In spite of this reliance, East Germany was left behind in the wave of economic prosperity that washed over Central Europe until 1990. In October of that year, the Berlin Wall came down and East Germany achieved political and economic union with West Germany.

In the meantime, the West German economy had become one of the most powerful and fastest growing in the world. In 1980 about 45 percent of West German workers were employed in the country's industrial sector – a much higher proportion than in most advanced countries. Most of this industry was export-oriented and contributed strongly to West Germany's healthy balance of payments. Nearly half of West Germany's merchandise exports in the 1980s came from the automobile, chemical and machinery industries. These three industrial sectors alone employed more than one in five West German workers in 1985.

A solid financial infrastructure

Since then, in spite of this pronounced emphasis on industrialization, the region as a whole has followed the gradual shift among developed countries into the services sector. Frankfurt has become Europe's second largest financial center, adding further luster to the prosperous banking industries of Switzerland, Austria and Liechtenstein. By 1990 the proportion of West Germans employed in the industrial sector had dropped to less than 40 percent, with the figures for Switzer-

Six-cylinder status symbol *(right)* BMW's headquarters copy the engine design of the car that contributed to West Germany's wealth and reputation. A united Germany faces the challenge of raising industrial standards to uniformly high levels.

Unfashionable and unreliable *(left)* Trabant cars were abandoned by the thousand in favor of Western vehicles after reunification. The quality of design and workmanship in Trabants is a typical example of how much socialist state-run industry lagged behind its Western neighbor.

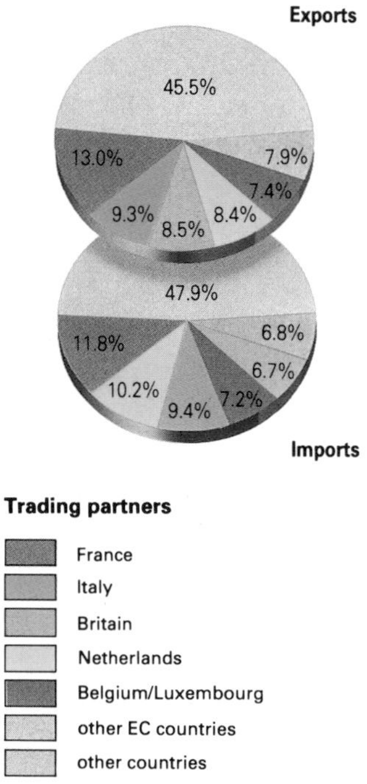

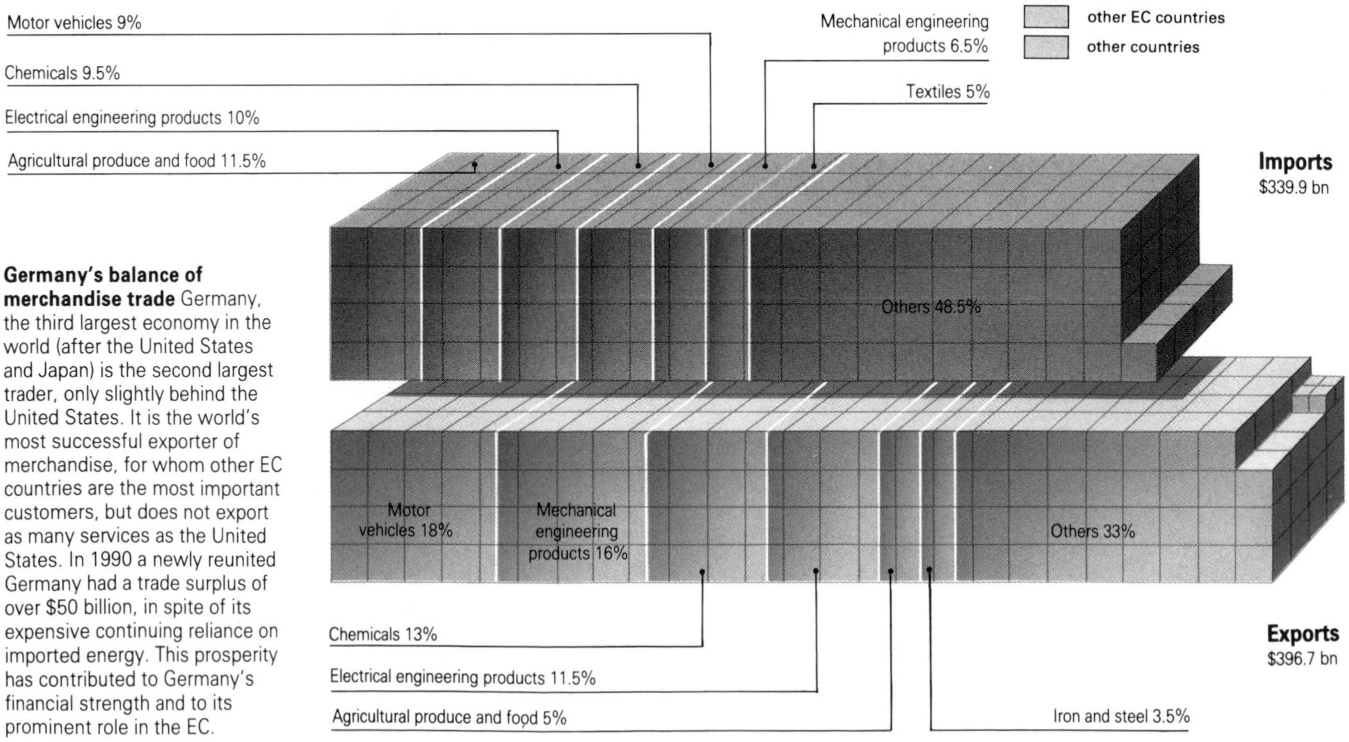

Germany's balance of merchandise trade Germany, the third largest economy in the world (after the United States and Japan) is the second largest trader, only slightly behind the United States. It is the world's most successful exporter of merchandise, for whom other EC countries are the most important customers, but does not export as many services as the United States. In 1990 a newly reunited Germany had a trade surplus of over $50 billion, in spite of its expensive continuing reliance on imported energy. This prosperity has contributed to Germany's financial strength and to its prominent role in the EC.

SWATCH, THE REVIVAL OF SWISS WATCHMAKING

Switzerland is widely regarded as a model Western economy. Although it lacks natural resources, the country has prospered by targeting international markets with high-quality goods, and by continually adapting its products to suit them.

The revival of the Swiss watchmaking industry in the 1980s is a good example of the national talent for adaptability. In 1970 the Swiss share of the world watch market was about 40 percent, but the industry was based almost entirely on local workmen producing mechanical parts. When cheaply produced electronic wristwatches were put on the market by the Japanese and others, the Swiss watch industry nearly collapsed. Between 1970 and 1983, 43,600 people lost their jobs, and the Swiss market share contracted from 40 percent to 17 percent by 1981.

Swiss watchmaking reorganized itself and fought back. Using heightened market awareness and imaginative design, the industry reinvented itself with the introduction of the Swatch. By reducing the number of parts and assembling them in one operation, the Swiss could engage in mass production while allowing their designers to create up to 100 stylish new Swatch models each year. Financial support came from the commercial banks, which put up some SF 600 million in the early and mid 1980s. The success of Swatch has also boosted the value-added end of the Swiss watchmaking industry by generating cash for investment and providing economies of scale.

land and Austria being 35 percent and 37 percent respectively.

The region's economy also had to adjust to growing industrial competition from some developing countries. West German shipbuilding was a notable casualty, with a world market share of 20 percent in 1950 dwindling to less than 4 percent in 1990. Other established industries faced competition from Japan and Southeast Asia, including Swiss watchmaking and German manufacturing of automobiles, audio equipment and cameras. Across the region companies responded to competition with labor shedding and "upward restructuring", concentrating on producing high-quality luxury goods and customized equipment for industry. The automobile companies

Mercedes-Benz and BMW and the machine-tools industry provide typical examples of how this strategy works.

Central Europe is now a high-wage area with a well trained and efficient labor force and excellent productivity. German industries have not relocated abroad on a large scale, in part because of this emphasis on high-quality production and engineering, and in part because of a flexible domestic industrial structure that makes extensive use of subcontracting. What has flowed abroad is German capital. The savings ratio in Central Europe is comparatively high, and funds from the region support economic projects all around the world. In 1990, West Germany was also the world's third largest source of official development assistance (foreign aid) contributing a total of $6.32 billion.

The rise of the free market economy

The restructuring of the economies of Central Europe has been accompanied by a shift in economic ideology. This has been most evident in East Germany, which had a socialist command economy before its dissolution in 1990. Elsewhere, the ideological shift has followed the more familiar Western pattern of less government intervention, greater faith in the free market economy and privatization (already proposed for Austria's railway system). Before German unification, budget deficits were cut back in West Germany by Chancellor Helmut Kohl and Austria has set itself the target of a budget deficit no greater than 2.5 percent of GDP by 1994. Against such a background, unemployment is forecast to remain high (at 5–12 percent) when compared with 1950s' totals. Inflation, by contrast, continues to remain low in Central Europe, though the unification of Germany created some inflationary pressures. In Germany, low inflation and a strong deutschmark are matters of national pride, even of national identity.

Further reforms are likely in agriculture, where a reduction in subsidies poses a threat to farmers throughout the region. The strength of the German economy means that it is required to take a lead in the European Community (EC) and to contribute sizable funds to the poorer countries of the community; meanwhile, both Switzerland and Austria expect to join an expanded EC later in the 1990s. In all respects, the region is likely to remain at the heart of Europe.

THE ADVANTAGES OF AFFLUENCE

According to the World Bank and the United Nations, Swiss citizens were the richest in the world in 1990, with average per capita incomes in excess of $30,000. In West Germany and Austria average incomes were $22,000 and $19,000 respectively, but in both these countries the cost of living was less prohibitive than in Switzerland, where (in the same year) house prices in some cities started at $500,000. In East Germany, average per capita incomes for the same period were about $8,000.

Sharing out the benefits

The distribution of income and wealth in Central Europe is more even than in most parts of the world. Class distinctions and class consciousness are not as strongly developed as in other European countries, because of the leveling effects of wartime destruction in Austria and Germany. The average pay of a professional worker in West Germany in 1990 was only 2 to 3 times higher than a worker without professional training. In East Germany income differentials have been less marked still, with even the most highly trained individuals earning only 1.5 to 2 times that of a person without technical or professional training. However, the wage of an East German individual or a household was only a partial guide to their standard of living. Less than 30 percent of East German families owned a private house in 1989, with the majority living in apartment blocks owned by the state or housing cooperatives. Housing was provided as a basic service and was heavily subsidized by the government for social reasons.

In spite of the fairly uniform high quality of life in the region, there are still

SKIING DOWNHILL

The beauty of the Alpine landscape and its easy accessibility from neighboring countries have made Austria one of the most important holiday destinations in Europe, particularly during the skiing season. It was one of the first countries affected by mass tourism in prospering postwar Europe. Between the late 1950s and the early 1980s the number of foreign visitors increased from 4 million to 21 million. Tourism is vital to this small, landlocked country, lacking in natural resources. It generates about 18 percent of Austria's GNP (and more than 45 percent in the Tyrol region). Austria's net receipts from tourism cover about 75 percent of the country's (nontourism) trade deficit.

Winter holidays have become increasingly popular since the early 1970s, leading to the development of new resorts and the expansion of skiing facilities into areas of higher altitude. (The number of ski-lifts increased sixfold between 1960 and 1980.) This growth has created problems including congestion and environmental damage. Day trips into Austria and competition from the ski industry in other countries have reduced the demand for accommodation, and overcapacity is now a problem in some areas of the Tyrol. The destruction of Alpine landscapes by winter sports has contributed to a decline in summer tourism in Austria, also dating from the mid 1970s.

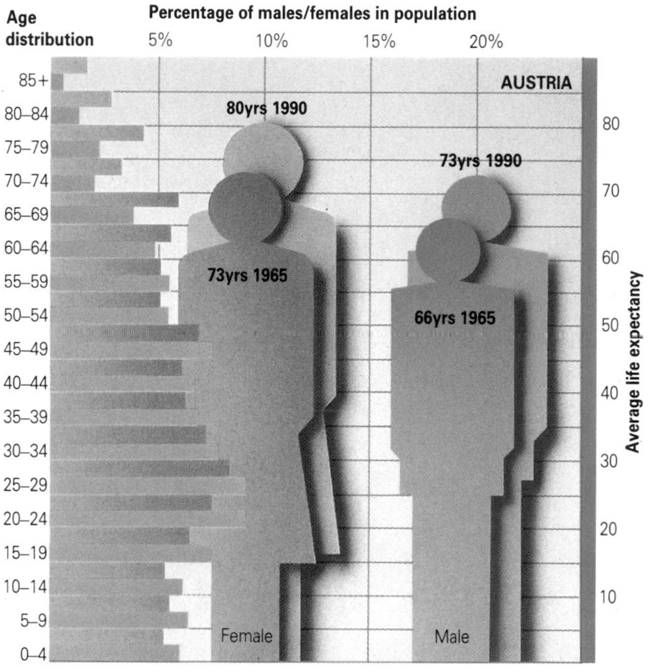

Attention to detail (*left*) has gained the Swiss an international reputation for the quality of their services. Here, an instructor at the Lausanne Hotel School demonstrates a series of formal table settings. Hotel staff are trained to be highly skilled professionals, attracting the wealthy clients – tourists, consumers and investors – who sustain Swiss prosperity.

Life expectancy and age distribution (*above*) A long history of stability and prosperity makes Central Europeans among the world's most healthy and well cared for. These figures for Austria are slightly lower than those in either Germany or Switzerland. Throughout the region, women still outlive men by a considerable span. Infant mortality rates since 1965 have reduced dramatically.

variations in funding and in services according to locality and social class. In Germany, the states of Hessen, Bavaria and Baden-Württemberg are noticeably the richest. In Switzerland and Austria the main differential is the urban–rural divide. Gender also makes a difference. Women did not get the vote in Swiss national elections until 1971 and they are still excluded from some local elections, though their standard of living is high. In East Germany, by contrast, women under the socialist regime had a poorer standard of living, but had equal rights in politics and in the workforce. In 1989, the share of women in total employment in East Germany was 49.8 percent; in West Germany it was 39.6 percent. In 1990 this gap began to close as large numbers of former East Germans were made redundant in a united Germany.

Education and healthcare systems

Educational and standards of vocational training levels are uniformly high in Central Europe. In 1989 72.5 percent of the West German workforce had technical or higher education qualifications or had served apprenticeships; 78.7 percent in East Germany. Vocational training is given a strong emphasis in Germany, where the adaptability of a highly trained labor force is of critical concern to employers. Almost a third of Germans and Austrians continue into postschool education, compared with a quarter of the Swiss population. Higher education is funded by a mixture of federal and regional government spending and by a system of student loans and grants-in-aid.

Standards of healthcare are also high in Central Europe. Infant mortality rates are as low as anywhere in the world (save Japan) and most citizens can expect to live to 75 and beyond. In East Germany the state was responsible for a nationalized system of healthcare provision, where treatment was free at the point of delivery. Elsewhere in Central Europe healthcare expenditure as a proportion of GDP is close to the average figure in the Organization for Economic Cooperation and Development (OECD), and private semipublic insurance systems provide care. Hospitals are run by state and local governments and various benevolent organizations, including the Church. All the countries of Central Europe face the problems associated with a rapidly aging population. The Swiss are trying to meet this problem by setting up a system of professional healthcare services in the community in order to release scarce hospital beds.

The dominant feeling in Germany is that work and welfare issues are well attended to for those with full citizenship rights. By contrast, large numbers of "guest workers" from Turkey and other (mostly Mediterranean) countries are not so well treated. Their formal citizenship rights are well catered for – pensions, sick leave, etc. – but the guest workers often face discrimination in the housing market and are disproportionately confined to low-paid menial jobs. As unemployment grows in Central Europe, some of these communities are also coming under attack from a growing racialist Right who resent sharing employment prospects with them.

When East meets West

When the economies of East and West Germany were united in 1990, economists and politicians were faced with the difficult task of restructuring the stagnant economy of East Germany without unduly damaging that of West Germany, the main engine of growth of the European Community. This task was not helped by the poor quality of official statistics about the East German economy. Most economists had assumed that the East German economy was more efficient than it proved to be when more detailed information became available in 1990. After all, the East German economy had been celebrated as the model of the communist economic community (COMECON). When the facts were known, it turned out that the average labor productivity in East Germany was less than one-third of that in West Germany.

The East German economy had been organized before unification according to political criteria. Firms were divided into giant groupings called *Kombinate* – in 1989 some 200 of these accounted for 95 percent of the country's total output. The *Kombinate* were controlled from above, with relatively little discretion being allowed to managers at a local level. To make sure that production targets were maintained, most plants were overmanned and hoarded intermediate products far beyond levels that would be considered efficient in a market economy. Inefficient enterprises were not usually allowed to fail. Employment was a constitutional right, though in many *Kombinate* disguised unemployment was the norm.

From communism to capitalism

The unification process meant that the East German economy was subjected to rapid structural reorganization. A treaty creating a monetary, economic and social union between the Federal Republic of Germany and the German Democratic Republic was signed on 18 May 1990. Four main factors have eased the process of reorganization. First, a nonconvertible currency (the GDR mark) was replaced by a stable international currency (the deutschmark), managed by a strong central *Bundesbank*. Access to international financial markets followed. Second, private property rights could be provided in the former East Germany according to the tried and tested model of West Germany. Private property rights are considered an important way of giving people an incentive to work hard and to accumulate private wealth. Third, the reorganization of East Germany's agriculture and industry could be paid for in part by West German funds and by monies borrowed on world markets. In 1992 the net transfer of funds from West to East Germany was an estimated DM 180 billion ($34 billion). Finally, the citizens of East Germany could be sheltered from the full costs of economic restructuring by virtue of West Germany's social insurance systems.

It will take some time for the transition to capitalism to be secured. In the two months after monetary union, recorded

Starting over (*below*) The demolition of an old building in former East Germany leaves a gaping hole. Poor standards of construction left many living in substandard housing. Reconstruction involves replacing accommodation as well as obsolete factories.

Berlin gets a facelift *(above)* The Brandenburg Gate, Berlin's arch of triumph and the only remaining gate of the original city of Berlin, undergoing cleaning and extensive restoration work in 1991. Following reunification, builders and architects moved in all over the city to repair and restore its infrastructure.

industrial production in East Germany fell by more than 40 percent and by the end of 1990 unemployment had increased more than six-fold to 650,000. A further two million workers were on short-time work, with still others being laid off as local trade unions pushed for rapid wage equalization with the West. By spring 1992 more than one-third of the labor force in East Germany was regarded as unemployed. An enormous change in attitudes and institutions is required in East Germany if its economy is to be rebuilt. Consumers are now reluctant to buy goods made in that part of the country (the Trabant car is a typical example). Legal and financial services will have to be built up from next to nothing, together with educational systems geared to a market economy.

Finally, there are the considerable costs that West Germany must bear. There is fear in some quarters that German funds will be withdrawn from the EC's social fund and from joint-European defense initiatives. Some also fear that the costs of unification will spur inflation in Germany, so that the deutschmark becomes less acceptable as an international means of payment. All this seems unlikely, however. The *Bundesbank* is committed to a firm policy of money management in the newly united Germany and Germany's rising budget deficit is still less as a percentage of GNP than the average figure among its Western peers.

The economics of racism

In the early 1990s Germany was already home to 1 in 13 of the world's refugee population – more than 1.4 million people – and was facing further demands for asylum from victims of the civil war in former Yugoslavia. This new wave of refugees came at a time when Germany was still trying to deal with the economic challenges of unification and when many Germans were unemployed, especially in the eastern *lander*. Although economic and political migrants tend to add a great deal to the economy of the host country over a number of years, in the short run migrants old and new (Turks and Slavs) are often resented as unwelcome competitors for the few jobs on offer.

Until economic growth returns to a united Germany, one of the most visible problems associated with the unification of Germany is the growth there of racial hatred and a related intolerance of non-Germans. In 1992 alone there were more than 2,000 acts of racial violence, with up to 24 racially motivated killings being notified to the authorities.

It is important to emphasize that the German government and most of the German people do not share this intolerance. Article 16 of the German Constitution offers a blanket promise of asylum to all victims of persecution, and it represents a generous coming to terms with Germany's Nazi past. Nevertheless, racial hatred is a growing problem in Germany. Although violence against non-Germans is perpetrated by small groups of ultra-rightists, it has its roots in the wider economic and political problems associated with unification.

Berlin, 8 November 1992 over 300,000 people attend an antiracism rally. Posters call for the protection of Article 16, guaranteeing asylum to victims of persecution.

ARTIKEL 16
BEWAHREN

FROM MARX TO THE MARKET

INSTABILITY AT THE CROSSROADS · REJOINING THE WORLD ECONOMY · WELFARE SOCIALISM

Throughout their history, the economies of Eastern Europe have suffered in the clash of interest between rival empires. Much of the region remained heavily dependent on agriculture well into this century, with only the north enjoying world trade comparable with its Western European neighbors. After 1945, most Eastern European countries fell under Soviet influence and adopted planned economies with a new emphasis on heavy manufacturing and trade with the Soviet Union. For a time this brought rapid growth, but in the long term socialism failed to deal with the region's economic problems. The revolutions of 1989 brought in new regimes with new policies. All across the region governments struggled to develop free enterprise while dealing with the side effects of poverty and ethnic tensions.

COUNTRIES IN THE REGION

Albania, Bosnia and Hercegovina, Bulgaria, Croatia, Czech Republic, Hungary, Macedonia, Poland, Romania, Slovakia, Slovenia, Yugoslavia (Serbia and Montenegro)

ECONOMIC INDICATORS: 1990

	UMIE* Hungary	LMIE* Poland	LMIE* Romania
GDP (US$ billions)	32.92	63.59	34.73
GNP per capita (US$)	2,780	1,690	1,640
Annual rate of growth of GDP, 1980–1990 (%)	1.3	1.8	1.2
Manufacturing as % of GDP	27	20	n/a
Central government spending as % of GNP	55	40	34
Merchandise exports† (US$ billions)	7.1	8.9	n/a
Merchandise imports† (US$ billions)	6.1	7.4	n/a
% of GNP received as development aid	–	–	–

WELFARE INDICATORS

Infant mortality rate (per 1,000 live births)			
1965	39	42	44
1990	15	16	27
Daily food supply available (calories per capita, 1989)	3,644	3,505	3,155
Population per physician (1984)	310	490	570
Teacher–pupil ratio (primary school, 1989)	1 : 13	1 : 16	1 : 21

Note: The Gross Domestic Product (GDP) is the total value of all goods and services domestically produced. The Gross National Product (GNP) is the GDP plus net income from abroad.

** UMIE (Upper Middle Economy) – GNP per capita between $2,465 and $7,620 in 1990. LMIE (Lower Middle Income Economy) – GNP per capita between $610 and $2,465.*

† Hard currency only (Polish figures for 1989)

INSTABILITY AT THE CROSSROADS

The economies of Eastern Europe have a long history of lagging behind their Western neighbors. The region enjoys a strategically powerful location astride routes linking western Europe, Russia and the Middle East, but trade was frequently interrupted by rivalries and warfare. Conflict between the Russian, Ottoman and Austro-Hungarian empires fragmented trading patterns in the 18th century and impaired the region's economic development. The region also has a history of a north–south divide, with the industrial capacity of the northern countries generating relative prosperity compared with the agricultural south.

As early as the 18th century some manufacturing had developed in Silesia (Poland) and Bohemia (the Czech Republic). By 1900 these areas had constructed extensive railroad networks and Silesia had become one of Europe's leading powerhouses of heavy industry. However, the southern part of the region (modern Romania, Bulgaria, Bosnia and Hercegovina, Macedonia, Slovenia, Croatia and Albania) remained heavily dependent on farming. Most of these countries traded agricultural exports to western Europe in return for manufactured goods, but they played little part in world trade. Communications were poor, leaving many communities isolated.

This remained largely true even after World War I, when warring between empires stopped and the region became a group of independent nation-states. Trade was dependent on western Europe, with the Eastern European countries borrowing heavily from abroad to finance economic growth. Lacking a diversified economic base, the region suffered badly during the worldwide recession of the 1930s. Mass unemployment, depressed agricultural prices and the decline of manufacturing industries added to political instability and prompted the rise of authoritarian governments.

The Soviet economic orbit

With the imposition of Soviet rule following World War II, socialist regimes were established in all Eastern European countries, while all except former Yugoslavia and Albania became part of the Soviet

In the picture (*below*) Foto World in Warsaw is one of many joint ventures set up between Eastern European and Western companies. Following a series of peaceful revolutions in the region, businesses flocked to exploit growing new markets.

Map of GDP per capita *(above)* This is the poorest region in Europe, with no country achieving a GDP per capita of over $5,000 in 1990. Within this relative poverty, the split between the industrialized cities and the poorer rural areas is still quite pronounced.

economic orbit. A free-market philosophy was replaced by central planning, industries were nationalized and priority was given to heavy manufacturing rather than making consumer goods. In 1949 the Council for Mutual Economic Assistance (Comecon) was set up, with the aim of coordinating economic planning among the five East European members of the Warsaw Pact (Poland, Czechoslovakia, Romania, Hungary and Bulgaria). Huge military industrial complexes were built to serve Soviet needs, while each country in the region was allocated a different product in which it was to specialize. Hungary made buses, Czechoslovakia manufactured railroad locomotives, and East Germany made machine tools. After Stalin's death, the five Soviet satellite states enjoyed some autonomy from Moscow and a small private sector was permitted, but always on a limited scale.

Planning success and failure

On the surface these planned economies were successful, at least for a time. The region enjoyed steady economic growth during the decades after 1945 and saw considerable improvements in transport and power supplies. The five Warsaw-pact members together with the Soviet Union formed a distinct economic zone with its own guaranteed markets, free from external competition. In the mid 1980s no less than two-thirds of Eastern European trade was within the Comecon bloc. Inflation was low and unemployment nonexistent in all countries of the region except Yugoslavia, where strict central planning was not enforced.

However, the appearance of progress concealed serious problems. The region's isolation from international trading meant it was not exposed to important technical innovation, notably in computer technology and microelectronics. Individual enterprise was generally discouraged by the centralized system, though Hungary was a notable exception after the mid 1960s. This system provided little motivation for workers. Nor could they buy high-quality goods with their earnings; production of consumer goods was both divorced from popular demand and lacked effective quality control. Countries suited to farming (such as Romania) found themselves saddled with large and inefficient industrial sectors while agriculture was neglected. By the late 1970s these problems were creating signs of decline in every country in the region, generating deep resentment at Moscow's longstanding dominance.

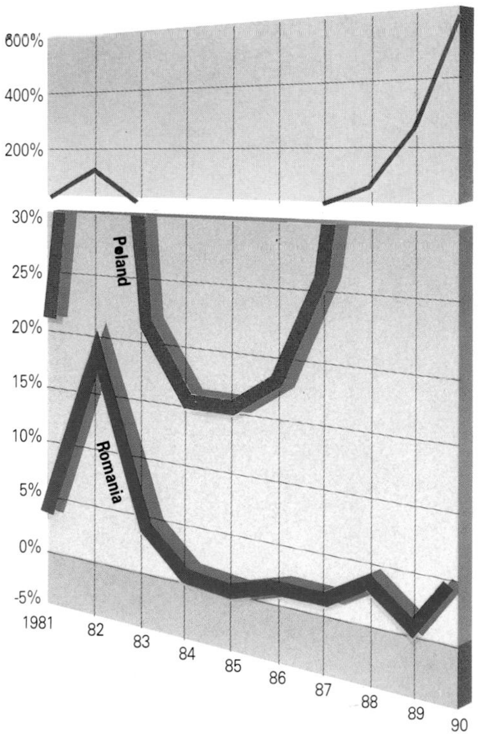

Profile of inflation *(above)* Romania's inflation rate soared in the early 1980s as the country faced problems in servicing its international debt. In Poland similar problems threatened the leadership's stability.

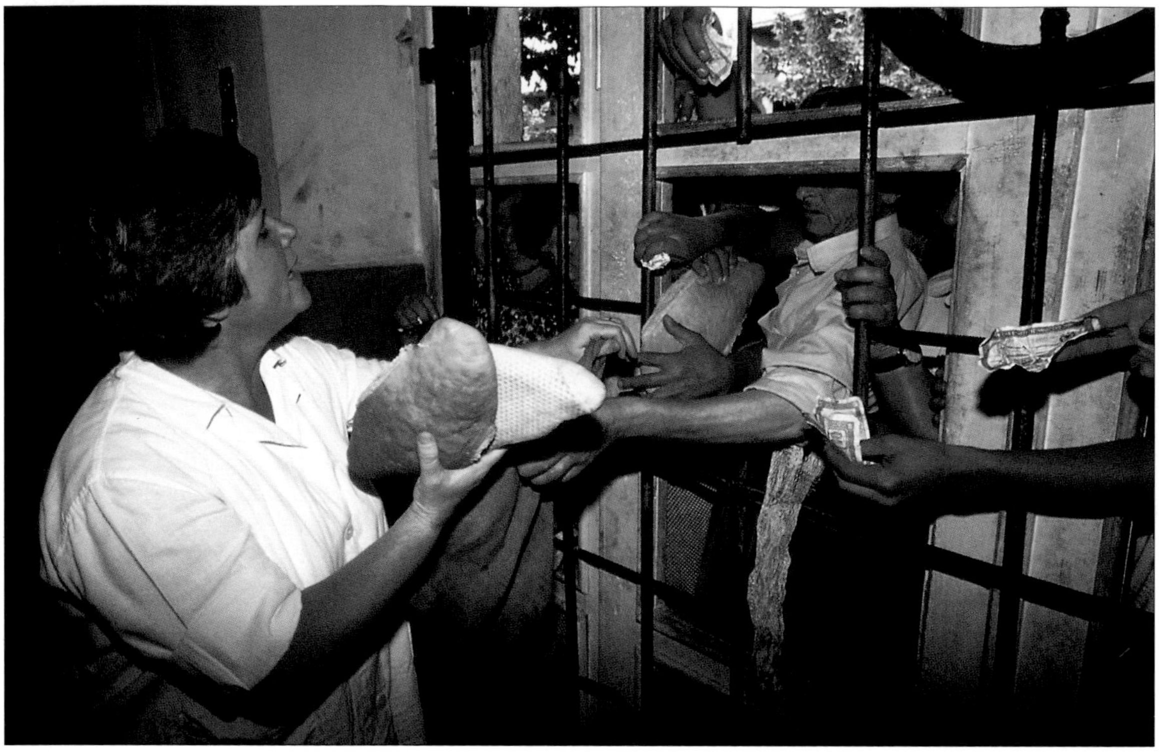

Held back by bars *(left)* Albanians scramble for bread at this private bakery in the capital Tiranë. By the early 1990s, the Albanian economic system had broken down, food in the shops was scarce and extremely expensive, and most people existed on food and aid from donor nations. This often had to be delivered by armed guards to protect against theft and hijacking by black marketeers trading in stolen food.

Gambling on a better future *(right)* Citizens in the Romanian capital, Bucharest, take part in one of the country's growing number of illegal lottery and gambling syndicates. As the economic situation in Romania worsens, the games are proliferating as desperate people hope to win a quick and easy fortune.

REJOINING THE WORLD ECONOMY

During the 1980s the planned economies of Eastern Europe were in desperate need of structural reform. In its absence they slid steadily toward collapse. Productivity began to decline as governments, short of capital, were unable to provide factories with urgently needed new equipment. At the same time, transport systems suffered neglect, and began to waste resources. Exports to the West fell as production quality lagged behind international standards. The result was falling revenues and a shortage of vital hard currency.

The breakup of Comecon

Similar problems were also occurring in the Soviet Union, and this compounded Eastern Europe's difficulties. The flow of subsidized energy (particularly oil and gas) and raw materials from Moscow to the Warsaw-Pact nations began to dry up, with disastrous consequences. In desperation Eastern European nations began to turn to the capitalist world from which they borrowed heavily; partly to pay for energy imports and partly in an effort to modernize outdated production. On the eve of the 1989 revolutions the countries of the region owed no less than $62.9 billion to the West, with Poland and Hungary being by far the largest debtors.

The exception among Soviet satellite states was Romania, where the government insisted on repaying those debts already accumulated, bringing great suffering to its people. Yugoslavia, which was not a member of Comecon, suffered political and economic problems of its own, in part reflecting the more federal structure of its government. State-determined prices kept inflation artificially low in the rest of the region, but Yugoslavia experienced runaway inflation and mounting unemployment.

The revolutions of 1989 destroyed the basis of the Comecon system and during the following year alone trade between Comecon countries fell by one-fifth. Most Eastern European countries recognized the need to take part in world trade outside the enclosed Communist world, but being competitive in the international market proved to be extremely challenging. The Comecon years left the region with a legacy of interdependent transportation networks as well as a shared electricity grid and integrated oil and gas pipelines. This made it extremely difficult for the new regimes to control their energy sources and distribution networks.

More worrying, the failure of the region's manufacturing industries to match the standards of their new capitalist business rivals meant the greater part of the region's production was obsolete and uncompetitive. At the same time, exporting to Western countries was hampered by the imposition of tariffs and import restrictions. The governments of Eastern Europe urgently needed more favorable trading arrangements with the West; they also needed massive new investment from outside, on top of the high levels of debts already accumulated.

The gap widens

As the dust settled after the 1989 revolutions, a new pattern of economic progress soon became discernible. The three northern countries – Poland, Czechoslovakia and Hungary, traditionally the strongest

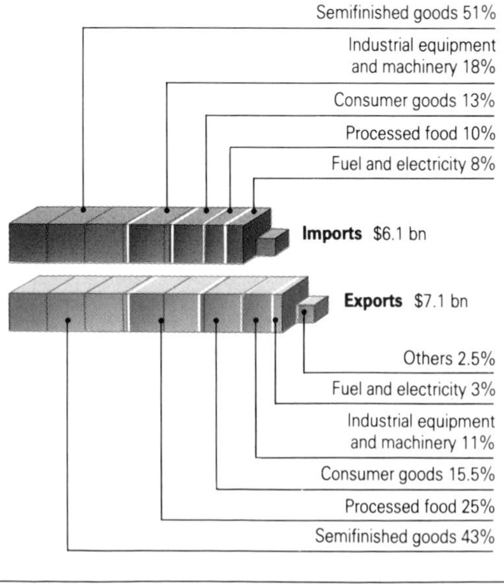

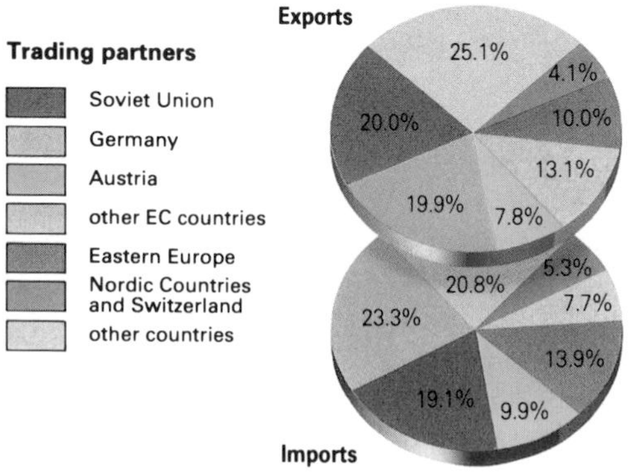

Hungary's balance of merchandise trade In 1990 Hungary had a small visible trade surplus. The former Soviet Union and Eastern European countries were already less important as an export market than the European Community.

economies in the region – soon obtained assistance from the World Bank and the International Monetary Fund (IMF). Both institutions insisted that financial aid should come with conditions to ensure the transition from state socialism to a market economy. The three northern states were required to demonstrate their commitment to change by introducing political and economic reform, and establishing the framework of democratic government. As part of this arrangement they achieved the important step of becoming associate members of the European Community (EC), which improved their ability to export more widely. By contrast Romania, Bulgaria and Albania did not evolve smoothly into parliamentary democracies and aid was withheld. All three countries suffered from some degree of internal ethnic conflict – and were more cautious in introducing free-market reforms. As a result they found themselves comparatively isolated from western Europe.

Inevitably, these events widened the existing north–south divide. Without financial assistance the southern states risked increasing hardship and unemployment which in turn threatened to undermine political stability. This was particularly the case in former Yugoslavia, where ethnic tensions proved explosive. The southern part, including Macedonia and Bosnia and Hercegovina suffered a dramatic slump in fortunes, while Slovenia – and to a lesser extent Croatia – enjoyed stronger economic and cultural links with western Europe, offering the possibility that they could leap the divide and become closely attached to the EC. However, even among the more fortunate northern states of the region, adjustment to the free market has proved far from easy, particularly during the 1990s' world recession. In the early part of the adjustment, at least, the whole region suffered growing unemployment and increasing poverty.

ALBANIA COMES IN FROM THE COLD

Nearly 30 years of self-imposed isolation has made Albania Eastern Europe's maverick economy. A member of Comecon only briefly (1947–62), Albania remained largely aloof from Soviet influence. It did, however, establish what turned out to be wholly impractical trading links with China, whom it regarded as an ideological mentor. Since the other countries of the region began to look toward the West, Albania has also proved to be the most reluctant to introduce market reforms and rejoin the world economy.

During the period of Soviet influence, the rest of Eastern Europe regarded urban–industrial development as the building block for a prosperous socialist society. Albania, however, under General Secretary Enver Hohxa (1945–85) made efforts to industrialize the countryside in the belief that this would offer protection from the evils of Western capitalism and city life. In this, at least, he was probably influenced by the teachings of Mao Zedong, and Albania remained an agrarian–peasant society.

The aim of this policy was to make Albania economically self-sufficient, but the consequence was that the country became the poorest state in Europe, with a standard of living comparable to Bangladesh or Indonesia. Yet the country is rich in natural resources, including oil, coal and metal ores, which a more reform-minded government could use to rebuild the economy. Some European states have offered much-needed aid, and trading links, especially with Germany and Italy, are growing. However, development has lagged so far behind other European economies that trading in the world market is unlikely to be easy. The scale of Albania's crisis is indicated – and worsened – by the steady flow of young economic refugees from the country.

WELFARE SOCIALISM

The postwar governments of Eastern Europe saw social welfare as a means to demonstrate the success of their political systems. Throughout the era of communist rule they claimed to have achieved a more equal distribution of wealth and higher living standards than before they gained power. They insisted that – in contrast to the West – unemployment, drug addiction and homelessness had been eradicated. In many key welfare areas, such as infant mortality and public expenditure per head, Eastern European states boasted that they had surpassed capitalist countries, proving the superiority of socialism.

While these claims were sometimes exaggerated, they contained an element of truth. Eastern European countries did for a time create increasingly egalitarian and collectively organized economies. Proportionately, more public spending was devoted to education, healthcare and housing projects than in some leading Western states where the levels of Gross Domestic Product (GDP) per capita were considerably higher. Albania, despite being the poorest country in Europe, expanded its educational system faster and enrolled a higher proportion of students than Spain or Greece.

At the same time, the governments of the region provided their people with more extensive pension and sickness allowances than many wealthier European nations. They were also unusually lavish in terms of allocating resources to the arts – theater, music, museums and book publishing – though this funding was strictly dependent on recipients falling in line with government ideology.

Where socialist claims were most vulnerable to criticism was in the way they concealed complexities in the picture, and in their reluctance to admit that the system was capable of decline. Welfare provision was far less uniform across the region than officially indicated, with social services more extensive in the wealthier states of Poland, Czechoslovakia, Hungary and former Yugoslavia (especially Slovenia and Croatia) than in poorer Romania, Bulgaria and Albania. At the same time, people living in urban areas tended to enjoy higher standards of living than those in the countryside, provoking mass migration to the cities.

Decay in the system

The region's leaders were also unwilling to admit that, from the 1970s, standards of welfare began to fall. This was very clearly shown in the provision of housing. Socialist principles considered accommodation to be a basic right, irrespective of ability to pay. To achieve this, largescale building projects were undertaken from the 1950s until, on average, governments in the region owned more than half of all housing. This allowed rents to be kept very low, ranging from 2

Pro-life campaigning *(above)* An antiabortion poster pinned to the door of a Catholic church in Warsaw. Under Soviet influence, abortion was encouraged throughout the region. As the Catholic church regains influence, the tide of opinion is turning the other way.

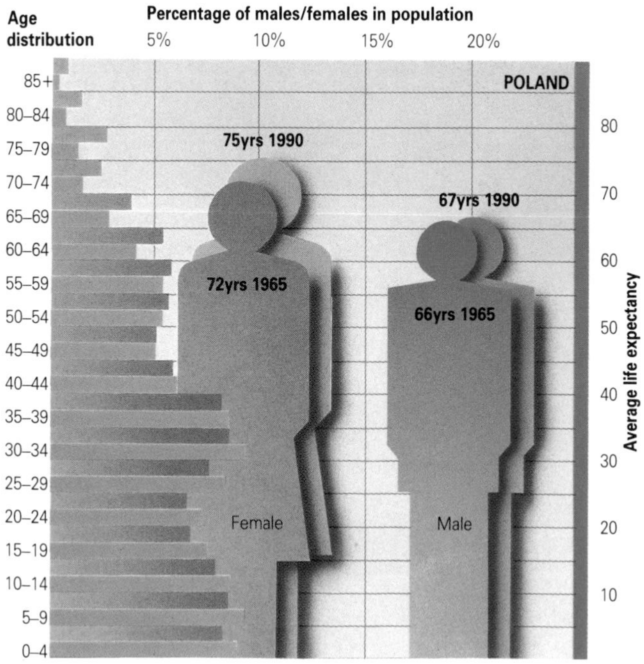

Flying the flag for Slovakian consumers *(above)* Like most stores throughout the region, the Prior department store in the Slovakian capital, Bratislava, has begun to stock Western consumer goods. Before Eastern Europe's revolutions in the late 1980s, most of the goods on sale in state stores were cheap domestic and regionally made products. Foreign goods were only available in special hard currency shops. Now Western goods are everywhere.

Life expectancy and age distribution *(left)* Life expectancy in Poland has risen comparatively little over the 25 years from 1965 to 1990, there have even been times during that period when life expectancy began to fall. In Poland and throughout the region average life expectancy is still significantly shorter than in most Western countries, particularly for men. Birth rates dropped during the 1970s and 1980s, but are rising again.

to 3 percent of average national income in Czechoslovakia to 4.5 percent in Bulgaria.

However, in the 1970s, when the region's economies began to stall and governments found their income was falling, it became increasingly hard to afford new construction. Old buildings became run down and were not replaced, bringing accommodation shortages that were especially acute in large cities such as Warsaw, Sofia and Budapest. Here it was by no means unusual for newly married couples to have to live with their parents in cramped conditions because nothing else was available. In Hungary studies linked the country's suicide rate, which was the highest in Europe, with overcrowded housing conditions.

Healthcare followed a similar pattern of rapid decline during the 1980s. In the hospitals, old equipment became run down and obsolete, while high-technology Western replacements could not be provided because of shortages of hard currency. At the same time, ideological priorities required hospital staff to be paid low wages in comparison with other workers, forcing many doctors to enter the illegal "shadow economy", where bribes and gratuities were paid for urgent or specialist treatment. In Poland by the late 1980s nearly one-third of all hospitals were considered unsuitable for use.

Welfare in reverse

The breakdown of Eastern Europe's welfare systems was accelerated by debt problems. Poland and Hungary, which were the largest borrowers and had become partially dependent on Western institutions, found themselves obliged to introduce economic reforms, including reductions in state subsidies. Consumer prices rose steeply, creating a new underclass of vulnerable groups, including the elderly, those with large families and some ethnic minorities, such as Hungary's large gypsy population. All across the region there were increases in alcohol abuse, poor nutrition and other forms of unhealthy living. Most striking of all, life expectancy, which had been increasing in the 1950s and 1960s, and which continued to rise in the West, actually began to fall in Eastern Europe. This slow collapse in the very welfare systems that had been held up as proof of the socialist achievement undoubtedly played an important part in the downfall of the region's Marxist regimes in 1989.

WOMEN'S WORK IN POLAND

The collapse of communist rule in Poland, though widely welcomed in the country, has been of uncertain benefit to Polish women. A leading aim of the socialist government was to secure full employment for all the population, irrespective of gender. This was largely achieved – though women were rarely represented equally at high levels – and 90 percent of Polish women of working age were employed before 1989.

Working was often a necessity rather than a right. A labor-intensive economy and inefficiently organized workforce produced a chronic labor shortage with a resulting high demand for female labor. At the same time the economy was a low-income one, and in most households two wages were essential to balance the budget. Yet working undoubtedly suited many women.

One consequence of the collapse of communism has been that many women have lost their jobs. In 1989, 52 percent of the workforce was female, but after three years of postcommunist rule the percentage had fallen to only 45.4. This was partly because the industries where women tended to dominate, such as textiles, proved the least able to compete on the world market.

At the same time, it became more difficult for women to go out to work. The already overburdened childcare facilities supported by the socialist regime were cut back in an effort to cut costs and mothers came under pressure to stay at home. Traditional Roman Catholic attitudes promoting large families also enjoyed a resurgence of influence. For those women who wanted or needed to work, the end of communism has undoubtedly brought new hardships.

Privatizing Hungary

Since 1989 Hungary, like its Eastern European neighbors, has embarked on a thorough overhaul of its economy. At the heart of these changes, central planning has been abandoned and state control of the means of production has been replaced by private ownership. Hungary's economic future has been staked on these reforms, which are intended to bring to its people a standard of living comparable to those of western European countries.

Goulash communism

The country has had a head start in converting from socialism to a market economy. Pre-1989-Hungary, like Poland and Yugoslavia, already possessed a growing private sector. As early as 1968, important reforms were introduced to bring greater flexibility to the Hungarian economy. Mostly this was an effort to appease the widespread discontent that followed the failed 1956 Hungarian revolution. The "New Economic Mechanism" dating from that era allowed individuals to create small businesses and cooperatives. At the same time, decision-making in state-run industries was devolved from central ministries to local factory managers who were more in touch with the daily problems of manufacturing. These changes – which became known as "Goulash Communism" – brought relative prosperity to the country, making it the envy of other Eastern European states.

Building on this advantage, Hungary quickly took the lead within Eastern Europe in terms of moving toward a market system. Soon after the country's revolution in 1989 a new enterprise law was introduced which allowed state industries to be privatized. Efforts were made to free prices from state regulation, and a stock market – the first in the region – was established. Hungary moved quickly to replace the state bank with commercial banks, which soon began to play an important role in funding new small businesses.

Attracting Western support

Western investment was crucial to the success of privatization. Most potential investors were impressed by Hungary's relative political stability and its progress

Barbie goes to Budapest (*right*) Trams in the Hungarian capital advertise one of the classic American consumer goods – Barbie dolls. After decades of controlled supply, Eastern Europeans are being introduced to the free market and mass advertising.

toward parliamentary democracy, as well as by its developed infrastructure and skilled but cheap labor force. In 1992 nearly half of all foreign investment to Eastern Europe went to Hungary. Much of this took the form of support for joint-venture schemes. The Hungarian government offered attractive incentives to foreign corporations, including tax benefits, the ability to own 100 percent of Hungarian companies and the right to export profits. By 1992 over 5,000 joint ventures had been established in the country, with German corporations at the forefront, followed by Austrian investors who often had historical, political and economic ties with Hungary.

Although Hungary was certainly the most successful Eastern European state in adapting to the world market, it still faces considerable problems. Freeing prices from state control proved more difficult to achieve than the government anticipated. By 1992, 90 percent of producer prices had been liberated, but most consumer prices remained artificially fixed. Despite this, high inflation broke out, causing widespread hardship.

In the early 1990s the government also had to come to terms with the fact that many state-owned industries proved impossible to privatize, as they were too outdated and unprofitable to attract investors. Particularly affected were the large industrial cities east of Budapest, where many iron, steel and chemical plants had to close down, throwing one-third of the labor force out of work.

As trade with other Comecon states fell and trade with the Soviet Union virtually collapsed, selling to Western countries began to pose new problems. Hungary's famous bus manufacturer, Ikarus, is a typical example of the country's export difficulties. Ikarus must improve the quality of its buses to make them attractive to the West, yet the cost of doing so threatens to price them out of the world market. Even in Hungary, the most Westernized of the region's economies, embracing capitalism will not prove easy.

Birth of a stock exchange (*below*) The first stock exchange in Eastern Europe was set up in Budapest. It started on a small scale (not many companies had been floated on the market) but is growing all the time as new companies start up.

THE SHOCK OF CAPITALISM

FORCED PROGRESS · THE EMPIRE STRIKES BACK · THE NORTH–SOUTH DIVIDE

The economies of the republics of Northern Eurasia have long been closely knit together. As Russia came to dominate the region after 1700, a distinctive economic style became evident among them, with the state playing a vital role, trying to bring about rapid modernization. After the Bolshevik revolution of 1917 the new Soviet economy became increasingly centralized. Policies were isolationist, with little foreign trade except with satellite allies. Rapid growth was achieved at first and the Soviet Union became an economic superpower. However, this achievement was not sustainable and by 1991 socialist planning collapsed, as did the Soviet Union itself. In the 15 newly independent republics there is an emphasis on free market policies and trade with new foreign partners. An innovative and unpredictable era has begun.

FORCED PROGRESS

As it began to edge on to the international scene at the beginning of the modern era, Russia – though rich in natural resources and an important exporter of flax, hemp, fur and timber – was economically underdeveloped compared with its western European neighbors. Its lack of entrepreneurial energy and innovation threatened the empire's military effectiveness in its many wars. Peter the Great (1682–1725) was the first ruler to try to force development by pursuing policies of rapid modernization from above. British and Dutch experts were brought to Russia and the tzarist government established new manufacturing plants, notably ironworks, turning the region into one of the world's leading iron producers within a single generation.

Such rapid growth could not be sustained for long. By the mid 19th century the Russian empire, which had expanded southward and eastward into central Asia was still economically underdeveloped. Only 7 percent of the population were employed in the urban–industrial sector, compared with 50 percent in England during the same period. Again the government took the lead in investment and development, creating a huge rail network that culminated in the Trans-Siberian railroad (constructed from 1891

Home-grown designer capitalism (*below*) comes to Moscow with a fashion show that draws on Russia's Cossack and Communist heritage. A sign of the changing times, such a show cuts across the former emphasis on drab, inexpensive, utilitarian clothes.

COUNTRIES IN THE REGION

Armenia, Azerbaijan, Belorussia, Estonia, Georgia, Kazakhstan, Kirghizia, Latvia, Lithuania, Moldavia, Mongolia, Russia, Tajikistan, Turkmenistan, Ukraine, Uzbekistan

ECONOMIC INDICATORS: 1990

	UMIE* Latvia	UMIE* Russia	LMIE* Uzbekistan
NMP (US$ billions)	12.6	680.2	38.5
NMP per capita (US$)	4,694	4,579	1,857
Labor force employed in agriculture (%)	16.2	13.2	32.0
Labor force employed in industry (%)	29.8	30.9	16.8
Merchandise exports as % of NMP (including to other ex-Soviet States)	70.0	26.6	n/a
Merchandise imports as % of NMP (including from other ex-Soviet States)	74.9	36.1	n/a

WELFARE INDICATORS

Infant mortality rate (per 1,000 live births)			
1970	17.9	23.0	31.0
1989	11.0	18.9	43.3
Population per physician (1988)	49.9	46.7	35.1
Students in higher education (per 1,000 population, 1989)	170	193	163

Note: Net Material Product (NMP) is a measure of economic performance often used by communist countries. It is defined as the total net value of goods and productive services produced by the economy. It excludes economic activities such as public administration, defense and personal and professional services.

** UMIE (Upper Middle Income Economy) – GNP per capita between $2,465 and $7,620 in 1990. LMIE (Lower Middle Income Economy) – GNP per capita between $610 and $2,465 in 1990.*

Map of NMP (*above*) Net Material Product was the standard measure of economic performance used by the former Soviet Union. It was calculated as the total value of goods and productive services generated by the economy in any given year, excluding the value of administration, defense and personal services. Isolated from the world economy from 1917 to 1991, the region has none of the world's top 500 banks or companies.

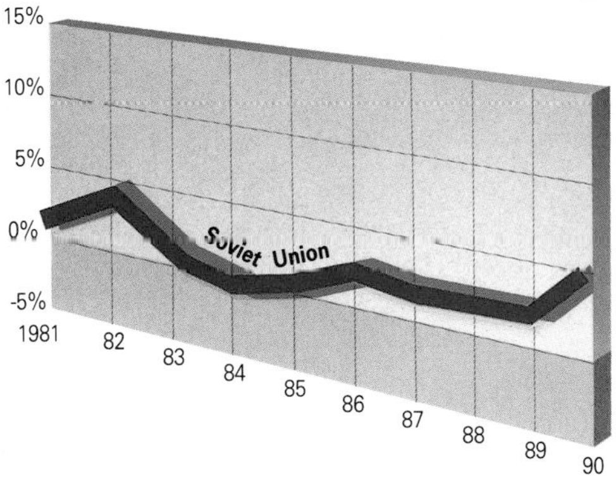

Profile of inflation (*above*) Intervention by the central planners of the former Soviet Union kept inflation low and figures were often manipulated to bolster the region's image. Sharp increases followed the collapse of the Soviet Union in 1991.

to 1915) connecting the industrial heartland west of the Urals with the largely untapped resources of Siberia in the east. Improved transportation and communications gave a fresh boost to the economy. Although the new infrastructure struggled with bad weather and the sheer distances involved, by the outbreak of World War I the Russian empire was an emerging industrial power.

The Communist state

The pressures of rapid economic change played an important part in provoking the Bolshevik revolution of 1917. The leaders of the revolution aimed to create a classless and socially just society, and the role of the state in economic development became greater than ever before. Under the leadership of the first head of the Soviet Union, Vladimir Ilich Lenin (1870–1924), all banks and property were nationalized, though private enterprise was allowed to remain in the countryside, where peasants sold their own produce at market prices. Under Joseph Stalin (1879–1953) this practice was abandoned and the state established collective farms.

From 1928 the economy was directed through a series of Five Year Plans. State terror was widely used to force the cooperation of the workforce, with millions uprooted from the countryside and moved into large industrial complexes. State ownership was extended throughout the region, even to Outer Mongolia, which had become part of the Soviet orbit. Driven by the need to increase the country's military strength, the emphasis was on heavy industry – particularly manufacturing arms and weapons. Housing, agriculture and public services suffered neglect. Yet these policies transformed the country, enabling it to play a vital role in the defeat of Nazi Germany.

The post-Stalinist economy

Significant changes occurred after Stalin's death in 1953. Greater priority was given to housing and rural development and state terror was gradually abandoned as a tool of economic policy. At first these changes were welcomed by Soviet citizens, since they brought with them a higher standard of living. In the long term, however, they exposed weaknesses in the economic system. With state terror removed, the people lacked an incentive to work. Innovation was stifled and the Soviet Union failed to keep pace with developments in the capitalist world, particularly in high technology. The transportation system was increasingly inefficient, while the economy suffered under the military budget maintaining the Soviet Union as a superpower. By the early 1980s the economy was threatening to stall. A major crisis was looming.

THE EMPIRE STRIKES BACK

As discontent and criticism of the Soviet regime reached a peak in the late 1980s, the weaknesses of the state-run economy became common knowledge both at home and abroad. The Soviet economic system resembled a giant corporation with an overbureaucratized center. In Moscow the state planning agency (Gosplan) and the economic ministries controlled the economy of the entire Soviet Union. Their Five Year Plans made decisions for factories thousands of miles away, specifying which items should be manufactured and the precise quantities to be produced. Little attention was paid to how much public demand existed, nor to the actual factory costs of production. Consequently goods were often manufactured at a loss, while the absence of any kind of quality control encouraged waste. The highly centralized system also stifled local initiatives to improve the product or the system as the crucial decisions were made by officials too distant to comprehend local issues.

The economy functioned best when organizing prestigious priority projects in which the leadership showed personal interest, such as weapons production or channeling investment to exploit the oil and gas resources of western Siberia. Lower-profile manufacturing and production of consumer goods including clothes, furniture and foodstuffs were dogged by poor workmanship and inefficient distribution, causing shortages. It was clear that the economic system was in urgent need of reform, yet change from within proved difficult to achieve, especially as the ideology of the system allowed little in the way of objective self-assessment or admission of failure. During the late 1950s Soviet Premier, Nikita Khrushchev (1894–1971), tried to tackle the overcentralized planning system but his efforts came to nothing. Only a generation later, when total national production had actually begun to shrink, was a thorough and radical effort made to regenerate the economic system.

Attempted restructuring

Mikhail Gorbachev, who assumed power in March 1985, initiated a program of *perestroika* or economic restructuring. One strand of this policy was to modernize factory equipment, much of which had not been updated since the 1930s. At the same time, smallscale private enterprise was encouraged in the form of cooperatives, especially in the service sector which had never functioned well under the old Soviet system. An effort was also made to decentralize, with local factory managers given greater control over production. Industrial plants were encouraged to be financially independent, while the more efficient among them were to be rewarded with greater government investment and higher pay for workers. This last measure introduced a kind of state-controlled profit motive.

Lastly, the Soviet Union was opened up to the world economy. Until the mid 1980s more than half of Soviet trade had been with the socialist states and military allies that made up the COMECON bloc. From 1987 most Soviet enterprises were

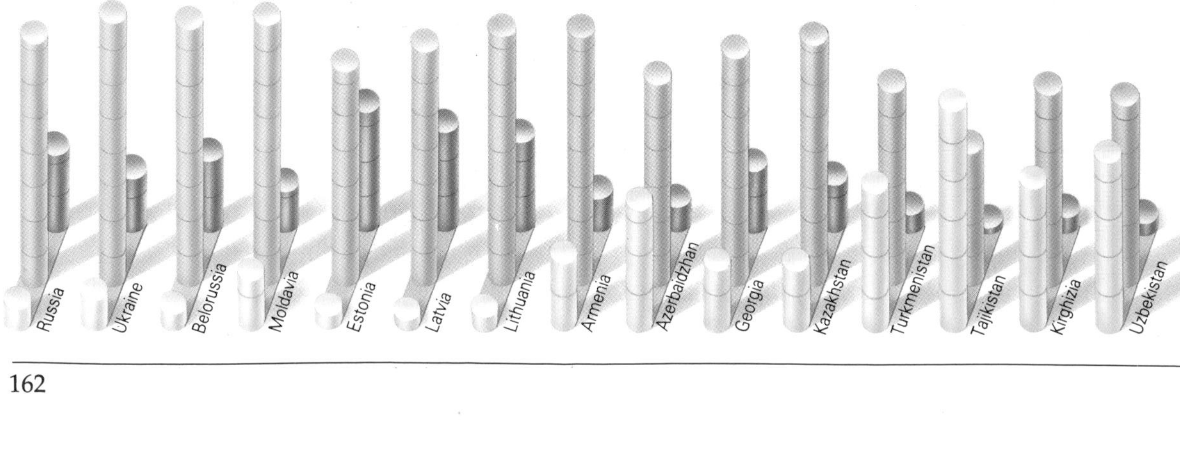

Income distribution in the Eurasian republics Incomes are higher in the Baltics – Latvia, Estonia and Lithuania – which broke away early from the Soviet Union. The southern republics are very poor.

Income distribution (10% units)

more than 200 rubles per month

75–200 rubles per month

less than 75 rubles per month

OPENING THE DOOR TO TRADE

In 1987 nearly 70 years of isolation from the capitalist world economy were ended when Mikhail Gorbachev opened the Soviet Union to trade with Western companies as part of his *perestroika* program. He hoped that numerous joint-venture schemes would develop between foreign and local enterprises. Western companies would be invited to contribute vital management skills and high technology in exchange for access to the Soviet Union's wealth of resources and to its market of 280 million people. In spite of these high hopes, joint ventures were slow to develop and by 1991 only 3,000 had been established, accounting for a paltry 2 percent of trade with the West.

After the collapse of the Soviet Union the independent republics opened the door to Western trade even wider. Restrictions on where Western companies could operate were lifted and there were moves toward creating free-enterprise zones. The Russian Pacific coast, for example, was designated as an area for Japanese investment.

These initiatives encouraged Western companies to take greater interest in the region, but foreign enthusiasm was dampened by the world recession. The republics most likely to attract investment are those with the most to offer in terms of resources and communications, such as Russia, Ukraine and the Baltic states. In the short term, at least, the central Asian republics may become even more isolated.

Turning culture into cash *(left)* Hand-painted trinkets are for sale at an artist's shop in Tsalinograd, Kazakhstan. Small enterprises such as this are already flourishing, and may serve a future tourist trade.

The Trans-Siberian express market *(below)* Passengers traveling from Mongolia sell goods from the train to local people along the journey to Moscow. Some foods and other products are available in China, across the southern border, but not in Russia.

prompted to enter into joint ventures with capitalist investors. These changes, it was hoped, would bring the region into the modern market economy, with enhanced efficiency, improved technology and greater commitment from the workforce.

Unfortunately the *perestroika* program did not cure the region's economic problems; if anything it hastened decline. The Soviet Union's entrenched centralized bureaucracy hampered the independence of the cooperatives and the managers of state factories. Little economic initiative occurred except in the black market, perhaps because the country's culture had for so long been set against the idea of private enterprise.

In spite of well-intentioned efforts to the contrary, the old structure of centralized economic decision-making remained largely unaltered. For example, armaments production continued despite the ending of the Cold War and in the full knowledge that the state could no longer afford new weaponry. The reason given was that it proved impossible to retool arms factories to produce consumer goods; nor could they be closed, as this would have created widespread unemployment. In St Petersburg no fewer than one in four of the city's labor force were dependent on the arms production at the Kirov military–industrial complex.

Dissent and fragmentation

As *perestroika* continued, the attempted reforms themselves began to have a destructive effect on the economy. Elements within the previously loyal bureaucracy grew resentful at challenges to their power and prestige. Claims were made of deliberate obstruction and sabotage from within the economic administration. Corruption, too, became a growing problem. The transport system deteriorated, bringing further waste, especially of perishable foodstuffs. By the summer of 1991 it was clear that six years of *perestroika* had failed to bring regeneration, and that the state was continuing to suffer falling production and widespread shortages. In the wake of these realizations, the government acknowledged a huge growth in the Soviet budget deficit, which increased from 15 billion roubles in 1985 to 200 billion by 1991. In short, the planned economy had shown itself to be beyond reform. This disastrous failure undoubtedly contributed to the collapse of confidence among the country's ruling elite that played such an important part in the disintegration of the whole Soviet Union at the end of 1991.

Learning to dance *(above)* Ballet was part of the curriculum for kindergarten children such as these in Khabarovsk, eastern Russia in 1988. Generous state-funding for the arts, assured under the Communist system, is now threatened.

THE NORTH–SOUTH DIVIDE

One of the main aims of the founders of the Soviet Union was to create an equal and just society and to ensure the wellbeing of the population. During three generations of Soviet state rule, average living standards certainly improved, helped by the growing urbanization and industrialization of the country. At the same time, free healthcare and education became available to all Soviet citizens, irrespective of social or ethnic background. Improved healthcare caused a leap in average life expectancy from 32 years before the 1917 revolution to as much as 70 years in the 1970s.

By the late 1980s illiteracy had largely been eradicated and the region could boast greater numbers of students entering higher education than probably any other region in the world. Unemployment was virtually nonexistent, as the state placed a premium on the right of every worker to have a job. At the same time the centrally controlled wage structure ensured that income differentials between professions remained much smaller than in market-economy states.

Spreading power around

Soviet leaders also strove to create social equality between different regions of the country, and between the cities and the countryside. The economic planners in Moscow were particularly concerned with the five mainly Muslim republics of central Asia (Turkmenistan, Uzbekistan, Tajikistan, Kirghizia and Kazakhstan), which lagged behind the European part of the country in terms of development. Largescale investment was made in these republics in an effort to give them a manufacturing base; they were also allowed to retain most of their contributions to the federal budget. Local people were promoted to key positions within their republics so as to create upward mobility into the local Communist Party, government administration and the professions.

These measures had some limited success, but the north–south economic divide proved an enduring one. Central Asians did begin to rise through their republics' hierarchies – but Russians continued to hold numerous key posts. At the same time poverty remained more common in central Asia than in European republics. In 1991, on the eve of the collapse of the Soviet Union, it was estimated that 11 percent of the country's total population lived below the poverty line while in the five central Asian republics the proportion was 40 percent. Despite the efforts of the country's rulers huge economic disparities also existed between the towns and the countryside. In central Asia, as throughout the Soviet Union, rural areas remained significantly poorer than the cities.

Disadvantaged farmers

One reason for the enduring north–south divide was the government's policy of paying more to industrial workers than to agricultural laborers, reflecting an ideological preference for the work of the proletariat. Despite the investment program designed to create an industrial base, central Asia remained predominantly agricultural. Consequently its population enjoyed none of the favorable treatment which, in some northern industrial complexes, extended to providing workers with public services ranging from housing to kindergartens. The five central Asian republics also suffered from high birthrates, which meant a greater proportion of their populations were too young to contribute to the economy. In 1989 the average birth rate in the whole Soviet Union was 10 births per thousand, while in central Asia the proportion varied from 23 per thousand in Kazakhstan to as many as 38.7 per thousand in Tajikistan.

Nor was it possible for central Asians to migrate to wealthier areas, which would be the normal pattern in Western economies. The Soviet state's commitment to full employment tended to keep them within their republics. Indeed, for some decades central Asia was a recipient of labor, as Russians and other European nationalities were sent south to provide managerial and administrative skills. Only from the mid 1970s did this migration become reversed. Between 1976 and 1988 as may as 1.6 million Russians and other Europeans left central Asia, with the exodus considerably increasing after the five republics became independent in 1991.

The collapse of the Soviet Union was of doubtful economic benefit to the central Asian states. It put an end to Moscow's generous investment in employment and education and its beneficial financial policies, as well as threatening to halt the supplies of Siberian oil and gas that had previously been provided at well below market costs. At the same time, the southern economy faced the daunting prospect of restructuring after years of central planning, with the added pressure of a rising population. The future promised to be a challenging one.

THE BLACK ECONOMY

The Soviet system always included a mainly private "second economy" that existed alongside the state sector and provided the products that it was largely unable to deliver. Some aspects of this parallel economy, such as private agriculture, were only tolerated by the regime, while others, ranging from car repairs to dentistry, were accepted as forming an integral part of the system. In all, the "second economy" contributed a staggering 10 percent of total national production throughout the Soviet era.

Since the collapse of the Soviet Union in 1991 the "second economy" has expanded rapidly, until it is well on the way to displacing the first economy. At the same time, however, illegal black market enterprises have also flourished. These range from trade in sought-after foreign goods (jeans, video-recorders) to organized crime, including prostitution, drug-trading and selling goods pilfered from state factories. The "Mafia type" black-market sector was estimated to be worth as much as 500 billion roubles in the early 1990s, and to have spawned no fewer than 150,000 rouble millionaires. It quickly became a major problem for the region's post-Soviet leaders. The challenge in all the republics is to find a way of replacing the discredited planned economy with the advantages of a market system, while avoiding the worst excesses of capitalism.

Black market in a suitcase *(above)* A speculator sells vodka illegally to a passerby at a figure far above the market price. Huge profits can be made by street vendors as they try to meet the demand for alcohol and other goods in short supply. Foreign-made clothes, shoes, electronics, and drugs are all commonly sold from suitcases.

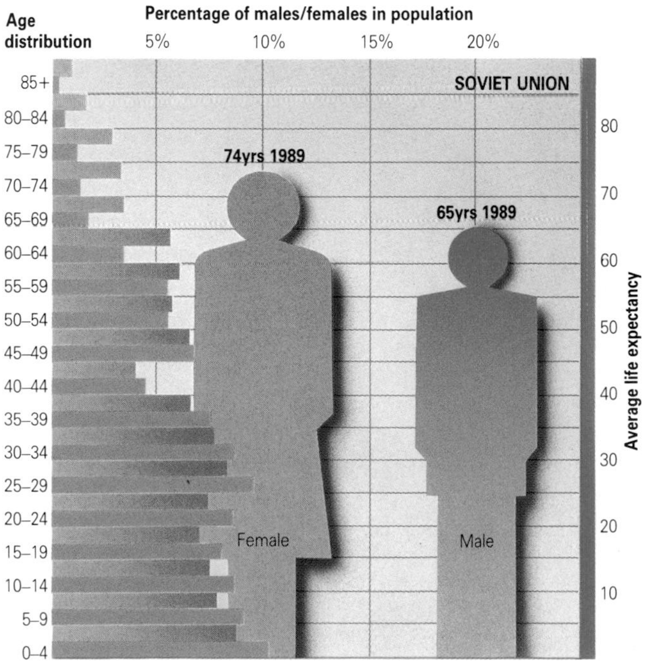

Life expectancy and age distribution *(left)* Life expectancy in the Soviet Union in 1989 was slightly lower than the average for Europe and North America in the same year. Women could expect to live almost a decade longer than men. The result over the long term has been that a high percentage of elderly women in the region are widows. Population growth slowed after the postwar baby boom of the 1950s, creating a pattern familiar to most developed countries of steadily falling birthrates and increasing numbers of elderly people.

Economic sovereignty and its limits

The rejection of communism that followed the failed coup of August 20th 1991 dissolved the glue holding together the last of the European multiethnic empires. The leaders of the 15 independent republics that emerged from the ruins of the Soviet Union abruptly found themselves in control of their countries' economies for the first time. A wealth of new possibilities blossomed, followed closely by a host of new problems.

Governments all across the region began exploring how to use their new economic sovereignty. Setting up new financial institutions was a priority, including banking and tax systems, national currencies, and border controls that brought the possibility of protectionist tariffs. Each republic sought to find a niche for itself within the global economy, and to foster new trade partnerships across previously closed frontiers. The republics of central Asia began developing ties with Turkey, China and Iran, while the three Baltic states (Latvia, Lithuania and Estonia) looked toward the Nordic countries and the European Community. All across the region there was a move to the free market, though individual states soon began to follow different paths toward this end. The Muslim republics of the south showed interest in east Asian models of economic growth (Singapore and South Korea). At the same time the European states (Russia, Belorussia, Ukraine, Moldavia) considered a range of possibilities, from letting the market forces take control to imitating the Nordic countries' combination of market economy and exemplary welfare policies. One aim shared by all the republics was the wish to escape the old system of central planning. Yet this did not prove easy to accomplish.

Unpicking the network

A leading feature of Soviet rule had been the encouragement of specialization in different parts of the region. For example, Uzbekistan became the Soviet Union's main source of cotton, while Azerbijan produced equipment for the oil industry, and Georgia grew citrus fruits. Such a system entailed considerable internal trade and created an extensive economic interdependency between republics that would not be easy to escape. This was true even of a large republic such as Ukraine, which possessed a significant manufacturing base and a population of 52 million. Before 1991, almost 40 percent of Ukraine's net material product (NMP, its total industrial and agricultural production excluding any nonproductive services) took the form of exports to other republics. As its coal industry declined, Ukraine had grown increasingly reliant on oil and gas supplies from Russia, provided at well below international market prices. After the 1991 disintegration Russia ceased selling fuel cheaply.

Russia seemed to suffer least from the collapse of the Soviet empire. The richest republic in natural resources, possessing significant mineral deposits as well as three-quarters of the land area of the former Soviet Union and half its population, it is responsible for 61 percent of manufacturing and agricultural output in the region and 90 percent of oil production, mostly based in Siberia. In fact the dissolution of the soviet system meant that Russia simply stopped trying to subsidize the poorer republics. Russia was also less dependent on inter-republic trade than its neighbors – in 1988 exports to other republics made up only 18 percent of Russian NMP. Its wealth of resources – especially oil and gas – provided useful bargaining chips to secure trade agreements with Western states.

Although Russia enjoyed the brightest prospects in the region, transformation to a market economy still did not promise to be easy. In January 1992 President Boris Yeltsin introduced measures to allow widespread privatization of the state sector, but problems soon emerged as little capital was available. Western investment was encouraged, but foreign companies showed some reluctance. The freeing of price controls brought hyperinflation and threatened social unrest. At the same time much of the country's production suffered from overmanning and obsolete equipment. Extensive economic renewal would not be achieved overnight.

The cost of *perestroika* An old man in Tallinn, Estonia, counts his money carefully before making a purchase. The end of state price controls caused enormous increases in the cost of basic necessities. Old People were particularly badly affected.

"Lenin is a cheater" (*right*) One of Russia's new homeless underclass makes his opinions known outside a shack not far from the Kremlin. Outspoken criticism of the early Soviet thinkers has become common, but poverty and upheaval makes those trying to manage the transition unpopular as well.

brainless bone-head
Lenin IS A cheater
КПСС ЭТИМИ
ПУЗЫРЯМИ 73г.
ДОМА НЕТ.

The consumer-goods revolution

All across the former Soviet Union industrial plants that used to make a single product are attempting to transform into market-sensitive businesses to serve the region's new consumers.

A large number of public-sector firms are being turned over to local management teams and these enterprises are expected to run at a profit and to sell their goods in markets which are no longer guaranteed by the state. In the long run this should encourage such factories to diversify their production bases and to improve the quality of the goods that they are trying to sell.

Some engineering plants are already beginning to manufacture components for automobiles, refrigerators, televisions and washing machines. New forms of contract are developing to link such enterprises together and turn them into efficient producers of components for new consumer-goods industries. In the short-term, however, the re-equipping of deregulated public-sector factories is proving very difficult. The new managers of such factories often lack the managerial skills that would be taken for granted in Europe, Japan and the United States and the cost of retooling factories can sometimes be prohibitive. Survival in the new world of the postsocialist economy is by no means guaranteed. The risk of failure is high, and an emerging private sector is offering them stiff competition.

Heating elements for washing machines, part of the new product range at the Tselinogradselmash industrial plant in Akmola, Kazakhstan. The plant was formally a single-product manufacturer of agricultural machinery.

STRIKING IT RICH

EMPIRES IN THE DESERT · THE MAINSTAYS OF WEALTH · INVESTING IN CARE

The countries of the Middle East contain some of the greatest extremes of wealth and poverty to be found in any part of the modern world. In spite of its rich cultural heritage and the extent of its former empires, the region lay outside the heartland of capitalist development in the 17th, 18th and 19th centuries. It was only with the exploitation of its oil resources in the second half of the 20th century that the Middle East wielded economic power again on the world stage. On a national scale, the oil-rich states of the Gulf are immensely more wealthy than neighboring states such as Afghanistan and Yemen which have no significant oil deposits. On a human scale, income, education and healthcare are by no means equally distributed even within the wealthier states, and poverty is still rife in almost every country.

COUNTRIES IN THE REGION

Afghanistan, Bahrain, Iran, Iraq, Israel, Jordan, Kuwait, Lebanon, Oman, Qatar, Saudi Arabia, Syria, Turkey, United Arab Emirates, Yemen

ECONOMIC INDICATORS: 1990

	HIE* UAE	UMIE* Saudi Ar.	LMIE* Jordan
GDP (US$ billions)	28.27	80.89	3.33
GNP per capita (US$)	19,860	7,050	1,240
Annual rate of growth of GDP, 1980–1990 (%)	−4.5	−1.8	4.3
Manufacturing as % of GDP	9	9	12
Central government spending as % of GNP	13	n/a	39
Merchandise exports (US$ billions)	15.0	44.4	1.15
Merchandise imports (US$ billions)	9.6	24	2.66
% of GNP donated as development aid	2.65	3.9	–†

WELFARE INDICATORS

Infant mortality rate (per 1,000 live births)			
1965	103	148	114
1990	23	65	51
Daily food supply available (calories per capita, 1989)	3,309	2,874	2,634
Population per physician (1984)	1,020	730	860
Teacher–pupil ratio (primary school, 1989)	1 : 18	1 : 16	1 : 28

Note: The Gross Domestic Product (GDP) is the total value of all goods and services domestically produced. The Gross National Product (GNP) is the GDP plus net income from abroad.

** HIE (High Income Economy) – GNP per capita above $7,620 in 1990. UMIE (Upper Middle Income Economy) – GNP per capita between $2,465 and $7,620. LMIE (Lower Middle Income Economy) – GNP per capita between $610 and $2,465.*

† Jordan is a recipient of development aid.

Bringing in cars by the boatload (*above*) at the port of Dammam, Saudi Arabia. With plenty of cheap domestic fuel to run them, this is one of the few places in the world where large American-made luxury automobiles are as popular as more economical Japanese models.

EMPIRES IN THE DESERT

The Middle East has played a pivotal role in the world economy for almost as long as records exist. Some 7,000 years ago, its farming villages produced the agricultural surpluses that allowed the rise of the great civilizations of Mesopotamia, Babylon and Assyria. In the centuries that followed, powerful trading networks were forged between Mesopotamia (Iraq), Anatolia (Turkey), Syria, Persia (Iran) and India. By the time Islam began to spread in the 7th and 8th centuries AD, the region contained many distinct trading centers. The advent of the Turkish Ottoman empire in the 14th century brought all these within one centralized economic area. After the Turks captured Constantinople in 1453, renaming it Istanbul, the city became the wealthiest in the region. It was the hub of a complex economic system dominated by flows of tribute from conquered peoples, and by trade with Europe and Asia.

The impact of oil

During the 17th, 18th and 19th centuries, the Middle East languished economically. This began to change in 1908 after oil was struck by a British consortium in Iran at the Masjid-al-Sulaiman well. The discovery of commercially exploitable deposits of oil on the Gulf island of Bahrain in 1932 (the first oil strike in the Arab world, and one which revitalized the Bahraini economy after the collapse of its pearl-fishing industry) was followed by strikes in Kuwait and Saudi Arabia in 1938. Throughout the 1930s and 1940s, American and British oil companies continued to obtain concessions for oil-prospecting in the region. They were given exclusive rights of drilling and ownership of all the oil produced, in exchange for an initial payment and a limited share of profits or a fixed royalty.

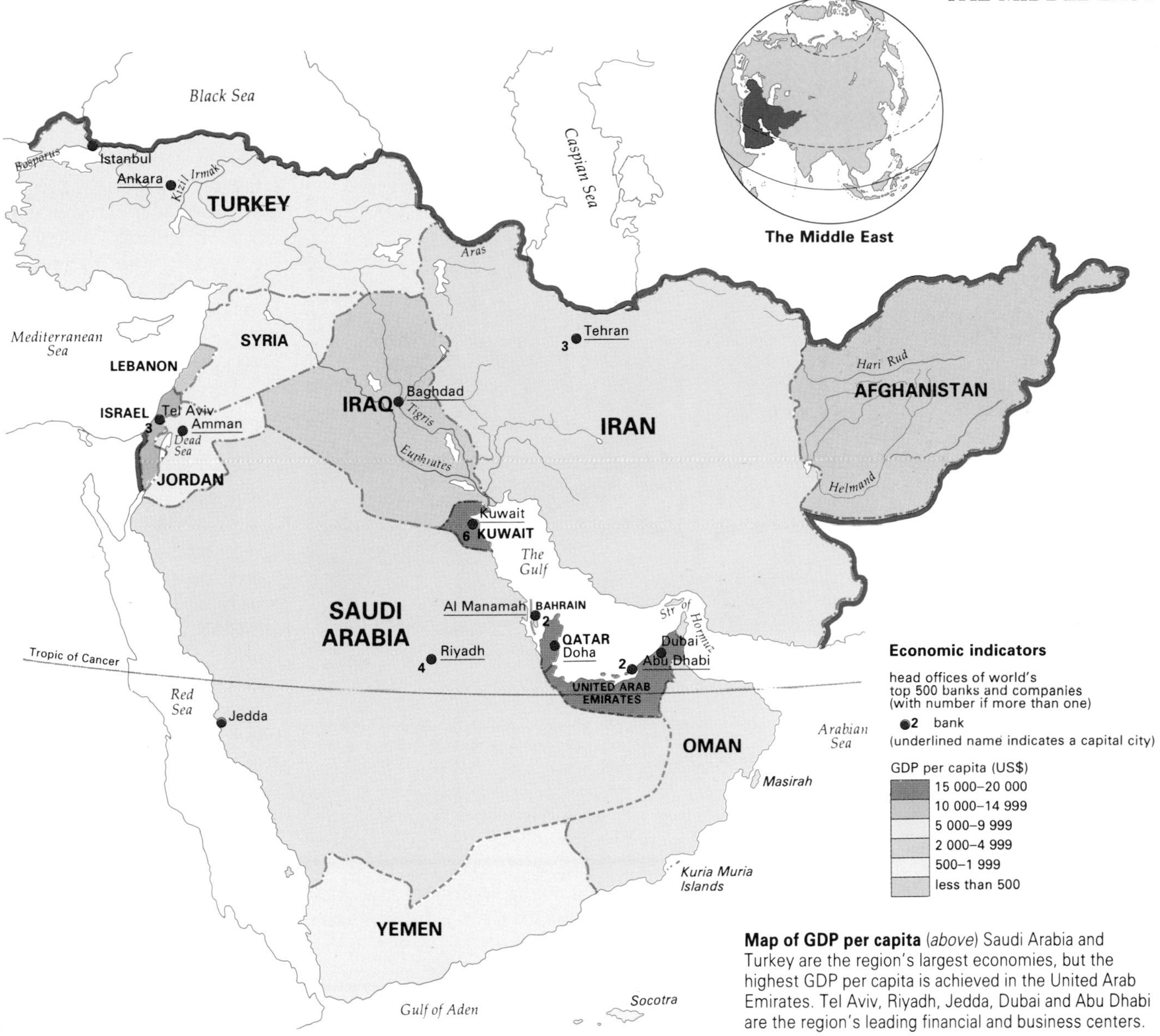

Map of GDP per capita *(above)* Saudi Arabia and Turkey are the region's largest economies, but the highest GDP per capita is achieved in the United Arab Emirates. Tel Aviv, Riyadh, Jedda, Dubai and Abu Dhabi are the region's leading financial and business centers.

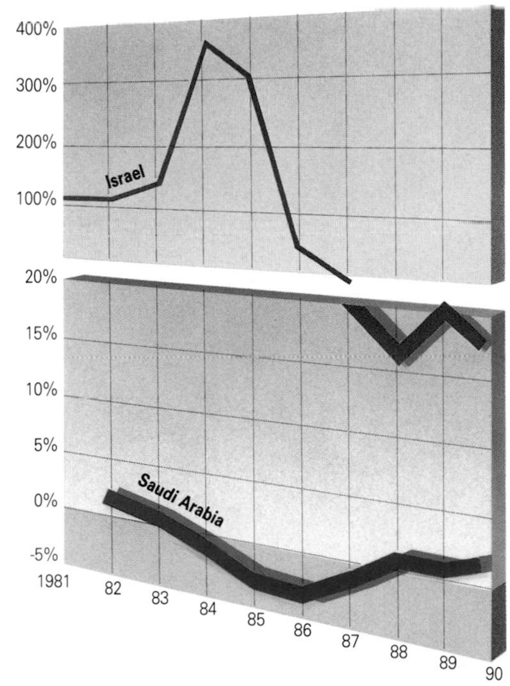

Profile of inflation *(above)* Saudi Arabia is one of the few countries in the world that has experienced recent negative inflation. Inflation rates in Israel are consistently high, but costs to the consumer are partially offset by index-linked wage rises.

After World War II, a fierce struggle born of growing nationalistic awareness developed between local governments and the oil companies over the concessions. Governments demanded more money from the companies, claiming they had sovereignty over the oil, and that the foreign companies were behaving like old-style colonialists. The companies argued that they took all the risks, invested capital in the countries and created wealth out of nothing. Saudi Arabia led the fight and, in late 1950, negotiated a new deal with the oil giants based on the principle that the profits would be split equally. Similar deals followed with Kuwait and Iraq.

In the first year alone, Saudi revenues doubled from $56.7 million to $110 million. But the oil states could not control pricing, which was determined by the foreign companies, such as Texaco, British Petroleum and Royal Dutch Shell. On 9 September 1960, the leading oil producers – Saudi Arabia, Iran, Iraq, Kuwait and Venezuela – formed the Organization of Petroleum Exporting Countries (OPEC) in protest at the cut in prices imposed that year by the oil companies.

By the 1970s, OPEC (with 13 member states, seven from outside the Middle East) had acquired tremendous economic and political influence. Oil had become the world's most important commodity in international trade and industry. In 1973, during the Arab–Israeli War, OPEC's Arab states flexed their muscles to political ends: they raised oil prices, reduced production and placed an embargo on the United States because it was supplying arms to Israel. Faced with such threats, the European Community (EC) quickly adopted a pro-Arab stance. For Western economies, however, the price rises of 1973–74 and 1979–80 had devastating effects, triggering inflation, worldwide recession and, finally, a reduced demand for oil. For the oil-exporting states, it meant an unprecedented inflow of money to fund development programs, buy armaments, and begin a period of extravagant spending in the West.

The spice trade survives *(above)* in a traditional souq or market in Oman. The region is still an important trading center for spices, but exports relatively little of its own produce. Less than 4 percent of Oman's GDP comes from agriculture.

THE MAINSTAYS OF WEALTH

The Middle East contains just under 60 percent of the world's known oil reserves. Since World War II, these and natural gas have been the mainstay of the economies of Saudi Arabia (whose oil reserves are estimated at more than 169 billion barrels – about a third of the world's total), Kuwait, the United Arab Emirates (UAE), Oman, Qatar and Bahrain. It was, in fact, Middle Eastern oil that helped fuel the recovery of a devastated Europe after 1945. Three other countries – Iran, Iraq and Syria – also produce oil, but have more diversified economies. In contrast, Afghanistan, Israel, Jordan, Lebanon, Turkey and Yemen, have no major oil reserves and have to rely on other economic activities.

The region's second most important economic activity – after oil – is agriculture, despite the harsh natural environment and the limited supplies of easily available water. In Iraq, for example, agriculture employs more people than any other sector of the economy, though oil accounts for 98 percent of exports, and Iraq is a net importer of food. In northern Iraq and Syria, water taken from the rivers Tigris and Euphrates enables thirsty crops, such as wheat, barley, vegetables and, especially, cotton, to be grown with considerable success.

Agriculture also forms the basis of Turkey's economy, and since World War II the country has made major economic strides, expanding its textile industry and exploiting its mineral reserves of coal, iron, copper and zinc. Turkey lies in the league of top 10 wheat-exporting countries, and is the world's largest supplier of figs, hazelnuts, raisins and oriental tobacco. A massive new project, the Ataturk dam in the Tigris and Euphrates basin, will irrigate a further 129,499 sq km (50,000 sq mi) of land, but is causing concern among Turkey's neighbors Iran, Iraq and especially Syria, who are dependent on the Euphrates for 90 percent of their water supply.

The Middle Eastern country that has, preeminently, turned to technology in the cause of economic growth is Israel. Having limited natural resources, Israel uses intensive farming, mechanization and advanced water engineering, such as "drip irrigation", to transform agricultural production. Although the number of people working on the land (particularly in kibbutzim, Israel's agricultural settlements), has dropped from 11 percent in 1950 to 5.4 percent in the mid 1980s, Israel still earns 10 percent of its income from exported agricultural products, such as cotton, citrus fruits, avocados, dates and melons. Its other major exports include weaponry, precious gems and jewelry.

The politics of trade

None of the Middle Eastern states is economically independent. Their trading patterns and links with the rest of the world often reflect the politics and ideological color of the region. Israel's economic survival is due largely to the financial aid given by the United States, and the support of Jewish people living in other parts of the world. Between 1948 and 1979, American Jews donated more than $3 billion through the United Israel Appeal alone. American money has also come from those wishing to invest in – rather than donate to – the country. Between 1951 and 1981, American Jews bought almost $5 billion worth of State of Israel Bonds. This money has helped Israel to drain malarial swamps, build oil pipelines, develop solar energy and create steel mills. The main donor of aid to Israel (often loans at preferential rates) remains the United States' government, which lent $77 billion between 1948 and 1992, much of it earmarked for the military.

Israel's balance of merchandise trade *(below)* In 1990 Israel ranked among the world's top 50 trading nations, on an equal footing with Argentina and Czechoslovakia. Exports include cut diamonds, electronics and machinery, textiles and agricultural products; energy is a significant import. The United States is Israel's most important trading partner.

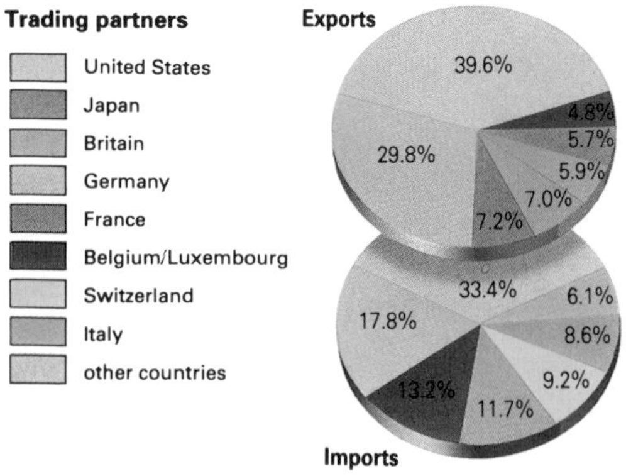

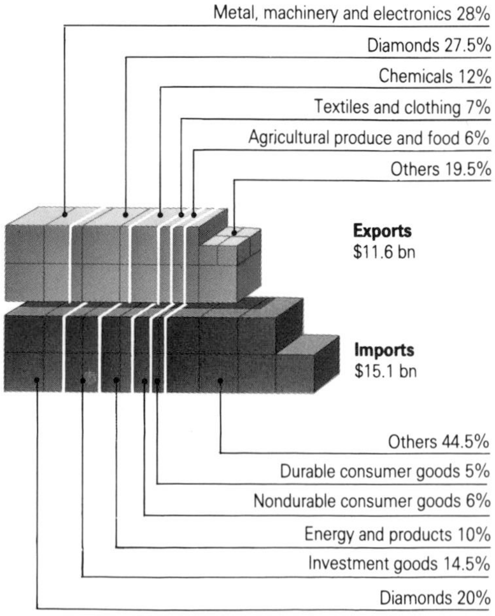

The great professional chasm *(left)* Korean laborers work under a Thai foreman directed by a British engineer in San'a, Yemen. Foreign workers form a huge proportion of the workforce; Asians in unskilled jobs, and Europeans or Americans at professional levels.

The reasons for the pro-Israeli bias of the United States are complex. American Jews – like most diasporan Jews – have emotional and psychological links with Israel. There is an influential Jewish lobby that argues its case for Israel, but it is not always successful. In 1992, for example, the United States' government withheld $10 billion in aid until Israel ceased building new settlements in the Occupied Territories. In the end, the United States' government supports Israel for its own reasons.

Syria, by contrast, has maintained strong trading links with the former Soviet Union and East European countries, while Afghanistan, occupied by the Soviet Union in the 1980s, was obliged to regard it as a main political and economic partner. Jordan, with its large Palestinian population and lack of natural resources treads a tightrope, retaining trade links with the United States, but also relying on aid and imports from Saudi Arabia and the Gulf States, as well as remittances from Jordanians working abroad.

Islamic banking

The laws of Islam have a clear influence on the region's commerce, especially in banking. Earning profit is allowed by Islamic (Sharia) law, but interest payments on loans are considered un-Islamic. This can create awkward situations. In Saudi Arabia, for example, the banking system is part Islamic, part ad hoc. Formal payment of interest is frowned upon, and may be replaced by "commissions" or "service fees". In the UAE, simple interest is allowed, while in Yemen, Sharia law is overriding.

THE DECLINE OF OPEC

The high-water mark in OPEC's power and influence came in 1979–80. With the overthrow of the Shah of Iran in 1978, and the collapse of the Iranian oil industry, the international demand for oil was high. To benefit from market forces, individual OPEC countries raised oil prices and production, so that by 1980, prices stood at a new peak of $26 a barrel for Arabian Light. OPEC revenues reached a maximum of $287 billion. The outbreak of the Iran–Iraq war in 1980 pushed prices even higher, as oil exports from the two countries dried up. This, however, triggered a new world-wide recession, and a cut in demand for OPEC oil. OPEC's output dropped from a peak of 31 million barrels per day in 1979 to some 18.5 million barrels per day in 1984.

In 1985, Iraq – still at war with Iran – refused to restrict its oil production; at the same time, other OPEC members failed to adhere to official price fixing and quota agreements. Saudi Arabia, which had adjusted its own oil supply to achieve market stability, decided to go it alone in the market. Oil prices fell again in 1986 – to below $10 a barrel – and although OPEC countries agreed to a new price, their power to influence the global oil market had all but evaporated.

INVESTING IN CARE

The vast wealth that the oil-rich Middle Eastern governments have accrued from exporting petroleum (and investing abroad) has revolutionized their standard of living. This is especially evident in their systems of healthcare, education and social welfare. Healthcare in some states is as progressive as any offered in the West. Most states are keen to improve their hospitals and to adopt the most advanced equipment. Physicians, especially those in large hospitals in the capital cities, have often been trained in the West. The size of the state seems to bear no relation to the quality of care. Tiny Qatar, with a population of only about 60,000, has an advanced state-run health service offering free care to its citizens – even flying them overseas for medical

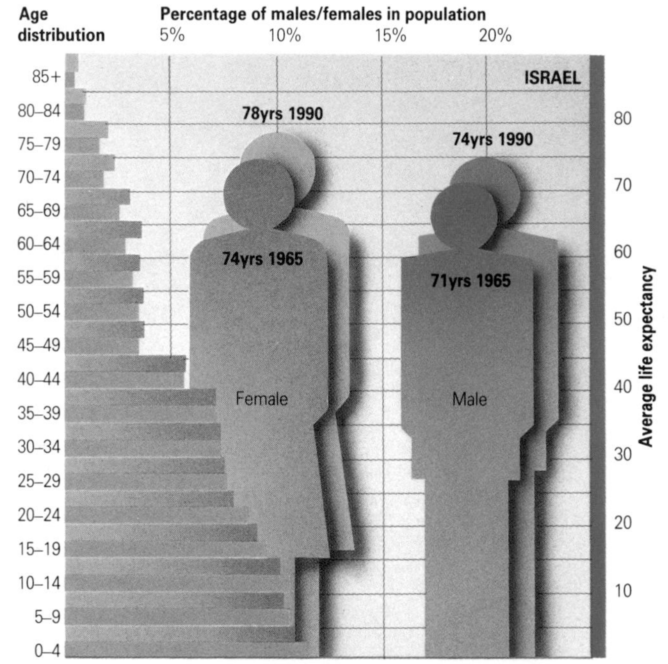

Life expectancy and age distribution (*left*) Life expectancy for Israeli men is now among the highest in the world, while women – though they live longer than men – do not live quite as long as in western Europe or North America. Israel's combined average life expectancy (76) is the highest in the region, followed by Kuwait (74); the lowest is Afghanistan, which at 43 is the second lowest in the world. The Israeli fertility rate (2.8 children per woman) is the region's lowest.

High-tech care (*below*) a cardiologist and two nurses tend a patient after heart surgery in Jedda, Saudi Arabia. Western-style hospitals have been established by the oil-wealthy countries, and have contributed to the region's improved life expectancy. Many medical staff are foreign; other nationals are likely to have trained abroad. These nurses wear masks to preserve their modesty, not for reasons of hygiene.

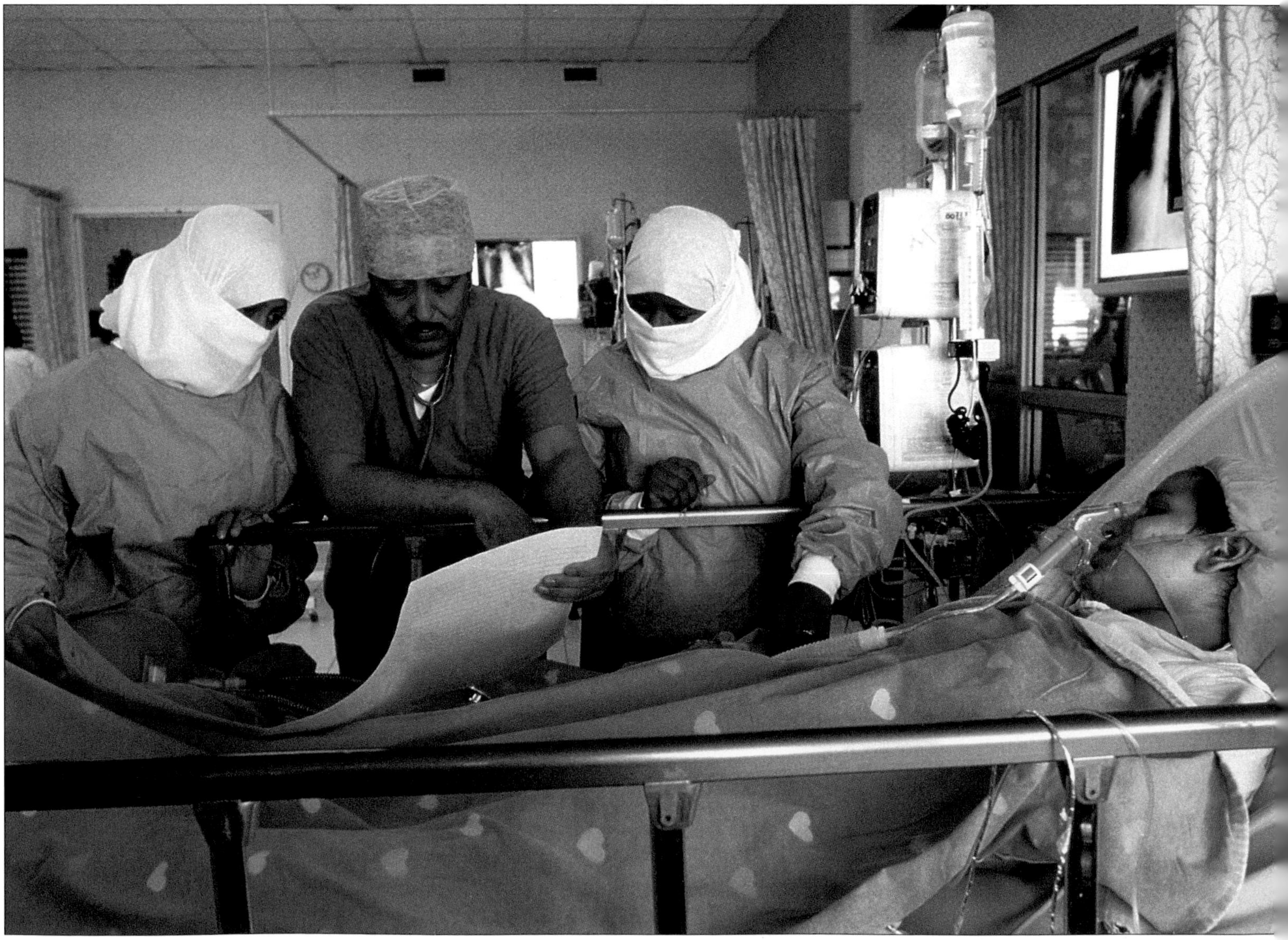

treatment if necessary. (A 660-bed general hospital in the Qatari capital Doha has facilities for computer diagnosis and helicopter ambulances.)

Kuwait, too, boasts a comprehensive system of social benefits and medical care. Before 1984 healthcare was provided free, but since then approximately 40 percent of the cost is borne by the patient. In 1985, Kuwait spent more than $350 million to support 1,600 doctors, eight hospitals and a host of local clinics. (Kuwait also has a private health service.) Saudi Arabia has a welfare system that pays state benefits in the event of unemployment, injuries at work, sickness, maternity, disability and old age. It offers free medicine and medical care to all its citizens. A series of Five-Year Plans, initiated in 1970, brought new hospitals, health centers and rural clinics to many parts of the country.

Facilities in the countries without high earnings from oil are generally not of this standard (Afghanistan is a particular case in point). The single exception is Israel, which has one of the best doctor–patient ratios in the world. In 1991, some 16 percent of Israeli government expenditure was allocated to housing, social welfare and healthcare.

Mixed privilege (*left*) These women students at Kabul University, Afghanistan, belong to the elite few in higher education. Literacy in the country is only 24 percent, one of the lowest rates in the world, and as few as 16 percent of school-age children regularly attend classes. Women students rarely go abroad to study, as men often do, and are much less likely to receive a technical education.

Women in the economy

Traditionally, Islamic and Muslim societies make a strict division between the public role of men and women, making it extremely difficult for women to play an active role in the formal economy. However, new employment opportunities for women in healthcare and social work, particularly, reflect the transforming influence of Western ways. They also reflect the need of certain Muslim governments to make use of the talents and energies of women in the cause of social and economic progress. Islamic values, such as modesty, are still guarded, though the degree of severity varies from society to society. In Saudi Arabia, Iran and the Gulf states, Islam still exerts a powerful influence. In Yemen, for example, women doctors bow to tradition by wearing a veil in public while in Abu Dhabi – one of the United Arab Emirates – many women visiting a doctor (always another woman) will still keep on their burqas, or face masks, even though they may take off their clothes.

The women of Bahrain and Kuwait are among the most emancipated, working on the stage, in television, as sales staff and secretaries. These occupations bring them into contact with men, and are therefore barred to women in more fundamentalist states. In Abu Dhabi, in the sphere of banking, the sexes do not mix and although hundreds of women work in banks, they do so in segregated quarters that deal only with women. Iraq, Jordan, Israel and Turkey, by contrast, have much more liberated attitudes to women in the workplace.

Learning experiences

Education is crucial to the economic future of all the Middle Eastern states, but particularly to the oil-rich states which are currently dependent on Westerners to provide technical expertise in their expanding and advancing economies. Many of the states – including Iraq, Kuwait, Iran, Saudi Arabia and Israel – provide free state education for all or part of a student's career. Taking advantage of this service is not always compulsory – in Saudi Arabia, for example, attending school is still a matter of choice. Literacy rates vary dramatically around the region: 61 percent of Kuwaitis are literate, compared with 10 percent in North Yemen and between 5 and 15 percent in Saudi Arabia. Women tend to have lower literacy rates than men. In 1985 literacy rates for men in Afghanistan, were 39 percent, compared with 8 percent for women. Kuwaiti men achieved 76 percent literacy compared with 63 percent for women.

In most of the region, schools are generally secular, though some religion is taught as well. In Iran, dominated by Shi'ite Islamic culture, mixed schools have been abolished, though men and women occupy the same classes in universities. In all Iranian schools there is an emphasis on Shi'ite Islamic law and doctrine. Israel deals with the thorny question of Jewish education by having two systems of state schools: one secular, and one religious. Arab–Israeli children attend separate, state-run schools where they study Arabic language, history and culture.

Throughout the Gulf states, women are admitted to all universities. In 1985, 90 percent of students at the University of Bahrain were women because Bahraini and Kuwaiti families send their sons overseas to study. Some Saudi students gain scholarships for study abroad.

THE REBUILDING OF KUWAIT

The Iraqi invasion of Kuwait in August 1990, and the subsequent Gulf War, devastated the country. Apart from costs to the oil industry – the damage to Kuwait may cost $60 billion to repair. Those involved in rebuilding Kuwait set themselves achievement targets grouped in three main stages. The first was to restore basic services – such as water and electricity – and to extinguish the fires burning at the well-heads. The second stage was to establish a new social order in which ethnic Kuwaitis made up the majority of the population. Before the invasion, 60 percent of Kuwait's population of 1.3 million were foreign laborers – an imbalance that created social tensions. After the war, amid recriminations over possible and actual collaboration with the enemy, approximately 200,000 Palestinians, 150,000 Egyptians and 600,000 Asians were forced to leave Kuwait. This dealt a blow to several of the region's economies: Egypt, for example, lost about $500 million in remittances, and Jordan about $400 million.

The third stage was to draw United States' and European companies into a program to build a new economy out of the ruins. Their brief included putting in place facilities such as air bases, power stations and a petrochemical plant. Consequently, America has won some $2 billion worth of contracts; Britain about $600 million.

Counting the cost

Warfare has long been endemic in the Middle East. Before the Gulf War of January 1991, which ranged a coalition of Arab and Western nations against Iraq over its invasion of Kuwait, there was an eight-year war between Iraq and Iran, the 1979 Soviet invasion of Afghanistan, and a succession of Arab–Israeli wars. The civil war in Lebanon, which tore that country apart, only ended in September 1991 with the disbanding of all private militias. In addition, there is the ongoing struggle of the Palestinians and Kurds to achieve self-determination.

Prolonged and widespread warfare has been extremely costly to the region, both in economic and human terms. Defense spending is one of the major drains on the economies of the Middle Eastern states, reducing the amount that can be spent on basic needs, such as water, food, housing and education within the region. In 1985, Israel (itself a major arms exporter) spent more than a quarter of its annual budget on defense; by 1991, defense and foreign debt accounted for 60 percent of its budget. Other high defense spenders include Oman (22.8 percent of GNP in 1985), Iraq (20 percent), Saudi Arabia (18.2 percent) and Syria (17.7 percent). By contrast, Turkey spent 5.9 percent of its GNP on the military. The most important suppliers of weaponry were the United States, supplying mainly Saudi Arabia and Israel; the former Soviet Union, supplying Iraq and Syria; and France, selling arms to Iraq and Saudi Arabia.

Legacy of devastation (*right*) One year after the Iraqi invasion, the badly burned structure of one of Kuwait's modern luxury buildings still awaited repair. More urgent tasks included quenching the burning oil wells and confiscating an arsenal of discarded weapons.

Out of service (*below*) a Kuwaiti engineer examines the damage caused to an electricity plant during the Iraqi invasion. Most basic services such as water and electricity were disrupted by bombing or sabotage.

Devastation in every aspect

The damage caused to Middle Eastern economies by these various wars is staggering. The Iran–Iraq War struck at the resource-base, international trading and balance-of-payments position of both countries. In Iran, a considerable portion of oil revenues went toward the war

effort, rather than being invested in industry and paying for imports of basic goods. Iraq amassed foreign debts estimated at between $60 and $80 billion (mostly to Saudi Arabia and Kuwait). By 1988, at the end of the war, Iraq was importing about $30 billion worth of food, mainly from the United States and Turkey, and inflation was running at between 40 and 50 percent. The total cost of the war is estimated to be $452.6 billion for Iraq and $644.3 billion for Iran. The loss of productive manpower on both sides of the Iran–Iraq War – between 100,000–150,000 Iraqi dead and 400,000–600,000 Iranians – acted as a serious brake on economic expansion. Conscripts were also taken off the land, resulting in a decrease in food supply.

Iraq's 1991 invasion of Kuwait was equally disastrous, economically, for surrounding countries. A near bankrupt Jordan was particularly badly affected. It lost remittances from Jordanians (and Palestinians) working in Kuwait; suffered the withdrawal of some $500 million in grants from Kuwait and Saudi Arabia and saw its export market in Saudi Arabia collapse. With the enforced closure of the Jordanian port of Aqaba it also lost its transit earnings as an entrepôt for Iraq. Syria, on the other hand, while losing remittances caused by the forced repatriation of thousands of Syrians from Kuwait, benefited by its support of the coalition force (against Iraq's Saddam Hussein) by receiving huge amounts of aid and credits from Saudi Arabia, the United States, Europe and Japan.

ONE STEP FORWARD, TWO STEPS BACK

RUNNING TO STAND STILL · THE DEBT CRISIS · MASSIVE POPULATION PRESSURE

Two different economic worlds come together in Northern Africa. The countries along the Mediterranean coast are geographically and historically linked to the richer economies of Europe. They are officially recognized as middle-income economies, though the 1980s slump in oil prices caused a dramatic drop in the revenues of Algeria and Libya. South of the Sahara conditions are much worse. Poverty and famine are widespread from Mauritania to Somalia, and the economic position is worsening. The gross domestic product (GDP) per capita of these countries is still declining and dependence on overseas aid is on the increase. Local political upheaval, population pressure, drought and other consequences of environmental damage pose further threats to life and prosperity on a massive scale.

COUNTRIES IN THE REGION

Algeria, Chad, Djibouti, Egypt, Ethiopia, Libya, Mali, Mauritania, Morocco, Niger, Somalia, Sudan, Tunisia

ECONOMIC INDICATORS: 1990

	UMIE* Algeria	LIE* Egypt	LIE* Ethiopia
GDP (US$ billions)	42.15	33.21	5.49
GNP per capita (US$)	2,060	600	120
Annual rate of growth of GDP, 1980–1990 (%)	3.1	5.0	1.8
Manufacturing as % of GDP	12	16	11
Central government spending as % of GNP	n/a	40	35
Merchandise exports (US$ billions)	13	2.98	0.3
Merchandise imports (US$ billions)	9.5	10.3	1.08
% of GNP received as development aid	0.4	15.9	14.6
Total external debt as a % of GNP	53.1	126.5	54.2

WELFARE INDICATORS

Infant mortality rate (per 1,000 live births)			
1965	154	145	165
1990	67	66	132
Daily food supply available (calories per capita, 1989)	2,866	3,336	1,667
Population per physician (1984)	2,340	770	78,780
Teacher–pupil ratio (primary school, 1989)	1 : 28	1 : 24	1 : 43

Note: The Gross Domestic Product (GDP) is the total value of all goods and services domestically produced. The Gross National Product (GNP) is the GDP plus net income from abroad.

** UMIE (Upper Middle Income Economy) – GNP per capita between $2,465 and $7,620 in 1990. LIE (Low Income Economy) – GNP per capita below $610.*

RUNNING TO STAND STILL

European colonialism made a lasting impression on the economies of Northern Africa. Until after World War II France dominated most of the region; it pulled out of its last colony, Algeria, in 1962. The British occupied Egypt until 1922 (maintaining a presence in the Suez zone until much later) and Sudan until 1956. Italy controlled Somalia and Ethiopia, and all three European powers maintained a presence in Libya until the early 1950s.

Under these colonial regimes most countries in the region produced a few primary exports for European markets using cheap local labor. Morocco supplied France with fruit and wheat, Tunisia supplied olives, and Algeria specialized in wine and cereals. Egypt and Sudan supplied British textile mills with cotton. As a result the colonial economies were overspecialized, dependent on exports of raw materials and had low levels of industrial development. Capital came from Europe or from European settlers, and profits were returned to them.

In the 1960s the economic development of the newly independent northern African states varied according to their resources and their experience of decolonization. In Libya – a poor desert country that was heavily dependent on Western aid during the 1950s – the discovery of oil transformed the economy, generating $3 million in 1961 and $1.2 billion in 1969. In Morocco, economic strategies set up by the French were continued after their departure in 1956, particularly the ambitious river regulation projects to provide irrigation.

Outgrowing the economy

One of the main problems for all these governments was that economic development could not kept pace with population increases, which canceled out some of the benefits of whatever progress they made. The Algerian population, for example, increased from 12 million to 20 million between 1966 and 1981 and the number of Moroccans rose from 14 million to 22 million. Feeding these swelling populations was a major challenge. In 1969 Morocco exported twice as much food as it imported, but by 1982, despite a threefold increase in exports, food imports were twice that of exports. In Egypt successive governments tried to stimulate economic growth by investing in hydroelectric power, land reclamation projects and irrigation to reduce the impact of drought. However, neither the socialist government of the 1960s nor the pro-Western administrations of the late 1970s found it easy to generate enough revenue to provide for a population that was growing by 1 million people per year.

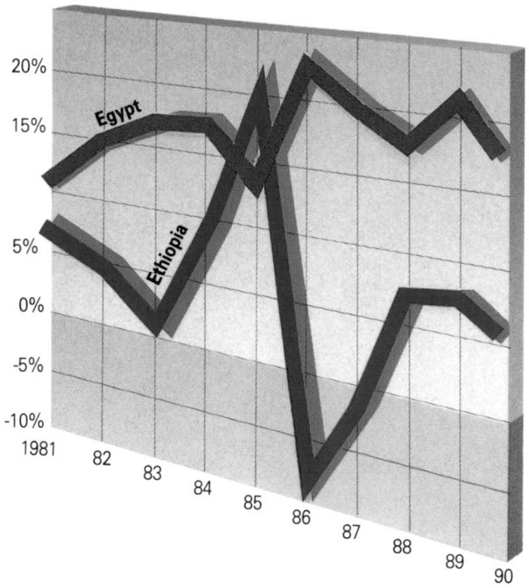

Profile of inflation *(above)* Egypt experienced consistently high inflation throughout the 1980s. In Ethiopia, inflation varied from over 20 percent to minus 10 percent. Its low average rate of 1.4 percent through the decade derived largely from the collapse of the economy under the pressures of famine and war.

War and instability

Political instability and regular outbreaks of war exacerbated all these problems as did increased government spending on arms at the expense of other sectors. The Arab–Israeli wars of 1967 and 1973, for example, forced the closure of the Suez Canal, reduced foreign investment in Egypt and led to huge increases in military spending – up to 40 percent of gross national product (GNP). Morocco has been fighting a territorial war in the Western Sahara since the mid-1970s; by 1980 this conflict was costing 40 percent of the country's national expenditure.

In Ethiopia, one of the countries most damaged by drought and famine, the Marxist regime that seized power in 1974 intensified border disputes with Somalia, leading to outright war in 1977–78. The conflict often prevented much-needed aid from getting through. In the mid 1970s, 19 percent of government spending went to the military, while agriculture – particularly coffee, which accounted for 58 percent of the country's GNP – received only 3 percent.

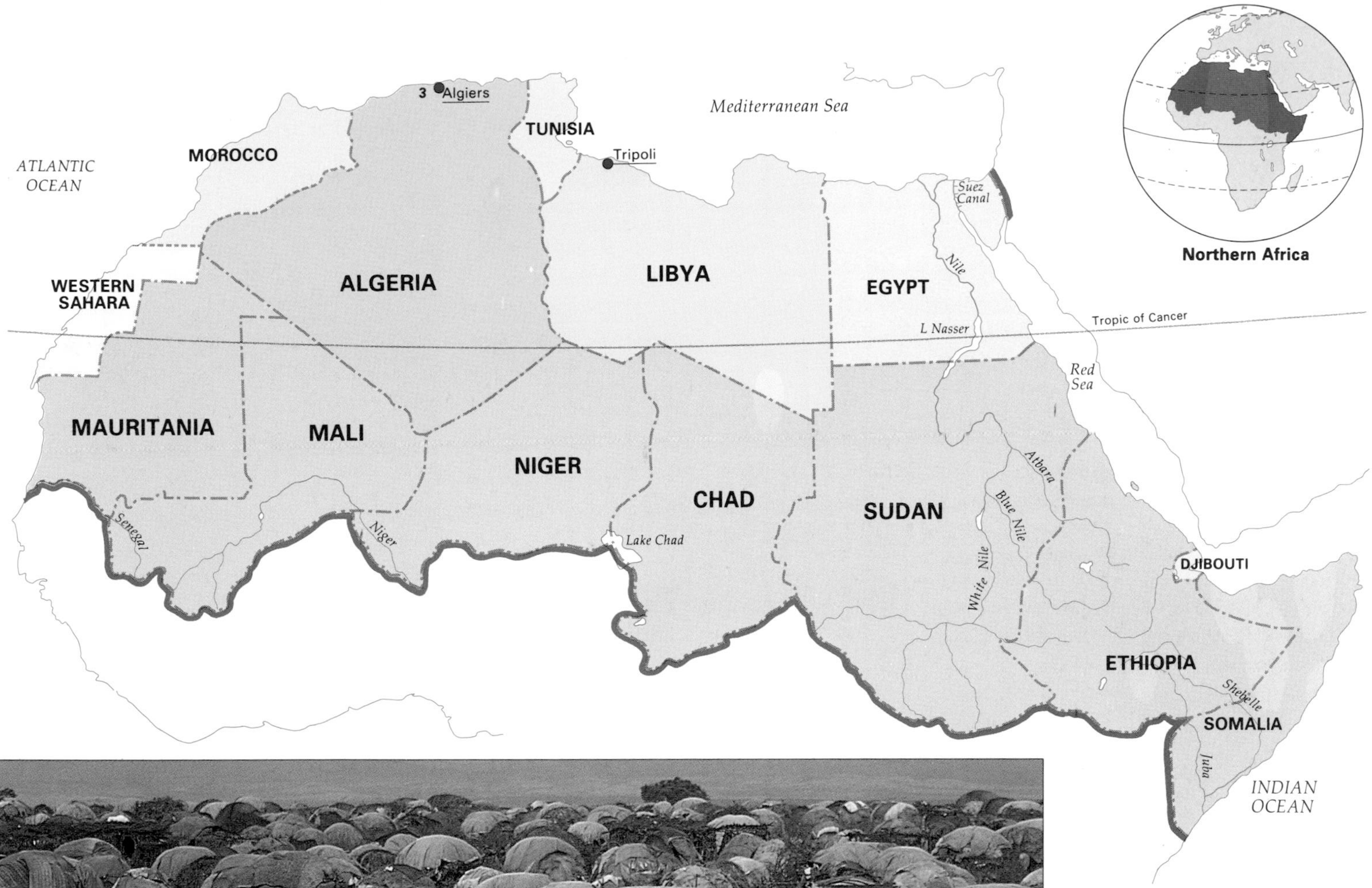

Economic indicators

head offices of world's top 500 banks and companies (with number if more than one)

●3 bank

(underlined name indicates a capital city)

GDP per capita (US$)

- 5 000–9 999
- 2 000–4 999
- 500–1 999
- less than 500
- no data available

Map of GDP per capita (*above*) Libya, with one of the region's smallest populations (4.0 million), has the highest per capita GDP; while populous Ethiopia (49.2 million) is one of the world's three poorest countries. In Africa, total external debt is often in excess of a country's GDP: by nearly 300 percent in Somalia and over 200 percent in Mauritania. Chad's GDP growth was one of the slowest in the world from 1965–80 but it improved significantly in the 1980s.

Refugees in Ethiopia (*left*) flock to camps to escape the poverty and violence of their homelands. Famine, drought and war have disrupted the country's agricultural economy causing mass migration away from the most fertile land. Disease is often endemic in the camps that shelter these desperate people and only foreign aid provides some slender and short-term hope against the deaths of millions.

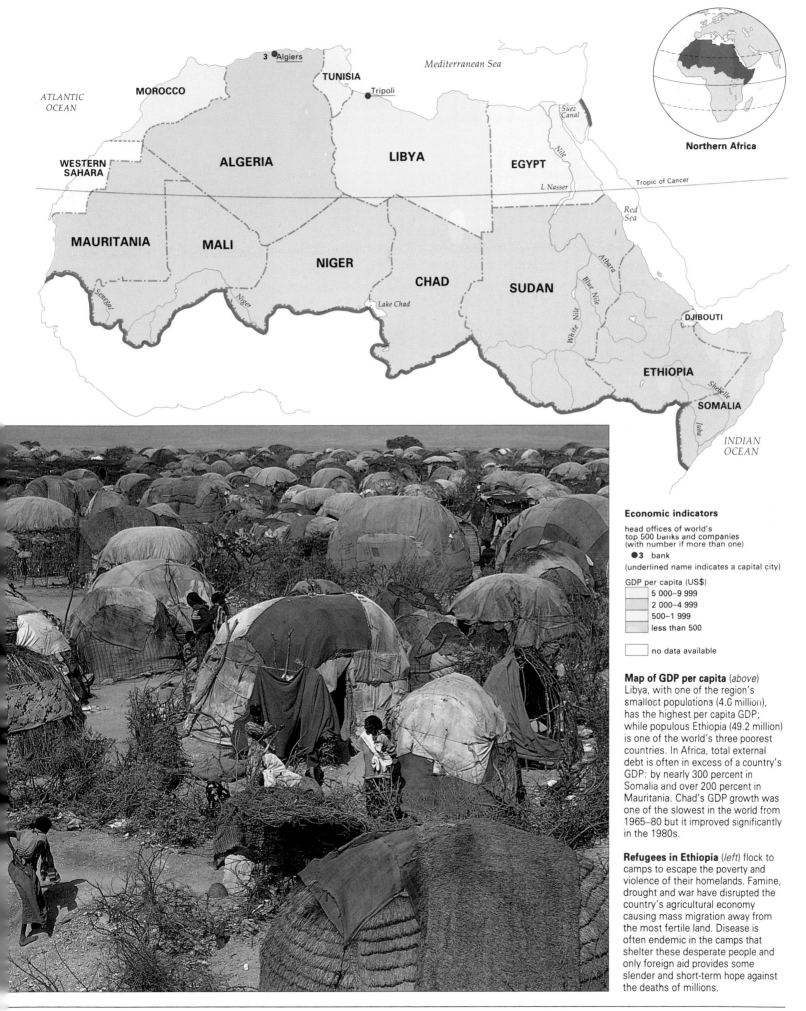

THE DEBT CRISIS

Indebtedness, environmental crises, famine and warfare intensified in most parts of Northern Africa in the 1980s. Almost without exception, GDP grew more slowly in the 1980s than in the 1970s, while dependence on overseas aid continued to increase. By the early 1990s, despite attempts to diversify into new products and to encourage private sector manufacturing, the Mediterranean African economies remained overwhelmingly dependent on a few unprocessed exports – minerals, oil and natural gas, and agricultural produce. The economies south of the Sahara remained excessively reliant on subsistence agriculture, which is at the mercy of an unregulated and unpredictable natural water supply.

Concerted attempts to escape from the poverty trap were made in the 1980s and early 1990s. Although Libya remained anti-Western, its neighbors adopted a pragmatic pro-Western stance. Egypt and Algeria, for example, began to abandon public-sector investment in favor of private enterprise. Tourism and other new industries are becoming established there, funded by both public and private capital. In 1988 tourism generated more than $5 billion in new revenue in both Morocco and Egypt.

Outside intervention

In spite of these initiatives, most of the Mediterranean economies have accumulated crippling foreign debts. In 1988, Egypt owed a total of $50 billion – the sixth highest debt in the developing world. Since its isolation from the Arab world following its recognition of Israel (1979), Egypt has relied heavily on Western loans: United States' aid to Egypt between 1975 and 1985 approached $11 billion, though much of this debt was written off by the United States in return for support against Iraq in the Gulf War (1991). Egypt's oil production grew steadily in this period – from 4 percent of export revenue in 1974 to 58 percent in 1980 – but the 1986 oil price collapse reduced this income by two-thirds. Traditional exports could not compensate for this unexpected loss of revenue. A shrinking agricultural sector produced just $250 million worth of cotton in 1989, compared with $357 million in 1985, despite a price increase of 32 percent.

Morocco's balance of merchandise trade (*below*) Morocco is one of the world's 50 largest traders, surpassed in the region only by Algeria, Egypt and Libya. It imports 2 percent of the world's total goods. France, the former colonial power, dominates trade with Morocco and helps to limit its visible trade deficit.

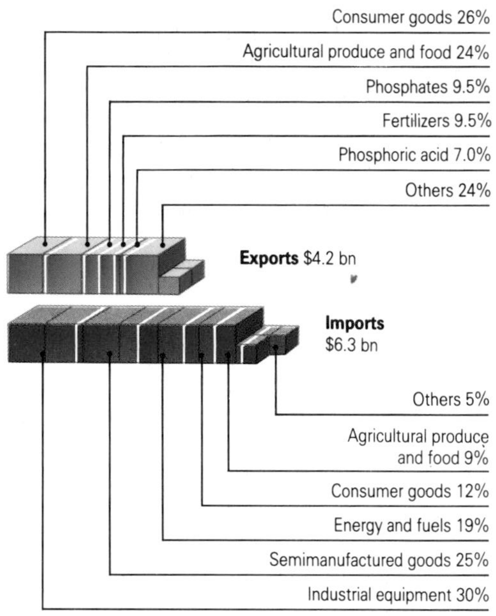

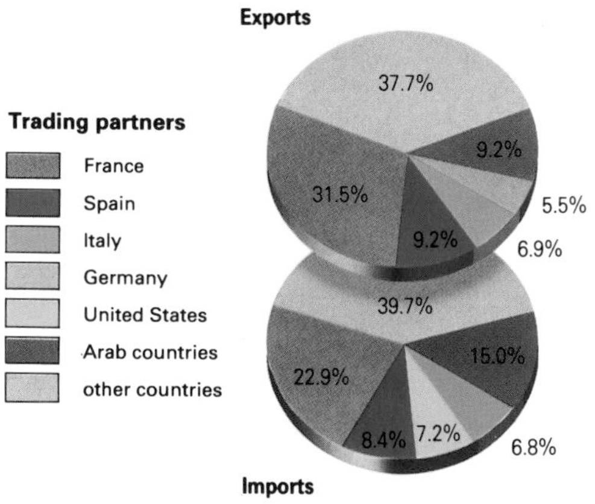

In 1987, the International Monetary Fund (IMF) negotiated a rescheduling of Egypt's debt in exchange for economic reforms, based on an increase in private enterprise and a removal of government subsidies on food and fuel. Fear of political unrest has so far prevented the Egyptian government from implementing all these reforms. Morocco, which was $20 billion in debt in 1988 has experienced similar difficulties; Tunisia's IMF-sponsored reforms have been more successful.

Algeria has followed another course in trying to reduce its debt, which in 1988 stood at $25 billion. Depressed prices for oil and gas, which together brought in 97 percent of foreign exchange, made interest payments an impossible burden.

A crop of Moroccan tomatoes at harvest time (*above*). Agricultural production grew by an average rate of 6.7 percent in Morocco during the 1980s, making it the most significant contributor to the overall expansion of the economy.

Unwilling to involve the IMF, the government imposed drastic cuts in imports. As 70 percent of imports were foodstuffs, this policy created dramatic shortages. Prices soared and violent demonstrations broke out in October 1988, forcing the government to introduce new reforms. The policy of economic liberalization, designed to reduce the size of the public sector and diversify the country's economic base, was accelerated and multiparty municipal elections took place in June 1990. These resulted in an over-

Aid arrives (*above*) at the port of Mogadishu, Somalia, during the famine of 1985. Urgently needed to prevent mass starvation, the food had to be transported to refugee camps at the risk of confiscation by soldiers and local gangs for black marketeering.

whelming majority for the newly established Islamic fundamentalist party. The same party dominated the 1992 parliamentary elections, prompting the government to suspend its democratic reforms. This provoked further political unrest culminating in the assassination of President Boudiaf in July 1992.

Political problems have also affected the oil-rich Libyan economy. Since Colonel Qaddafi's "Islamic-socialist" revolution in 1969, Libya has been in permanent conflict with Western powers and some of its African neighbors. Following a clash between American and Libyan fighter jets in 1982, President Reagan halted all exports to Libya except medicine and food, and banned imports of Libyan oil. In 1986 the Reagan administration banned all trade with Libya and froze the country's assets in the United States. The simultaneous slump in oil prices reduced Libyan oil revenue from $23.2 billion in 1980 to $5 billion in 1988.

MALI: IN PARTNERSHIP WITH FRANCE

Most of Mali's 8 million inhabitants are dependent on subsistence agriculture. It is a poor and land-locked country dominated by desert and semidesert land where farming is at the mercy of irregular rainfall. The river Niger forms a principal economic axis, providing irrigation, transport and a supply of food. Fishing in the Niger has always been a significant contributor to local revenue – in 1988 alone it yielded 100,000 tonnes of fish. Unfortunately, like all aspects of the Malian economy, the catch is notoriously unpredictable and fluctuates according to rainfall.

Despite the difficulties, an increasing proportion of Malian fish is exported to Europe, where a large market exists for exotic foodstuffs. Preserving a perishable product for long-distance travel is extremely difficult. Freezing is too expensive and Malians rely instead on the traditional method of smoking.

France, the former colonial power, still retains political, trading and economic links with Mali. In 1988, 40 percent of Mali's exports went there. France is also the major donor of overseas aid to Mali. In 1986, France provided FF8 billion ($1.5 billion) through the IMF to fund improvements in agriculture. In 1990, Mali's outstanding debt to France of $240 million was canceled by the French government.

Famine and drought

In the poorer economies of the region, population pressure has increased the deterioration of farmland into desert while political unrest has destroyed entire economies. In Ethiopia, a drought-induced famine struck on an unprecedented scale in the mid 1980s. Overseas aid flooded into the country but frequently became a strategic weapon in the ongoing civil war. Millions died and millions more were forced to flee as refugees. In 1992, this destructive cycle of famine and war repeated itself in Somalia, already in the grip of an intertribal conflict which destroyed the capital and reduced the economy to ruins.

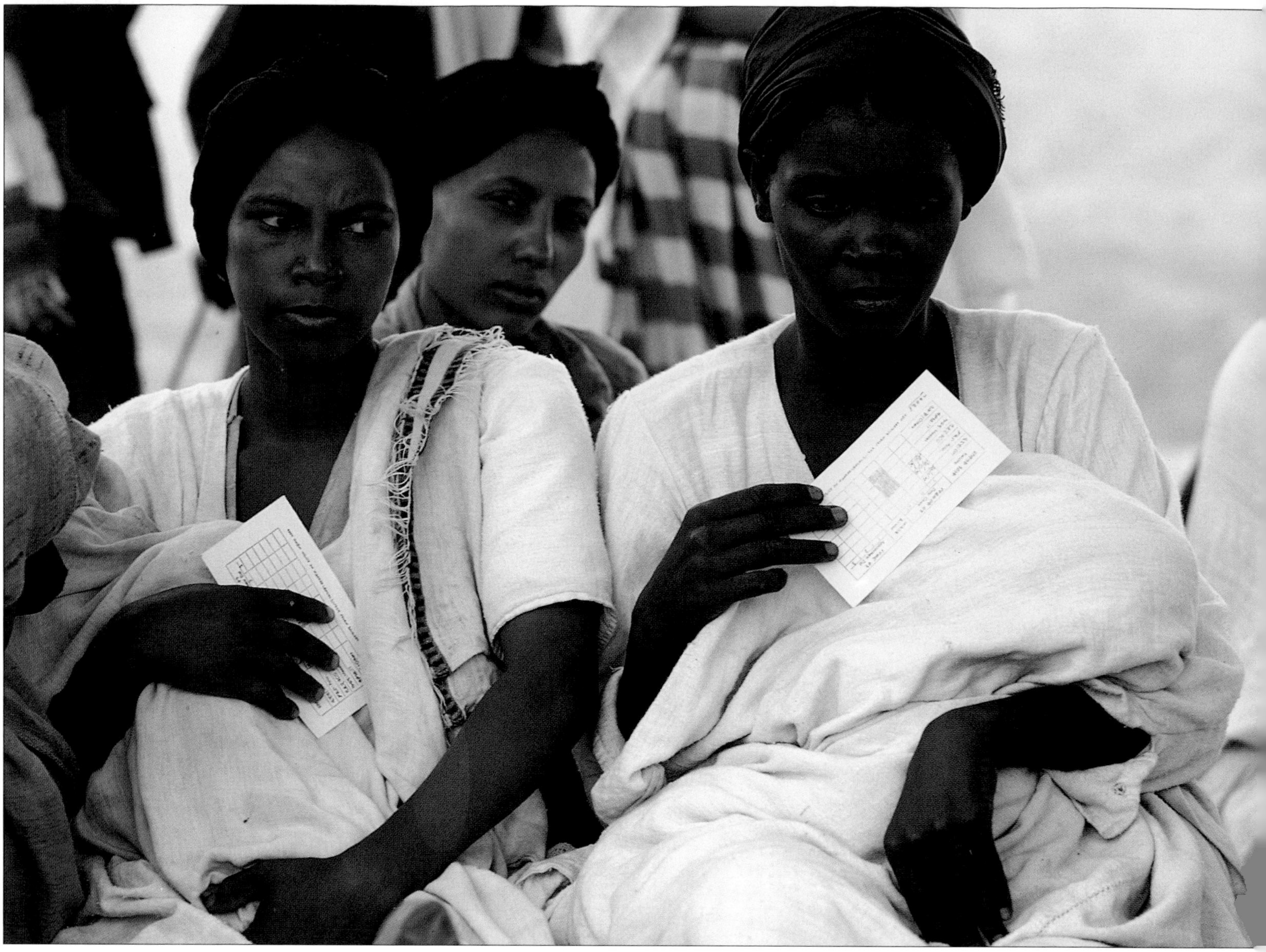

MASSIVE POPULATION PRESSURE

Many Northern Africans experience a degree of poverty unimaginable in the developed world. In 1990 Libya, the region's wealthiest country, had a GDP per capita of $5,310; the figure for the poorest, Ethiopia, was just $120. By comparison the United States had a GDP per capita figure of $21,700, Japan's was $25,430 and Germany's was $19,530. With such restricted funding, social services in Northern Africa were already under tremendous pressure. In addition, rapid population growth constantly increases demand on healthcare and feeding programs, education, housing and water supply, most of which depend entirely on public expenditure.

Health and survival

Life expectancy at birth remains low compared with the West, and infant mortality is high. For every 1,000 babies born from Mauritania to Somalia, at least 160 die before their first birthday. North of the Sahara, infant mortality is about 70 per 1,000 compared with below 10 per 1,000 in high-income economies. However, these factors have barely inhibited population growth, and providing food for all these mouths has become one of the region's greatest problems. In 1992 Algeria imported 75 percent of its food, Mauritania 50 percent, while in Somalia and Ethiopia 3 to 4 million people were at risk from starvation.

Trained medical personnel and supplies are especially lacking in the poorer countries, and leprosy, tuberculosis, malaria and other diseases remain endemic. International assistance comes from agencies such as the World Health Organization, *Médécins sans Frontières* and the Red Cross. In Egypt, both the Coptic Church and the Islamic Leagues perform community services, offering medical advice and running local schools.

In the 1980s, many of the countries north of the Sahara neglected education facilities in their drive for economic development but began to divert more resources to them in the 1990s. In 1992 Egypt devoted 13 percent of its budget to education; Algeria and Tunisia channeled 16 percent of government spending into education, Libya 22 percent and Morocco 25 percent. Educational facilities south of the Sahara are usually free but less accessible. Scattered populations, long distances and lack of transport make it difficult for children to attend, and in Chad enrollment stands at about 50 percent of school-age children. Most schools are secular except in Ethiopia, where public education is inadequate and religious instruction is more prevalent. A mass literacy campaign was sponsored by the military government of Somalia in the 1970s. Despite this, adult illiteracy rates are still over 50 percent in many areas.

A widespread shortage of work

The prospects for the young in the region are not high, regardless of education. Even in the relatively developed Mediterranean economies, there are not enough jobs to provide full employment. In Tunisia, between 20 and 30 percent of the

Affluence for a privileged few (*above*) Electric appliances on display in a store in Cairo, Egypt. The country has benefited from close ties with the United States since 1979. In 1992 it received $5.6 billion in foreign aid compared with $0.9 billion donated to Ethiopia.

Stiff with apprehension (*left*). Ethiopian women await the next in a series of inoculations sponsored by an international healthcare organization. Healthcare for rural residents of the sub-Saharan countries is almost entirely provided by foreign volunteers.

Life expectancy and age distribution (*right*) Improved life expectancy in the region still lags far behind the rest of the world. These figures for Ethiopia, and similar life expectancy in Mali are among the lowest recorded in any country. Birth rates remain very high – nearly 50 percent of the population is under 16 in 6 countries in the region.

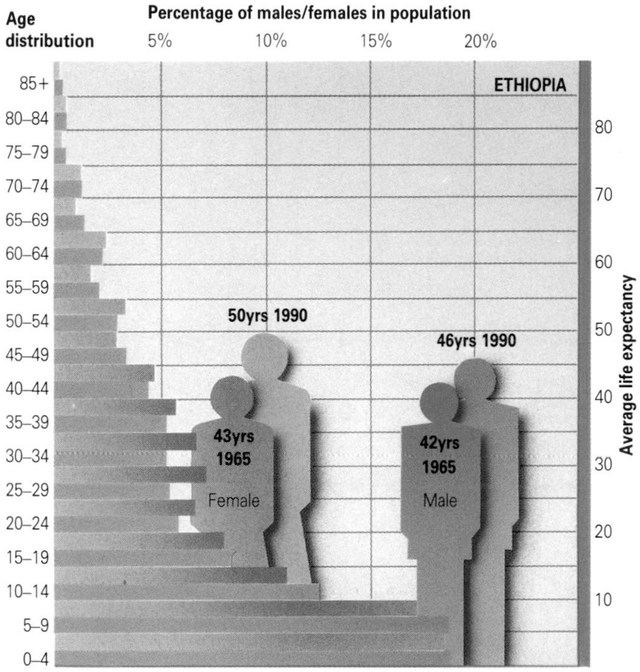

economically active population was unemployed in the mid 1980s, with the same number underemployed. Unemployment among young men rose from 29 percent in the late 1960s to nearly 50 percent in 1985. Egypt's surplus of skilled workers results in 2 to 3 million Egyptians – nearly a quarter of its workforce – working abroad in other countries around the Persian Gulf. Libya was host to many of the region's migrant workers. Over half a million foreigners worked alongside Libya's own workforce in the early 1980s, but 120,000 of these were expelled or laid off in 1985 due to a combination of political and economic factors.

In the subsistence agricultural economies south of the Sahara, employment figures based on a modern urban–industrial system are meaningless. In Sudan, the situation is marginally better, but the reduced number of migrant workers throughout the Gulf states in the mid to late 1980s meant that workers returned home to face worsening conditions in an economy crippled by debt and drought.

Welfare for women

The shortage of resources in Northern Africa has put the region's women at an even greater disadvantage than men. In Algeria, 63 percent of women were illiterate in 1985, compared with 37 percent of men. The low enrollment of girls in Moroccan secondary schools (37 percent) has prompted new programs to raise attendance, leading to the growth of private schools. In Niger, most students in primary and secondary schools are boys. Few women in the poorest countries aspire to more than domestic work.

Official statistics show that men outnumbered women by 10 to 1 among the working population of Egypt, but a report published by the United Nations Conference on Women in 1985 stated that women contributed much more to the economy than was usually acknowledged. The number of Sudanese women in the workforce has not grown since the 1950s. Male workers emigrated in search of work and women stayed at home with their families. In the mid 1980s, 22 percent of women were heads of their households living on remittances from male relatives abroad. In the early 1990s, many women in Somalia and Ethiopia were war widows with no male relatives to support them and were entirely reliant on government and foreign aid.

ETHIOPIA: A SYMBOL OF DESPERATION

Famine and warfare in Ethiopia have joined with climatic conditions and rising populations to make it one of the poorest countries in the world. Like much of underdeveloped Africa, its economy is based on subsistence agriculture and suffers from the lack of investment, communications, schools and other public services. Since the 1970s these problems have been compounded by intervals of political upheaval and fighting that have impoverished the government and unleashed chaos in the country. Farms and fledgling industries lie neglected in most areas. Hundreds of thousands have died of hunger or in the fighting, but populations continue to rise. Numbers will probably triple – from 52 million people to 156 million by 2025.

Deadly cycles of drought have accompanied this unrest. The former stable system of small farms was abandoned in the early 1970s in favor of exportable cash crops. A program to provide herdsmen with new wells to supply water encouraged the expansion of herds beyond the land's capacity to support them. These two factors made the region more vulnerable in dry years, when production from both farms and herds fell by 50 percent. The famine of 1973–74 was estimated to have killed 200,000; that of 1984–85, nearly a million, despite the vast flow of international aid culminating in more than $60 million generated by benefit rock concerts. In 1992, facing the prospect of civil war and still dependent on food aid, the prolonged crisis in Ethiopia was upstaged by the tragically similar events in its neighbor Somalia.

Sudan's spiral of debt

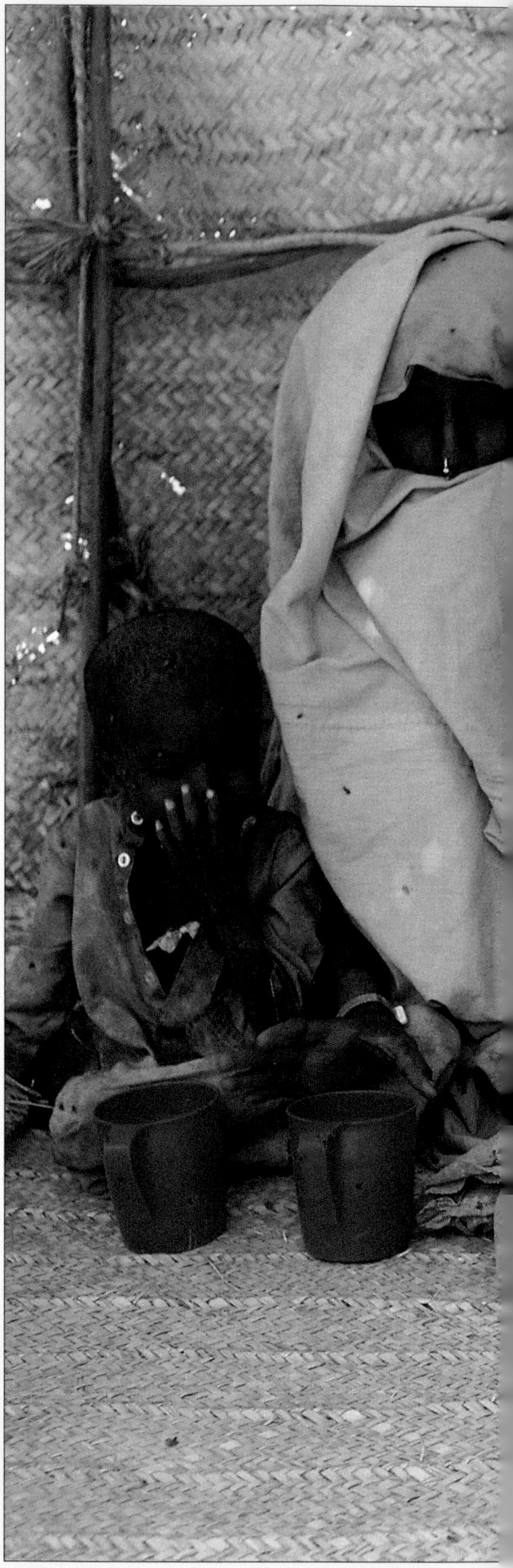

Ready for export (*left*) Bitumen – a natural form of asphalt – awaits collection in Port Sudan. It is one of the few commodities that Sudan exports to an international market. Trade generated only 0.3 percent of Sudan's total revenue in 1992. Export earnings are much too low to help pay off the country's debt.

Saved – for now (*right*) Sudanese women and children at a Red Cross food station in the province of Red Sea Hills. Sudan was the world's 18th largest recipient of foreign aid in 1992, but prolonged crisis meant that more aid was needed to keep the nation from starving. "Emergency" aid has become a permanent fixture.

According to the World Bank, 24 of the world's 26 "severely indebted" low-income countries are in Africa. Compared with countries such as Brazil and Mexico, which owe over $100 billion each, African debts seem small. In relation to their ability to pay, however, the burden is much greater. In mid 1990 Sudan's total external debt was $13 billion, the sixth highest in Africa; as early as 1986, the cost of servicing these loans consumed 180 percent of the country's annual export revenue and the situation grows worse.

Throughout Africa, the spiral of indebtedness began in the mid 1970s and was influenced by conditions in the developed world. Oil price rises in 1974 produced recession in the richer, oil-dependent economies of Europe and North America. Demand for domestic credit fell, and a surplus of capital in Western banks was redirected in the form of loans with interest to countries in the developing world embarking on ambitious new development schemes.

Between 1973 and 1977 over $3 billion flowed into Sudan, but development projects took much longer to show results than anyone expected. By 1978, Sudan was unable to keep up repayments. Starved of new investment, commercial agriculture collapsed. Annual cotton production fell from 248,000 tonnes in 1971 to 141,000 tonnes in 1978. New export crops such as sorghum (used for making bread and as a source of oil, starch and sugar) were unable to compensate and the economy was plunged into a balance-of-payments crisis with inflation hovering above 20 percent.

The failure of reform

In 1978 Sudan approached the IMF to reschedule its debts. The IMF imposed an economic recovery program designed to achieve price stability, encourage industrial output, reduce the need for imports and expand the traditional agricultural sector through a program sponsored by the World Bank. However, these policies had little impact and food riots broke out in 1981. Despite further reforms and rescheduling, total foreign debt rose from $2 billion to $8 billion between 1978 and 1982 and GDP per capita fell from $468 to $288. Inflation soared above 40 percent, and on 6 April 1985 the government was ousted by a military coup.

There are several reasons why the IMF's recovery program failed. Corruption was endemic in the Nimeiri government (1971–85) and IMF policies were often ignored. Rising populations and emigration to seek work in the Gulf states reduced the number of the country's male adult workers, leaving mostly women and children at home – 45 percent of the population was under 15 years old. Sudan suffered three years of drought culminating in a massive famine in 1984–85. During the same period, the rise of fundamentalism in the region resulted in the introduction of Islamic laws in Sudan – including the traditional ban on usury (charging interest). This alarmed Sudan's creditors, causing the loss of foreign investment, badly needed debt relief and other foreign aid. To make matters worse, political unrest in the south intensified into a fullscale civil war. Violence prompted huge numbers of people to move north at the same time as Sudan began to receive over 1 million Ethiopian refugees fleeing violence and famine in their own country. The burden was too much for Sudan to bear, and in spite of

the fact that it received over 600,000 tonnes of food aid in 1988, the United Nations estimates that 250,000 people starved to death during that year alone.

Under American pressure, the IMF supplied further funds to Sudan. In 1984, Sudan owed the IMF $18 million; by 1988 the figure had reached $900 million, and by 1992 the World Bank estimated Sudan's total external debt as over $15 billion. One of the lessons of this tragic saga is that loans on these terms are not sufficient to solve entrenched economic problems. Indeed, the provision of credit on this scale may even encourage governments to adopt short-term holding strategies to the detriment of long-term planning. The IMF has since been criticized for its role in Sudan, on the grounds that it represented American, not African, interests and abandoned its commitment to sustainable development in the face of political unrest. It is still unclear how Sudan can ever repay its loans.

Egypt's building boom

The construction of new cities in Egypt is a visible reminder of the population pressures apparent across north Africa. In Egypt the crude birth rate fell from 43 per 1,000 in 1965 to 31 per 1,000 in 1990, but the total population of the country nearly doubled in this period to 52 million. By the year 2025 the population of Egypt is expected to reach 86 million, with the vast majority of people being forced to live in the Nile delta and in the Mediterranean coastal belt. Population densities on the habitable lands of Northern Africa are already very high and more and more of this land is destined to be taken out of cultivation and used for housing and city growth.

If there is a silver lining to this cloud of population growth, it is that "with every new mouth comes a new pair of hands". Countries adapt to population pressure upon the land by tilling agricultural land more intensively and by providing more employment off the land. Nevertheless, rapid population growth is rarely a blessing for poor countries. In the short run, resources are diverted from investment in other areas to provide for the educational, healthcare and housing needs of an increasingly youthful (and dependent) population. About a quarter of Egypt's population in 1990 was aged between 0 and 15.

Ramadan New City under construction on the outskirts of Cairo, Egypt.

THE POVERTY TRAP

THE IMPACT OF CASH ECONOMICS · SERVICING A LARGE INTERNATIONAL DEBT · FIGHTING HUNGER AND ILLITERACY

The regional economy of Central Africa is geared to the supply of primary resources to Europe and North America, much as it was in colonial times. Most exports are agricultural products and minerals, often with unstable world prices and the industrial base remains largely undeveloped. Despite the strategic importance of the region's resources to the economies of the developed world, few Central African countries enjoy a positive balance of trade with the West, and almost all have accumulated crippling international debts since the mid 1970s. Austerity programs supervised by the International Monetary Fund (IMF) have further impoverished rural populations. Most inhabitants have seen their standard of living fall as already inadequate healthcare and education provisions have been cut back.

COUNTRIES IN THE REGION

Benin, Burkina, Burundi, Cameroon, Cape Verde, Central African Republic, Congo, Equatorial Guinea, Gabon, Gambia, Ghana, Guinea, Guinea-Bissau, Ivory Coast, Kenya, Liberia, Nigeria, Rwanda, São Tomé and Príncipe, Senegal, Seychelles, Sierra Leone, Tanzania, Togo, Uganda, Zaire

ECONOMIC INDICATORS: 1990

	UMIE* Gabon	LMIE* Cameroon	LIE* Tanzania
GDP (US$ billions)	4.72	11.13	2.06
GNP per capita (US$)	3,330	960	110
Annual rate of growth of GDP, 1980–1990 (%)	2.3	2.3	2.8
Manufacturing as % of GDP	7	13	10
Central government spending as % of GNP	n/a	21	n/a
Merchandise exports (US$ billions)	2.47	1.2	0.3
Merchandise imports (US$ billions)	0.76	1.3	0.94
% of GNP received as development aid	3.0	4.3	48.2
Total external debt as a % of GNP	86	57	282

WELFARE INDICATORS

	Gabon	Cameroon	Tanzania
Infant mortality rate (per 1,000 live births)			
1965	153	143	138
1990	97	88	115
Daily food supply available (calories per capita, 1989)	2,383	2,217	2,206
Population per physician (1984)	2,790	13,990	24,970
Teacher–pupil ratio (primary school, 1989)	1 : 46	1 : 51	1 : 33

Note: The Gross Domestic Product (GDP) is the total value of all goods and services domestically produced. The Gross National Product (GNP) is the GDP plus net income from abroad.

** UMIE (Upper Middle Income Economy) – GNP per capita between $2,465 and $7,620 in 1990. LMIE (Lower Middle Income Economy) – between $610 and $2,465. LIE (Low Income Economy) – below $610.*

THE IMPACT OF CASH ECONOMICS

The scramble to colonize Africa, which began in the 1880s, was motivated largely by economic factors: the enormous growth of capitalism in western Europe created a demand for new resources and markets to sustain rapidly growing industrial economies. Using the coastal bases established earlier for slave trading, the major European powers pursued their economic ambitions by subduing the African peoples, and then exploiting the region's resources.

In parts of the region, such as the Congo Free State (later the Belgian Congo and now Zaire), companies were granted concessionary rights by the colonial powers to exploit all the resources of the subjugated territories. These companies were purely parasitic on African labor and resources, and acted as agents for the colonial governments. In areas regarded as fit for permanent European settlement, such as Kenya, the most favorable land was allocated to settlers and existing African ownership was simply ignored. The peoples in the western parts of the region suffered less during this period than those in the central and eastern areas. The western territories were not deemed fit for permanent European settlement and there were no powerful concession companies there, so local people retained most of their land rights.

Erosion of village life

The economics of colonialism had a profound effect on the traditional way of life in African villages. The European powers imposed taxes and made industrial goods available for sale – both of which required villages to abandon traditional subsistence farming in favor of activities that generated cash. To meet the demand for money, Africans had to sell their labor to European settlers, usually by migrating to work in colonial-run mines and plantations. Traditional village life disintegrated. At the same time, the growth of European economic enterprises led to the decline of the region's handicraft indus-

Cash on delivery *(above)* during a sale of cattle in Sierra Leone. Colonialism brought cash economies to replace the traditional barter system practiced by the local people, and cash has replaced livestock as the measure of wealth and status.

tries. Colonial factories monopolized local raw materials and their finished products were in competition with the traditionally produced goods.

Constraints on industrialization

Throughout this period of limited industrialization there was no widespread transfer of technology and skills from Europe to Africa. The colonial powers saw no need to change the status quo by educating the workforce – a move that might threaten their ability to use the region as a source of raw materials. In this way, colonialism not only destroyed the old way of life, it also failed to establish the economic and social structures to build a new one. This task was left to the governments of the newly independent states in the years after World War II.

Following decolonization in the 1950s and 1960s, the new nations of Central Africa retained strong economic links with their former colonizers. The relationship between France and its old colonies was particularly close, and France continues to support the West African franc. For the most part, the independent states lacked the capital to invest in industrialization and continued to act mainly as suppliers of commodities and primary products to European and North American markets.

By the late 1970s the nations of the region were facing a number of problems and prosperity remained as elusive as ever. Rapid population growth outstripped economic expansion, often leading to ever-increasing levels of personal impoverishment. The oil price rises earlier in the decade had caused recession in many developed countries and this in turn affected Central African economies as their export markets declined and foreign aid was cut. A few countries, in particular Nigeria and Zaire, attempted programs of rapid industrialization financed by international loans made possible by recycling oil revenues. However, the funds they borrowed were not always invested wisely and future generations continue to be burdened by high levels of interest repayments.

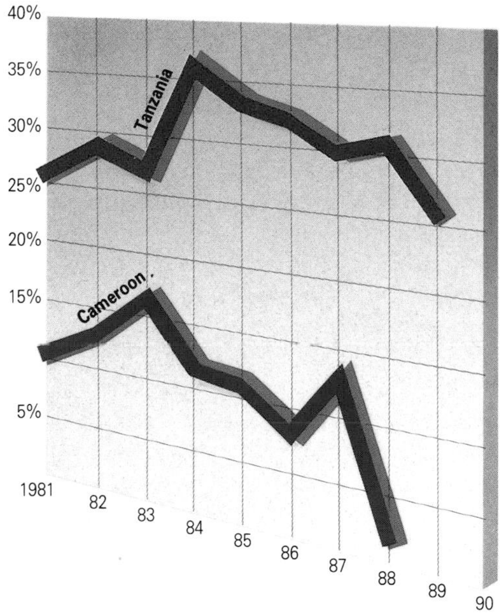

Profile of inflation *(above)* Despite sharp increases in 1981–83 and 1986–87, inflation in Cameroon has remained among the lowest in the developing world. In Tanzania it was much higher but has gradually decreased from a peak in 1984.

Map of GDP per capita *(below)* The rate of growth of Gabon's GDP from 1965–80 nearly equaled South Korea's, but six of its neighbors remain among the world's 20 poorest countries. Foreign debt consumes 81–264 percent of GDP in 12 countries.

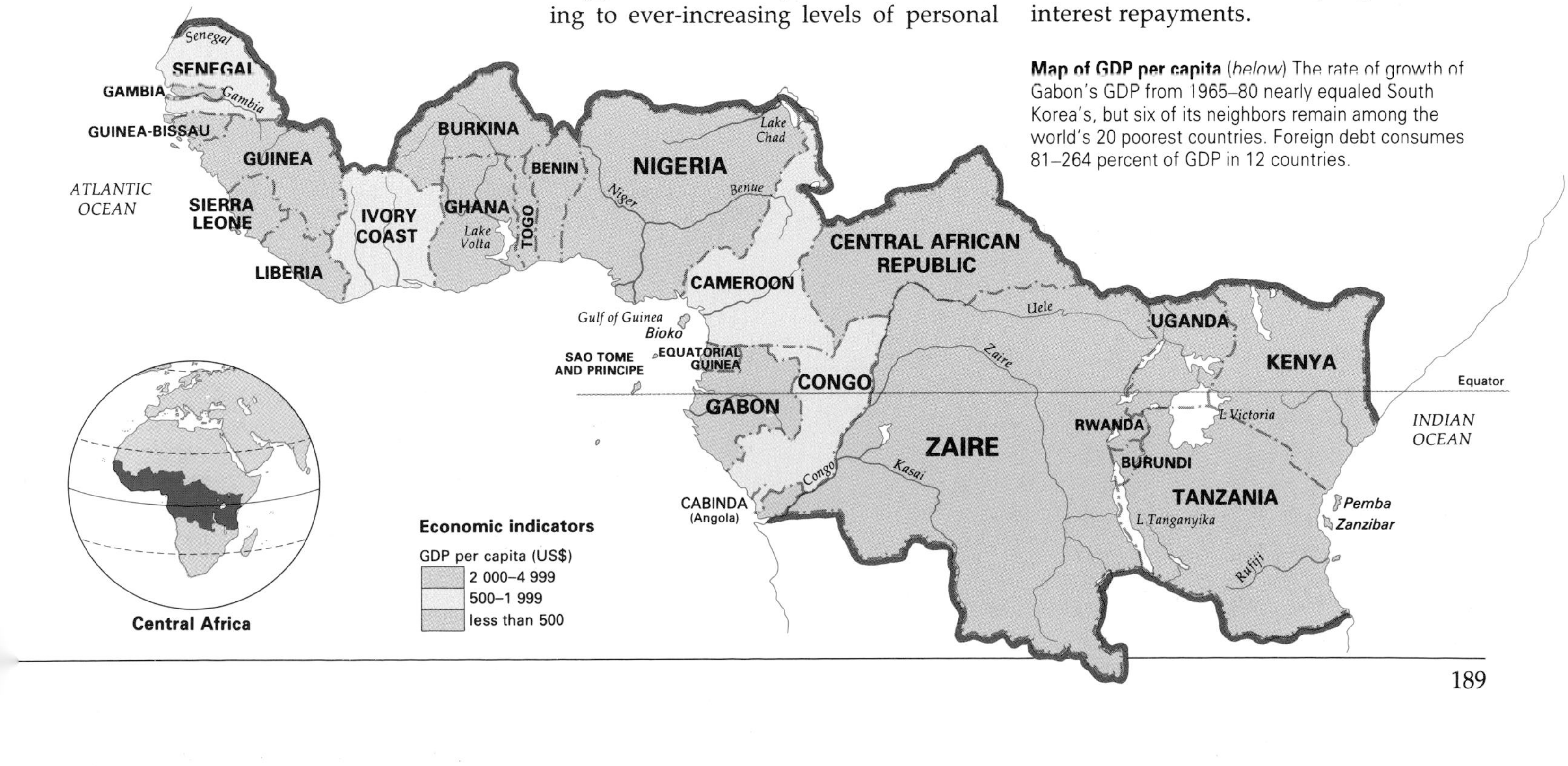

SERVICING A LARGE INTERNATIONAL DEBT

In the early 1990s, almost three decades after most of the region achieved independence, its export economy still revolved around producing a narrow range of primary products for the European and North American market. During the 1980s the volume of trade shrank slightly, and inflation was generally high. Stagnation and shrinkage was mostly due to dependence on commodity exports (whose value fell in the recessionary markets of high-income countries) and to the accumulated burden of international debt. In 1990 Nigeria, for example, owed a total external debt of over $36 billion; Tanzania owed over $5 billion of which $140 million was owed to the IMF.

Western economic control

A fundamental problem of balance-of-payments for most Central African countries is that they have failed to regain economic control of their natural resources, which remain in the hands of Western multinational corporations. Even where the industries have been taken into state ownership, foreign companies tend to be responsible for exploiting these resources – either because the host nation lacks the capital or technical expertise necessary, or because the commodity is of special importance to the Western power concerned. Zaire, for example, provides the American aerospace industry with 90 percent of its cobalt, and the United States has placed great emphasis on ensuring its supply of this vital mineral. Control like this is usually not in the best interests of Central African countries. Kenya sometimes has to import huge quantities of corn and wheat from the United States and South Africa because the large companies that control its agriculture concentrate on the production of cash crops for export rather than food crops for Kenyans.

A number of countries in the region also continue to depend heavily on a single resource. In Congo, for example, oil revenues finance half of the country's budget. Guinea is the world's second

Prosperity bypass (*right*) A modern highway separates the urban infrastructure of Lagos, Nigeria, from shantytowns on its outskirts. In this, the only Central African country with a GDP above $15 billion in 1992, the majority remain among the region's poorest.

TANZANIA'S UJAMAA PROGRAM

In the early years of Tanzania's independence, its development policy emphasized producing crops for export and encouraging foreign investment. In 1967 the government announced a new self-sufficient socialist strategy. An important part of the strategy for reducing export dependency was rural development, to be achieved through the establishment of collective "self-help villages" or Ujamaa – the Swahili word for family. Drawing upon traditional ideas and structures, the Ujamaa villages were intended to be created and managed by the people who lived and worked in them, but before long became subject to direct government intervention.

By the late 1970s the Ujamaa program, which had come to rely on government money, was in difficulties: Tanzania's financial situation had deteriorated as the value of its exports fell and the cost of manufactured imports rose. The country's economic problems continued into the 1980s, despite the introduction of a number of austerity measures. In 1986 a plan for economic recovery – designed according to World Bank and IMF guidelines – went into effect. Agricultural production has improved and some industrial enterprises have prospered, but the recovery of Tanzania's economy in the 1990s has become dependent on international support.

largest producer of bauxite, which accounts for over 90 percent of its export earnings. Countries that depend heavily on a narrow resource base are vulnerable to world commodity price fluctuations beyond their control. The burden of debt that has built up in recent years means that even when conditions are favorable, revenue from exporting is spent on servicing external debt, rather than on investment in industrial diversification.

More than half the exports of Central Africa go to the European Community (EC). Internal transactions within the region and trade with other African countries accounts for about 10 percent of exports, and the United States takes another 10 percent. Only Nigeria, the Congo and Cape Verde are not heavily reliant on European trade. Nigeria and the Congo are both major oil-exporting nations and the United States is their most important market; for the islands of Cape Verde, the African mainland accounts for half of all exports. Despite the importance of the region's raw materials and resources to the economies of Europe and North America, in 1990 only a handful of countries – including Nigeria, Ivory Coast, Zaire and Cameroon – enjoyed a positive balance of trade.

Loading cocoa in Ghana for export *(above)* Four of the world's top 10 cocoa exporting countries are in Central Africa. Ghana, the second largest of these, produced 295,000 tonnes in 1992 mostly for Western confectionery and food processing.

The interest-payments burden

Maintaining payments on international debt continues to be a major drain on financial and other resources throughout the region. Even for those nations with a positive balance of trade, external debt consumes a significant proportion of export earnings. Ivory Coast, which had a total foreign debt of almost $18 billion in 1990 was spending 13.3 percent of its export earnings on interest payments alone. In the same year, the total external debt of six countries – Tanzania, Congo, Zaire, Sierra Leone, Nigeria and Ivory Coast – was greater than their gross national product (GNP).

Most Central African countries, with the guidance of the IMF, are implementing programs aimed at reducing the balance of payments deficit, honoring debt repayments and revitalizing stagnant economies. The IMF has made these programs a condition of its continued financial support, but any real benefits will only emerge in the long term.

In recent years the burden of debt and increasing levels of poverty have encouraged popular demands for democratic government within the region, spurred on by the rapid political changes that took place in Eastern Europe in 1989. Benin abandoned its Marxist–Leninist political and economic policies in December 1989, moving to a multiparty political system and a free market economy. These ideas are now spreading across the region from west to east. Tanzania and Kenya are set to abandon their long-standing one-party political systems and work for greater openness in their economies in 1992.

Zaire's balance of merchandise trade Richly endowed with high-value natural resources, the country relies for its trading strength on exporting metals and minerals. Zaire runs a visible trade surplus, exporting mostly to its former colonial power, Belgium.

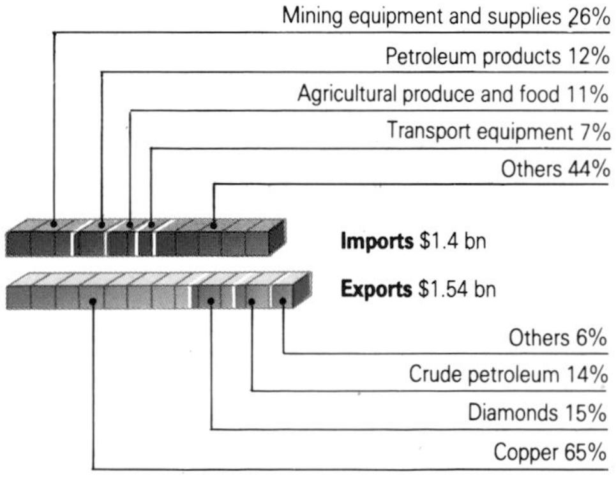

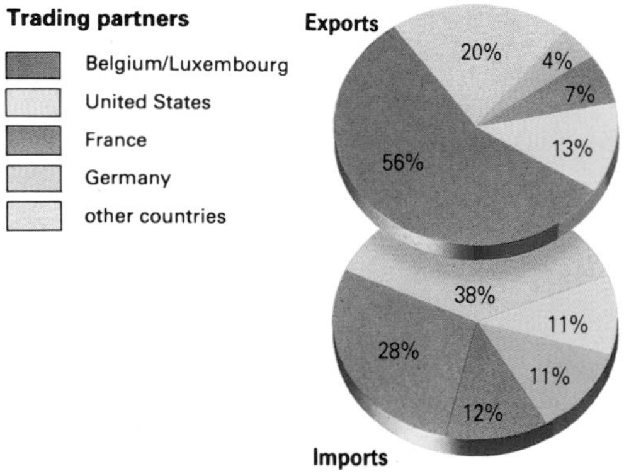

Core of the workforce *(above)* Tanzanian women with a harvest of maize. According to a 1989 United Nations report, 56 percent of Tanzania's GDP came from agriculture, with women doing half the planting, 60 percent of harvesting and 70 percent of weeding.

FIGHTING HUNGER AND ILLITERACY

Statistical measures of a country's wealth give very little idea of how income and prosperity are distributed through the population. In most of Africa, wealth is concentrated in the hands of the urban elite at the expense of the rural sector and the urban poor. An extreme example of uneven distribution is provided by Zaire's President Mobutu, who is believed to be one of the five richest heads of state in the world. Although he has a vast personal fortune amassed from hi interests in his country's strategic companies, Zaire has one of the world's lowest gross domestic product (GDP) per capita figures and a huge external debt.

Village healthcare and nutrition

In Central Africa approximately 70 percent of the population is rurally based and depends on subsistence agriculture complemented by cash-crops and village handicrafts. Women play a key role in the rural economy, not only in domestic and handicraft work, but as agriculturalists, often maintaining small plots of land to provide food for the family or for sale in the local marketplace. Most villages do not have electricity or piped water, and little more than a third of the region's population have access to a safe water supply. The daily ritual of fetching water and fuelwood can be a lengthy task that occupies time that could more profitably be spent tending crops or animals.

Modern educational and healthcare systems were first established by European missionaries, and mission schools, clinics and hospitals still play an important role throughout the region. Medical facilities tend to be concentrated in larger villages and towns, and rural people often have limited access to healthcare. To overcome this problem, in some parts of the region nurses and healthworkers are trained to diagnose and treat the more common diseases, and then sent out to the villages to hold temporary clinics.

THE AIDS CRISIS

The AIDS epidemic in Central Africa has implications far beyond the illness and death of individuals. It also strikes at the economic health of the region, largely because it is men and women in the economically active 15–45-year-old-age group who are primarily affected. Illness drains family resources due to the cost of medicines and the patient's inability to work. If a parent dies household food production is likely to fall and to compensate, children may be withdrawn from school to work the land. A widow may face claims from her husband's family for the household's land rights. The death of both parents often leaves orphans dependent on their grandparents or the state; the elderly are left without children for support in their old age, and become an additional strain on state resources.

The region's ability to cope with the crisis is extremely limited. It is now recognized that the spread of AIDS is a rural as well as an urban problem. The costs of preventive health education and screening, together with the care of victims, have overstretched already inadequate health services, and despite some success with local self-help projects, AIDS threatens to overwhelm the region's healthcare systems.

Only those people whom they cannot treat are referred to a doctor. This policy has been successful in bringing medicine to remote communities and also maximizes the use of the few doctors in the region. Drugs are available from pharmacies in the larger settlements, but are relatively expensive. A course of treatment can easily absorb any surplus cash that a family has earned.

Despite Kenya's success with family planning programs since 1982 (the number of children per family has dropped from 7 to 4 or 5) rapid population growth continues to be a problem. As well as stretching immediate resources, population pressure creates environmental change that can reduce the productive capacity of the land. This has caused growing impoverishment, and only nine countries in the region – the Seychelles, Cape Verde, the Congo, Ivory Coast, Gabon, Guinea-Bissau, Gambia, São Tomé and Liberia – are able to meet their people's calorie consumption requirements. In the region the average calorie consumption is about 96 percent of what is needed to sustain health.

Low levels of nutrition, together with limited access to safe water and healthcare, take a heavy toll on the health of the region's population. A measure of how human wellbeing is affected by the social environment is the infant mortality rate – in Central Africa the average figure is over 10 times higher than in the United States.

Urban unemployment

As conditions in the countryside deteriorate, many villagers, particularly young men, have migrated to the towns and cities in search of work. In some countries in western Africa, gold-mining sites act as magnets, drawing in men from a wide area. The low level of industrial development in most countries in the region, however, means that urban employment opportunities are extremely limited. When people arrive in the cities, the best they can usually hope for is insecure work in the informal sector of the economy such as street-trading; it is quite common for people from the countryside to be forced into crime, prostitution or begging in order to survive. The urban unemployed are normally between 15 and 24 years of age – in Nigeria and Kenya 70 percent of the unemployed fall into this age group – and young women tend to fare worse than young men. Some Central African countries also have large numbers of educated people for whom underdevelopment means that there is little prospect of finding employment that will make the best use of their skills.

In the early 1990s, most Central African countries were cutting back state services and subsidies to reduce balance of payments deficits and honor interest payments on foreign debt. National health and education services have suffered accordingly. Living standards throughout the region are falling – with young people suffering the most – and hopes of reducing the birthrate through improved social conditions remain distant.

Aid to education *(above)* An adult education class in a village in Senegal, funded by international aid. Outside intervention here in recent years has changed the average educational attainment significantly. Literacy in Senegal was 32 percent in 1992, compared with under 20 percent in four neighboring countries. However, lack of funds from national governments across the region means that few domestically funded educational facilities are available, and primary school enrollment remains extremely low in most countries.

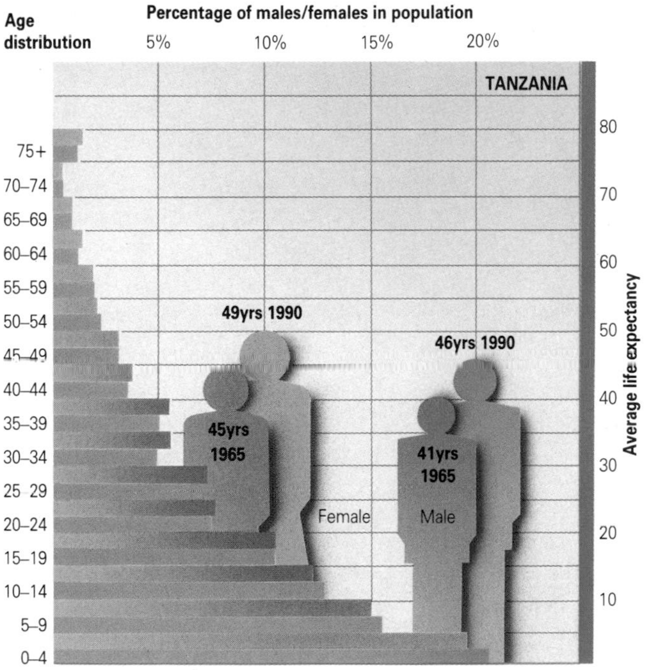

Life expectancy and age distribution *(right)* People in the Central African region have some of the lowest life expectancies in the world. These figures for Tanzania are only marginally better than for Sierra Leone (the lowest in the world) but far behind life expectancy in Kenya. Half of the world's 20 fastest-growing and youngest populations are in this region.

Band Aid in Burkina

The story is now legend. One evening in the late autumn of 1984, the London-based Irish rock musician Bob Geldof, watching television at home, was horrified by the picture of a starving child in Ethiopia, at the height of what was then Africa's worst ever famine. With friends from the music industry – some of them internationally famous – he recorded and distributed a Christmas song to raise funds to pay for emergency aid. The project, nicknamed Band Aid, rapidly grew far beyond Geldof's original aims and was able to finance a much wider range of activities throughout the continent.

The enormous public response to the Christmas record, and to the Live Aid concert that followed seven months later, enabled Band Aid to broaden the scope of its intervention from famine relief to longterm development, and to widen its geographical field of interest. The development specialists on the Band Aid committee, appointed to administer the funds, decided that 40 percent would be used on immediate disaster relief and the remaining 60 percent should be spent on longterm development activities. The aim was to support projects that would help people to develop their own skills and the facilities in their communities so as to avoid the worst effects of future droughts and to escape the poverty trap. With these ideas in mind, key considerations included local community participation, the distribution of benefits among the population, local education and literacy, and the sustainability of the project in the long term.

Rural development projects

In the landlocked Central African country of Burkina, 15 projects presented by local nongovernmental organizations were accepted by Band Aid for funding after a visit by Geldof to the country in 1986. At the time, Band Aid was already supporting 12 projects in Burkina, as a result of applications made directly to the London office. The total amount allocated was over $4.75 million; a huge expenditure in a country whose gross national product (GNP) per capita in 1990 was $330, one of the lowest figures in the world.

The projects supported in this initial phase were mostly concerned with meeting the basic needs of local communities: clean water and adequate nutrition. These were provided through small dam construction and market gardening, activities that fitted in well with the progressive, community-based rural development program being implemented by the country's revolutionary leader, Captain Thomas Sankara.

In 1988 Band Aid made the decision to decentralize its administrative structure and devolve power to local committees. In Burkina the *Comité National Band Aid* was established. The *Comité* went on to select a further 16 projects for funding from three main categories: agriculture, herding and health; low-cost appropriate research; the strengthening and support of local development organizations. New projects were submitted in the years 1989–91 to encompass women's activities, children's welfare, smallscale animal rearing, nutrition and village health.

Learning to build *diguettes* (*left*) Market gardening projects funded by Band Aid in Burkina have focused on building these small earth banks called *diguettes* which follow the natural contours of the land. They help the land to hold water during the rainy season by preventing rapid "runoff" which can also cause serious soil erosion.

Red-nose day in Central Africa (*below*) Since the success of Band Aid numerous other charities have run successful fund-raising campaigns for locally-based African relief projects often supervised by Oxfam or the Save the Children Fund. The British charity, Comic Relief, raises money through organizing comic stunts by the general public and charity performances by celebrity comedians, and by selling red noses.

Raising international awareness

Band Aid's greatest strength was its independence from government, which allowed it to direct its activities to those it saw as most in need, and at the same time speak frankly with donor nations and other international organizations. Its greatest achievement was to awaken interest and concern among the populations of the developed world (and particularly among young people) for the peoples of Africa and the Third World in general. This concern has been sustained through subsequent fund-raising initiatives such as Sport Aid and Comic Relief.

THE COLOR OF MONEY

THE LEGACY OF COLONIALISM · FORGING A NEW IDENTITY · THE WELFARE RIFT

Southern Africa encompasses the continent's most powerful economy, South Africa, as well as two of its poorest countries, Malawi and Mozambique. South Africa's industrial and military superiority has dominated the region for almost a century. Its headstart in industrialization made it a major center of employment for migrant workers from neighboring countries, and its treatment of these workers became the subject of international concern in the 1970s and 1980s. Mounting political and economic conflict between white-ruled South Africa and governments in the rest of the region created conditions of extreme instability, disrupting development programs and hastening environmental degradation and famine. Yet the region is rich in natural resources and has vast potential for economic development.

THE LEGACY OF COLONIALISM

Until the mid 20th century most of the economies of Southern Africa were shaped by the interests of European colonial powers, principally Britain and Portugal. They exploited the region as a source of raw materials and as a market for imported manufactured goods, with the result that industrial development was mainly limited to mining and processing raw materials.

Riches in South Africa

In the late 19th century large deposits of diamonds and gold were discovered in South Africa, attracting high foreign investment. The dynamic combination of mineral wealth, international investment and cheap black labor (sometimes coerced) from all over the region produced spectacular economic growth. South Africa achieved political independence from Britain in 1931, but the white ruling class, descendants of colonial settlers, continued to rule there. By 1945 manufacturing – supported financially by France, the Netherlands, Germany and particularly Britain – had overtaken mining as the country's leading economic sector.

This relatively early industrial development was unique within the continent. The other countries in the region became dominated, both economically and poli-

Heart of a modern economy (*below*) The transportation and financial infrastructures in Johannesburg equal those in many Western capitals, allowing the city to generate a GDP of $90 billion in 1992. However, the benefits do not extend to all citizens.

COUNTRIES IN THE REGION

Angola, Botswana, Comoros, Lesotho, Madagascar, Malawi, Mauritius, Mozambique, Namibia, South Africa, Swaziland, Zambia, Zimbabwe

ECONOMIC INDICATORS: 1990

	UMIE* S Africa	LMIE* Zimbabwe	LIE* M'bique
GDP (US$ billions)	90.72	5.31	1.32
GNP per capita (US$)	2,530	640	80
Annual rate of growth of GDP, 1980–1990 (%)	1.3	2.9	−0.7
Manufacturing as % of GDP	26	13	n/a
Central government spending as % of GNP	35	41	n/a
Merchandise exports (US$ billions)	23.4	1.3	0.092
Merchandise imports (US$ billions)	17	1.09	0.68
% of GNP received as development aid	–	5.5	65.7
Total external debt as a % of GNP	–	54.1	384.5

WELFARE INDICATORS

Infant mortality rate (per 1,000 live births)			
1965	124	103	179
1990	66	49	137
Daily food supply available (calories per capita, 1989)	3,122	2,299	1,680
Population per physician (1984)	n/a	6,700	37,950
Teacher–pupil ratio (primary school, 1989)	n/a	1 : 38	1 : 61

Note: The Gross Domestic Product (GDP) is the total value of all goods and services domestically produced. The Gross National Product (GNP) is the GDP plus net income from abroad.

** UMIE (Upper Middle Income Economy) – GNP per capita between $2,465 and $7,620 in 1990. LMIE (Lower Middle Income Economy) – GNP per capita between $610 and $2,465. LIE (Low Income Economy) – GNP per capita below $610.*

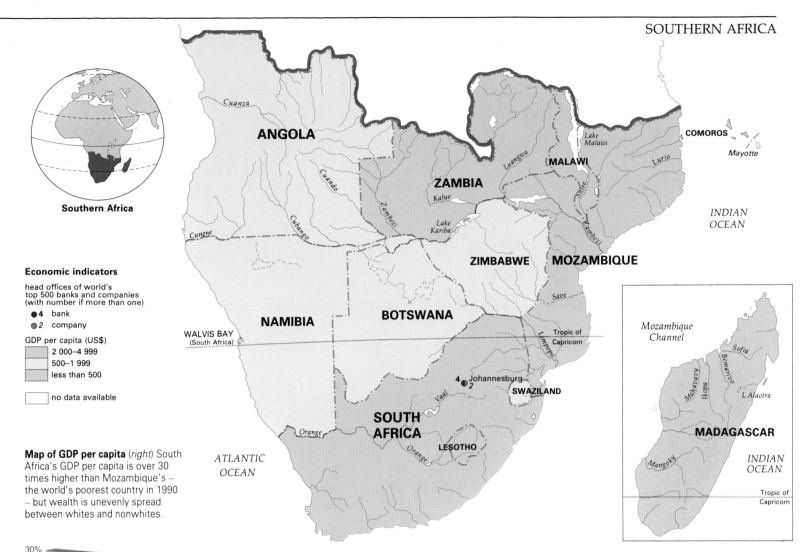

Southern Africa

Economic indicators

head offices of world's top 500 banks and companies (with number if more than one)

- ●4 bank
- ●2 company

GDP per capita (US$)

- 2 000–4 999
- 500–1 999
- less than 500
- no data available

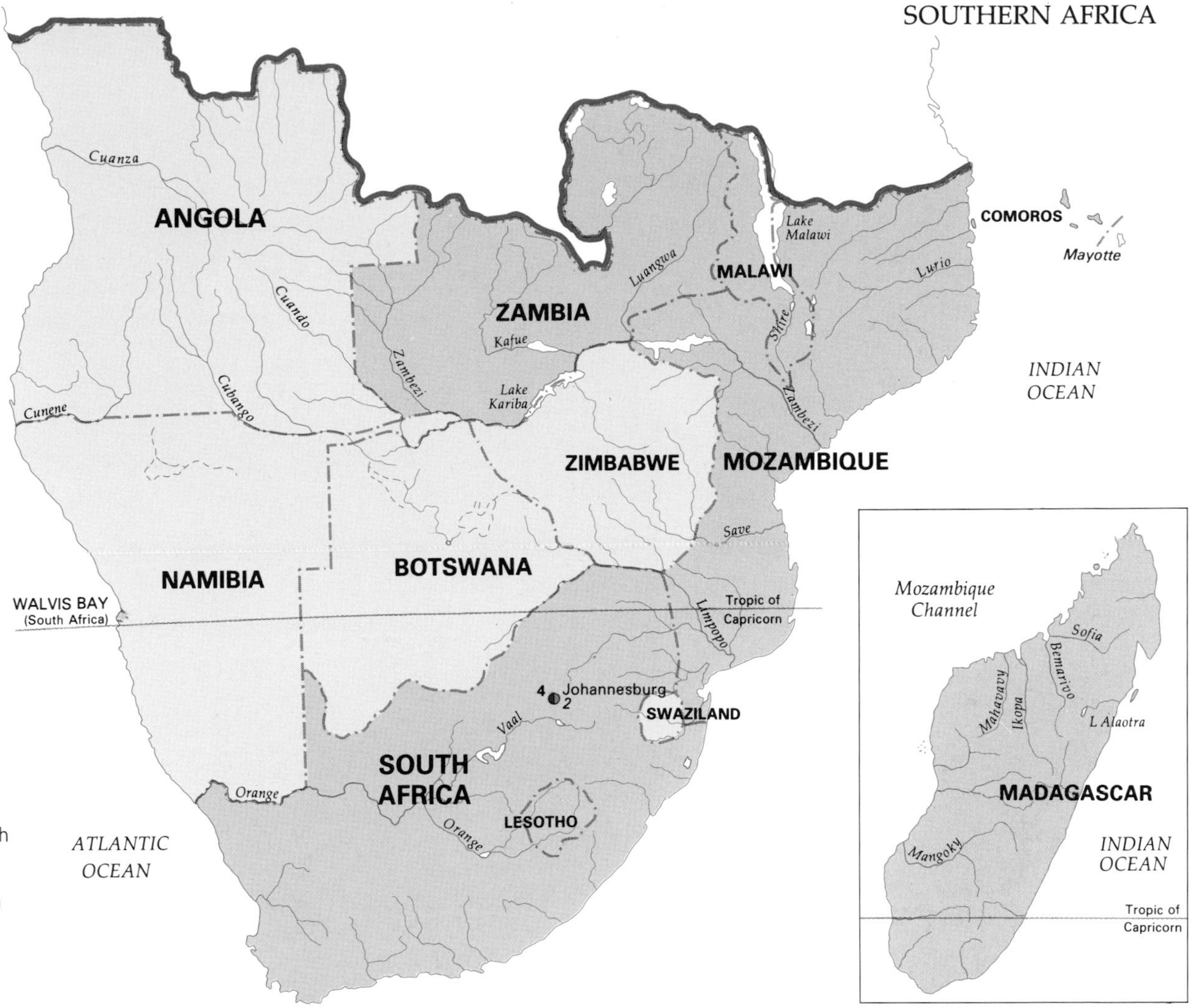

Map of GDP per capita *(right)* South Africa's GDP per capita is over 30 times higher than Mozambique's – the world's poorest country in 1990 – but wealth is unevenly spread between whites and nonwhites.

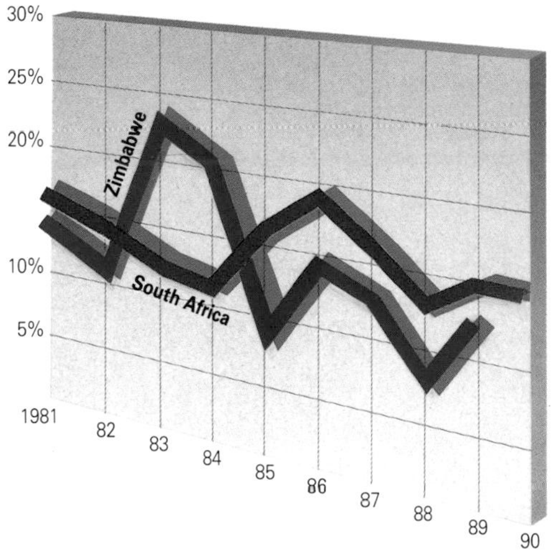

Profile of inflation *(above)* Inflation in both countries has rarely fallen below 10 percent since 1980. Constant price changes accompanied the restructuring of Zimbabwe's economy following independence and the effect of economic sanctions on South Africa.

tically, by white-ruled South Africa. Their economies remained predominantly agricultural and were heavily dependent on remittances from migrants who worked in the mines, farms and towns of South Africa. Namibia's economy in particular was completely subordinated to the interests of South Africa, which had gained control of the country after a League of Nations' mandate in 1919. South African and other foreign investment in Namibia's rich mineral resources produced rapid economic growth after World War II, though this mainly benefited the white elite. South Africa did not relinquish control of Namibia to the United Nations until 1989.

The quest for independence

After World War II, political factors played an increasingly influential role in the region's economic development. During the 1960s Britain withdrew from most of its former colonies and the nationalist movements that were emerging throughout Africa as a whole came into regular conflict with South Africa's colonialism and white-minority government. The Portuguese colonies of Angola and Mozambique and British-ruled Southern Rhodesia (Zimbabwe) were the last parts of the region to gain independence. Diamond extraction in Angola, and plantation agriculture in both Angola and Mozambique (producing coffee and rice under harsh conditions of forced labor) were a vital source of revenue to Portugal, particularly as its own fortunes declined. It was not until 1975, after prolonged colonial wars, that nationalist governments there finally took control of their own economies. Zimbabwe did not manage to achieve independence until 1980.

Angola, Mozambique and Zimbabwe responded to independence by adopting ambitious development programs. The main aims were to reduce external economic dependence (by, for example, nationalizing important industries) and to make sweeping improvements to social welfare provision for the majority black populations. Despite some early successes, principally in improving education and healthcare, these programs generally proved to be unworkable. Furthermore political tensions within the region were growing. The "frontline states" were an informal alliance comprising Botswana, Tanzania (to the north of the region) Zambia and, after 1975, Angola, Mozambique and Zimbabwe committed to fighting apartheid and promoting black majority rule. These political goals diverted scarce financial resources that could have been invested in production, infrastructure and social services into military spending to withstand South Africa's increasingly aggressive policies. At the same time, international opposition to South Africa's political ideology of apartheid was mounting. By the 1980s worldwide condemnation of the policy was so intense that South Africa found itself politically and economically isolated from its former overseas trading partners.

FORGING A NEW IDENTITY

The 1980s were a period of declining prosperity throughout Southern Africa. The decade opened with the creation of the Southern African Development Co-ordination Conference (SADCC) by nine independent states: Angola, Botswana, Lesotho, Malawi, Mozambique, Swaziland, Tanzania, Zambia and Zimbabwe (Namibia became a member in 1990 after gaining independence). A successor to the earlier frontline states, SADCC aimed to achieve collective economic self-reliance and reduce external economic dependence, particularly on South Africa.

Uniting for growth

The SADCC countries faced formidable economic challenges. The legacy of colonial economic policies left most countries dependent on exporting primary commodities, and importing expensive manufactured goods. This resulted in an unequal balance of trade that put the region at an even greater disadvantage. World recession during the 1980s led to a drop in commodity prices and a rise in the price of imports, driving the SADCC countries into heavy external debt. A dramatic fall in the price of copper, Zambia's major export, had a devastating effect on the country's economy. Even Malawi, which pursued rigorously conservative economic policies and welcomed foreign aid and capital, was badly hit by world recession.

In 1984 Zambia agreed a "structural adjustment program" with the International Monetary Fund (IMF) and the World Bank. Similar programs were subsequently introduced in Angola, Lesotho, Malawi, Mozambique and Zimbabwe. In return for loans, the countries were required to make fundamental economic changes to reduce public spending and budget deficits. Further economic changes were intended to liberalize government controls and increase incentives to the private sector. While these measures should help to promote more buoyant economies in the long term, reductions to public spending in the short term damaged welfare programs.

Diversifying in Namibia *(above)* Namibia Breweries is one of the country's few flourishing non-mineral-based industries. Brewing was probably introduced by the large numbers of German farmers who settled in South West Africa in the late 19th and early 20th centuries.

Botswana is exceptional among SADCC states for its high rates of economic growth (which have averaged almost 14 percent a year since the 1970s) and its successful diversification into mineral exploitation (mainly diamonds and coal), financial and other services, construction, transport and commercial farming. By the early 1980s its economic performance exceeded that of all nonpetroleum producing countries in Africa. Zimbabwe is also unusual within SADCC for its well-

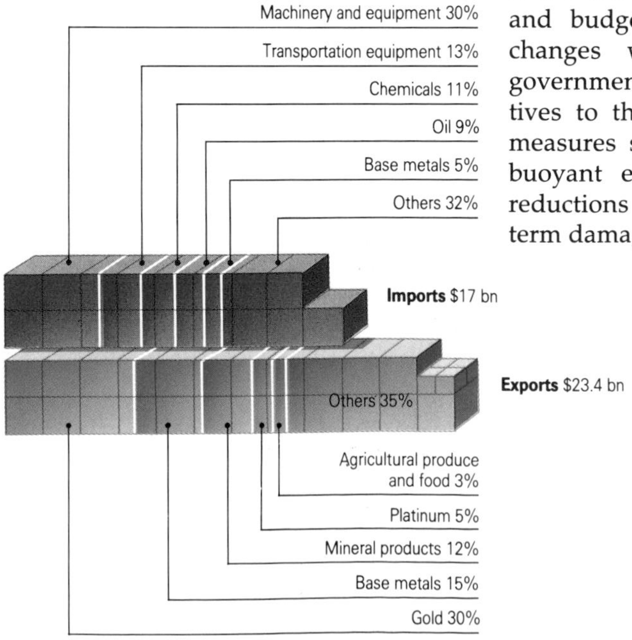

South Africa's balance of merchandise trade South Africa is the region's only major trader. Gold, base metals and minerals are the most important exports, while machinery and heavy equipment are significant imports. South Africa enjoyed a comfortable trade surplus in the 1980s in spite of sanctions imposed by Europe and the United States. The lifting of sanctions in the early 1990s in return for political concessions and guarantees of future antiracist reform should encourage further expansion.

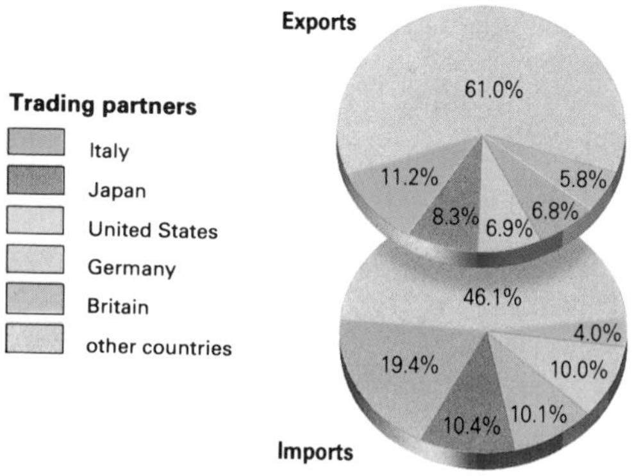

established and diversified manufacturing industry. This has given the country some protection against fluctuations in the world economy. By the end of the 1980s Zimbabwe's range of exports, including tobacco, food products, textiles, metallic and nonmetallic mineral products, and transportation equipment was among the most diverse in Africa.

South Africa's economic stranglehold over the region persists. In spite of recent progress, most countries continue to depend on South Africa for a significant proportion of their trade and as an employment center. In Lesotho, for example, more than half the adult male labor force is employed in South Africa's gold and coal mines, and many thousands of women also work in South Africa in domestic service or agriculture. Virtually all the goods for sale in Lesotho's small commercial centers are imported from South Africa and paid for by the earnings of migrant workers.

South Africa's recession

In 1980 South Africa was one of the world's most profitable trading nations and Africa's leading industrial economy. Nevertheless, the fall in gold prices, two years of severe drought and an inflation rate of over 13 percent pushed the country into severe recession by the mid 1980s. The worsening political crisis within the country, caused by growing international pressure for the abolition of apartheid, led to a sharp fall in foreign investment. In addition, the imposition of economic sanctions by the British Commonwealth, the European Community (EC) and the United States, including a ban on new investments and imports of South African goods, severely damaged the country's trading position. Unemployment, which was already rising due to the world recession and the mechanization of mines, reached new heights. Black workers were particularly badly affected. Although no accurate figures are available, it has been estimated that black unemployment or underemployment in 1986 reached 1.7 million people, or 23 percent of the workforce.

Impoverished by war *(above)* Refugees in Mozambique shelter in abandoned railroad cars. Economic devastation in the late 1980s was the result of deliberate targeting of farmland and factories by antigovernment forces supported by South Africa.

In spite of these difficulties, the South African economy has proved remarkably resilient. A negative growth rate in 1985 climbed to 3.2 percent by 1988. In the face of sanctions, the country has successfully developed new markets in Asia, the Pacific Rim, Latin America and even Eastern Europe following the end of the Cold War. Nevertheless, at the beginning of the 1990s the country was still beset with serious economic problems, including continuing high inflation and high levels of external debt and government spending.

THE AGONY OF MOZAMBIQUE

Chronic political instability and severe drought brought Mozambique to the point of social and economic collapse during the 1980s. Since 1981, South Africa has used the antigovernment forces of the Mozambique National Resistance (MNR) as an agent of economic devastation; this, coupled with drought, caused an estimated 100,000 people to die of starvation between 1982 and 1984.

Mozambique signed the Nkomati Accord with South Africa in 1984 in an attempt to secure peace and regenerate the economy. Nevertheless, war intensified over the next five years as the MNR battled to capture the most productive farmlands. Damage to crops intended for export and to industrial production brought economic activity to a virtual standstill. In addition to strategic economic targets such as farmland, factories and transportation, the fighting has also destroyed hundreds of villages, schools and health centers. By mid 1989 almost one-third of the country's population faced starvation and some 7.7 million needed food relief. The tragedy of starvation has been worsened by widespread disease. As a result Mozambique has one of the highest infant mortality rates in the world, and more than one million refugees have fled from their ravaged homes to neighboring countries, including over 600,000 to Malawi.

THE WELFARE RIFT

Since independence, most Southern African countries have tried to improve access to the employment opportunities and health and welfare services that were formerly reserved for white settlers. Within South Africa, however, standards of living continue to be sharply defined by class and race. Conditions in the country's urban and rural slums are closer to those in early industrial Europe than to an advanced industrial state nearing the end of the 20th century.

A legacy of discrimination

White South Africans, who make up one-sixth of the population, earn almost two-thirds of the national income. Successive apartheid laws have intensified this inequality by confining black people to

Beneficiaries of injustice (*above*) Middle-class white students leave a girls' high school in Cape Town, South Africa. In 1990 black students outnumbered white by more than 8 to 1, but white students benefited from 4 times more educational spending per capita. Education consumed 6 percent of GDP in the early 1990s and would have to mushroom to permit equal spending on black students. About 20 percent of South Africans over age 16 have had no formal education.

Life expectancy and age distribution (*right*) South Africa has the region's highest average life expectancy, raised by the white minority. In contrast, three countries in the region still have an average life expectancy below 50 years old. South Africa also has a significantly lower birthrate than its neighbors. In 1992, 37 percent of South Africans were under age 15, compared with over 40 percent in nine other countries in the region.

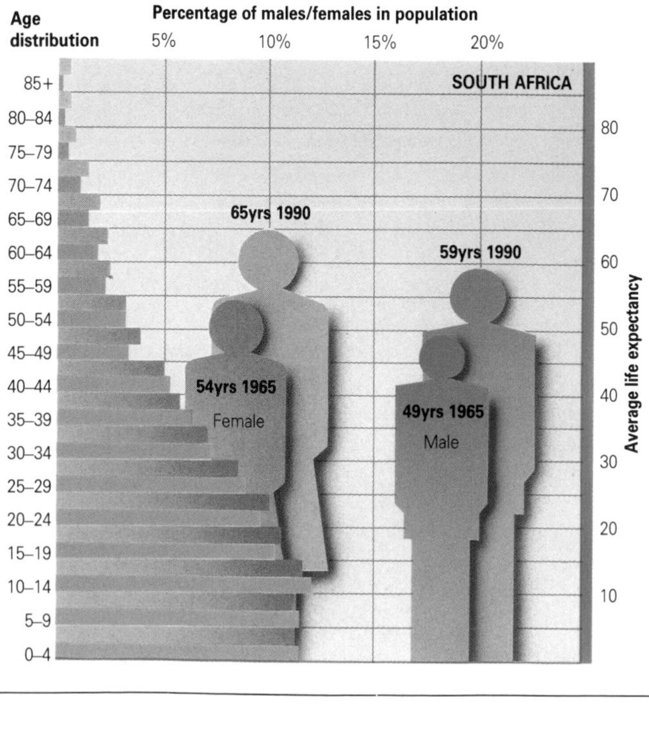

Family planning posters *(above)* on the walls of a mother-and-baby clinic in Lesotho. Improved healthcare has reduced infant mortality, but many families in the region continue to have 6 or 7 children. Populations will mushroom in the early 21st century.

TRANSFORMING HEALTHCARE IN ZIMBABWE

In colonial Zimbabwe infants, young children and women in their childbearing years were most vulnerable to disease and death. Mortality also varied by area, race or class. Just before independence, the mortality rate for white infants of 17 per 1,000 was close to that of industrialized countries. Among the black population diarrheal diseases, pneumonia and tuberculosis accounted for an estimated infant mortality rate of 120 per 1,000. This pattern of disease was rooted in practices that confined the black population to unproductive communal farmlands or to poor living and working conditions in the industrial towns or plantations.

Since independence the underlying causes of ill health have been tackled through a series of economic and social reforms including minimum wages for all, food subsidies, a land resettlement program, expanded education and the provision of drought relief. The healthcare system, which was previously geared to white urban populations, has been redirected toward primary healthcare in rural areas. This has included an expanded national village health-worker program), increased maternal and child healthcare, and improved village water supplies and sanitation. Recently, the healthcare program has been weakened by drought, recession and pressure from the IMF to reduce the country's budget deficit.

particular areas of cities or separate homelands – except where they are required to serve the needs of white-controlled urban economies or commercial agriculture. Housing, healthcare and education facilities are all sharply segregated and provision for the black minority is very much poorer than in white areas.

The government's social spending on nonwhites has traditionally been well below that for the white minority. During the 1980s, a chronic shortage of adequate housing for black Africans was compounded by government restrictions on housing subsidies except for the poorest households. Although private-sector housing increased, house prices were typically far beyond the means of all but a few black professionals. By the end of the 1980s, an immediate doubling of housing provision was necessary simply to cope with the backlog of homeless people.

Modern healthcare is concentrated in the white urban centers. In the homelands where the black population lives, malnutrition and disease are widespread and children are particularly at risk. From 1981–85 the infant mortality rate for black South Africans averaged between 94 and 124 per 1,000, a rate that is significantly higher than some in neighboring countries such as Botswana (72 per 1,000) and Zimbabwe (76 per 1,000).

State investment in black education has also been considerably lower than that for whites. In 1982 only 23 percent of teachers in black schools held appropriate qualifications; pupil/teacher ratios were 42:1 for black students, 27:1 for colored students, 24:1 for Indian students and 18:1 for white students. Drop out and failure rates among black students continue to be high, while the employment opportunities available to them are severely limited. Despite real gains in wages between 1970 and 1985, wages for black and many colored and Indian South Africans remain very low compared with white incomes. State pensions are also meager and are available only to a small minority. The political reforms of the early 1990s abolished some of the central pillars of apartheid. Nevertheless, it is likely to be many years before equality between South Africa's racial groups is achieved. The reforms did not, for example, extend voting rights to black people.

Change through independence

Improvements to health, work and welfare in most countries of the region have largely depended on how far they have succeeded in reducing their economic dependence on South Africa. Rapid economic expansion and urban growth in Botswana since the 1980s has increased access to employment opportunities and social services. Nevertheless, social and economic inequalities persist. For example, the economic benefits of beef production – one of the country's major exports – are restricted to only about 5 percent of the population, chiefly based in towns. By contrast, in a country of erratic rainfall and poor soils, some 50 percent of rural households continue to depend on arable farming supplemented by payments from urban migrants.

The restructuring of the old colonial economy has been a primary goal of President Robert Mugabe's government in Zimbabwe. Regional reorganization and a policy for growth have promoted investment in the communal lands, where the problems of overcrowding and environmental decline have been partly remedied through land redistribution and conservation measures. Massive welfare spending has improved provision of education and welfare services. However, like other countries in the region, Zimbabwe suffers very high unemployment and is having to curb its social spending in line with austerity programs run by the International Monetary Fund (IMF).

The factors restricting economic growth and development in Southern Africa have been intensified by political struggle and by South Africa's policy of regional destabilization. The two principal trouble-spots of Angola and Mozambique won their independence only after long wars that seriously disrupted their economies. Recovery was constrained by the mass exodus of the commercially and politically important Portuguese community, so that ambitious welfare programs were quickly stifled by lack of funds. Drought and conflict with South Africa intensified their economic plight during the 1980s, leaving a cruel legacy of famine, environmental degradation and hundreds of thousands of refugees.

The politics of trade

The economies of Southern Africa form an integrated system, though trade between the countries is dominated by – and highly favorable to – South Africa. During most of the 20th century, as investment and production became concentrated within South Africa, the other countries became service economies that provided it with cheap labor, raw materials and a local market for its products.

The formation of the Southern African Customs Union (SACU) in 1910, comprising South Africa, Botswana, Lesotho, Namibia and Swaziland, helped South Africa to consolidate its position as the region's dominant economic power. The SACU agreement is theoretically reciprocal, though in practice only South African exports to member countries have enjoyed preferential status. South Africa's command of major trade and transportation routes also gives it an important advantage over its neighbors. Consequently, one of the primary goals of the Southern African Development Coordination Conference (SADCC) has been to reduce its members' dependence on South African transportation networks by constructing alternative road and rail services to the coast through Angola, Mozambique and Tanzania, as well as new infrastructure for energy supplies. Since 1986 SADCC has emphasized stimulating trade within member countries which, at that time, accounted for only 5 percent of their total external trade.

Threat and counterthreat

SADCC's activities posed a direct threat to South Africa's economic ascendancy and to its ambitions to create a "constellation of Southern African states". International opposition to apartheid reinforced the challenge. Foreign donors such as the EC actively supported SADCC projects and gave economic and military aid to its members. After the Soweto disturbances of 1976 and South Africa's refusal to accept the United Nations plan for Namibian independence, they also imposed economic sanctions against South Africa.

South Africa responded to the threats to its political system and economic superiority with an aggressive policy of deliberate regional destabilization. This had the twin aims of undermining SADCC's economic initiatives and weakening black majority governments. During the 1970s and 1980s South Africa gave financial and military assistance to rebel forces in Angola, Lesotho, Mozambique and Zimbabwe. It also used sabotage, among other methods, to disrupt economic activity in the SADCC states. Transport and communications lines were repeatedly destroyed, including the Benguela railroad across Angola and the Zimbabwe–Maputo line. Power supplies were also sabotaged, such as oil pipelines, the oil depot at Beira, the refinery in Angola's capital, Luanda, and power lines from the Cahora Bassa Dam in Mozambique.

During the 1980s South Africa sought agreements with neighboring black states that would prevent the use of their territories as bases for either the African National Congress (ANC) or the South West Africa People's Organization (SWAPO). This last organization was formed in 1960 to resist South Africa's administration of Namibia. Assurances were given in return for an end to South African support of antigovernment organizations. Accordingly, the Nkomati Accord was signed with Mozambique in 1984 and a similar agreement reached with Angola. Despite these agreements, South Africa continued its policy of political destablization in the two countries, which by the 1980s were among the poorest in the world. The United Nations estimates that 1.3 million people died in Angola and Mozambique from 1980–88 as a direct or indirect result of the wars, and that South Africa's policy of aggression and retaliation cost the SADCC countries $62.45 billion over the same period.

The withdrawal of South African troops from Angola in 1988, agreement over Namibian independence in 1989 and the recent political reforms in South Africa have opened a new era in the region. At the beginning of the 1990s, while negotiation proceeded over a new, more democratic South African constitution, the government has been trying to establish the country as a legitimate international and regional economic power. President F. W. de Klerk has emphasized the "constructive role" that the new South Africa can play in fostering an effective and more equitable economic region. Meanwhile, the SADCC countries face a daunting task of economic reconstruction after more than a decade of instability and war.

Waging a war of terror Renamo, the Mozambique national resistance, made this attack on a settlement just over the border in Malawi. Renamo drew on the support of the South African military during the 1980s to destabilize Mozambique and its neighbors.

KULIMA
MOAGEM

THE STRUGGLE FOR SELF-SUFFICIENCY

FROM COLONIZATION TO INDUSTRIALIZATION · LAYING THE FOUNDATIONS OF A MODERN ECONOMY
INEQUALITY AND UNEVEN DEVELOPMENT

The Indian subcontinent has an extremely diverse economy, though most of the region is very poor. Government welfare programs have improved life expectancy, literacy and general healthcare in many areas, but the number of people living in absolute poverty continues to rise. Since India, Pakistan and Sri Lanka won their independence in 1947–48, industrial development has brought about great economic changes, though in the poorest areas the economy still depends on agriculture. India now manufactures most of its capital goods (equipment used to make consumer goods) and both Pakistan and Sri Lanka are attempting to achieve the same. However, a combination of trade deficits, repayment of interest on debts and internal political conflicts continues to strain economic development.

Ancient wealth of the East *(above)* Sacks of spices on a market stall in Karachi, Pakistan. Once an exotic and valuable commodity, spices were the basis of ancient trade in the region, eventually attracting the interest of the British and Dutch East India Companies and firing colonial ambitions.

COUNTRIES IN THE REGION

Bangladesh, Bhutan, India, Maldives, Nepal, Pakistan, Sri Lanka

ECONOMIC INDICATORS: 1990

	LIE* B'desh	LIE* India	LIE* Pakistan
GDP (US$ billions)	22.88	254.54	35.5
GNP per capita (US$)	210	350	380
Annual rate of growth of GDP, 1980–1990 (%)	4.3	5.3	6.3
Manufacturing as % of GDP	9	19	17
Central government spending as % of GNP	15	18	24
Merchandise exports (US$ billions)	1.49	16.1	4.95
Merchandise imports (US$ billions)	3.38	20.5	6.94
% of GNP received as development aid	9.2	0.6	2.9
Total external debt as a % of GNP	53.8	25.0	52.1

WELFARE INDICATORS

Infant mortality rate (per 1,000 live births)			
1965	144	150	149
1990	105	92	103
Daily food supply available (calories per capita, 1989)	2,021	2,229	2,219
Population per physician (1984)	6,390	2,520	2,900
Teacher–pupil ratio (primary school, 1989)	1 : 60	1 : 61	1 : 41

Note: The Gross Domestic Product (GDP) is the total value of all goods and services domestically produced. The Gross National Product (GNP) is the GDP plus net income from abroad.

** LIE (Low Income Economy) – GNP per capita below $610 in 1990.*

FROM COLONIZATION TO INDUSTRIALIZATION

The economic history of the Indian subcontinent has been deeply influenced by the area's long tradition of international trading and by the external influence of Mediterranean and Middle Eastern civilizations. From the 16th century onward, resource-based economies in many areas were exploited and expanded for trading purposes by European (and particularly British) colonizing forces. The export of opium (traded for Chinese tea) and the exchange of agricultural products for manufactured goods formed the basis of this trade. It continued well after India and Ceylon (now Sri Lanka) became independent in 1947 and 1948 respectively.

During the colonial period the local economy suffered greatly at the hands of the colonizing forces. Natural resources and trading profits alike left the region, and the local population was subject to land revenues and military taxes. However, some of the infrastructure left behind gave a boost to local enterprise after independence. For example, the British built an extensive transport and communication network and established a number of largescale industrial plants making iron and steel and textiles for domestic use as well as for export. Using these facilities, half of independent India's exports were of manufactured goods rather than raw materials by the end of 1947. The biggest obstacles facing industrial development were the lack of chemicals and heavy engineering industries, the low level of employment in factory industries and a heavy reliance on manufactured goods from Britain. Poor health and literacy among the workforce and the lack of financial systems to raise funding were also major problems. Agriculture was an unstable platform to support economic growth due to its susceptibility to unreliable rainfall, including drought, and to fluctuating markets.

Promoting an independent economy

During the 1950s the new governments of India, Pakistan and Sri Lanka aimed to bring about economic development to relieve poverty and make their countries

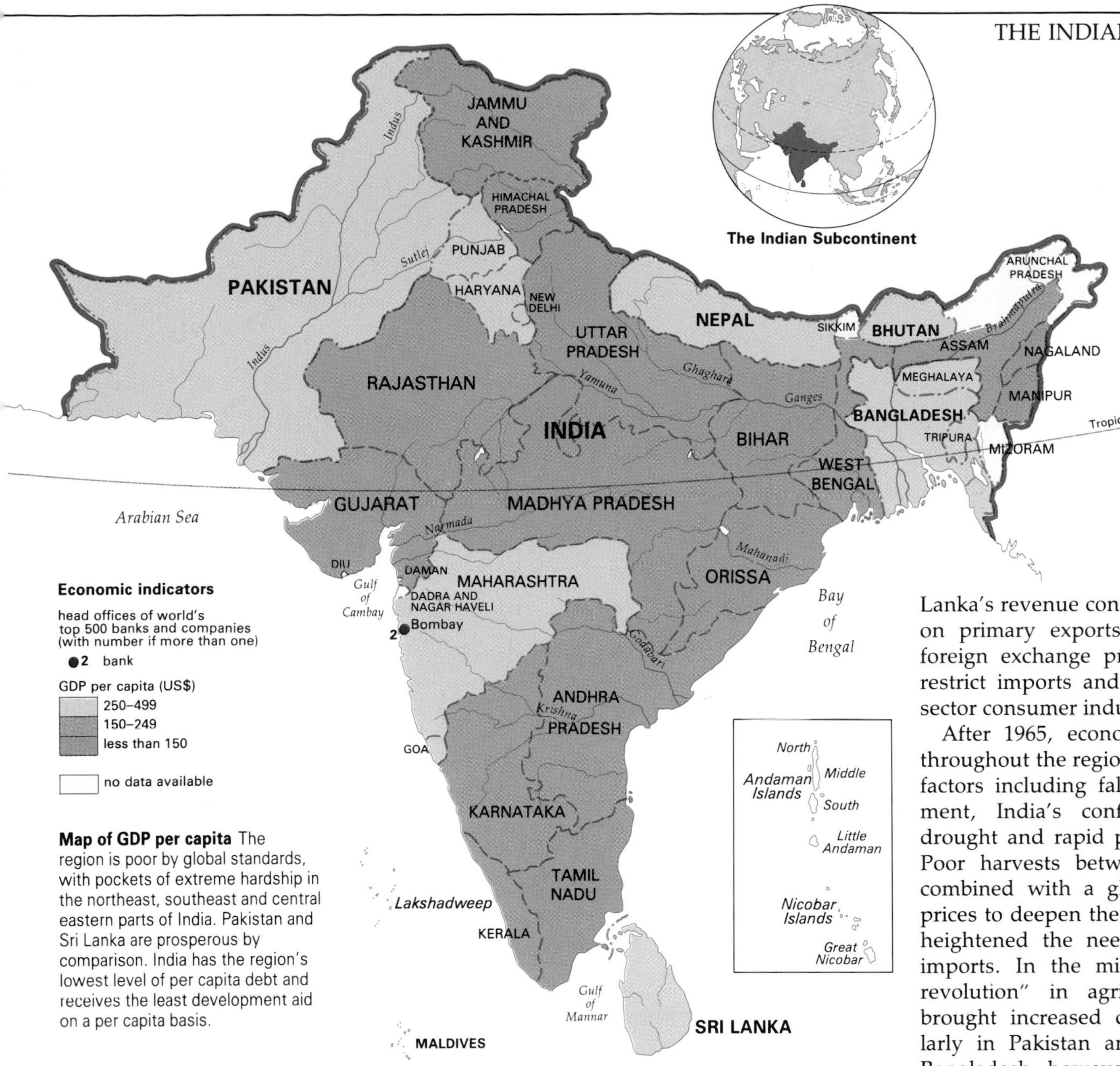

Map of GDP per capita The region is poor by global standards, with pockets of extreme hardship in the northeast, southeast and central eastern parts of India. Pakistan and Sri Lanka are prosperous by comparison. India has the region's lowest level of per capita debt and receives the least development aid on a per capita basis.

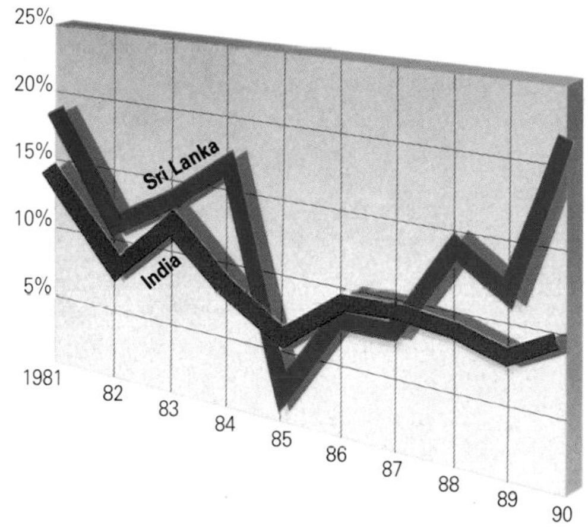

Profile of inflation (*above*) India's inflation was sharply reduced in the mid 1980s, but rose slightly in the early 1990s following economic liberalization. In Sri Lanka, the effects of a destructive civil war followed closely by the world recession, sent inflation soaring; it is now by far the region's highest.

more self-sufficient. In India, the first prime minister Jawaharlal Nehru (1889–1964) advocated Soviet-style centralized economic planning, though he maintained a nonaligned political position. State-owned industries, such as iron and steel, heavy engineering and chemicals, were developed to limit dependence on foreign goods, reduce the longterm balance of payments deficit, and increase national economic autonomy. Nehru also advocated strong control over private industry, discouraged foreign investment, and introduced land reforms to develop agriculture.

Pakistan and Sri Lanka, by comparison, had fewer industrial resources. The area that became East Pakistan (later Bangladesh) was dependent on jute growing and processing, but had few jute factories of its own. Partition dealt a severe blow to the industry since East Pakistan could no longer process its raw jute in Calcutta (over the new border in India). Both Sri Lanka and Pakistan exported agricultural products in exchange for imports of industrial machinery and manufactured goods. Later, supported by foreign aid, Pakistan began to manufacture goods that it had previously imported, particularly machine tools and chemical products. Sri Lanka's revenue continued to rely mainly on primary exports (notably tea) until foreign exchange problems forced it to restrict imports and to develop private-sector consumer industries.

After 1965, economic growth slowed throughout the region due to a number of factors including falling rates of investment, India's conflict with Pakistan, drought and rapid population increases. Poor harvests between 1971 and 1974 combined with a global increase in oil prices to deepen the recession. They also heightened the need for aid and food imports. In the mid 1970s the "green revolution" in agricultural technology brought increased crop yields, particularly in Pakistan and northwest India. Bangladesh, however, did not benefit to the same extent, neither did it recover economically from its secession from Pakistan in 1971. A combination of war-related disruption, intense poverty, susceptibility to natural hazards and severe population pressure has forced Bangladesh to remain a predominantly agricultural economy dependent on large influxes of foreign aid.

The economies of Nepal, Bhutan and the Maldives were never directly governed by Britain and remained quite isolated from developments in the rest of the region. In Nepal, manufacturing industry has been slow to develop due to competition from Indian goods, but tourism has proved to be a good source of foreign revenue. Since 1958 Bhutan has relied almost entirely on India for its economic development, achieved by improving Bhutan's basic infrastructure, ser vices, agricultural sector and processing industries. The Maldives, one of the poorest countries in the world, has a subsistence economy based on fishing and a small amount of tourism.

LAYING THE FOUNDATIONS OF A MODERN ECONOMY

Strategies for growth across the region achieved mixed success in the 1980s and early 1990s. India benefits from a large and varied resource base and manufactures the majority of its own consumer goods, though demand exceeds supply. Manufacturing growth rates have been quite high since the early 1980s, and heavy industries now account for almost half of India's gross domestic output. Nevertheless, several of these industries are inefficient by international standards. Agriculture has kept pace with population growth and in the early 1990s India was a net exporter of cereals.

Pakistan has seen an increase in both economic growth and real wages since 1977. However, lack of investment in transportation, communications and basic infrastructure has tended to discourage private-sector enterprise. Agriculture has continued to grow steadily with record harvests in the early 1980s, but this has caused problems in other areas. The high levels of mechanization needed to sustain this pattern of growth have caused unemployment, encouraging some segments of the population to seek job opportunities in the Middle East.

Sri Lanka also increased its food production during this period. In the early 1980s the government specifically promoted increased agricultural output, and Sri Lanka became self-sufficient in rice in 1985. However, the export of food products has suffered from a decline in non-oil commodity prices in the 1980s and increased protectionism in some Western countries. A variety of successful domestic manufacturing industries, including ceramics, textiles and rolled steel, have helped to compensate for this loss, but tourism – an important source of revenue – has been disrupted by the civil war in the late 1980s and early 1990s. Bangladesh has grown less well and continues to rely upon agriculture for most of its gross domestic product (GDP). In 1990 modern factory industries accounted for only 5 percent of GDP and the Bangladeshi economy continues to remain heavily dependent upon foreign aid.

Trade and aid

The direction of the subcontinent's trade has changed markedly in recent years since Britain lost its position as south Asia's major trading partner. Trading with the Organization for Economic Cooperation and Development (OECD) countries increased significantly during the 1980s. While an overall trade deficit has become an increasing threat to the region's economic growth, India managed to sustain a trade surplus in the 1980s with the former Soviet Union, and domestic oil production has enabled it to reduce oil imports from the Middle East.

The main exports of Sri Lanka and Bangladesh continue to be dominated by cash crops (rubber, tea, coconuts and jute), which have suffered greatly from a global decline in market prices. Imports of petroleum products, chemicals, machinery and manufactured goods have

Illegal kerb trading (*above*) is carried on outside Calcutta's stock exchange. Just inside the building traders perch in tiny booths equipped with telephones to link them with brokers elsewhere. Financial trading in India is not yet computerized.

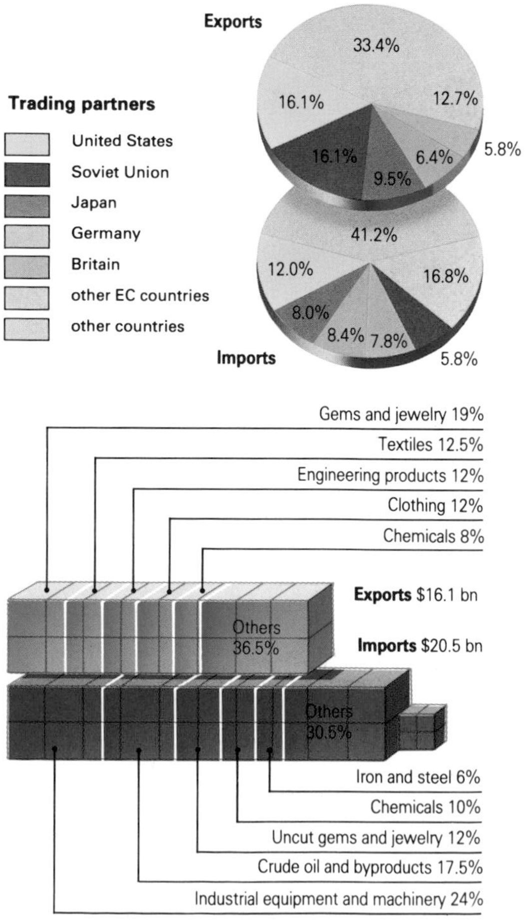

India's balance of merchandise trade (*right*) Like the rest of the region, India imports more than it exports; but is self-sufficient in food. Gems and jewelry remain important exports, but trade is no longer dominated by Britain or the former Soviet Union. Partners now include the United States, Japan and Germany.

Hollywood in Bangalore *(above)* The movie industry is big business in India, employing over 2 million people. Many films are exported to China, where their romantic plots and musical accompaniment make them popular. At home, the government taxes profits at 60 percent.

placed severe strain on the balance of payments in both countries, leading to increased levels of foreign aid, borrowing and interest payments. Sri Lanka responded to this problem mainly by lifting restrictions on international trade. Bangladesh, however, suffering from severe difficulties in exploiting its jute crop and hampered by its lack of economic infrastructure, has been forced into even greater levels of dependence upon foreign aid. In Pakistan, high levels of government spending on arms has combined with other economic problems to squeeze the national budget. As a result, it has had to resort to World Bank funds.

In the mid 1980s, the Indian government introduced a new wave of funding for projects to develop industry and the infrastructure that supports it. Rajiv Gandhi's 1985 budget cut import duties on machinery and materials used to construct buildings, roads and manufacturing plant in order to make it easier to import foreign equipment for industrial expansion. It also reduced licensing restrictions (imposed in the late 1940s and early 1950s to protect and regulate new industries) and introduced tax incentives for exporters. The level of borrowing needed to sustain the policies introduced by the budget resulted in constraints on the funding available for health, education and rural development. These constraints, and a related shift by some Indian companies toward the manufacture of luxury goods rather than mass produced commodities for the less wealthy, has meant that the vast majority of the Indian population has not benefited from this development strategy.

The role of agriculture

There is still much inequality in the spread of individual wealth across the subcontinent, caused not only by early colonial intervention, but also by recent economic developments. One example of this has been the appropriation of "green revolution" agricultural technologies by rural elites who are able to use their class or caste connections to obtain the latest supplies and information. In Pakistan, many large farmers who used to rent out land have taken it back for tractor cultivation, making many tenant farmers both landless and unemployed. In Bangladesh, too, higher caste groups have taken over cooperatives to ensure their access to agricultural supplies. Some used the resulting profits for moneylending and black marketeering. Both these factors have contributed to the fact that 75 percent of Bangladesh's population is now effectively landless. Even longterm economic development is influenced by the interests of various urban, industrial and rural elite sections upon whom governments depend for electoral support. The more needy, meanwhile, struggle to make their voices heard.

THE PRICE OF A CUP OF TEA

Sri Lanka is the world's largest tea exporter. Its export economy has been dominated by this crop since it replaced the island's blight-damaged coffee plantations in the 1870s. To ensure that sufficient people were available for year-round picking, pruning and processing the British gradually imported cheap Tamil labor from South India throughout the late 19th and early 20th centuries. Despite the recent Sinhalese-Tamil tensions in Sri Lanka, gangs of resident Tamil women still carry out most of the tea picking whereas men prune and plant. Labor costs which may amount to 60 percent of cultivation costs and 40 percent of total expenditure are minimized since wages tend to be low and living conditions poor.

Export earnings from tea are subject to damaging price fluctuations on the international market. Only 9 percent of the tea grown is consumed domestically and when international prices slump, as in 1984-85, over two million people dependent upon the industry are affected. Britain was the main export target until the 1960s, but today, Pakistan, Iraq, Egypt and the United States are all major buyers. A quarter of Sri Lanka's tea is exported in bag or packet form and international brokers such as Lipton and Brooke Bond handle the largest tonnages.

INEQUALITY AND UNEVEN DEVELOPMENT

Despite the fact that the number of people in absolute poverty is increasing in the Indian subcontinent, significant improvements in healthcare and life expectancy have been achieved in most areas. Some of the most notable advances have occurred in Sri Lanka where a high level of state expenditure has gone into the provision of basic healthcare, education and welfare. Schemes include government-subsidized rice for the population, guaranteed price schemes for food producers and land colonization programs for the landless. As a result, Sri Lanka sustains a relatively high quality of life compared with the rest of the Indian subcontinent, and life expectancy at birth there has risen from 43 years in 1946 to 71 years in 1990.

Elsewhere, life expectancy at birth has also increased significantly. In India, for example, it rose from 27 years at independence to 59 years in 1990. General standards of health have also improved since independence. Partly this is because food production is more reliable than it was in the middle of the 20th century and the incidence of famine has decreased. However, high levels of poverty mean that average food intake is still low in many areas, despite government welfare measures such as the establishment of subsidized "fair price" shops.

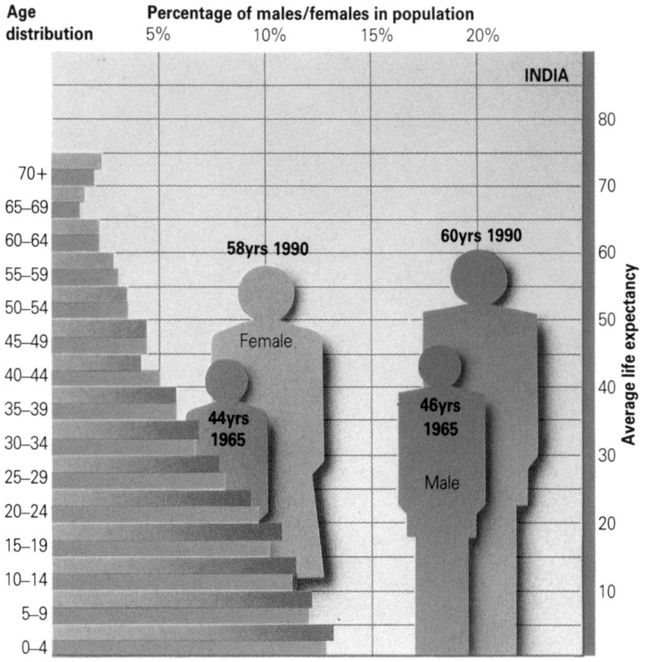

Life expectancy and age distribution *(left)* Life expectancy in India is average for the subcontinent but strikingly low compared with developed countries, in spite of recent advances in healthcare. Unlike most other countries in the world, in India men are likely to live longer than women. Life expectancy in Sri Lanka, by contrast, is almost as high as in developed countries, with women outliving men. Throughout the subcontinent, the large number of people under the age of 25 reflects the high birthrate.

The economics of relief *(right)* Food is distributed to people in a relief camp in Dhaka, Bangladesh, following a major flood. Poverty is the result of the lack of economic development exacerbated by a large population and frequent natural disasters. By the 1990s Bangladesh was the world's second largest aid recipient, receiving more than US$2 billion annually.

Government welfare policy also emphasizes the importance of free basic community healthcare, improved doctor to patient ratios and better medical facilities in rural areas. Even so, access to healthcare remains extremely unequal. It is biased strongly toward urban areas and care for wealthy elites. Many of the rural poor are unable to afford the traveling expense or time away from work to attend distant clinics. Country health centers are frequently understaffed and poorly equipped. As a result, mortality rates remain high, especially among young babies. In India alone, it is estimated that around 5 million children die each year from preventable causes.

Challenging social divisions

The benefits that come with secure employment are also unequally distributed throughout the population. India's Scheduled (lower) castes and tribal groups tend to remain at the bottom end of the economic hierarchy. To improve their situation, the Indian government has implemented a "positive discrimination" policy so that a proportion of jobs in the public sector are reserved for them. Dissatisfaction with the extent of these policies has led a number of disadvantaged groups to agitate for better terms. Meanwhile, higher castes resent the relative rise in status of the Scheduled castes who, traditionally perform ritually polluting tasks. The pressure of ill-feeling has vented itself in a violent backlash of prejudice and resentment against the lower castes.

Although formal education has a relatively well-established history in India, Bangladesh, Pakistan and Sri Lanka, the

Filling the public sector *(left)* Information and practice papers for the Indian civil service exams are available at a stall where vacancies are posted informally. In 1990, 18.7 million Indians worked in the public sector, half of them in the civil service.

BANGLADESH LIVING ON FOREIGN AID

Bangladesh (formerly East Pakistan) achieved independence in 1971 after a damaging civil war. The new state was left with little capacity to generate its own economic growth, since most of the major sources of investment were concentrated in former West Pakistan, from which it had just separated. Foreign aid provided the initial funds for repairing the country's damaged infrastructure and for rehabilitating the 10 million refugees who had fled to India during the war. As time went on, rapid population growth, food shortages and the inability of the economy to create significant revenue of its own produced a cumulative reliance upon international aid.

By the early 1990s, Bangladesh's domestic policies had become dominated by aid, and a number of elite groups had taken the opportunity to divert incoming funds away from the needy and into their own pockets. Many aid-related projects have come to be tied to the interests of these groups, but few are willing to invest the profits back into local industry. Instead, the state has become the main source of capitalist growth in Bangladesh, but its own funds are largely dependent upon foreign loans.

Bangladesh's expenditure on development, imports and investments depends largely upon financial aid while food aid provides the basic staple diet for six major urban centers. Even the steel, chemical and textile industries, potential sources for economic growth depend on raw material imports bought with aid, highlighting the near impossibility of Bangladesh achieving self sustaining economic growth in the near future.

system has tended to benefit mainly the upper castes and classes. By the 1990s, however, almost all Indian and Sri Lankan villages had access to a primary school, and Sri Lanka had achieved an adult literacy rate of 88 percent, the highest in the subcontinent. India's, by comparison, was only 48 percent. Better rural education facilities are steadily being provided in Bangladesh, Pakistan, Bhutan and Nepal. In Bangladesh, for example, government expenditure on education ranks below defense (less than one-fifth of the total) but above debt servicing, subsidies, social services, justice and the police.

Pockets of poverty, patches of wealth

Within India, rural poverty is lowest in Punjab in the northwest and highest in Bihar and the surrounding northeast. Himachal Pradesh, on the northeastern border of Punjab, boasts the lowest incidence of urban poverty, while the governments of Andhra Pradesh and Kerala in the south, and West Bengal in the northeast, have been the most successful in relieving local poverty. Bangladesh, starting from a much weaker position than its neighbors, has a severe eastern–northwestern divide in terms of the prosperity brought by industrial development. The eastern division benefits significantly from the services and facilities based in the country's two major cities, Dhaka and Chittagong; the northwest has no comparable urban centers. In 1970, Bangladeshis living in urban areas earned five times more per capita than those in rural areas, and this disparity has increased over time. In addition, two-thirds of Bangladesh's food aid rations go to the major cities. Within these cities, priority groups such as defense workers, civil servants and the police get the lion's share. The remaining third is distributed in rural areas to a population which, although resourceful, is fighting an uphill battle for survival.

Women in the economy

Across the Indian subcontinent, economic well-being varies with class, caste and geography; but within all these groupings there is one additional division – gender. South Asian women are frequently denied access to wealth, waged employment and property ownership in a way that men are not; and female children tend to have less access to healthcare and nutrition. All these are factors which, along with reported cases of female infanticide, help to account for the region's rising ratio of men to women.

This trend is the result of deeply ingrained cultural and social practices, which often limit the economic participation of women. Many Muslim and Hindu women go veiled in public and in some areas women are secluded in their houses between the onset of puberty and marriage. Particular types of work such as agricultural labor and trading are frequently out of bounds to women, and social contact is limited.

Women of lower castes and classes tend to be less restricted in the types of work that are socially permitted to them. They are frequently involved in work outside the home while their higher caste counterparts are restricted by the fact that they are not allowed to perform ritually polluting or physically dirty jobs. Women's wages tend to be substantially lower than those for men, though in India this disparity has decreased in recent years, except in the Punjab. Nevertheless, many employers feel strongly against hiring women and they are at a particular disadvantage when applying for higher income jobs.

In addition, many parents are opposed to educating girls. Wealthier parents may regard education as a way of increasing the girls' value for marriage but poor

Backbreaking work (*below*) Women sweep the floor in a plywood factory in Bhutan, one of the poorest countries in the world. A practical, widespread, if physically demanding solution to childcare is adopted by strapping children to their backs as they work.

Going to market in Jaipur (*right*) Middle-class Indian women, in spite of increasing education, are more likely to participate in the economy as consumers than as producers. Those who wish to work may be frustrated by the job shortage as much as by social opposition.

families cannot afford the cost of school clothes and equipment. An emphasis on early marriage, often between children, added to the need for girls to help at home, further lessens their chances of going to school. As a result, levels of female literacy in rural areas are significantly lower than those of men. There are some exceptions to this general rule. In Kerala in the south of India local authorities have promoted education for women for many years and female literacy levels there now stand at 90 percent.

Women throughout the subcontinent receive less medical treatment than men, and if they are seriously ill they often have to make do with cheaper, traditional forms of care. Many women suffer from anemia and malnutrition, especially when nursing or pregnant, and there are high female mortality rates in childbirth. In Bangladesh, more than 14 percent of girls are severely malnourished compared with 5 percent of boys. Female life expectancy – unlike the dominant trend in the west – is lower than that of men in all countries except Sri Lanka. In India, the number of women who die during childbirth (5 per 1,000 live births in 1980, not counting miscarriages and abortions) is among the highest in the world.

Nevertheless, healthcare for women has improved over the years. Child immunization linked with basic healthcare and nutrition programs have been encouraged throughout the region. In addition, state departments, nongovernmental organizations and international aid foundations have funded welfare programs. These include training for midwives, nurses, female doctors and local helpers; prenatal, delivery and postnatal care; child feeding and daycare centers for working women and programs that offer food in return for labor.

There is still a long way to go before women in the subcontinent are in a position to win real control over their own economic affairs. However, local women's movements are growing and are increasingly well organized. One notable example has been the Chipko movement in the Himalayan region of India. There, women are expected to collect forest litter and firewood so they depend on the trees for survival and are more aware of their value than their menfolk. The Chipko movement encourages villagers to stand up in opposition to timber companies to protect their forest-based livelihoods.

City transportation

Local transportation through the streets of Dhaka and other cities throughout south Asia is controlled by an army of rickshaw wallahs. In New Delhi three-wheeled scooters work as auto-rickshaws, but in Calcutta and Dhaka, cycle and hand-pulled rickshaws are the norm. Rickshaw wallahs throughout India and Bangladesh often work long days for low wages, carrying all manner of goods and people around cities not always designed for motorized forms of transportation. These cities could not function without their services.

The rickshaws themselves are rarely owned by their operators. Most are owned by small, family companies and lent out to the rickshaw wallahs for a sizable share of the profits. In some cases a rickshaw wallah can buy his own rickshaw from the manufacturer with the aid of a bank loan. Efforts are afoot in many south Asian cities to provide loans on more favorable terms to some rickshaw wallahs from government-owned or cooperative banks.

Rickshaw wallahs pulling highly decorated rickshaws through the crowded streets of Dhaka in Bangladesh.

CATCHING UP

REVERSALS OF FORTUNE · THE OPEN DOOR · THE IRON RICE BOWL

The Ming emperors who ruled China in the 16th century governed the most populous and economically developed country in the world. However, political instability gradually undermined the economy and by the early 1800s China had been surpassed by the industrial nations of the West. This long period of decline was halted by the communist government of Mao Zedong after 1949. His revival was given new impetus by the market-oriented reforms of the 1980s, which allowed China's economy to grow at the unprecedented rate of almost 10 percent per annum. If population growth can be controlled, and if a new generation of effective leaders can be found – two major challenges – it is possible that China will be a world economic power once again by the end of the next century.

COUNTRIES IN THE REGION

China, Hong Kong†, Macao‡, Taiwan

ECONOMIC INDICATORS: 1990

	LIE* China
GDP (US$ billions)	364.9
GNP per capita (US$)	370
Annual rate of growth of GDP, 1980–1990 (%)	9.5
Manufacturing as % of GDP	38
Central government spending as % of GNP	n/a
Merchandise exports (US$ billions)	61.3
Merchandise imports (US$ billions)	52.6
% of GNP received as development aid	0.6
Total external debt as a % of GNP	14.4

WELFARE INDICATORS

Infant mortality rate (per 1,000 live births)	
1965	90
1990	29
Daily food supply available (calories per capita, 1989)	2,639
Population per physician (1984)	1,010
Teacher–pupil ratio (primary school, 1989)	1 : 22

Note: The Gross Domestic Product (GDP) is the total value of all goods and services domestically produced. The Gross National Product (GNP) is the GDP plus net income from abroad.

** LIE (Low Income Economy) – GNP per capita below $610 in 1990.*

† Colony of UK, to be returned to China in 1997.

‡ Colony of Portugal, to be returned to China in 1999.

Affluent consumerism for the masses (*above*) at a new shopping mall in Beijing. Until the late 1980s, most Chinese would have been barred from entering, and the range of luxury goods – beyond the means of ordinary people – reserved for tourists and officials.

REVERSALS OF FORTUNE

In 1800, the Chinese economy was virtually self-sufficient and isolated from the rest of the world except for a trickle of trade through the southeastern port of Guangzhou (formerly Canton) northwest of Hong Kong. Britain's victory in the First Opium War (1839–42) put an end to this isolation. China was forced to open the eastern coastal cities of Xiamen, Shanghai, Guangzhou, Fuzhou, and Ningbo (called treaty ports) to British trade and to cede Hong Kong as a British dependency.

In the next hundred years the Western powers acquired more Chinese territory and the volume of trade between China and the West increased enormously. Considerable foreign investment in mines, textiles and railways occurred in the treaty ports and domestic entrepreneurs began to emulate the foreigners. By the 1930s eastern China had acquired a significant amount of industry. Shanghai, a small fishing town in 1840, had become the country's largest urban metropolis with a huge textile industry and a thriving port; 40 percent of all of China's industrial output was produced there.

Nevertheless, the Chinese economy of the 1930s remained massively underdeveloped. Although industry had grown rapidly, it still accounted for only about 19 percent of national income (compared with 45 percent in Japan in the same year) and only a small fraction of firms used modern equipment. The country's underdeveloped transportation network severely restricted import and export trade with the rest of the world and for a time China was immune to fluctuations in world trade. Famines, such as the one that killed close to a million people in Shanxi province in 1930, were commonplace. In addition, the fragile and incomplete industrialization that had taken place by the late 1930s was first halted and then reversed by the Japanese invasion (1937–45) and the subsequent civil war (1945–49) between the bitterly feuding Nationalists and Communists.

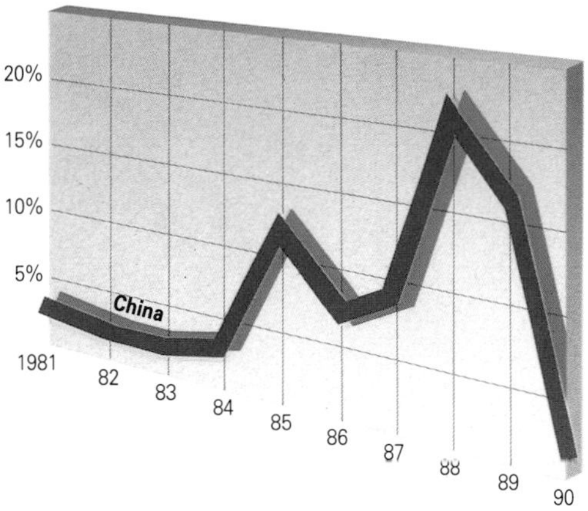

Profile of inflation *(above)* Inflation in China began to rise as more bold market reforms were introduced in the mid 1980s. The sharp rise of 1987–88 forced the government to cut back credit and imports, and economic growth decreased as well as inflation.

Map of GDP per capita *(below)* Economic growth has been most spectacular along the south coast of China, where average personal incomes can reach nearly double that in Beijing. Hong Kong's future as the region's financial center is uncertain; China takes it over in 1997.

Mao's qualified success

Following the Communist victory in 1949 and under the leadership of Mao Zedong (1893–1976), China reverted to isolationism. Mao charted a course that sympathetic Western observers hailed at the time as a unique strategy for economic development because it emphasized developing the rural sector rather than urban economic expansion. Most experts now agree that it was actually modeled on Stalin's policies in the Soviet Union. Over the three decades, the majority of the Chinese population became literate for the first time, mortality rates fell sharply and China developed both heavy industry and nuclear weapons. But Mao Zedong was unable to do much to raise living standards. He presided over the terrible famine of the early 1960s, and by the time of his death in 1976 millions of peasants still lived in conditions of abject poverty and hunger.

Taiwan (ruled by the Nationalists) and Hong Kong (a British colony) pursued very different economic policies. After a period of successful land reform in the early 1950s, the Taiwanese authorities introduced a mixed economy which combined the best elements of free market capitalism with limited state intervention. Hong Kong, by contrast, became a capitalist stronghold and was almost entirely dependent on international trade. Despite these considerable differences, both economies grew astonishingly quickly throughout the postwar period.

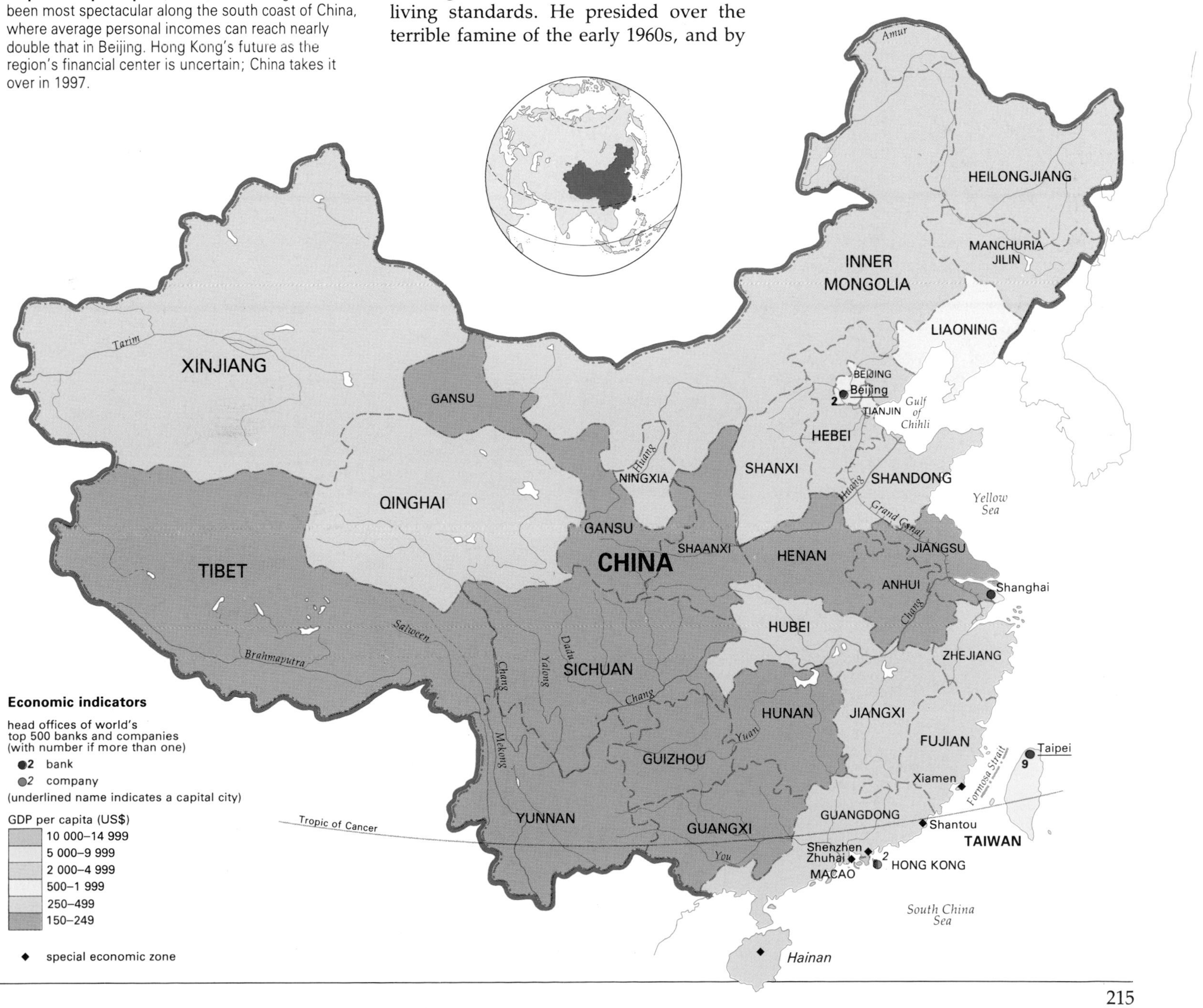

THE OPEN DOOR

Mao's death allowed Deng Xiaoping and those members of the Communist party who had always been skeptical of Mao's utopian vision to introduce a series of sweeping economic reforms. One of the most radical was the reopening of China to foreign trade – the "open door" policy. It involved making successive devaluations of China's over-valued exchange rate, granting permission to foreign firms to set up joint-venture companies, and establishing Special Economic Zones along the coast near to Hong Kong. Foreign and Chinese companies were encouraged to establish plants and offices within these zones through tax incentives and the removal of a host of legal restrictions. The first four, established in 1979, were at Shenzhen, Zhuhai and Shantou in Guangdong province and Xiamen in Fujian province. In addition, 14 further coastal cities (Dalian, Qinghuangdao, Tianjin, Yantai, Qingdao, Lianyungang, Nantong, Shanghai, Ningbo, Wenzhou, Fuzhou, Guangzhou, Zhanjiang and Beihai) were given special status in 1984, followed by the entire island province of Hainan in 1988.

Profiles of success

China's successful liberalization of its trading policy has been supported by two other factors. First, China has benefited from a combination of low wages and relatively high levels of labor productivity; the East Asian work ethic seems as powerful in China as it is in Korea and Japan. Second, many Chinese living in Singapore, Hong Kong and Taiwan retained some contact with their village of origin even during the Maoist era and most were only too happy to invest their money and skills in what they saw as the new China.

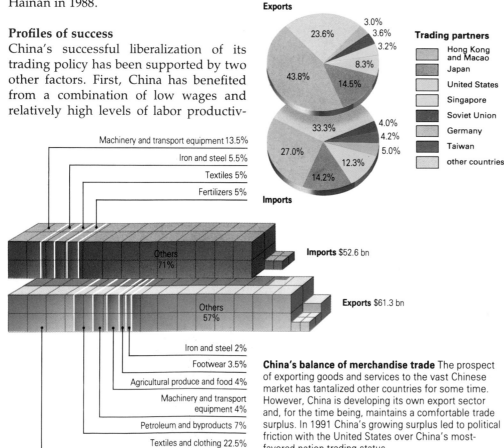

The open door policy was remarkably successful in the 1980s and early 1990s. Exports, for example, increased in value from $10 billion in 1978 to $62 billion by 1990. China's most important trading partner is Hong Kong (which accounts for a third of all trade) followed by Europe, Japan and the United States. As trade performance has been so good, and given China's continuing reluctance to borrow heavily, the economy has avoided the problems of debt and dependency that have afflicted many developing countries in the 1980s. Total external debt was only about 11 percent of gross national product (GNP) in 1989. Nevertheless, China has benefited from a closer association with international organizations, notably the World Bank and the United Nations Development Program. Both have provided

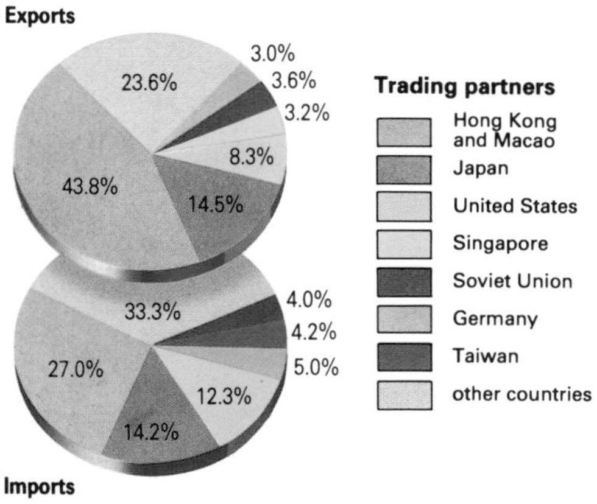

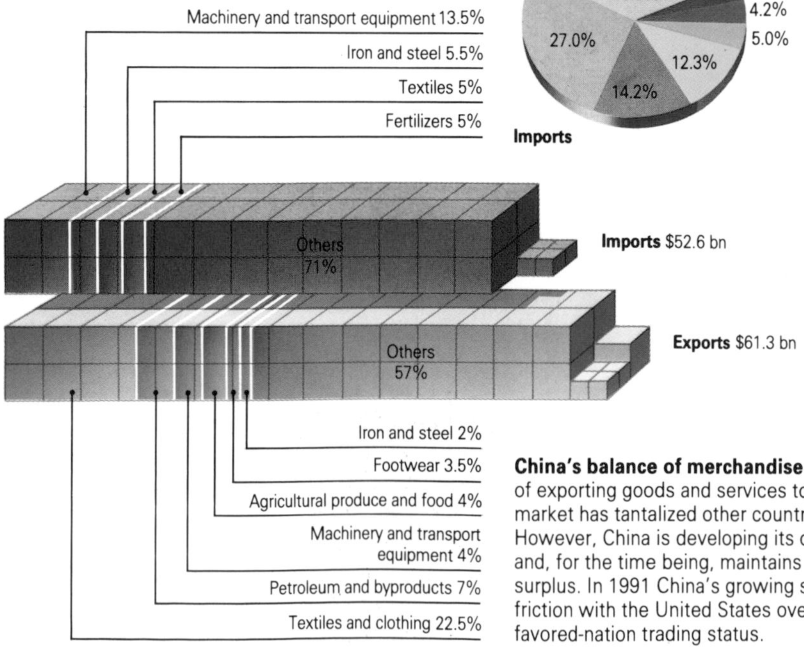

China's balance of merchandise trade The prospect of exporting goods and services to the vast Chinese market has tantalized other countries for some time. However, China is developing its own export sector and, for the time being, maintains a comfortable trade surplus. In 1991 China's growing surplus led to political friction with the United States over China's most-favored-nation trading status.

Far from the commercial boom (*above*) rural Chinese continue to farm. However, their plots are now likely to be privately worked, and surplus crops may be sold for profit at local markets. Capitalism has made a less dramatic impact in rural areas but wealth is increasing.

THE HONG KONG MONEY AND BRAIN DRAIN

In the early 1980s Hong Kong was the epitome of a free market capitalist economy. Accordingly, the agreement signed by Britain to return the colony to China in 1997 sent shock waves through the Hong Kong business community who feared that their assets would be confiscated by China's authoritarian socialist regime. Others in Hong Kong were concerned that they would lose their freedom of speech and movement, fears that were confirmed in June 1989 by the massacre of supporters of China's Democracy Movement. As a result, there has been a steady outflow of capital and some of the colony's most skilled workers have fled to Singapore, Australia and Canada. In 1990, Hong Kong citizens were leaving at a rate of 1,200 every week.

China's leaders have publically reiterated their commitment to maintaining Hong Kong's economic system virtually unchanged after 1997. However, most senior politicians, including Deng Xiaoping (born in 1904), are unlikely to live beyond the end of the century so their guarantees carry little weight. Unless China can inspire more confidence it seems that the brain drain will continue.

Hong Kong's airport (*left*) serves both passenger and cargo planes in severely crowded conditions. A US$15.5 billion project has been proposed to build new facilities on the island – in 1990 Hong Kong received more international passengers than either Tokyo or New York.

expertise and funds for poverty relief in Gansu province, one of the poorest parts of the country. China has also successfully attracted direct investment by foreign companies in its industrial sector, most notably in the fields of oil exploration, services and motor vehicles.

Integration into the world economy is most marked in Guangdong province. Because of its position it dominates China's trade with Hong Kong. Massive investment by Hong Kong Chinese in textile factories and assembly production has played a critical part in ensuring that Guangdong's economy has grown much faster than the Chinese average. By the early 1990s, Hong Kong and Guangdong were fast becoming part of a single economic region with no less than 2 million workers employed by Hong Kong firms on the mainland.

The industrial boom

The open door policy is not the only success story; China's industrial sector has also performed spectacularly. By 1990 over 70 percent of exports were industrial products. This reflects the rapid increase in the production of machinery, metal products and consumer goods during the 1980s, often caused by the meteoric growth of smallscale rural industry owned by private individuals or, more importantly, owned by rural townships but leased out to private managers. As a result, the share of state-owned industry in total industrial output fell considerably, though in 1990 this sector still accounted for more than a half of industrial production.

Despite these successes, Chinese industry in the 1990s is still suffering from energy shortages and high transportation costs because of limited investment in vital infrastructure before 1978. At any one time, as much as 20 percent of industrial capacity is idle. Even more serious, according to many economists, are the escalating losses made by virtually every state-owned company. Many Chinese and Western experts believe that the only solution is to privatize them. However, this could cause redundancy or unemployment for anything up to 50 million workers and might provoke unprecedented social unrest, leading to the fall of the Communist party. Even the most ardent reformers are predictably cautious about implementing such a program. It seems that, in spite of the problems, state-owned industry will continue to be tolerated until it imposes an unacceptable burden on the more dynamic sectors of the economy.

The one-child family (*above*) beams at passersby from a propaganda poster. Implemented as a desperate measure to control explosive population growth and raise standards of living, the stringent family planning program is deeply unpopular. The traditional preference for sons has proved difficult to overcome, and female infanticide – long outlawed – may be increasing.

THE IRON RICE BOWL

When Mao Zedong – the university-educated son of a wealthy peasant – came to power his followers were starving and mostly illiterate. One of the main objectives of his regime was to eliminate the wide inequalities in income, life expectancy and literacy found throughout Chinese society. In the villages, private ownership of land was abolished and replaced by collective farms to keep differences in incomes small. In the cities, private businesses were outlawed and wage payments were limited to a narrow band. Schools and clinics offering basic healthcare were established throughout the country. By the late 1970s, the standard of living throughout China's rural towns and villages was among the most consistent in the world.

The socialist regime had much less success in reducing the gap between living standards in the industrial cities and the countryside, and between different parts of China. By the 1970s the average income of an urban worker may have been as much as five times higher than that of peasants, in spite of comparable levels of literacy and life expectancy. The biggest failure of Mao's government was that it was able to do little to raise levels of material consumption. While the mainland came close to matching the improvements in life expectancy and literacy that Hong Kong and Taiwan had achieved after 1949, the lifestyle of a Chinese peasant was little better materially than in the 1930s. Famine killed close to 30 million people in the early 1960s and threatened many areas into the late 1970s. In poorer provinces such as Anhui, Gansu and Guizhou, peasants had barely enough food and clothes even in relatively good years. Conditions in these areas were far removed from the consumer societies that thrived in Hong Kong and Taiwan by the time of Mao's death.

Reform to banish famine

After the mid 1970s, the new leader Deng Xiaoping and other reformers decided that wide income differentials had to be restored in order to create new incentives for workers and peasants. The economic rewards of hard work, they argued,

RURAL INDUSTRIALIZATION IN TAIWAN

Since 1949, Taiwan has been one of the miracle economies of Asia. Not only has national income mushroomed but poverty has declined sharply and social inequalities have been reduced. Although Taiwan's development strategy (unlike China's) was orthodox in that it placed considerable weight on the promotion of urban industries, a key element in the miracle was the growth of small rural industries springing up in the wake of the land reform of the early 1950s. Land reform transferred agricultural profits out of the hands of the conservative landlord class and into the hands of progressive and entrepreneurial farmers who used it to invest in local plants producing chemical fertilizers and textiles. Later they diversified into consumer electronics and other more skill-intensive products.

These very successful industries relied initially on cheap farm labor. Low costs allowed the products to compete effectively in world markets, and the foreign exchange that they earned allowed Taiwan to purchase machinery and other major investment goods from the West. Rural industries provided higherpaid employment for farm workers raising living standards and, in turn, encouraging farmers to mechanize their businesses as a way of increasing profits. In the wake of this period of innovation and change the income gap between towns and the countryside narrowed considerably.

would gradually extend even to the poorest parts of the countryside. Nevertheless, the leaders were careful not to eliminate the social security system or to close the schools and hospitals set up by the Maoists. In fact, government spending on poverty relief was greater in the 1980s than it had been under Mao, and "the iron rice bowl" (the guarantee of work and food) remained a fixture. Low unemployment rates were maintained by strategic and widespread overemployment, often in positions that struck foreign observers as unnecessary, such as ticket collectors in shops.

The 1980s saw definite improvements in living standards. The specter of famine was effectively banished and the daily diets of peasants and workers improved enormously, regularly including meat and dairy products which were rare even in the late 1970s. In the very poorest parts of China conditions were considerably better, even though they still fell well short of those in prosperous Guangdong and Jiangsu provinces, to say nothing of Hong Kong and Taiwan. The gap in income between the towns and the countryside grew narrower because of the success of agricultural reform.

Education and the gender gap

Despite Mao's great success in spreading literacy, education remained a sensitive issue in China. A decade of ideological struggles – the chaotic period known as the Cultural Revolution (1966–76) – resulted in the widespread closing of schools and persecution of teachers and intellectuals. The education of a whole generation was disrupted, and many professionals, including scientists, were discouraged from building on their expertise. In the aftermath, the government placed great emphasis on scientific and technical education. Most Chinese graduate students abroad are scientists or engineers, though business and education studies are increasingly acknowledged as useful. Students compete fiercely for limited university places through a national examination. Less than one-tenth of one percent are successful. For those, all fees are paid by the government in exchange for a nonoptional agreement to carry out assigned work after graduation on a longterm or permanent basis. Urban schools are generally superior to rural schools, and urban students are more likely to go beyond the basic six-year primary education. Beijing and Shanghai are the leading educational centers housing a range of famous universities and colleges.

China remains an intensely patriarchal society and it is arguable that some of the gains made by women during the Maoist period in terms of equal pay, nursery facilities and equal access to education have been reversed. The imposition of a coercive system of family planning in which each household is allowed only a single child except in very special circumstances is bitterly resented.

State-sponsored daycare (*left*) was a fringe benefit of the communist regime, designed to maximize China's workforce – and output – by freeing women to participate as regular full-time workers. Controlling the nurseries also gave the state an opportunity for early indoctrination. Now nurseries continue to provide care for China's "Little Emperors" – children without siblings

Life expectancy and age distribution (*right*) Dramatic increases in life expectancy have resulted from China's rising prosperity. Adequate food has been a major factor but healthcare, though greatly improved, remains inadequate for many people. Famine in the early 1960s was particularly life-threatening to the elderly and the very young, but the subsequent baby boom is evident in the bulging numbers of young people between 18 and 30, born before the introduction of the one-child per family policy.

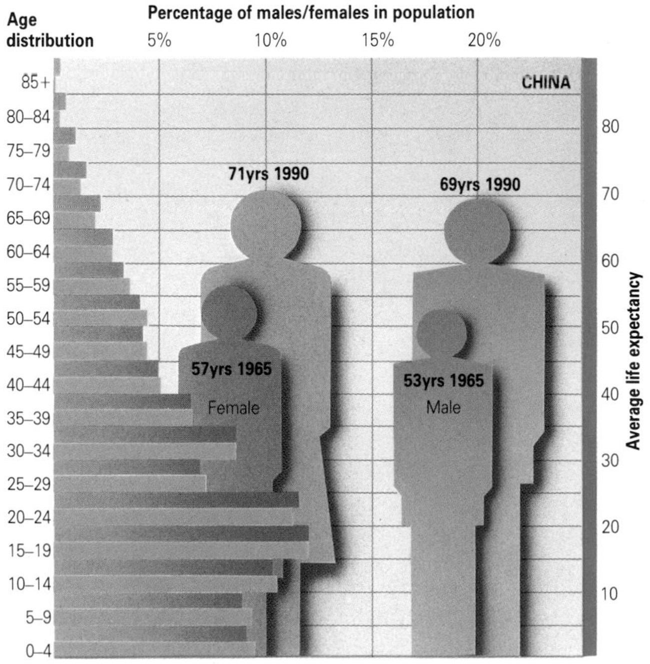

Socialism with Chinese characteristics

Mao Zedong believed that a low but uniform standard of living was preferable to the unequal distribution of wealth that had kept most Chinese poor and starving for 2,000 years. Since Mao's death, one of the most publicized features of China has been quick to ensure "socialism with Chinese characteristics" – senior statesman Deng Xiaoping's slogan for capitalism by another name.

The next "Little Dragon"

Guangdong's proximity to Hong Kong and the Special Economic Zones – and its distance from the national government in Beijing – has put it at the forefront of the provinces developing local market economies. On a visit to the area in January 1992, Deng Xiaoping predicted that Guangdong would be as successful as Hong Kong, Singapore, Taiwan and South Korea – the "Little Dragons" of Asia. Local government planners are considering a proposal for the economic union of Guangdong and Hong Kong before 1997, and are trying to get permission to open a stock exchange, as Shenzhen and Shanghai have already done. Former state-owned factories are now corporations issuing shares to private investors who receive dividends, though Guangdong retains ownership. To draw the line at fully fledged capitalism, however, individual investors are barred from owning more than one-half of one percent of total shares.

Opportunity or exploitation? *(above)* A young girl works Sundays in a toy factory in Shandong, northeast China. Child labor, seen as an evil of the old feudal China, is returning to the new China, as part of the fierce drive for individual prosperity.

Model socialist workers *(right)* The tallest women workers at a Shanghai silk-printing factory have new career prospects as fashion models. Luxury silk garments, politically suspect in the 1960s and rarely seen even in the mid 1980s, are recently in demand.

Informal financial markets are also thriving. Foreign tourists have always been able to exchange currency on the black market at a premium of between 10 and 70 percent above the official rate; apart from periodic crackdowns, the police receive weighty enough bribes to prevent them from interfering.

In the early 1990s new ventures were growing fastest in the rural industry sector where local governments established large numbers of new factories. Most of these are concentrated in the southern coastal provinces, especially around Guangzhou. Between 1980 and 1992 20,000 factories were built in Guangdong province, assisted by investments from Hong Kong companies totalling some $10 billion. Shunde County in Guangzhou province contains more than 500 of these new businesses, and its $36 million contribution to the Chinese

treasury in 1991 made it the nation's top-earning region.

In the late 1980s and early 1990s a struggle developed over the profits. In Wenzhou, a former treaty port in Zhejiang province, private entrepreneurs routinely avoided taxation. They were making over 100,000 yuan ($25,000) a year as early as 1985, when workers earning $1,100 a year were considered prosperous. In Jiangsu province, where industry is closely controlled, large sums were handed over to local government in the form of taxes and other payments, compulsory business registration fees and the threat of the withdrawal of police protection. Little of this illicit revenue was declared to Beijing but instead funded new hotels, factories and hospitals, and filled the pockets of officials.

Floating on a sea of corruption

In many parts of China now, the urban economy floats on a sea of corruption. Many goods have two prices and there is great scope for profiteering by buying at the low state price and selling at the free market price. Local governments are as active in this as private individuals. In 1985, Hainan Island used foreign currency allocated by Beijing to develop its stagnant economy, buying thousands of Japanese cars and selling them to other provinces at greatly inflated prices.

Towns on the Guangdong coastline have grown prosperous through smuggling goods between the mainland and Hong Kong. Products ranging from machinery and electronics – sometimes stolen – to human organs taken from executed prisoners are exchanged between them. It is estimated that half of the electronics sold in the New Territories (between Hong Kong and Guangdong) are smuggled across the border into China, depriving the treasury of some $650 million in import duties annually. Smugglers travel in custom-built speedboats, communicating with each other by mobile telephones, to evade the Hong Kong Marine Police who patrol the coastal waters. Some patrols have been turned back by armed Chinese military or police, and close communication is essential to prevent the two forces of the law opening fire on each other. Despite the losses to businessmen and the treasury, the courts take an equally relaxed view of smuggling; fewer than 30 percent of smugglers prosecuted are sentenced to jail.

ASIA'S LITTLE DRAGONS

PRIMARY CONCERNS · GROWING FAST · LONGSTANDING POVERTY AND NEW WEALTH

Southeast Asia was recognized as a major subdivision of the world economy only after World War II, when the region gained independence from its former colonial masters. Since then, Southeast Asia has transformed itself from a supplier of raw materials into a thriving manufacturing region with booming export sales. Despite a background of political conflict, particularly in former Indo-China, cheap labor costs and a powerful work ethic have encouraged foreign investment, especially from Japan and the United States. The communist states of Vietnam, Laos and Cambodia remained cut off from the world economy until the late 1980s. The other countries have pursued diverse economic philosophies, ranging from Singapore's rigid system of economic control to Thailand's "freewheeling" capitalism.

PRIMARY CONCERNS

Southeast Asia occupies an important strategic position linking China and east Asia with India and the Middle East. From the 15th century, the region became a vital connection in the emerging world economy, initially as a supplier of high-value spice and transshipper of Chinese silk, drugs and porcelain. Later it became a supplier of bulk primary goods such as rice, tin and rubber and a large market for manufactured goods from the West.

During the 19th century virtually the whole region passed under direct Western rule. Only Thailand – much reduced in size – retained a measure of political independence. Broadly based patterns of trade and production gave way to the production of a narrow range of primary products. After the signing of the Bowring Treaty (1855), Thailand also came under British economic control. The removal of tariff barriers opened the Thai economy to a flood of cheap British manufactured goods that pushed domestic manufacturing into rapid decline. Textile production was largely replaced by the export of raw cotton. Rice, which accounted for under 3 percent of export value in 1850, constituted 70 percent of exports in 1890 and dominated production.

By the late 1930s the economies of Southeast Asia were geared toward primary production. Trade and investment were locked into the imperial trading systems of Britain, France, the Netherlands and the United States. However, in Southeast Asia, as elsewhere in the world,

COUNTRIES IN THE REGION

Brunei, Burma, Cambodia, Indonesia, Laos, Malaysia, Philippines, Singapore, Thailand, Vietnam

ECONOMIC INDICATORS: 1990

	HIE* Singapore	LMIE* Thailand	LIE* Indonesia
GDP (US$ billions)	34.6	80.17	107.29
GNP per capita (US$)	11,160	1,420	570
Annual rate of growth of GDP, 1980–1990 (%)	6.4	7.6	5.5
Manufacturing as % of GDP	18	26	20
Central government spending as % of GNP	23	15	20
Merchandise exports (US$ billions)	52.6	22.9	25.7
Merchandise imports (US$ billions)	60.5	32.9	21.8
% of GNP received as development aid	–	1.0	1.6
Total external debt as a % of GNP	–	32.6	66.4

WELFARE INDICATORS

	Singapore	Thailand	Indonesia
Infant mortality rate (per 1,000 live births)			
1965	26	145	128
1990	7	44	61
Daily food supply available (calories per capita, 1989)	3,198	3,121	2,750
Population per physician (1984)	1,410	2,150	9,410
Teacher–pupil ratio (primary school, 1989)	1 : 26	1 : 18	1 : 23

Note: The Gross Domestic Product (GDP) is the total value of all goods and services domestically produced. The Gross National Product (GNP) is the GDP plus net income from abroad.

** HIE (High Income Economy) – GNP per capita above $7,620 in 1990. LMIE (Lower Middle Income Economy) – GNP per capita between $610 and $2,465. LIE (Low Income Economy) – GNP per capita below $610.*

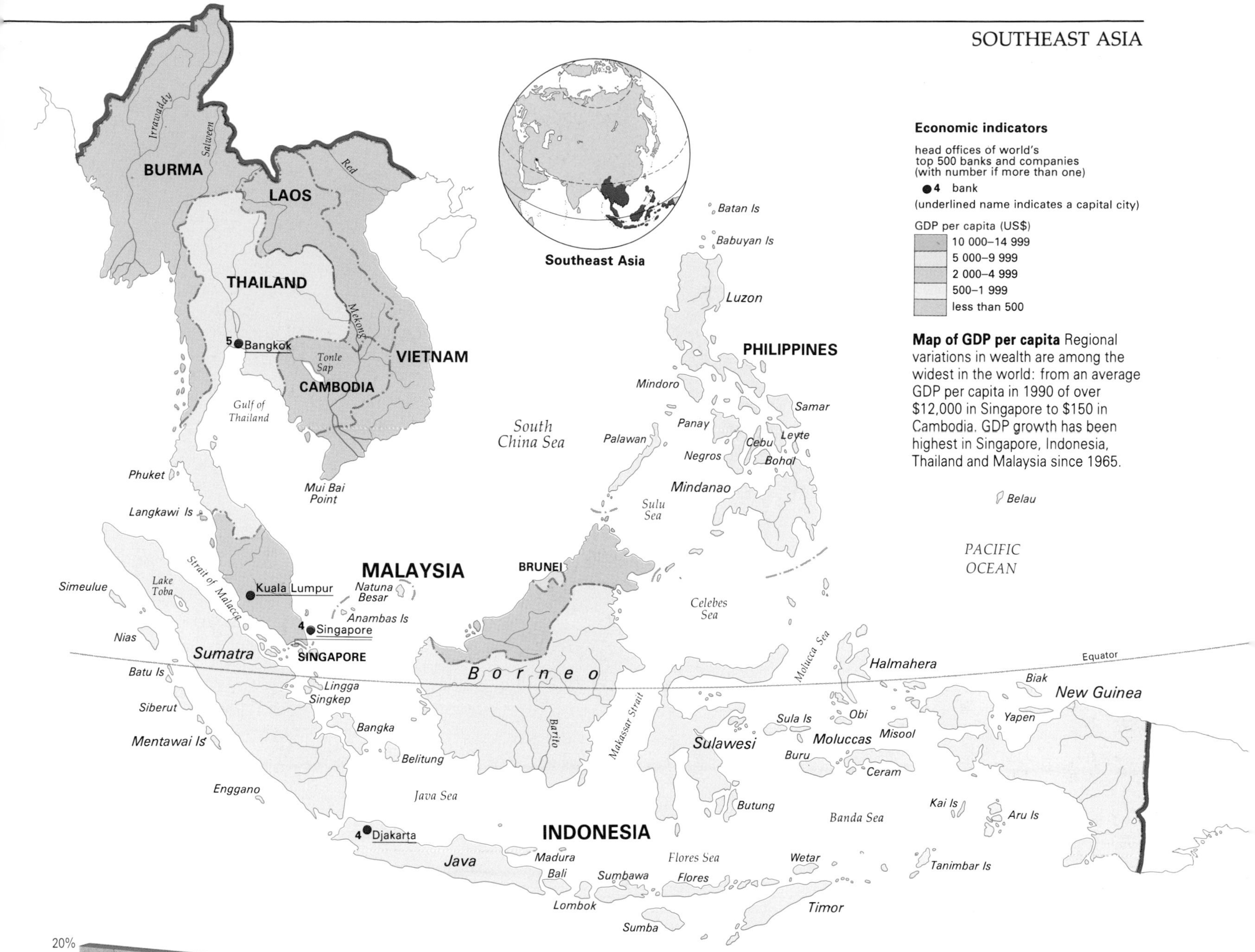

Map of GDP per capita Regional variations in wealth are among the widest in the world: from an average GDP per capita in 1990 of over $12,000 in Singapore to $150 in Cambodia. GDP growth has been highest in Singapore, Indonesia, Thailand and Malaysia since 1965.

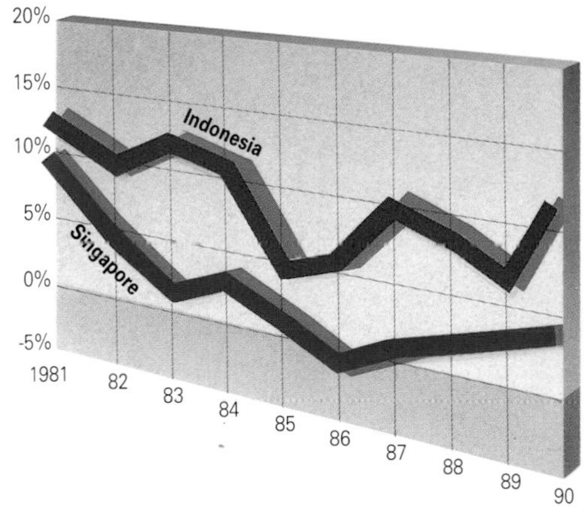

Profile of inflation *(above)* Both Indonesia's and Singapore's rates of inflation were higher at the beginning of the 1980s than at the end. Singapore achieved near-zero inflation from 1985–87 (–1.4 percent in 1986), in part because of its social controls and tight monetary policies.

Sea of wealth *(left)* Singapore's petroleum industry is one of its most valuable assets, contributing to nearly 25 percent of all trade. The country has some offshore oil reserves of its own, but is primarily involved in refining. The shipping in the bay is part of the general traffic through Singapore harbor, the largest port in Southeast Asia and second in financial importance only to Rotterdam in the Netherlands.

the colonial structures were beginning to crumble. World War II and Japanese occupation hastened the process. By the 1940s a new world order had emerged.

Capitalism versus communism

The Southeast Asian countries gained their independence between 1946 and 1958. Decolonization resulted in deep and lasting regional divisions. These became institutionalized in 1967 with the establishment of the Association of Southeast Asian Nations (ASEAN) by Indonesia, Malaysia, the Philippines, Singapore and Thailand (Brunei joined in 1984). The region became increasingly polarized between the pro-Western ASEAN states and the communist states of Indo-China: Kampuchea (Cambodia), Laos and Vietnam. Only Burma (Myanmar) adopted a nonaligned position.

American fears that the entire region would fall to communism, underlaid by a desire to secure the markets and resources of Southeast Asia as a sphere of American economic activity, led to the country's involvement in the protracted Vietnam war. The war exacted terrible social and economic costs on Vietnam. An estimated 2 million people were killed between 1954 and 1974; many more were maimed and made homeless, and about 70 percent of industrial capacity was destroyed.

The communist countries remained almost entirely isolated from the world economy until the late 1980s. Elsewhere in the region, huge amounts of American aid and military expenditure helped to boost the ASEAN economies, particularly the Philippines and Thailand. From the early 1970s, all the ASEAN states embarked on a period of rapid economic growth, characterized by expansion of manufacturing sectors and the emergence of authoritarian, often military, political regimes. Very high levels of military expenditure are still justified in terms of the threat of "communist subversion", though in practice this can mean simply opposition to the government.

GROWING FAST

The ASEAN economies are among the most dynamic in the world. Singapore, Hong Kong, South Korea and Taiwan are known as Asia's four "Little Dragons": newly industrializing countries with a spectacular record in economic growth over the last two decades. Recently Thailand too has achieved some of the world's highest growth rates. The region as a whole has vast potential for further development. It occupies a favorable strategic position, is richly endowed with resources and, with a youthful population of over 450 million, offers a large labor force and extensive market for domestic or imported goods.

The region remains a significant supplier of commodities such as rubber, tin, rice, palm oil and copra to the developed world. Since World War II it has also become a significant producer and processor of oil and natural gas. Japan, for example, is heavily dependent on Indonesian fuels, while Singapore is the region's most important processing and distribution center for petroleum and other primary goods. Since the late 1970s, however, low international commodity prices and the growth of manufacturing exports have greatly reduced the contribution of primary products to the region's export earnings.

Labor-intensive light industries such as electronics and clothing manufacture now provide the region's most valuable exports. All countries actively promoted the expansion of manufacturing industry during the postcolonial period, initially to replace imports with domestic production, later to generate exports. Singapore has followed a particularly clear program of export-oriented industrial development since the 1960s, though all the ASEAN states have adopted broadly similar policies.

The foreign factor

Since the 1970s, multinational corporations and foreign capital have flowed into the region, encouraged by the receptive policies of most governments and a more stable political climate. Furthermore, the

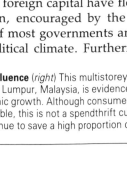

Levels of affluence (*right*) This multistorey shopping mall in Kuala Lumpur, Malaysia, is evidence of rapid new economic growth. Although consumer goods are widely available, this is not a spendthrift culture, and people continue to save a high proportion of income.

region offers foreign investors an abundant supply of cheap, well-disciplined and largely nonunionized labor. High profits can be made, especially as the region has managed to sustain excellent rates of economic growth during a period of international instability.

Under pressure from the International Monetary Fund (IMF) and the World Bank Indonesia, Malaysia, the Philippines and Thailand reformed their economies during the 1980s to allow market forces to operate more freely. The reforms – such as lifting trade and investment barriers, and reducing government intervention in the economy – gave a further boost to export manufacturing and direct and indirect foreign investment.

Since the 1980s Thailand and Malaysia – and to a lesser extent Indonesia and the Philippines – have become growing centers for labor-intensive manufacturing, mainly by foreign-owned companies. This reflects the decision by countries such as Japan, Hong Kong, South Korea and Taiwan to relocate their labor-intensive manufacturing to other parts of Asia in the face of rising domestic labor costs and concern over industrial pollution. Since 1979 Singapore has deliberately allowed wage levels to rise and encouraged the development of more skilled, capital-intensive manufacturing. Consequently, Singapore, also, is relocating its labor-intensive industries elsewhere in the region, particularly to neighboring Jahore in Malaysia and Bataan in Indonesia, creating a "triangle of growth". These developments have created new divisions of labor within Asia: first, between the more developed economies of east Asia, led by Japan, and the low labor-cost countries of Southeast Asia; and secondly between Singapore and the rest of Southeast Asia.

Future trends

Southeast Asia is rapidly becoming a Japanese sphere of influence in terms of trade and investment. Japan exports capital and manufactured goods to the region, importing almost exclusively raw materials in return, while Japanese plants in Southeast Asia produce manufactured goods for export to European and American markets. Japanese influence could even be set to expand into the communist countries.

In Vietnam, the reintroduction of elements of the market system, the lifting of the American trade embargo and the country's gradual reintegration into the world economic system seem to herald the end of the socialist–capitalist split within the region. Thailand's lead in investing in the former Indo-Chinese states has been followed by Malaysia, Singapore, Japan and other east Asian countries. Many analysts believe that the fresh influx of foreign capital, together with the cheap labor and raw materials of Vietnam, Laos, Cambodia – and perhaps Burma – will provide the focus for a new phase of dynamic economic development in Southeast Asia.

COMMERCE AND THE CHINESE COMMUNITY

The Chinese are Southeast Asia's largest minority: populations range from 76 percent in Singapore, which is effectively a Chinese city, through 15 percent in Malaysia to a regional low of 1.5 percent in the Philippines. Large-scale migration into Nang Yang ("the Southern Ocean") only began during the early 19th century, when migrants from the overcrowded provinces of southern China were attracted by the trade and investment opportunities then opening up in Southeast Asia.

Although most Chinese immigrants remained poor, a significant proportion established themselves in local trading, petty manufacturing and money-lending, acting as middlemen between the colonial powers and the indigenous populations. The Chinese flair for commerce enabled them to amass considerable assets and develop a business network that now dominates the domestic economies. For example, the small Indonesian Chinese population controlled 17 of the country's 25 largest businesses in the late 1980s. There are similarly high levels of Chinese ownership and control in the other countries of the region.

Despite their economic dominance, the Chinese have little political power. Indeed, they have been the object of much resentment and discrimination. Malaysia made a sustained effort to reduce Chinese economic power in the 1970s and 1980s, and the Chinese communities in both Indonesia and Vietnam have been severely persecuted. Nevertheless, Chinese enterprise and capital remain of crucial importance to the economies of Southeast Asia.

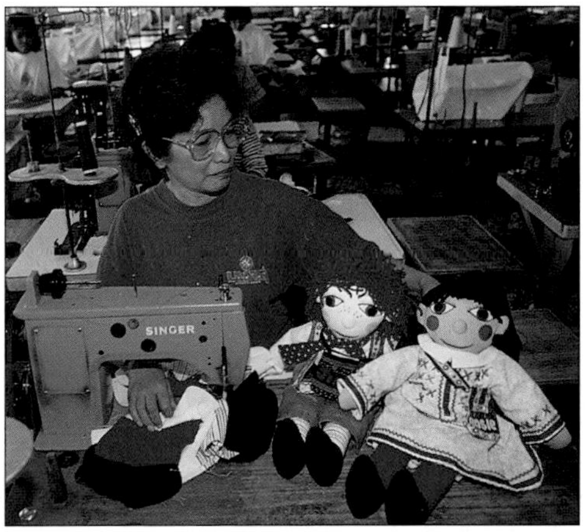

The rag-doll trade *(left)* Hand-sewn goods such as these soft dolls (made mostly by women) account for a large sector of the Philippine export industry. Women are most likely to be employed in casual or part-time jobs such as this one, but the official workforce is mostly male – 63 percent in 1990.

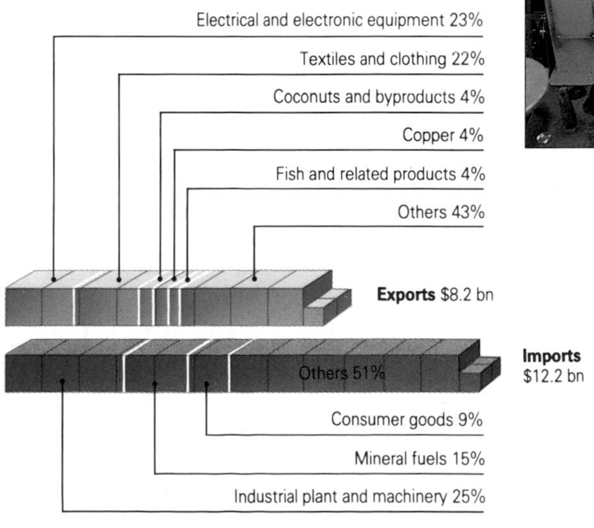

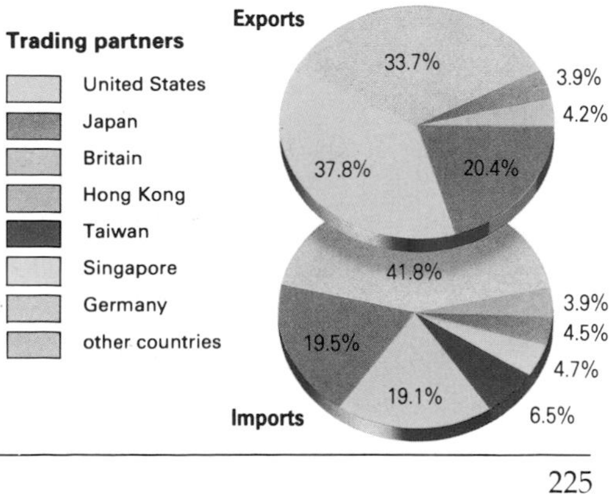

The Philippines' balance of merchandise trade The products of light industry – electronic equipment and textiles – are two of the Philippines' most important export sectors. A heavy industrial base has not been established in the country, so capital goods and fuels for energy are the chief imports. The United States continues to be a major trading partner across the region, though in the early 1990s Japan was the largest single source of imports.

LONGSTANDING POVERTY AND NEW WEALTH

Wealth is very unevenly spread both between and within the countries of Southeast Asia. Singapore ranks with many developed countries in terms of per capita income and general standards of living. On the other hand, Vietnam, Laos, Cambodia and Burma are among the poorest countries in the world. The gap between Southeast Asia's rich and poor countries has widened considerably over the last two decades.

Apart from Singapore, most of the region's population lives in rural areas and is dependent on agriculture. Although all governments have reiterated their commitment to reducing poverty and regional inequalities over the last 30 years, in practice national development programs have concentrated on achieving accelerated industrial growth in the urban centers. Rural areas have been neglected by comparison, with the result that their large populations are effectively excluded from a share in the economic and social benefits that have accompanied national economic growth.

While the economic differences between rural and urban areas are great, there are even sharper divisions within the cities. Rural poverty is propelling vast numbers of people into a relatively small number of cities: Southeast Asia has some of the highest rates of urban growth in the world. The urban centers have been unable to cope with such rapid population growth; many recent migrants can find neither adequate work nor shelter and are forced to live in appalling conditions in sprawling squatter settlements on the city fringe. Furthermore, welfare systems are poorly developed and often woefully underfunded. The poverty of large sections of Southeast Asia's urban populations is in sharp contrast to the prosperity of the elite who live and work in the luxurious downtown apartment and office blocks.

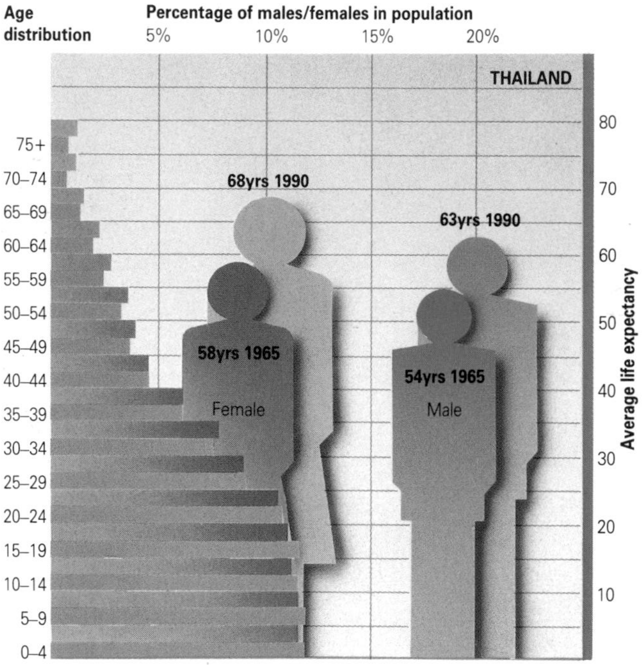

Bangkok by night (*right*) The glow of English-language neon signs in Thailand's capital reflects the number of foreign visitors: over 5 million in 1992, contributing more than $4 billion to the economy. Most are tourists, come to see the beautiful scenery and exotic temples; many are male and are clients of the sex trade, which flourishes in spite of its official nonexistence.

Life expectancy and age distribution (*left*) Life expectancy in Thailand, at 68 years for women and 63 for men, is about average for the region. Laos and Cambodia have the lowest life expectancy in the region, and Singapore (at a combined average for men and women of 74) has the highest. Thailand's birthrate has held fairly steady over the past few decades. In 1992, 32.7 percent of the population was under 15, well below the average figure which is better represented by 40 percent under 15 in the Philippines.

Wealth, poverty and ethnicity

Inadequate welfare systems and channeling of government resources into urban–industrial development mean that high levels of poverty and severe regional inequalities persist throughout the region, though trends are far from uniform. For example, the World Bank estimates that the number of people living below the poverty line in the Philippines rose from 43 percent in 1964 to 52 percent in 1985; in Thailand, the number of households living in poverty fell from 57 percent in 1962 to 24 percent in 1986, though the income gap between both social classes and different areas within the country had widened. A similar situation is reported in Malaysia, though here it is further complicated by marked ethnic differences in levels of income and employment opportunities.

The colonial administration of Malaysia encouraged an ethnic division of labor,

General issue for sale (*left*) Acquired, often illegally, from a nearby United States' military base in the Philippines, equipment from army stores is openly on sale. Trade on the black market is brisk – it is one of the region's fastest ways of making a large profit.

TOURISM AND THE SEX INDUSTRY IN THAILAND

Since the late 1970s tourism has become a major sector of the Thai economy, with tourist revenues generating the equivalent of 15–20 percent of total export earnings. The growth of tourism has been helped by Thailand's reputation as an exotic center for the sex industry. Amid the country's scenic and cultural delights, the "red light" districts of Bangkok and coastal resorts such as Pattaya and Phuket are now important tourist attractions.

Apart from the "sex package tours" marketed from Japan, Germany, the Netherlands and the United States, the role of the sex trade in tourism can only be measured indirectly. For example, there is a high proportion of male tourists, rising from 66 percent in 1977 to 73 percent in 1986. Increasing tourist traffic from Singapore and Malaysia comprises predominantly single men. The number of female prostitutes has also risen from an estimated 400,000 in 1974 to over 500,000 in the mid 1980s. These women's clients are as likely to be Thai as tourist: it has been estimated that about 95 percent of Thai men use prostitutes at some time in their lives. Households in the poorer rural areas of the north and northeast of the country are becoming increasingly dependent on remittances from prostitutes working in the resorts and cities.

The tourist and sex industries are suffering from international recession and the soaring rate of HIV infection. Since 1989 education campaigns sponsored by the government have tried to alter behavior and promote condom use. However, in 1991 over 15 percent of low-paid brothel prostitutes had contracted the HIV virus; rates as high as 63 percent were reported in some areas.

whereby the indigenous Malays were regarded as "natural rice growers", while Chinese and Indian immigrants were seen as labor for the modern industrial and commercial sectors. The ingrained socioeconomic divisions that resulted from this policy caused considerable tension, leading eventually to race riots in 1969. The Malay-controlled government then implemented a series of reforms – the New Economic Policy – that aimed to improve the economic and employment opportunities for the majority Malay population through "positive discrimination". Although successful in this respect, the New Economic Policy alienated the important Chinese community, who felt discriminated against, and may have contributed to a decline in economic growth and foreign investment. By the early 1990s, there were signs that the government was reducing the influence of racial politics on its economic policies.

The plight of Vietnam's boat people

Between 1976 and 1990 about 1 million refugees left Vietnam by sea, often packed into tiny fishing vessels and with no certain destination. The vast majority of these refugees were ethnic Chinese desperate to escape from harsh treatment by the Vietnamese government and the deteriorating economic conditions within the country.

By mid 1979 about 200,000 refugees had crossed into China, and perhaps the same number had reached Australia, Hong Kong, Taiwan or other countries in Southeast Asia. Thousands more were believed to have perished at sea, some the victims of pirate attacks. The recipient countries, particularly Indonesia and Malaysia, regarded the refugees as security risks and a drain on already scarce resources. These views were reinforced by the belief that the exodus was taking place with the complicity of the Vietnamese government. Commercial boat owners were perhaps the only group ultimately to profit from the exodus by sea. The owners of the Honduran-registered vessel, the "Southern Cross" reputedly made a profit of $485,000 for shipping 560 children and 690 adults from Ho Chi Min City to Indonesia in 1978.

Resettlement and repatriation

The Vietnamese government agreed to halt the exodus after a United Nations' Conference in 1978. Subsequently, the United Nations High Commission for Refugees (UNHCR) sponsored the Orderly Departure Scheme, under which a further 140,000 people had left Vietnam by 1988. Nevertheless, the illegal departures continued. The large numbers of refugees reached crisis levels in several Asian countries. Between 1976 and 1988 (when screening was initiated) more than 100,000 Vietnamese boat people were received by Hong Kong alone, one of the most popular destinations. Apprehended by the authorities close to the shore, many of the new migrants claimed to have crossed hundreds of miles of open sea from Vietnam. However, ocean patrols often assert that they cross China by land, boarding boats near Hong Kong harbor.

Following huge influxes during this generally receptive period, Hong Kong and Western nations, who were becoming increasingly unwilling to resettle refugees, tightened their immigration policies. Since the International Conference on Refugees from Indo-China of 1989, only those who could convince the authorities that they had fled Vietnam to escape persecution were regarded as refugees entitled to be resettled. Although many produce documents to try to substantiate their claims to status as political refugees, most of today's boat people – an estimated 80 percent – are screened and classified as "economic migrants" fleeing Vietnam's poverty. They will probably be kept in detention centers until they can be repatriated.

Since 1989 the UNCHR and the Vietnamese government have cooperated in various mass-information schemes to advise would-be boat people of the need to be recognized as refugees before they will be resettled. This, together with improving economic conditions in Vietnam, has stemmed the flow of migrants. However, the Vietnamese government is still faced with the prospect of reabsorbing the thousands of boat people who are likely to be repatriated over the next few years. Financial help includes a $120 million assistance program from the European Community (EC) and cash payments from the United Nations (UN). Although the UNCHR is officially opposed to compulsory repatriation, it will monitor the welfare of those who go back.

Confined in camps

The sufferings of the boat people are still far from over. During 1990 only about 5,000 agreed to voluntary repatriation. Pressure is now mounting for the remaining "economic migrants" to be repatriated forcibly. In early 1991 there were still some 112,000 Vietnamese boat people in camps, 54 percent of them in Hong Kong where they had fled, attracted by the higher standard of living and the possibility of work. The cramped conditions in all the camps are causing rising concern. Outbreaks of violence are becoming frequent as the boat people are faced with the difficult choice of returning voluntarily to Vietnam, or remaining in the camps with the ultimate prospect of forcible repatriation.

No refuge A Vietnamese family's hopes of a new life are dashed as Hong Kong police take them into custody after their vessel was intercepted. They will be detained in a camp until they are eventually sent back to Vietnam by air.

POLICE
PV 33

THE RISING SUN

HOPE FROM THE ASHES · THE POWER OF SUCCESS · THE PAIN AND PLEASURE OF HARD WORK

During the last 150 years the economies of Japan and Korea have followed closely related paths. At the end of the 19th century both countries moved rapidly from feudalism into the industrialized world. During World War II Japan's economy was shattered and the country's empire – of which Korea had been part – was lost. Immediately after the war Japan embarked on a second economic revolution. Growth since 1945 has been remarkable and by the early 1990s Japan had become the world's second largest economic power. Japanese companies are international giants, fueling growth across Southeast Asia. Korea's post-war economic development has also been dramatic, though division into a socialist north and capitalist south has meant the two economies have developed in different directions and at varying speeds.

HOPE FROM THE ASHES

Both Japan and Korea were jolted violently into the industrial world from virtual feudalism. In Japan two centuries of self-imposed isolation from the world were ended in 1853, when United States naval forces entered Tokyo bay, forcing trade concessions. The Japanese were shocked at the discovery of their country's weakness and a new and enduring "catch up" mentality began to emerge. New leaders embarked on a policy of rapid modernization. A financial system was constructed along Western lines and a series of government-run enterprises were established. These were later cast loose from the state and bought by a small number of capitalist families, forming what were to be distinctively Japanese economic institutions: powerful alliances of firms well connected with government that were known as *zaibatsu*.

Japan's growing economic strength was matched by military ambition. In 1876 the country imposed a Western-style trade treaty on Korea, which had been pursuing an isolationist policy of its own. Korea was annexed in 1910 and given modern banking and education systems so it might prove more profitable as a colony. By 1940 Japan's empire had extended into China and Southeast Asia. Conflict with the United States, however, proved a major miscalculation and led to the destruction of the economies of both Japan and Korea in World War II. Japan was subsequently occupied by United States' forces until 1952.

COUNTRIES IN THE REGION

Japan, North Korea, South Korea

ECONOMIC INDICATORS: 1990

	HIE* Japan	UMIE* S Korea
GDP (US$ billions)	2,942.89	236.4
GNP per capita (US$)	25,430	5,400
Annual rate of growth of GDP, 1980–1990 (%)	4.1	9.7
Manufacturing as % of GDP	29	31
Central government spending as % of GNP	17	16
Merchandise exports (US$ billions)	280.4	65.0
Merchandise imports (US$ billions)	216.8	69.8
% of GNP donated as development aid	0.31	n/a

WELFARE INDICATORS

Infant mortality rate (per 1,000 live births)		
1965	18	62
1990	5	17
Daily food supply available (calories per capita, 1989)	2,956	2,852
Population per physician (1984)	660	1,160
Teacher–pupil ratio (primary school, 1989)	1 : 21	1 : 36

Note: The Gross Domestic Product (GDP) is the total value of all goods and services domestically produced. The Gross National Product (GNP) is the GDP plus net income from abroad.

** HIE (High Income Economy) – GNP per capita above $7,620 in 1990. UMIE (Upper Middle Income Economy) – GNP per capita between $2,465 and $7,620.*

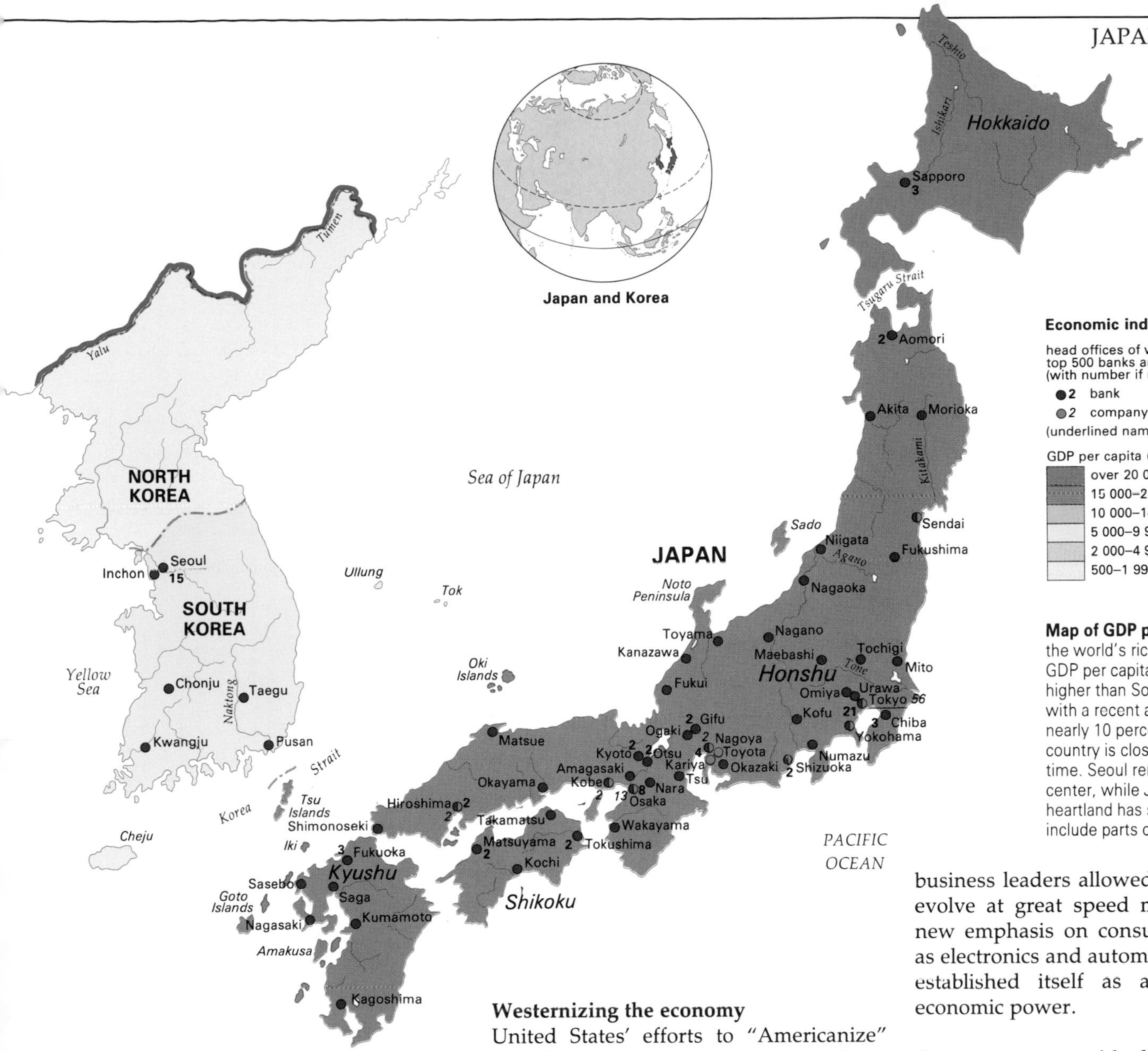

Economic indicators

head offices of world's top 500 banks and companies (with number if more than one)

- ●2 bank
- ●2 company

(underlined name indicates a capital city)

GDP per capita (US$)

- over 20 000
- 15 000–20 000
- 10 000–14 999
- 5 000–9 999
- 2 000–4 999
- 500–1 999

Map of GDP per capita As one of the world's richest nations Japan's GDP per capita is nearly 5 times higher than South Korea's. However, with a recent annual growth rate of nearly 10 percent, the smaller country is closing the gap all the time. Seoul remains its business center, while Japan's financial heartland has spread from Tokyo to include parts of the south.

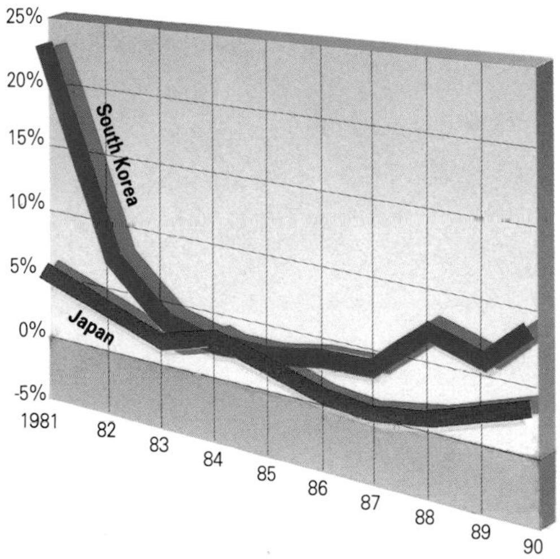

Profile of inflation *(above)* South Korea's high inflation fell spectacularly in the 1980s as the country's money supply was tightened. Even Japan's low inflation was affected by recession in the early 1990s, when Japan lowered its interest rates to help the world economy.

Lighting up the economy *(left)* Akihabara in Tokyo is a thriving center for discounted electronic goods. Consumer electronics are also some of the country's most successful exports, and accounted for nearly 4 percent of the export market in 1990.

Westernizing the economy

United States' efforts to "Americanize" Japan's economic system were abandoned after the superpower's attention was distracted by the growing communist presence on the Asian mainland. The alliances of firms regrouped as *keiretsu* and the Japanese state resumed its guiding role, protecting the home market with high import duties while encouraging competition between domestic companies to prepare them as international traders. Banks were encouraged to take a longterm view of their industrial clients, allowing firms time to research and develop new products. At the same time Japan's role as a United States resource base during the Korean and Vietnam wars brought in a valuable flow of dollars.

Within just 20 years these factors combined to create remarkable economic success. By the late 1960s Japan had overtaken the Soviet Union as the world's second largest economy (after the United States) and by the early 1970s the country was the leading producer of steel, shipping and other heavy manufactured goods. In the late 1970s and 1980s the foresight and adaptability of Japan's business leaders allowed the economy to evolve at great speed moving toward a new emphasis on consumer goods such as electronics and automobiles. Japan had established itself as a leading world economic power.

One country – two ideologies

Korea's recent economic development has followed a more complex pattern. In 1945 the Japanese occupation of the country came to an end. After the long struggle of the Korean war two states emerged on either side of the 38th parallel: a socialist north backed by China and the Soviet Union, and a capitalist south supported by the United States. The two states pursued radically different economic policies. Until the early 1970s the North Korean economy grew faster and its system of central planning brought higher standards of living to its population. However, the sharp increases in the cost of oil and the subsequent drop in commodity prices badly affected the North's economy and, increasingly, the country moved away from a trading role to one of self-sufficiency. South Korea, in the meantime, was gaining ground. In the early 1960s its rulers began to channel foreign loans and investment into industry. Within a decade South Korean firms were beginning to compete successfully in international markets.

THE POWER OF SUCCESS

During the 1980s Japan and South Korea continued their remarkable economic ascendence and by the end of the decade Japanese industrial output was only just behind that of the United States.

Neither country had any obvious potential for economic expansion. They both lacked significant deposits of natural resources and Japan relies greatly on imported fuel, food and raw materials for manufacturing. However, such problems have been more than overcome by the dynamic achievement of the two countries' manufacturing sectors. During the 1980s Japan attained a trade surplus of no less than $533 billion. Of the country's exports, over 30 percent went to the United States while the European Community (EC) accounted for a further 20 percent. The United States and the EC were the most important exporters to Japan over the same period, but the value of their trade was too small to prevent a huge imbalance in Japan's favor.

By the 1980s Japan's wealth was reflected in its growing importance as a financial power. In 1985 it became the world's largest creditor nation, overtaking the United States. Japanese financial institutions became important players in international markets and Tokyo became one of the world's three main financial centers, alongside New York and London.

Such rapid success brought new problems. United States authorities began to be alarmed at the vast quantities of goods being imported to America from Japan and South Korea, and applied pressure on both countries to alter some of their economic policies. At the same time Japan's achievement at home triggered changes that began to undermine the country's traditional social structure.

How did they do it?

Various theories have been offered to explain the exceptional performance of the Japanese and South Korean economies since World War II. Commentators have emphasized the "developmentalist"

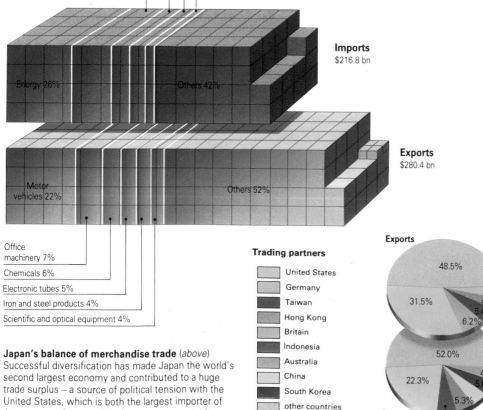

Rising yen, falling stocks (*right*) Numbers flash on screens on the Nikkei stock exchange, the world's second largest. Tokyo share prices declined in 1992 despite the strength of the yen and efforts of the government to bolster the market with public money.

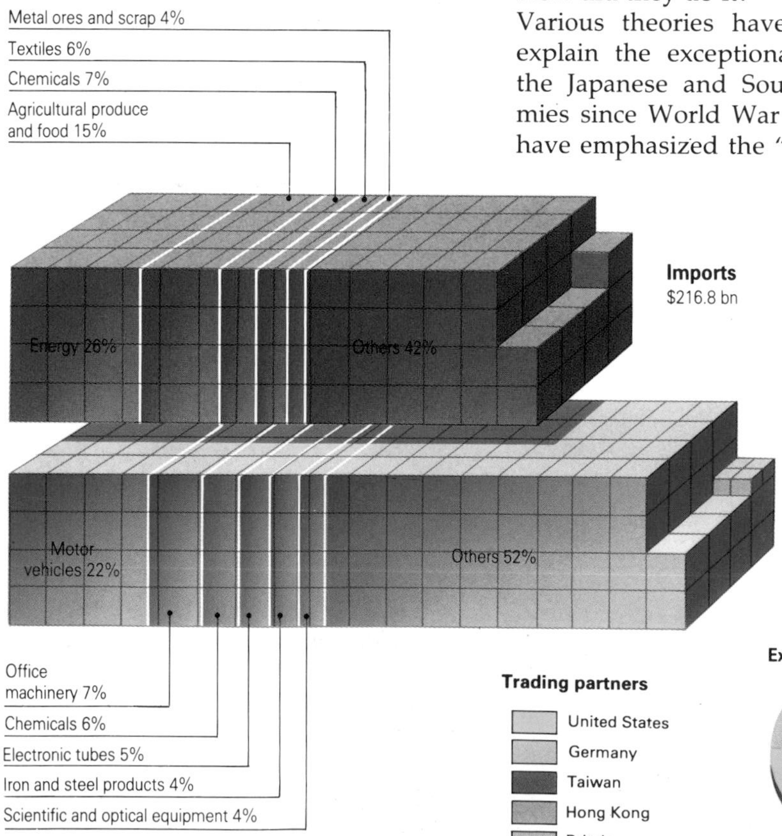

Japan's balance of merchandise trade (*above*) Successful diversification has made Japan the world's second largest economy and contributed to a huge trade surplus – a source of political tension with the United States, which is both the largest importer of Japanese products and the largest exporter to Japan.

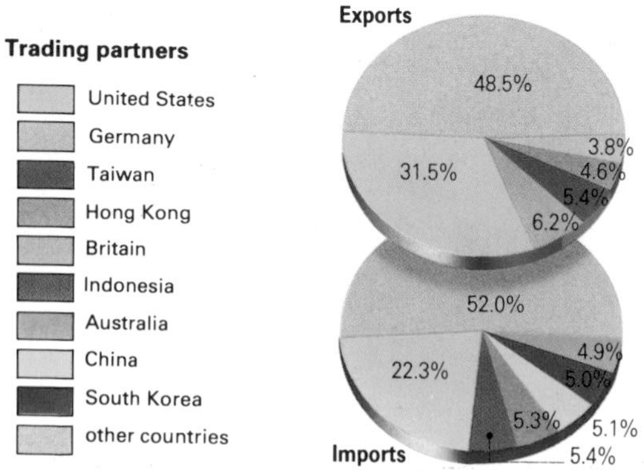

THE FUTURE FOR SOUTH KOREA

South Korea is one of the world's most indebted countries. Between 1964 and 1989 the country's foreign debt increased from $177 million to $43,183 million, a level surpassed among developing countries only by Brazil, Mexico, Argentina, India, Indonesia and Egypt. However, since the 1960s the South Korean government has played a guiding role in directing foreign borrowings into new industries. These have proved competitive exporters and so the country has been better able to carry its high level of indebtedness than other states in its situation.

In 1989 South Korea's debt-service ratio (the proportion of all earnings from exports that are needed simply to service the country's foreign debt) was only 12.7 percent. By contrast, the average debt-service ratio of the six debtor countries listed above was 37 percent. South Korea's export success has allowed it to increase capital reserves and move toward the construction of its own financial system, offering hope that any future economic development will be less dependent on foreign money. However, the existence of large foreign debt still threatens South Korea. It can only be serviced by continued success in international markets, which may be damaged by moves toward protectionism, or downturns in the global economy.

attitudes of their governments, which have promoted industrial competitiveness while at the same time using import duties to protect firms from foreign competition. Other analysts have focused on the distinctively local strengths of the region's manufacturering industries. Japanese companies have shown a particular talent for organizing production, while those of South Korea have made good use of the country's cheap but highly efficient workforce.

During the 1980s a third and more sinister theory emerged. It accused Japanese firms of carving out new markets for themselves by temporarily undercutting foreign competitors – even if this meant selling goods at a loss or "dumping" them – until they had sufficiently weakened rivals to secure firmly a share of business. At the same time, the theory suggested, a panoply of legal restrictions prevented foreign firms from competing in Japanese markets. This interpretation of events was strongly denied in Japan but proved popular in the United States where there was growing alarm at the country's huge trade imbalance in Japan's favor. Not only that, but America was becoming increasingly dependent on Japanese credit, a situation that threatened to destabilize the global economic system.

In 1985 the United States prompted the Group of Five industrial nations (G5) to act. Central banks in the United States, Japan, Britain, France and Germany began selling dollars to try to drive down the currency's value and make United States' goods more competitive. The yen soared, creating sharp increases in the cost of Japanese goods and causing a crisis within the Japanese manufacturing sector. However, Japanese companies quickly adapted to the new situation by establishing manufacturing bases in Southeast Asia, where costs were lower, which allowed them to continue trading competitively.

Cheap money

From February 1987 onward the Group of Seven (G7) industrial nations (G5 plus Italy and Canada) sought a different approach in Japan. The foreign exchange markets were stabilized but Japan was encouraged to maintain low interest rates in the hope that this would stimulate the domestic economy and lead to increased imports from the United States. The policy, however, did not have the desired effect. Borrowing money in Japan became so cheap that it fueled a speculative bubble. Many of Japan's manufacturing firms began to make more profits from financial dealings than from selling their products. Japanese money traveled across the world but mainly to the United States, deepening that country's indebtedness.

In fact, the speculative-bubble economy was short-lived. Japan's leaders became alarmed at the socially divisive and inflationary effects. Cheap money was seen to have extremely damaging consequences for the longterm competitiveness of the Japanese economy, and from 1989 interest rates were raised once more. By the early 1990s the Japanese financial sector was plunged into turmoil while its entrepreneurs and businessmen focused once more on manufacturing. In response, the country's visible trade surplus began to increase after several years of decline. Japan's economy, it seemed, was back on track.

Cut off from capitalism *(above)* North Koreans live in one of the world's few remaining centrally planned economies. Political ideology dictates a cult-like worship of the president, Kim Il-Sung, whose portrait is on the wall. Compared with their Japanese neighbors, this family owns significantly fewer consumer goods, but life expectancy and literacy have risen considerably since the 1960s.

THE PAIN AND PLEASURE OF HARD WORK

Until recently, Japan and South Korea displayed very few of the social divisions that have come to characterize industrial society in the West. The gap between rich and poor was narrow and levels of unemployment remained low, while the homogeneity of both populations allowed for few racial tensions. Recent years have seen significant changes.

The relatively equal distribution of wealth in Japan had its origins in the years after 1945, when a spirit of common sacrifice was important in rebuilding the shattered economy. This ethic endured for several decades and in the mid 1980s Japan boasted the lowest rich–poor income ratio of any capitalist country, with the richest 20 percent of the population earning only 4.3 times more than the poorest 20 percent. Japanese companies have played an important role in preserving the balance; the salary of the highest-paid employee is not more than 7.5 times that of the lowest. In the United States the multiple exceeds 100.

Japan's low level of income-polarization has meant that the rewards of economic growth are more widely distributed there than in any other industrial country, though there is still a huge difference between male and female earnings. In a 1990 United Nations' survey which measured literacy, life expectancy and average income in society as a whole, Japan emerged as the world's most developed country, scoring 99.6 out of a possible 100. On the same index South Korea scored 90.3 and North Korea 78.9.

The price of achievement

Such achievements are not without their costs. Japanese employees work longer

"EXAMINATION HELL": THE JAPANESE EDUCATION SYSTEM

Young Japanese schoolchildren routinely achieve the highest marks in international math tests and are considered to be as much as two years ahead of Western pupils in a range of science subjects. As many as 94 percent of schoolchildren progress from junior to senior high school, while 60 percent go on to some form of higher education, half of these at university.

The system is gruelingly competitive. Recruitment to prestigious companies is largely based on where candidates have studied. Successful entry to a respected junior school will play a part in gaining admission to a good senior school. Consequently, from children's earliest years their performance in examinations is regarded as having possible bearing on their adult lives. Parents usually send them to unofficial private schools, known as *juku*, which offer extra classes on Saturdays and weekday evenings. Japanese children are left with very little free time after they have endured the demands of both school and *juku*, as well as the extensive homework associated with both. They also have to meet the requirements of a compulsory school music or sports club. However, such a demanding system at least ensures that those who survive it are well qualified to take on the exhausting life of a Japanese "salaryman".

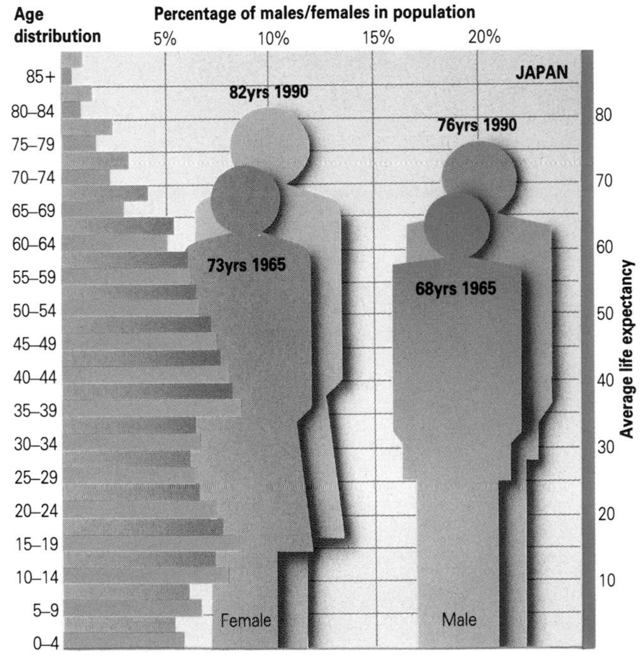

Commuting on the Bullet Train (*above*) First seen in 1964, on time for the Tokyo Olympics, the Bullet Train has become a fixture in the lives of "salarymen" reducing commuting time and helping them to avoid Tokyo's severe traffic jams. The train is well equipped to allow time-conscious commuters to work or catch up with the news on the miniature TV screens installed on the back of each seat.

Life expectancy and age distribution (*left*) The Japanese now have a higher life expectancy than any other people in the world. Some health experts credit their low-fat diet, which even now is changing as Western foods become popular. Low infant mortality rates make the age distribution among the most even in the world, though birth rates may fall as women's career prospects improve – further depleting the available workforce.

hours than any others in the Organization for Economic Cooperation and Development (OECD) countries, with those in manufacturing typically working 46 hours per week, compared with an average of 39 in the OECD. Managerial and professional workers tend to work harder still, hoping to demonstrate sufficient commitment to ensure their promotion up the "salaryman" career ladder. Not all are able to endure so demanding a life; it has been estimated that as many as 200,000 Japanese die each year from overwork.

Women rarely suffer such punishing expectations, nor do they share equally in the country's economic success. The number of Japanese working women has increased steadily during recent decades and by the mid 1980s the proportion in the labor force was only just below the OECD average, yet most were employed in the lowest paid and most menial jobs. In the mid 1980s female incomes were barely more than 50 percent of those of men and many women were still expected to leave work following marriage.

Showing the cracks

As living standards rose some workers were showing unwillingness to put in the punishing hours of work expected. However, it was the financial boom of the late 1980s that did most to undermine the traditional social order. Salaries in the financial services sector reached new heights, while the growing demand for specialist skills encouraged the previously little-known practice of job-hopping. At the same time property values increased rapidly, so that by the end of the 1980s modest homes in the main cities cost as much as 12 times annual salaries, forcing aspiring home-owners to take on mortgages for up to 90 years, with debt repayments spanning generations. As prices continued to rise, the gap between rich and poor began to widen. Homelessness became a growing problem, while owners of previously ordinary properties found themselves newly wealthy. A class of "new rich" was becoming established.

Coping with ethnic diversity

Another social change was the increasing ethnic diversity of the population. Before the 1980s Japan had been overwhelmingly homogenous. The only ethnic minority of any size were Koreans, most of whom had arrived during Japan's occupation of their country. In any case, they made up less than one percent of Japan's population. During the 1980s, however, new groups began to appear. Tokyo's rise as a financial center brought a growing influx of Western bankers.

At the same time immigrants from Southeast Asia and South America began to fill jobs at the bottom of the occupational hierarchy, many of them working illegally. A flourishing informal and casual labor force has begun to emerge, particularly in trucking, construction, painting and metal reprocessing. Day-labor markets have arisen in some cities and the uncertainty of such an existence has been associated with a growing tide of street vandalism and petty crime; phenomena previously all but unheard of in Japan. The decision to end the era of cheap money was motivated by a determination to halt such changes. Japan's leaders were alarmed that the country's dramatic economic growth was threatening political stability and the very national cohesion that had made such success possible.

Overseas development and aid

Japan's contribution to economic development in the Third World takes two main forms. Japanese companies have been important as investors setting up overseas factories. In addition, the government has been increasingly active as a donor of aid. During the 1980s, Japan consistently increased its payments to developing countries: it is now the world's third largest donor as measured by dollar contribution, though only 14th by percent of GNP. Nevertheless, its approach has been criticized as excessively self-serving and parsimonious.

The vast majority of Japan's direct investment abroad has been concentrated in Southeast Asia. Initially Japanese firms opened factories in this area as a way of overcoming protectionist import duties and entering local markets. Following the rise in the value of the yen after 1985 and the growing shortage of labor in Japan, a new incentive attracted Japanese investment – the area's cheap and plentiful workforce. Manufacturing in Japan and Southeast Asia has become increasingly interrelated, as Japanese transnational

Aid gone astray (*right*) Cans of Japanese tuna donated as food aid have found their way onto a market stall in Mali, one of the poorest countries in Africa. A major disadvantage of donating goods is the risk that they will be diverted in this manner.

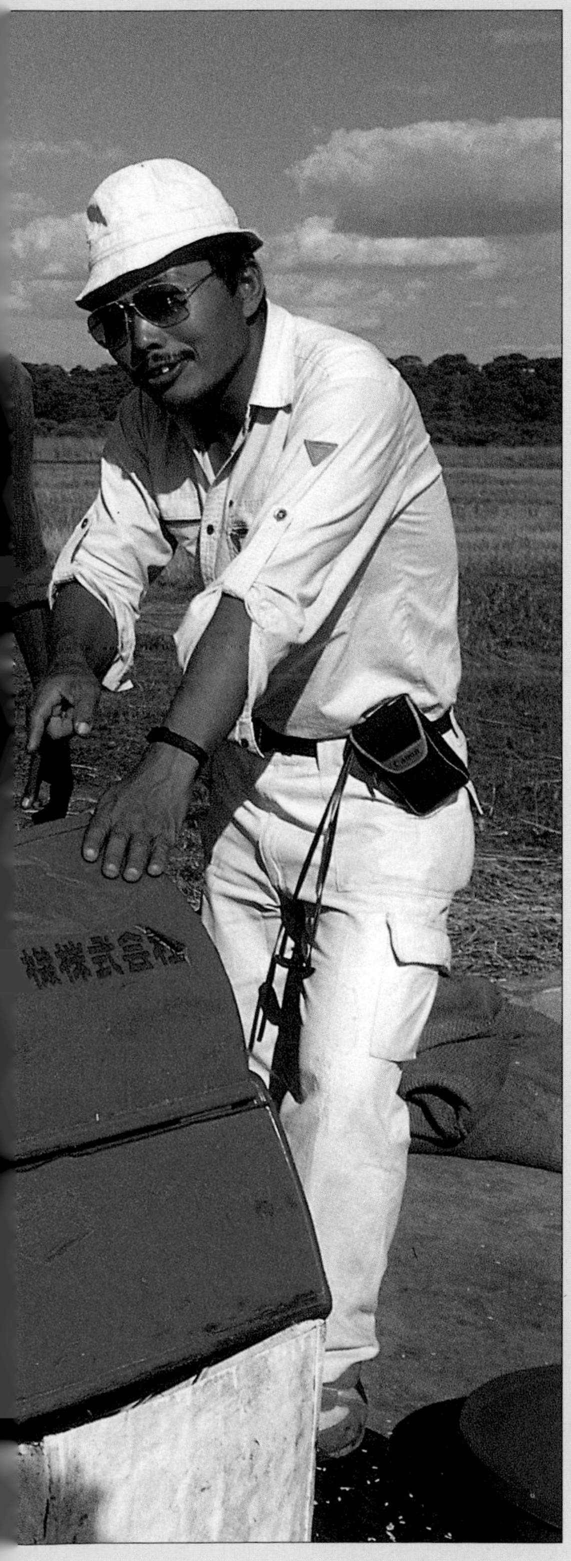

Cooperative development (*below*) A Japanese adviser with workers on a rice-growing project in Zambia. Development assistance to Africa is more likely to be agricultural than technical, focused on improving food production and raising standards of living.

corporations coordinate their activities across the area as a whole. In most cases production in Japan itself is concentrated on developing new, leading-edge products, while facilities in Southeast Asia are used to manufacture more established items that can compete in international markets only if their prices are low. These developments have raised the possibility of greater economic integration within Southeast Asia, and some commentators foresee the gradual transformation of the whole area toward economic and even political union, creating a stable platform for Japan's future growth. However, national rivalries remain potent forces in many eastern Asian countries.

The second way that Japan exercises influence over developing economies is through overseas aid. Until the 1960s Japan was itself a recipient of overseas aid from Western countries, and its role as a donor is quite a new one. By 1989, however, it had become (however briefly) the world's largest giver of aid. Now more than three-quarters of Japanese donations go to Southeast Asia. In spite of this apparent generosity, the aid programs have been widely criticized for being both miserly and more calculated to benefit Japanese interests than those of the developing countries involved.

While Japan certainly supplies large total volumes of aid, when these are measured against the country's GDP then Japanese contributions are revealed to be well below those provided by most OECD countries. Moreover, Japan has been criticized for favoring loans rather than straightforward nonrefundable grants. It also tends to offer tied aid that requires the involvement of Japanese firms in the receiving country. The Japanese government has also been attacked for the low priority it attaches to aid. Its Overseas Development Office, for example, is thinly staffed by international standards. Consequently there are few aid workers to provide intelligence on suitable projects, and aid projects are often the proposals of Japanese trading companies already operating locally. It is doubtful that organizations with a vested interest in the economy are best placed to make an objective decision about a country's most urgent needs.

In the late 1980s, partly in response to these criticisms, the Japanese government began reducing the proportion of its tied aid. At the same time Japan consistently increased its aid donations to the developing world during the 1980s, at a time when countries such as the United States and Britain were reducing theirs.

Venerable age

Women and men in Japan can expect to live longer than anywhere else in the world – women to an average age of 82 and men to an average age of 76. This achievement reflects well on the Japanese diet and healthcare system, but it also highlights an economic dilemma for Japan and for some other mature industrial societies.

In the developing world, a sizable claim is made on the national purse by a large population of dependent young people – boys and girls who often consume more than they produce. In Japan a similar claim is made by a large and fast-growing population of retired men and women. The private and public pension rights of these individuals, together with the often costly healthcare bills associated with geriatric illnesses, have to be funded by a younger generation now at work. Their premiums are rising as a consequence and this in turn raises the important new issue of intergenerational equity.

In Japan, the elderly are often venerated; elsewhere however, there are signs already that today's working population is anxious about the financial support it must offer to a large nonworking population of adults. Even family relations are bound up with the changing world economy.

Elderly Japanese lady writing against a background of blossom.

RESTRUCTURING THE EXPORT ECONOMY

UNTAPPED RESOURCES · REORIENTING TOWARD ASIA · A WORKING MAN'S PARADISE

The economies of Australasia still rely heavily on exporting minerals and agricultural produce rather than manufactured goods. Australia and New Zealand, protected by trade with the British Empire in the 19th and early 20th centuries and reliant on the European market, have had to restructure their economies following the formation of the European Community (EC). This forced the region to look for new trading agreements with Japan and Asia, to scale down agricultural exports, develop new industries and establish a more vibrant commercial banking policy. Hampered by physical remoteness and a restricted labor supply, many island economies are using aid for economic development. Antarctica and Oceania are rich in resources, but their fragile environments are threatened by prospective exploration.

COUNTRIES IN THE REGION

Australia, Fiji, Kiribati, Nauru, New Zealand, Papua New Guinea, Solomon Islands, Tonga, Tuvalu, Vanuatu, Western Samoa

ECONOMIC INDICATORS: 1990

	HIE* Australia	HIE* New Zealand	LMIE* Papua New Guinea
GDP (US$ billions)	296.3	42.76	3.27
GNP per capita (US$)	17,000	12,680	860
Annual rate of growth of GDP, 1980–1990 (%)	3.4	1.9	1.9
Manufacturing as % of GDP	15	19	12
Central government spending as % of GNP	26	35	29
Merchandise exports† (US$ billions)	41.2	9.5	1.14
Merchandise imports† (US$ billions)	38.4	7.12	1.29
% of GNP donated as development aid	0.34	0.23	–‡

WELFARE INDICATORS

Infant mortality rate (per 1,000 live births)			
1965	19	20	140
1990	8	10	57
Daily food supply available (calories per capita, 1989)	3,216	3,362	2,403
Population per physician (1984)	440	580	6,070
Teacher–pupil ratio (primary school, 1989)	1 : 17	1 : 19	1 : 32

Note: The Gross Domestic Product (GDP) is the total value of all goods and services domestically produced. The Gross National Product (GNP) is the GDP plus net income from abroad.

** HIE (High Income Economy) – GNP per capita above $7,620 in 1990. LMIE (Lower Middle Income Economy) – GNP per capita between $610 and $2,465.*

† Year ending June 1991.

‡ Papua New Guinea is a recipient of development aid.

UNTAPPED RESOURCES

The British and Dutch both laid claim to Australia in the 17th century, but following Captain Cook's voyage in 1770 the British took formal possession of New South Wales. British convicts were transported there from the late 18th century until well into the 19th century, when discoveries of precious metals and the development of agriculture attracted free immigrants to the region to improve their lot. Economic development of the region was largely dependent on European colonial ambitions during the late 19th and early 20th centuries. The region was one of the last parts of the world to be colonized and decolonization was slow. Parts of Polynesia, Micronesia (the islands of the west Pacific Ocean) and Melanesia (the Pacific islands northeast of Australia) are still overseas dependencies of Britain, France and the United States.

Between 1820 and 1850 companies funded by British capital began to exploit the agricultural and mineral resources of New South Wales and parts of Oceania, turning the area into a major supplier of raw materials to developed economies. Copper, discovered in 1842 and gold, discovered in 1851, spurred economic growth and attracted European settlers. The development of sheep farming established Australia's wool industry, but displaced the native population and eroded their traditional way of life. On several of the Pacific Islands, permanent European settlers acquired large amounts of land and established plantation societies. Trade linked the islands of Oceania to Australia and New Zealand and islanders were encouraged to produce cash crops for Australian and European land owners. Throughout the region, agricultural produce became the currency that was exchanged for tools, utensils, food and clothing.

New financial infrastructure

A banking system was established in Australasia between 1820 and 1850, and funds from overseas helped to finance the expansion of sheep farming, rapid residential and commercial development and railroad construction. During the long boom of 1851 to 1890, Australia and New Zealand remained principally exporters of

Traditional exports *(left)* Ranch hands load bales of wool into a truck ready for export. For a developed country, Australia exports a relatively high percentage of agricultural produce and other primary commodities, making the economy vulnerable to fluctuations in world demand and prices. The collapse of the wool market in 1990 left sheep farmers with tons of unsold wool.

Map of GDP per capita *(right)* Australian GDP grew slowly but steadily at an average of 3.4 percent per year during the 1980s, despite the impact of world recession and falling commodity prices. The current per capita figure is among the 20 highest in the world.

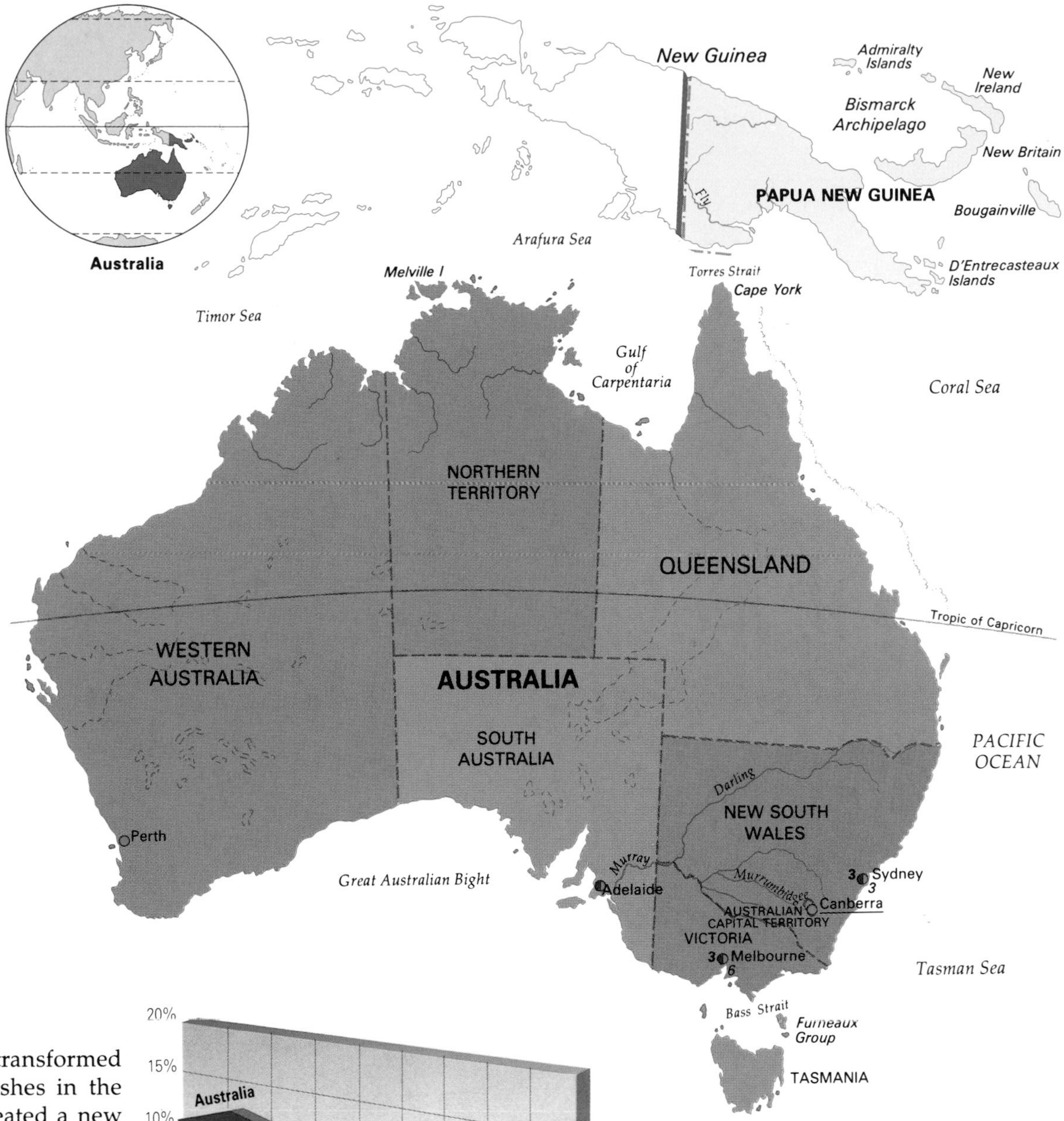

Economic indicators

head offices of world's top 500 banks and companies (with number if more than one)

- ●3 bank
- ●3 company

(underlined name indicates a capital city)

GDP per capita (US$)

- over 20 000
- 15 000–20 000
- 10 000–14 999
- 5 000–9 999
- 2 000–4 999
- 500–1 999

raw materials but became transformed into urban societies. Gold rushes in the second half of the century created a new wave of mining development. Combined with the lucrative agricultural sector, this made Australia one of the world's most prosperous countries by 1900, with New Zealand not far behind.

The depression of the 1930s reduced export earnings in Australia and New Zealand and cut off capital inflow, leading to economic contraction. In Australia, agriculture and mining remained vital but more diverse while manufacturing, boosted at the start of World War II, began to become more established. Despite the war, the standard of living remained high in Australia and New Zealand and exporting continued to earn considerable revenue.

Most of the island-states experienced minimal growth in the interwar years; their agricultural economies were at a standstill due to depressed world prices though a gold rush in the mountains of Papua New Guinea began a process of more rapid transformation. Increasingly, the islands with mineral resources began to exploit them for export. For example,

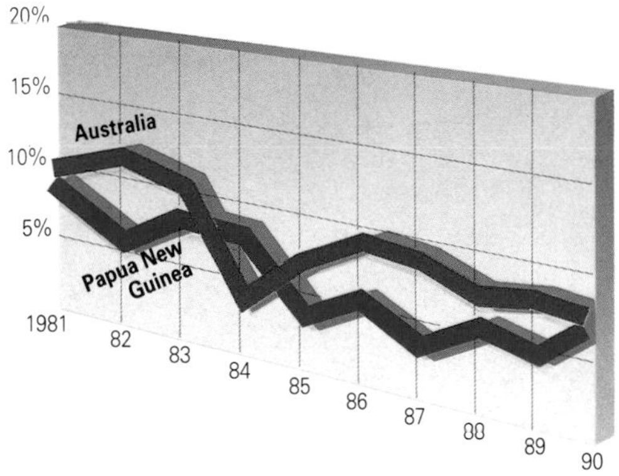

Profile of inflation *(above)* Inflation was consistently lower in Papua New Guinea than in Australia during the 1980s apart from a brief period in 1984. Both countries ran tight monetary policies throughout the decade to keep control of inflation.

New Caledonia became the world's largest producer of nickel, which accounted for 90 percent of its export revenue in 1960. Papua New Guinea developed an export trade in coffee, copra and cocoa, but increasingly copper became its most valuable commodity.

Apart from these exceptions, the majority of Pacific islands are short of natural resources, and the prospects for economic development are poor. Most of these states have only recently been decolonized, mainly in the 1970s, and there are still doubts about their economic viability. The island-states have tended to retain an agricultural base to their economies whereas, in the postwar years, Australia's and New Zealand's larger economies had greater success with diversification out of agriculture.

Late 20th-century decline

By the 1980s the region's economy was still dominated by Australia and New Zealand but their economic fortunes waned in the late 20th century. The EC's Common Agricultural Policy severely reduced Australia's trade with member countries. At the same time, prohibitive tariffs blocked trade with potential new markets in Asia, and powerful trade unions restricted industrial output at home. Australia slipped from having the world's highest gross national product (GNP) per head at the beginning of the 20th century to being ranked 18th in the world toward the end.

REORIENTING TOWARD ASIA

In the 1990s Australasia is beginning to come to terms with its position as a major supplier of resources close to the manufacturing boom-area of Southeast Asia, rather than regarding itself as an outpost of the British Empire separated from its ideal markets by the "tyranny of distance". Change in economic policy has been slow to take effect, but the key to recovery from the slump of the 1980s seems to be the emerging significance of Japan and Asia as trading partners for the more buoyant economies and as donors of development aid to the more fragile Pacific island states.

A major challenge to the region's economies is to apply strategic thinking to enable them to weather international fluctuations in the demand for raw materials. Australia, for example, has become one of the world's largest suppliers of minerals. It is the single biggest exporter of iron ore and aluminum, the second biggest exporter of coal, nickel and zinc, and an important supplier of lead, gold, tin, tungsten and uranium. As a commodity exporter, Australia is particularly vulnerable to fluctuations in international demand and prices. The 1990 collapse in the wool market, for example, left the industry in crisis and created a wool mountain costing A$ 1 billion ($690 million) to store. If the economy as a whole is to reduce this vulnerability, it needs to add value to its exports by part-processing them or using them in manufacturing industries. Australia, like the region as a whole, needs to restructure and diversify its domestic economy in order to gain greater international competitiveness and to develop new trading structures and markets.

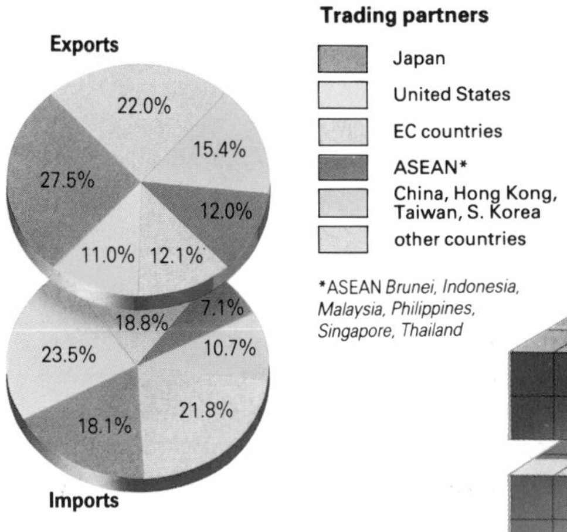

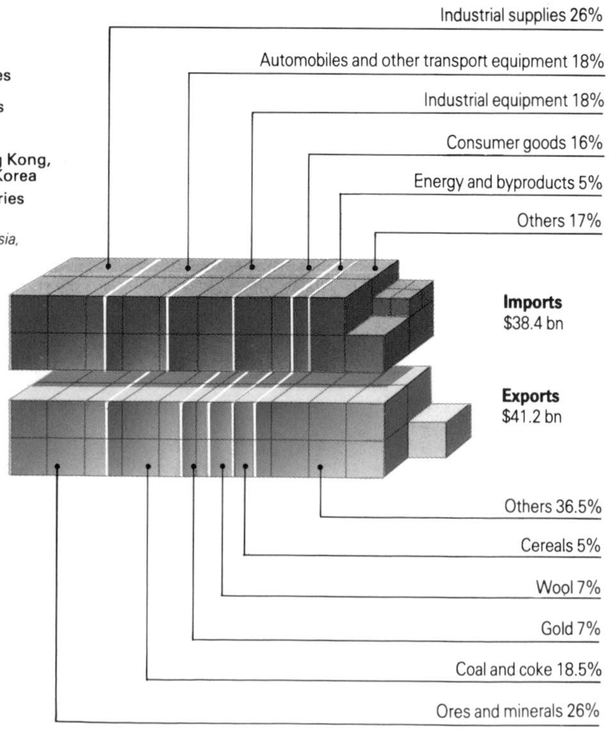

Australia's balance of merchandise trade Australia's three main trading partners are Japan, the United States and the EC. In recent years, however, the booming economies of Southeast Asia are rapidly becoming more important markets for Australia's raw materials. The bulk of imports are of manufactured goods.

Slimming down

Australia's Labor government of the early 1990s has encouraged freer trade by deregulating financial, transportation and other services and moving toward privatization in formerly public enterprises. Competition, rather than change of ownership, has led to greater efficiency. Many Australian businesses are not expected to survive such extensive economic restructuring. As businesses decline, the country should be left with a manufacturing base that is fit enough to survive in open competition.

Public ownership is declining everywhere in the region. Both Australia and New Zealand are becoming some of the world's most open and market-directed economies. Officially, agriculture and fisheries are at the core of their economic development, yet agricultural exports have all plummeted in the 1980s. Fisheries are rarely locally owned, though small states derive significant lease incomes from countries such as Japan and the United States. In reality the smaller states have become more dependent on remittances from overseas migrants and aid, a situation that has failed to stimulate productive investment.

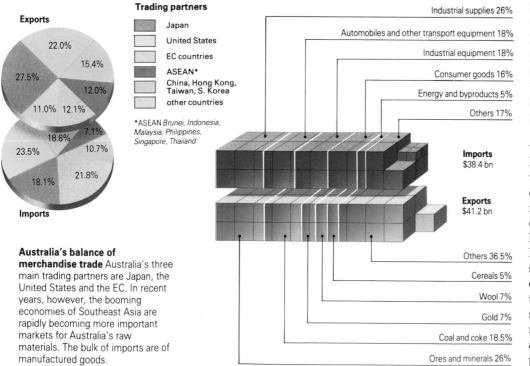

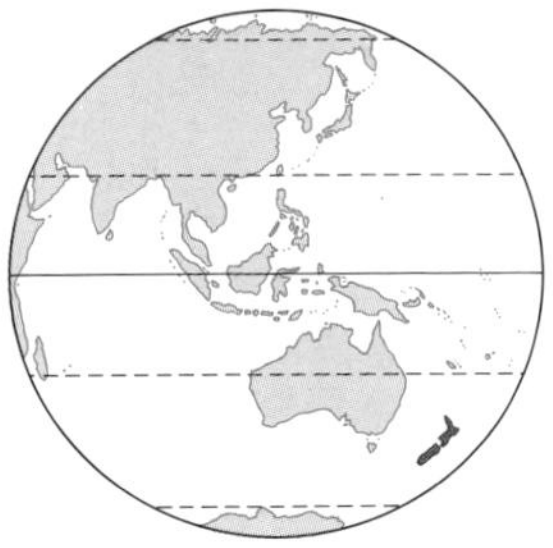

Alternative island economies *(left)* Villagers of the Solomon Islands gather round to watch money being made out of shells. Melanesian peoples have a long tradition of trade, both with neighboring villages and other islands. They have evolved elaborate exchange rituals, trading goods such as shells or salt for pigs.

Map of GDP per capita *(right)* Agricultural produce supplies 8.6 percent of New Zealand's GDP; twice the level in Australia. Low economic growth during the 1980s reflected problems with economic restructuring in New Zealand.

The wealth of the region has been based on primary resources, but in the 1990s their significance has dwindled in favor of manufacturing and services. In Australia, despite the growth of both output and exports, agriculture's contribution to the national income fell from 20 percent in 1950 to only 8 percent in 1970, and to 4 percent in 1990. This drop in income was partly offset by a rise in world demand for minerals; by 1990 Australia's three highest-earning exports were coal, oil and gold.

Islands fighting for survival

New Zealand and the island economies (except Papua New Guinea) continue, in spite of the changing world market, to invest in agricultural exports and commercial fishing. Their manufacturing sector also relies heavily on agricultural products and is dominated by processed food and drinks, including wine and beef. High wages and few economies of scale have slowed manufacturing growth where it has had to go without government support, and most of the small island economies have experienced problems in achieving rapid economic growth, in stark contrast to the expanding Asian economies of the Pacific rim.

In the last decade a number of highly developed manufacturing economies, notably Japan and the United States, have played a greater economic and political role in the region. Although the United Kingdom has largely withdrawn its influence, France, Australia and New Zealand have continued to exert a substantial pressure on political and economic change or the lack of it. Since 1987 Japan has become the largest donor of aid in the Pacific region and the single most important market for fish from the Pacific islands.

A number of the smaller island states continue to remain isolated from global economic fluctuations, supported by foreign aid and partly dependent on subsistence production. For many islanders, migration will offer greater opportunities than remaining at home. Deficient in capital, modern technology and human resources, independent island states have pursued the same official strategies of economic development as those of the colonial powers. Most of the countries in the region have adopted an economic management policy which endorses deregulation and reduces government intervention.

NEW ZEALAND AND THE EC

New Zealand's economy has always depended on a limited range of agricultural products, principally lamb, butter and wool. For much of the 20th century, trade followed the old colonial routes to Britain, aided by preferential tariffs and quotas for goods from Commonwealth countries. In 1973 this situation was transformed. The United Kingdom joined the EC and, following the guidelines of its Common Economic Policy, ceased to be a major customer.

The impact on New Zealand was shattering, and marked the start of a long period of economic decline. At the end of the 1970s two-thirds of all dairy products went to Britain; by 1988 this had fallen to less than a fifth. New Zealand was forced to develop new export markets in Asia, the Middle East and North and South America, but in the early 1990s exports to these new markets had still not compensated for the loss of revenue. New Zealand was still importing manufactured goods at high cost, and developed a serious balance-of-payments problem.

A restructuring of the agricultural economy followed. Farm subsidies were slashed, halving farm income. Friesian cows replaced Jerseys as butter exports declined and milk products were processed further into yogurt, cheese and delicatessen butter packs. Farms diversified into fruit and the tourist industry, while the government encouraged new export industries such as timber and woodpulp. Despite these efforts, recovery has been very difficult in a time of global recession.

"A WORKING MAN'S PARADISE"

Since the late 19th century Australia and New Zealand have been two of the more developed and affluent nations in the world. The educational systems established by settlers under British rule, and the social reforms that surrounded welfare provision in Australia earned the country the nickname "a working man's paradise". Traces of that heritage still remain in modern Australia's democratic and highly competitive society.

Health services across the region are primarily financed from government sources. In Australia and New Zealand, almost two-thirds of financial input is from the government, but both countries have moved toward "user-pays" principles. Australia's universal healthcare insurance system, Medicare, established in 1984, provides basic services free but makes direct charges to users for the remainder. New Zealand ended its free system in 1992 when fees were introduced. Both countries spend more than half their total health budget on institutional care in public hospitals. Facilities are generally excellent in urban areas and there are Flying Doctor services covering Australia's more remote areas. As well as providing emergency treatment, monitoring chronic conditions and moving patients to urban hospitals, the Flying Doctor runs antenatal and childcare services and special clinics. In the smaller islands of Oceania where there are more risks to health and facilities are less sophisticated, there is a corresponding drop in life expectancy. Melanesia, in particular, is plagued by resurgent tropical diseases such as malaria.

The region's schools are also primarily supported from public funds, supplemented by individual contributions for university education. Tertiary education is now available in Papua New Guinea, Guam and Fiji. The University of the South Pacific has an agricultural campus

Flying to the rescue (*above*) Australia's Flying Doctor brings primary healthcare and emergency treatment to scattered populations who may be up to a thousand kilometers (hundreds of miles) from hospital.

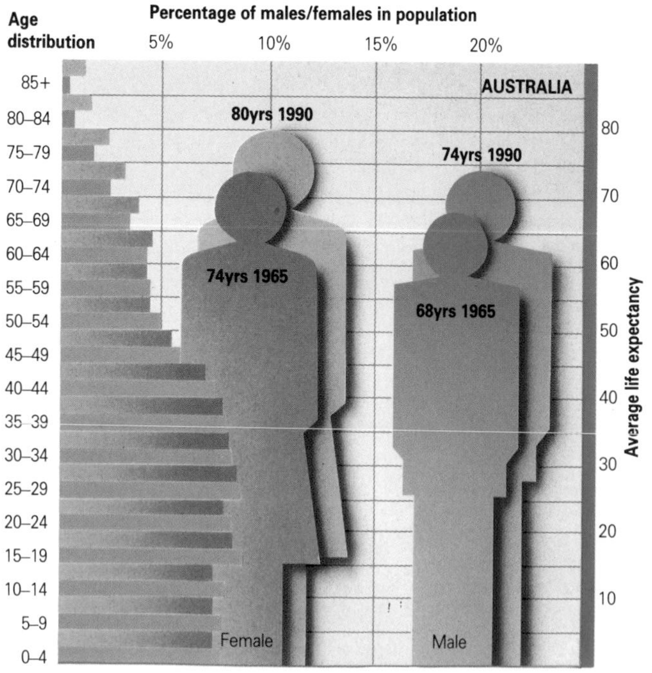

Life expectancy and age distribution (*right*) These figures, showing high life expectancy and low birthrates in Australia, contrast sharply with the high birthrates and relatively low life expectancy on the smaller islands.

Japanese gold The luxury hotels and apartment blocks of the Gold Coast in Queensland, Australia are now owned almost exclusively by Japanese leisure companies who moved in after a series of Australian financial failures of the late 1980s.

THE DEMISE OF THE AUSTRALIAN TYCOON

In the latter part of the 19th and much of the 20th century, Australia was a golden land for entrepreneurs. This was mainly because of government commitment to growth driven by financial speculation rather than linked to commodities or products. Toward the end of the 1980s, however, it became apparent that the economic philosophy that money makes more money was not working in the long term. The huge individual debts run up by some tycoons could never be repaid and the stock market crash of 1987 began a rapid decline for habitual risk-takers.

By the end of 1991, Alan Bond's financial empire was in ruins, he was fighting to stave off bankruptcy and was subsequently jailed. Christopher Skase, pioneer of Mirage's luxury Gold Coast resort, Sanctuary Cove, fled Australia for the sanctuary of Majorca, leaving behind him debts of more than A$87 million ($60 million). Brian Grey's attempt to give Australia a third domestic carrier, Compass, also collapsed at the end of 1991. Only the most shrewd tycoons survived (including Kerry Packer, the country's wealthiest man).

in Western Samoa and centers in 10 other countries. Primary education is not universal in parts of Papua New Guinea and the independent states of Melanesia, but otherwise literacy is almost universal.

Male bastions

Employment in the region's formal sector has favored men, especially in the higher echelons of both the public and private sectors. In the island-states both business and politics are largely male preserves and girls are unlikely to receive the same educational opportunities as boys. Even in Australia and New Zealand a culture of "mateship" slowed female access to services and employment until the late 20th century. Within the region today, only Australia and New Zealand have comprehensive social welfare systems that provide family allowances, workers' compensation, unemployment benefit and old age pensions to all citizens.

Average incomes vary considerably across the region. There are huge gaps in expectations between the two larger states and the islands; between men and women; and between urban and rural workers. Both Australia and New Zealand have average incomes of over $12,000 per capita, but Fiji, the next most affluent independent state, has an average income of $2,000 per capita. The least developed countries have average incomes of less then $1,000 per capita. Kiribati, an island group of 20 atolls in the mid Pacific Ocean, has less than half of that. At an international level income inequalities are substantial; they are even greater within individual countries. Urban incomes, especially in the small island-states, are several times those of rural areas, reflecting the significance of public-sector employment. Urban bias in the allocation of services has further emphasized rural–urban inequalities.

Welfare on the islands

In contrast to the well developed welfare services and high average incomes of Australia and New Zealand, Kiribati, Tuvalu, Western Samoa and Vanuatu have all been recognized by the United Nations as less-developed nations, with severe problems in achieving economic self-sufficiency. Australia and New Zealand are major donors of aid to those countries and to other island states. The gap between rich and poor is widened by the high birthrates in poorer parts of the region. Although population growth rates are less than 1.5 percent in Australia and New Zealand, they are relatively high in other parts of the region. Papua New Guinea, Vanuatu and the Solomon Islands have a population growth rate of 3 percent while the Marshall Islands, at 3.8 percent, have one of the highest in the world. In urban areas particularly, social services including education and health have not been able to cope with such rapidly growing populations.

In the central Pacific (Polynesian) states of Tonga, American Samoa, Western Samoa and the Cook Islands, population growth rates are much lower, primarily because of emigration, which has become a safety valve for high rates of natural increase and minimal economic growth. For the smaller Polynesian states – Niue, Cook Islands, Tokelau and also Pitcairn – more than half the ethnic population now lives overseas, mainly in New Zealand. Auckland has become the largest Polynesian city in the world.

Resource conflicts in Melanesia

In Melanesia (the group of islands northeast of Australia comprising Papua New Guinea [PNG], the Solomon Islands, Vanuatu, Fiji, and New Caledonia) conflicts over who should exploit and profit from mineral resources have become a source of serious political unrest. At independence in 1975, PNG was primarily an agricultural economy. Since then, mining has brought great wealth to the country, which now gains 80 percent of its export income from copper and gold. Mining has also brought conflict – over land, incomes and environmental damage – and brought the country to the verge of civil war in 1989.

The story of Bougainville island

Mining was not new to PNG in the late 20th century; there had already been two distinct phases in the colonial era. In the postwar years, the mining industry was quiescent until the discovery of the rich copper deposits of Bougainville island. The opening of the gold and copper mine at Panguna on Bougainville island in 1972 was the first real diversification of the economy – previously profits had belonged to colonial companies. Huge incomes from mining at Panguna, more than a third of the national income in the early years, contributed to the development of the local economy, increased the relative wealth of Bougainville (which already produced much of PNG's copra and cocoa), provided jobs, developed skills and established the country on a path of rapid transformation.

Government economic policy emphasized new growth, job creation and the reduction of dependence on Australia. However, conflict developed on Bougainville island when local landowners began to resent the limited incomes they received from exports. About 0.2 percent of the profits reverted to them, compared with 63 percent to national government and 5 percent to provincial government. Their case was supported by the villagers close to the mining site who lived in relative deprivation compared with the well paid mineworkers who had migrated from other parts of PNG and overseas.

The compensation payments received by landowners for the lease of and damage to the land was inadequate for longterm development and there were disputes about a better settlement. Local people resented how little prosperity the mine brought them. Following the pattern of capital-intensive industries, the mine stabilized its labor force in the 1970s, and local young people were unable to get prestigious employment there while established migrants remained in place. In 1988 the militant landowners closed the mine, sought Bougainvillean secession from the rest of PNG, established the Bougainville Revolutionary Army and fought a bitter and violent struggle with the PNG military forces. The conflict was still not resolved at the end of 1992 and the mine, the single most valuable component of the PNG economy, remained closed.

New mining sites

While the Panguna mine was being constructed, high mineral prices had also brought geologists to the most remote areas of the highlands. In 1968 gold and copper was discovered at Ok Tedi. By 1987 it had become the largest gold mine outside South Africa. Further new discoveries followed, mostly epithermal gold mines, associated with hot springs and ancient volcanic activity. Extraction from these areas required new geological techniques and chemical skills. The mine at Porgera, in the Enga highlands, began gold production in 1989 and Misima, in Milne Bay, started in the following year. Lihir, off the coast of New Ireland, could eventually become the largest gold mine in the country.

The Melanesian states of Vanuatu and the Solomon Islands have yet to be fully explored geologically, though there is now significant mining at Gold Ridge in the Solomon Islands. In New Caledonia long-established nickel mining has disfigured mountainsides and degraded river systems. In Fiji the Vatukoula gold mine has become a site of industrial conflict, but prospects for new copper mines are good. It remains to be seen if these resources can be exploited peacefully and without destruction. Experts fear that the disputes in Bougainville may have subsequent parallels in other mining areas of Melanesia.

Mine of discord The Panguna copper and gold mine on Bougainville island is Papua New Guinea's most valuable economic asset. It is also the cause of bitter disputes between local people and the government over how profits from the mine are distributed.

GLOSSARY

ACP 66 countries in Africa, the Caribbean and the Pacific region receiving a large proportion of the European Community's foreign aid. Their exports are largely given free entry to west European markets.

Age of empire The heyday of European imperialism (1850–1950).

Agricultural economy An economy where most people work as cultivators or PASTORALists.

ASEAN The Association of South East Asian Nations, formed in 1967. A regional association of noncommunist states, based in Jakarta.

Baker Plan A set of proposals first put forward by the United States' Secretary of State James Baker in 1985 to deal with the international DEBT CRISIS. The proposals linked economic reforms in the indebted countries to economic growth in the developed world.

Balance of Payments A statement of a country's transactions with all other countries over a given period. The CURRENT ACCOUNT of the balance of payments is made up of MERCHANDISE (VISIBLE TRADE), INVISIBLE TRADE (receipts and payments for services such as shipping, tourism and insurance), private transfers (remittances from workers abroad) and official transfers (such as payments to international organizations). The capital account consists of long and short-term transactions relating to a country's loans and borrowings. The overall balance consists of the current and capital accounts added together. Since the overall balance of payments must be in equilibrium, any surplus or deficit in the overall or basic balance of payments must be offset by changes in a country's foreign exchange reserves and its net monetary movements. Balance of payments statistics are difficult to collect and are subject to errors which are often presented as an omission item.

Benelux countries European states forming the Benelux Economic Union (Belgium, Netherlands and Luxembourg).

Birthrate The annual number of live births per 1,000 population.

Black economy The sector of the economy that avoids paying tax.

Brain drain The loss of well-educated labor to another country.

Brady Plan A market-based plan for dealing with debt in developing countries. Proposed by the United States' Secretary of State James Brady in 1988.

Branch plant A subsidiary of a major corporation.

Bretton Woods system The system of international economic management that lasted from 1945 to the early 1970s, and which emerged from the Bretton Woods Conference in 1944.

Capital Variously refers to machinery, investment funds or a particular employment relationship involving waged labor.

Capital goods Infrastructure or equipment, including machines, industrial plant, buildings and transportation infrastructure used to produce further goods and income.

Capitalism A political and economic system based on the production of goods and services for profitable exchange in which labor itself is bought and sold for wages. Capitalist economies can be more or less regulated by governments. In a capitalist MIXED ECONOMY the government will own some of the country's utilities and industries as nationalized companies. It will also act as a major employer of labor.

Cash crop A crop that is specifically grown for sale, often abroad.

Central Bank The government agency that oversees a country's banking system and that is often responsible for the conduct of monetary policy. Examples include the Bundesbank in Germany, the Bank of England and the Federal Reserve System in the USA.

Central government spending General government expenditure, not including spending by state and local governments.

City of London The financial center of Europe.

Collectivization The organization of the economy by collective control through agencies of the state.

Colonialism The occupation of foreign territory by a state for settlement and economic exploitation.

Colony A territory under the sovereignty of a foreign power.

COMECON The Council for Mutual Economic Assistance, formed in 1947 as an organization to further trade and economic cooperation between communist countries. It had 10 members before its collapse in 1989 – the Soviet Union, Bulgaria, Czechoslovakia, Hungary, Poland, Romania, East Germany, Mongolia, Cuba, and Vietnam.

Commercial banks Financial institutions linking lenders (through checkable deposits and savings deposits) to borrowers (including consumers, property buyers, firms and governments). In the FIRST WORLD, most commercial banks are privately owned; in some developing countries they are NATIONALIZED.

Commodity prices The prices charged for fuels, foodstuffs and raw materials like iron and bauxite.

Commonwealth A loose political grouping of some of the states that made up the British Empire.

Communism A social and economic system based on the communal ownership of property. It usually refers to the state-controlled social and economic systems set up in the Soviet-bloc countries and in the People's Republic of China.

Comparative advantage A country has a comparative advantage in the production of goods and services where its relative costs are lowest.

Competition A situation where a large number of buyers can choose to purchase goods or services from a large number of sellers. Sellers are encouraged to be cost efficient as a result.

Competitiveness A measure of a trader's costs (the cost of labor, energy, etc.) in comparison to those of a rival trader.

Constant prices Prices adjusted to offset for the effects of INFLATION.

Consumer goods Goods that are acquired for immediate use, such as foodstuffs, radios, televisions and washing machines.

Consumer societies Societies where basic needs (food, sanitation, shelter) are largely satisfied and where money is available to purchase commodities for pleasure.

Consumer sovereignty The idea that the "buyer is King and Queen" and that goods and services will be produced to meet the desires of consumers.

Convertible currency A currency that can be freely exchanged for another currency or for gold.

Countertrade The exchange of goods and services for other goods and services, excluding money. This includes barter trade.

Cultural Revolution A radical attempt to continue the communist revolution in China from 1966 to 1976.

Current Account The part of a country's BALANCE OF PAYMENTS which consists of VISIBLE and INVISIBLE TRADE (in goods and services) and private and official transfers to and from abroad.

Daily food supply available per capita The calorie equivalent of the net food supplies in a country, divided by the total population, per day.

Death Rate The annual number of deaths per 1,000 population.

Debt (foreign/external) The financial obligations owed by a country to the rest of the world, usually repayable in US dollars. Total external debt includes public, publicly guaranteed, and private long-term debt.

Debt crisis The widespread failure to meet loan repayments that has affected many indebted developing countries since 1980.

Debt rescheduling An agreement between an indebted country and its creditors to spread out debt repayments over a longer period than first agreed. COMMERCIAL BANK debt is rescheduled through the LONDON CLUB. Official debt (including government-to-government loans) is rescheduled through the PARIS CLUB.

Debt service Interest payments on outstanding debt plus any principal repayments due.

Debt service ratio Interest and repayments expressed as a percentage of a country's earnings from the export of goods and services.

Demand and supply The twin determinants of market prices.

Demand management An attempt to regulate economic activity and employment by means of direct government spending and by government policies on private spending (such as taxation policy).

Dependency ratio The percentage of the population aged under 15 and over 64.

Dependent countries Countries that rely heavily on other countries for foreign aid, bank loans, inward investment and political protection.

Depression A severe and prolonged downturn in economic activity lasting more than two years and associated with high unemployment.

Devaluation A fall in the exchange rate of a currency, sometimes formally announced by government.

Development An increase in the living standards of a group of people or countries, often defined in terms of a population's capability to meet its own basic needs and present and future aspirations.

Direct foreign investment Overseas investment by a multinational corporation.

Direct taxes Taxes levied on an individual's net income, on the profits of firms and on capital gains.

Dividends Payments to shareholders from company profits.

Domestic savings (gross) The GROSS DOMESTIC PRODUCT (GDP) minus government and private spending.

Economic agent An individual, household, firm, conglomerate or country engaged in economic transactions, including production and exchange.

Economic growth The rate of growth of a country's GROSS DOMESTIC PRODUCT over a given period of time. The fruits of such growth are often shared unequally among the population, which is one reason why economic growth and development are not always the same thing.

ECU European Currency Unit, a weighted basket of the currencies of all European Community member countries.

EFTA European Free Trade Association formed in 1959, comprising Austria, Norway, Sweden, Switzerland, Liechtenstein, Finland and Iceland

EMS European Monetary System, founded in 1979 to manage exchange rate fluctuations in the European Community (the EXCHANGE RATE MECHANISM), and to examine the prospects for a single European currency.

Entrepot An international trading center specializing in the importation and re-export of goods.

EC European Community, an alliance of western European nations formed to agree common policies in the areas of trade, aid, agriculture and economics. The six founder members in 1957 were France, West Germany, Belgium, Holland, Luxembourg and Italy. A further three – Britain, Ireland and Denmark – joined in 1973, Greece in 1981 and Spain and Portugal in 1986. East Germany became a member when it was reunited with West Germany in 1990.

Exchange Rate Mechanism An agreement that binds member countries to maintain their currency exchange rates between established lower and upper limits.

Exports Goods and services sold to other countries, bringing in foreign exchange.

First World A term sometimes used to describe the advanced industrial countries

Fixed exchange rate A situation where the price of one currency stands in a constant relation to other currencies (and usually to gold). Fixed exchange rates were the norm in the 1950s and 1960s and a country had to enter into formal negotiations with other countries and the INTERNATIONAL MONETARY FUND to secure an official devaluation of its currency.

Floating exchange rates A situation in which traded currencies find their own price in the open market and in relation to DEMAND AND SUPPLY factors. Most major currencies have floated since 1973, although governments will buy and sell their own currency from time to time in an effort to maintain its value within some sort of target range. The EXCHANGE RATE MECHANISM of the European Community is an example of a "managed float" exchange rate regime.

Floating interest rate Interest rates that vary over time.

Foreign exchange market A dispersed market in which currencies are bought and sold by ECONOMIC AGENTS, and in which the price of any currency is established.

Free market economy An economy in which transactions are entered into by private individuals and firms, with very little intervention by government. Private buyers and sellers carry out their business in the market-place.

Free trade A system of international trade in which goods and services are exchanged without tariffs, quotas or other restrictions.

Free Trade Agreement (FTA) A trade liberalization pact signed between the United States and Canada in 1989, and expected to extend to Mexico in the early 1990s.

Full employment A situation where the total available LABOR FORCE is gainfully employed, save for those individuals who are unable to work or are temporarily between jobs.

Futures A loose term which usually refers to agreements to buy and sell specific quantities of goods and currencies at a stated price and at a stated time in the future. Such forward dealing is often undertaken for speculative or insurance reasons and the contracts are made in futures markets.

GATT General Agreement on Tariffs and Trade, set up in 1947 to liberalize international trade and to prevent discrimination (except where agreed by signatory countries). The sixth round of GATT negotiations began in Uruguay in 1986.

GDP Gross domestic product, the total value of a country's annual output of goods and services, with allowances being made for depreciation. Growth in GDP is usually expressed in constant prices, to offset the effects of INFLATION. GDP is a very useful guide to the level of economic activity in a country.

GDP per capita A country's gross domestic product divided by its total population. If a country's GDP is very unevenly divided amongst its citizens, the average GDP per capita figure might not be a good guide to the economic position of a typical individual in that country.

GNP Gross national product, a country's GDP plus net income from abroad. A country's GNP will usually be similar to its GDP, but GNP will be significantly higher than GDP in countries which rely heavily upon wages remitted from nationals working abroad.

GNP per capita A country's gross national product divided by its total population. If a country's GNP is very unevenly divided amongst its citizens, the average GNP per capita figure might not be a good guide to the economic position of a typical individual in that country.

Gold standard A system of international economic management that lasted from 1870 to 1914 and which was resurrected, unsuccessfully, after World War I. Countries on the gold standard were required to convert their currencies freely into gold through their central banks. The gold standard system guarded against INFLATION at the cost of mounting economic stagnation.

Group of 3 Germany, Japan and the United States, the three most powerful economies in the world.

Group of 7 Canada, France, Germany, Italy, Japan, Britain and the United States, the seven most dominant FIRST WORLD economies.

Gross domestic product see GDP.

Gross national product see GNP.

Hard currency A currency used by international traders because they think it is safe from DEVALUATION.

Healthcare expenditures Spending on hospitals, health centers and clinics, health insurance schemes and family planning.

Heavy industry Largescale industries engaged in the production of goods for further use in the production process, such as the steel and chemical industries.

High-income economies (HIEs) The wealthiest countries in the world, where average per capita incomes were in excess of $7,619 in 1990.

Human Development Index (HDI) A measure of economic welfare devised by the United Nations Development Program.

IBRD The International Bank for Reconstruction and Development, an institution set up at the BRETTON WOODS conference of 1944 and now more usually referred to as the WORLD BANK. The IBRD is the single largest source of aid for developing countries, most of which is distributed through its cheap-loan agency, the International Development Association (IDA).

IDA International Development Association, the cheap-loan agency of the IBRD/WORLD BANK.

ILO International Labor Organization (of the United Nations), based in Geneva, Switzerland. The ILO was founded to improve the conditions of labor and living standards throughout the world.

IMF International Monetary Fund. The fund was suggested at the 1944 BRETTON WOODS Conference and it commenced formal operations in 1946–47. It is charged with maintaining and stabilizing exchange rates and with eliminating unwanted restrictions on international trade. The IMF can also provide funds to countries facing temporary difficulties in their BALANCE OF PAYMENTS. In return for such funds, the IMF usually requires countries to reform their economies by means of structural adjustment programs (including cuts in public spending and devaluation). Since 1969, the IMF has sponsored a new form of international reserve currency known as the SPECIAL DRAWING RIGHT.

Imports Goods and services purchased from other countries, usually involving the use of foreign exchange.

Import controls Government attempts to stem imports by means of taxes or tariffs, and by means of quotas and health and safety regulations.

Import-substitution industrialization (ISI) The process of building up a domestic industrial base in order to make the country more self-sufficient in manufactured goods and to save on the future cost of imported industrial goods.

Indirect taxes Taxes collected by means of a levy on public and private spending on goods and services, usually in the form of a sales tax.

Industrial output The level of production of manufactured and other industrial goods in an economy.

Industrial revolution The rapid transfer of a majority of the working population from agriculture to new industrial occupations. The first industrial revolution began in Britain in the late 18th century.

Infant mortality rate The annual number of deaths of infants aged under one year per 1,000 live births.

Inflation The annual rate at which prices are increasing.

Informal sector The part of the economy that is not subject to standardized agreements on the employment of labor and which does not always maintain conventional systems of bookkeeping and accounting. Characterized by face-to-face dealings, rather than by abstract economic negotiations involving employers' groups, unions and government.

Infrastructure The network of publicly and privately provided facilities that allows directly productive economic activities to take place. The infrastructure of an advanced industrial country includes transportation and telecommunications facilities, educational facilities (to train labor) and healthcare facilities (to ensure that labor is fit enough to work and reproduce itself).

Interest rate A measure of the price of money. Interest rates will tend to be high when a lender is fearful that a loan might not be repaid (the risk factor), or when high rates of inflation are eroding the real value of debt repayments.

Interfirm trade Trade between two or more firms in the same economic grouping; for example, trade between two different car companies.

International Monetary Fund see IMF.

International reserves (gross) A government's holdings of monetary gold, foreign currencies, SPECIAL DRAWING RIGHTS (SDRs) and IMF resources. Governments hold international reserves to help protect their own currencies in the FOREIGN EXCHANGE MARKETS and to provide funds for imported goods and services.

Intra-firm trade Trade between two or more branches of the same multinational corporation.

Investment Resources used for the production of future goods and services.

Investment bank A bank that helps companies to raise funds by selling their DEBT on the open market. Investment banks such as Morgan Stanley and Merrill Lynch also advise corporate clients on such things as industrial strategy and the takeover of rival firms. They earn substantial fee income from such activities.

Invisible trade Trade in services including banking, shipping, tourism and insurance. It is a significant revenue earner for countries such as Spain (tourism) and the United Kingdom (financial services). VISIBLE TRADE is trade in goods and mechandise.

Inward-looking economy An economy geared to producing goods and services mainly for itself.

Keynesianism The economic and political philosophy associated with John Maynard Keynes (1883–1946). Often used to justify government intervention in a MARKET ECONOMY.

Labor force The economically active population, including the armed forces and the unemployed. Does not include homemakers and unpaid caregivers.

Labor Union An association that protects the interests of organized labor. Also known as a TRADE UNION.

Laissez-faire The belief that an economy works best when the government is not allowed to interfere in market operations.

LDC Less developed country. The term is now being discontinued in favor of the World Bank categories LOW-INCOME ECONOMY, LOWER-MIDDLE-INCOME ECONOMY and UPPER-MIDDLE-INCOME ECONOMY. The less developed world is also known as the THIRD WORLD or the developing world.

Liberalization An attempt to make an economy more responsive to global market conditions.

LIBOR London Inter-Bank Offered Rate, the interest rate most often quoted by commercial banks lending to each other and to developing countries.

Liquidity The ease with which funds can be raised by the sale of assets. Also a measure of the volume of turnover in a financial market.

Literacy Usually defined as the ability to read and write a simple sentence.

Literacy rate The percentage of a population aged 15 and over who can read and write a simple sentence.

London Club An informal network of commercial banks responsible for rescheduling the private DEBTs of developing countries.

Lower-middle-income economies (LMIEs) Countries where average per capita incomes were between $611 and $2,565 in 1990.

Low-income economies (LIEs) The poorest countries in the world, where average per capita incomes were $610 or less in 1990.

Manufacturing industry Industry producing goods by means of the application of labor to raw materials.

Marshall Plan The United States-funded program (1948–52) for European Recovery after World War II.

Market A meeting-place for buyers and sellers of goods and services.

Market economy An economy in which most economic activities are transacted by private individuals and firms in largely unregulated markets.

Merchandise trade Trade in VISIBLE GOODS (both EXPORTS and IMPORTS).

Mercantilism An economic philosophy that encourages countries to put their own trading interests before the wider interests of the international trading community.

Mixed economy An economy that contains a large number of both NATIONALIZED INDUSTRIES (publicly owned) and private companies.

Modernization The attempt to make developing countries more like the developed countries.

Monetarism An economic philosophy that sees INFLATION as the main menace to economic growth and proposes a direct relationship between the rate of growth of the MONEY SUPPLY of a country and its subsequent rate of INFLATION.

Monetary policy The Government's method of control over the quantity of money in the economy. Monetary policy is related to interest and exchange rate policies.

Money-center bank A large, innovative COMMERCIAL BANK not dependent upon checkable deposits as its primary source of funds.

Money supply The amount of money put into circulation in an economy. Money can be defined, measured and supplied in different ways. A narrow definition of money concentrates on coinage and banknotes. A broader definition of the money supply includes checkable deposits in commercial banks.

Monopoly A situation where one producer of goods and services controls the market for its commodities. Monopolies are discouraged in many countries because higher than necessary prices can result from a lack of competition.

Multilateral organizations International institutions that represent more than one country, such as the WORLD BANK, the IMF and UNCTAD.

Multinational corporations (MNCs) Very large businesses with offices or manufacturing plants in more than one country, and often in a good many countries. Sometimes called transnational corporations or global corporations.

Multiplier effect The knock-on effect of an initial economic decision.

National income The total economic activity of a country.

Nationalized industries Industries owned by the public, usually by the government, for strategic reasons.

Net Material Product see NMP.

New Deal An attempt to lift the United States' economy out of depression in the mid 1930s by means of increased government spending by the administration of President Franklin D. Roosevelt.

NIC A newly industrializing (or industrialized) country, such as South Korea or Taiwan.

NMP Net material product, a measure of total economic activity used pre-1992 in the socialist economies of Eastern Europe and the former Soviet Union. It is generally reckoned that NMP measures about 85 percent of a country's GDP, from which it differs mainly by excluding revenue from certain services.

OAPEC Organization of Arab Petroleum Exporting Countries, set up in 1968.

OECD Organization of Economic Cooperation and Development, set up in 1961 to promote the economic growth of its (now 24) rich member countries. A talking-shop for the advanced industrial world, based in Paris.

Official debt Foreign debt owed to governments and multilateral organizations, rather than to commercial banks.

Official development assistance The technical term for foreign aid.

Offshore banking The development of branch banks away from the country of origin of the headquarter bank. An attempt to serve international markets and to avoid national banking regulations.

Oligopoly The control of a market by a few independent firms.

OPEC Organization of Petroleum Exporting Countries, set up in 1960 and based in Vienna.

Outward-looking economy An economy geared to production for the world market.

Overemployment A situation where people are employed to do jobs that create little real wealth.

Paris Club An informal network of officials from developed countries charged with rescheduling the OFFICIAL DEBTS of some developing countries.

Pastoral economy An economy heavily dependent upon the raising and management of livestock.

Pax Americana The "American Peace" imposed at the end of World War II, which ensured that the capitalist world economy between 1945 and 1970 was to the liking of the United States.

Pension A regular payment to a person retired from work.

Pension funds Financial institutions that invest the savings of people in the workforce for repayment when they retire. Pension funds invest heavily in STOCKS and SECURITIES and are powerful players in the modern world economy.

Perestroika President Mikhail Gorbachev's program for the economic restructuring of the former Soviet Union during the second half of the 1980s.

Petrodollars Dollars earned from the sale of petroleum products; especially associated with OPEC members following the oil-price rises of 1973–4.

Population growth The rate (or total number) by which the total population of a country grows over a period of time, usually one year. The population growth rate will be high where the BIRTHRATE is significantly in excess of the DEATH RATE.

Poverty line A measure of deprivation that varies from country to country. In LOW-INCOME ECONOMIES the poverty referred to is an absolute poverty, where a certain percentage of the population lacks sufficient food to eat and resources to provide for shelter. In the advanced industrial world people are often considered to be in poverty if they earn less than 60 percent of the average wage. Their basic needs will be met by local welfare systems but they suffer poverty relative to their compatriots.

Primary education Education that teaches reading, writing, arithmetic and some other basic skills.

Private sector The part of the economy that is owned and operated by private individuals and firms.

Privatization The sale of publicly owned assets to private individuals and privately owned institutions.

Productivity A measure of economic output in terms of the quantity of economic inputs (labor, machines, land, etc.) needed to produce it.

Profit The return to owners of capital after all costs have been paid for. Often paid to shareholders in the form of dividends, and also used for reinvestment.

Profiteering Taking unfair advantage of trading conditions to make excessive PROFITS.

Public sector The part of the economy that is owned by, and operated by or on behalf of, the state.

Quota An impediment to FREE TRADE in the form of a limit to the quantity of goods that can be imported in a given year. For example, 20,000 cars from country A in year B.

Real interest rate The price of money (or the cost of a loan) after allowance has been made for INFLATION.

Real terms Economic figures that have been adjusted for INFLATION.

Recession A period of decline in national economic activity sustained over two or more quarters.

Regional policy An attempt to deal with the economic problems of the poorer regions of a country.

Rescheduling debt Drawing up a new agreement to pay back a DEBT over a different period of time to the one originally stated.

Reserve currency A stable currency that governments and international financial agencies are willing to hold as part of their gold and foreign exchange reserves.

Restructuring A significant reshaping of the component parts of an economy, such as the mix between the PUBLIC and PRIVATE SECTORS or between agriculture and industry.

Science park A site for the joint production of high-technology goods and services by small companies and a research university.

Secondary education Education that builds upon at least four years' previous instruction in basic or primary schools.

Second World A term sometimes used to describe the developed socialist countries (including the former Soviet Union).

Security A term loosely used to refer to STOCKS and SHARES, but which more exactly refers to something given by the borrower as a safeguard for a loan. Such a guarantee, or security, can often be traded in securities markets (including the mortgage market).

Self-sufficient economy An economy which largely meets its own needs, importing and exporting very little to other countries.

Service economy The part of the economy not accounted for by agriculture and industry (including manufacturing). It includes banking, tourism, leisure and retailing. The services offered will vary from country to country.

Shares Stakes in the capital of a company, on which dividends are paid.

Shareholders The ECONOMIC AGENTS (individuals and institutions) that own a company through their subscribing a sum of money to the company's CAPITAL in return for a portion of the PROFIT. The sum of money advanced buys a designated number of SHARES at the prevailing price.

Socialism An economic and political system in which a majority of the economy is owned by the people and where inequalities of wealth are meant to be low.

Soft loan Money lent below market interest rates and for a longer period of time than most COMMERCIAL BANKS would consider. This is the main form in which foreign aid is made available.

Special Drawing Right (SDR) An international reserve currency, introduced by the International Monetary Fund (IMF) in 1969 and intended to take the place of gold and national currencies in settling international trade balances. The SDR is a form of "paper gold", backed by a MULTILATERAL ORGANIZATION. All members of the IMF are allocated SDRs, roughly in proportion to a member country's existing subscription with the IMF.

Special Economic Zone A small regional economy exempted from the usual range of government regulations.

Stock A stake in the CAPITAL of a company akin to a SHARE, but fully paid up and therefore easy to transfer in the STOCK EXCHANGE.

Stock exchange A market for buying and selling STOCKS, SHARES and SECURITIES. It is extremely important in countries such as Australia, Britain and the United States, where a substantial part of company finance is raised through the sale of such assets.

Structural adjustment program A package of economic reforms implemented in many indebted developing countries at the request of the IMF and the WORLD BANK. Such reforms vary from country to country, but generally include currency DEVALUATION, trade and investment liberalization, the removal of subsidies and tighter fiscal policies. The main aim of structural adjustment programs is to make economies more open and OUTWARD-LOOKING and more directly led by price signals emerging from the market-place. In practice, cutbacks in government spending have tended to penalize poor people dependent on state welfare policies.

Subsidy Public money used to depress the price of goods or a service.

Supply-side economics A belief that economic activity can only be increased in the long term by making the suppliers of goods and services more efficient. Government spending to increase demand in the short term is discouraged as inflationary.

Sustainable development Economic activity that can be sustained over generations without causing irreversible environmental damage.

Tariff A tax or duty imposed on imported goods and services.

Tax haven A, usually small, independent country that legally aids individuals and firms in minimizing the taxes they pay on income or CAPITAL.

Terms of trade A measure of EXPORT prices in terms of IMPORT prices, often expressed as an index number (eg 100). If EXPORT prices are rising faster than a country's IMPORT prices, its terms of trade are improving (moving above 100).

Tertiary education College-level education (post secondary school).

Third World A term first used to refer to ex-colonial countries which were neither fully capitalist nor fully socialist. Now used to refer to the poorer, less industrialized countries of the developing world.

Trade balance The record of a country's MERCHANDISE TRADE. Part of the CURRENT ACCOUNT balance.

Trade dependency The extent to which EXPORTS and IMPORTS affect a country's GDP – high dependency is where trade accounts for a large proportion of revenue and spending.

Transaction An economic exchange or business decision.

Trade union see LABOR UNION.

Transfer pricing A system of invoicing between branches of a MULTINATIONAL CORPORATION that minimizes the total taxes due in all countries of operation.

UNCTAD United Nations Conference on Trade and Development, first convened in Geneva in 1964. The main talking-shop for developing countries.

Unemployment A state of being out of paid work (including self-employment) whilst being willing and able to work.

Upper-middle-income economies Countries where average per capita incomes were between $2,566 and $7,619 in 1990.

Visible trade Goods shipped from one country to another, tangible EXPORTS and IMPORTS.

Wall Street The financial center of New York City in the United States.

Welfare state The part of government that provides public services for its citizens, including education, healthcare and benefit payments.

W.H.O. World Health Organization

World Bank see IBRD.

Further reading

Brett, E. A. (1985) *The World Economy Since the War* (London: Macmillan)
Corbridge, S. (1993) *Debt and Development* (Oxford: Blackwell)
Daly, M. and Logan, M. (1989) *The Brittle Rim: Finance, Business and the Pacific Region* (Harmondsworth: Penguin)
Dicken, P. (1992) *Global Shift* (2nd Edition) (London: Paul Chapman)
Dornbusch, R. and Fischer, S. (1990) *Macroeconomics* (5th Edition) (New York: McGraw-Hill)
Friedman, M. and Friedman, R. (1980) *Free to Choose* (Harmondsworth: Pelican)
Galbraith, J.K. and Salinger, N. (1980) *Almost Everyone's Guide to Economics* (Harmondsworth: Penguin)
George, S. (1989) *A Fate Worse Than Debt* (Harmondsworth: Penguin)
Gill, S. and Law, D. (1988) *Global Political Economy* (Hemel Hempstead: Harvester Wheatsheaf)
Gilpin, R. (1987) *The Political Economy of International Relations* (Princeton: Princeton University Press)
Hobsbawm, E. (1969) *Industry and Empire* (Harmondsworth: Penguin)
Iliffe, J. (1987) *The African Poor* (Cambridge: Cambridge University Press)
Knox, P. and Agnew, J. (1989) *The Geography of the World Economy* (London: Edward Arnold)
Kornai, J. (1992) *The Socialist System* (Oxford: Oxford University Press)
Krugman, P. (1992) *The Age of Diminished Expectations* (Cambridge, Mass.: MIT Press)
Sen, A. K. (1984) *Resources, Values and Development* (Oxford: Blackwell)
Thurow, L. (1992) *Head to Head: The Coming Economic Battle Among Japan, Europe, and America* (New York: William Morrow)
Wallace, I. (1990) *The Global Economic System* (London: Unwin Hyman).
Wolf, E. (1982) *Europe and the People Without History* (Berkeley: University of California Press)
World Bank (annual) *World Development Report* (Oxford: Oxford University Press/World Bank)

Sources used for data panels and standard artwork

Data in the data panels come mainly from the World Bank's World Development Report (Oxford: OUP/World Bank; annual). Most of the data come from the Report published in 1992 and refer to 1990 unless otherwise indicated. Data on merchandise exports and imports come from the Economist Intelligence Unit and are based on customs statistics for 1990. The standard artwork on merchandise exports and imports, and the direction of trade statistics, are also based on data taken from the Economist Intelligence Unit. Data on Northern Eurasia have been taken from The Economist: Pocket World in Figures, 1993 Edition (London: Random Century). The standard artwork on inflation is based on the General Consumer Price Index published by the International Labor Office in its Year Book of Labor Statistics (Geneva/ILO: 1991 edition). Finally, the standard artwork on life expectancy is based on data in the 1992 World Development Report of the World Bank (Oxford: OUP/World Bank).

Acknowledgments

Picture credits

Key to abbreviations: A Arcaid, Surrey, UK; **C** Colorific!, London, UK; **COP** Christine Osborne Pictures, London, UK; **CPL** Comstock Photo Library, London, UK; **E** Explorer, Paris, France; **HL** The Hutchison Library, London, UK; **IB** The Image Bank, London, UK; **IP** Impact Photos, London, UK; **KP** Katz Pictures, London, UK; **M** Magnum Photos Limited, London, UK; **NP** Network Photographers, London, UK; **PP** Panos Pictures, London, UK; **RHPL** Robert Harding Picture Library, London, UK; **SAP** South American Pictures, Suffolk, UK; **SP** Select Photo Agency, London, UK; **SPL** Science Photo Library, London, UK; **TSW** Tony Stone Worldwide, London, UK; **Z** Zefa Picture Library, London, UK

t=top; c= center; b=bottom; l=left; r=right

1 HL/Melanie Friend **2** HL/Robert Francis RHPL/Peter Scholey **4** RHPL/Robert Francis **6–7** HL **8–9** Z **10** HL **10–11** Z/Scholz **12–13** M/Rene Burri **14** SAP/Marion Morrison**15** TRIP/Dave Saunders **16** PF **16–17** ET Archive **18** C/F Ward **18–19** C/Kay Chernush **22** IP/Sergio Dorantes **22–23** Z **24** COP **26** PP/Jimmy Holmes **26–27** KP/ICS/Randy G Taylor **28** HL **30–31t** M/Chris Steele-Perkins **30–31b** IB **32** IP/Conant **32–33** PP/Chris Stowers **35** M/Alex Webb **36** IB **36–37** PP/Klass **38** TRIP/Eye Ubiquitous/Waterlow **38–39** C/Valdes **40–41** PP/Rob Giling **44–45** Hot Shots/Mach II/Bill Marsh **46** Z **48** KP/SABA/Christopher Morris **48–49** Hot Shots/Brian Thompson **50** Hot Shots/Brian Thompson **51** Canapress Photo Service/Bill Becker **52–53** M/Gilles Peress **54** IB/Marvin E Newman **55t** M/Michael K Nichols **55b** KP/JB Pics/James Marshall **56** FSP/Gamma Liaison/Barr **56–57** HL/Liba Taylor **58 NP 58–59** KP/JB Pics/Fritz Hoffmann **60–61** M/Michael K Nichols **62–63** KP/Gerd Ludwig **63** IB/Kay Chernush **64–65** TSW/Aldo Torelli **65** M/Fred Mayer **66–67** HL/Jeremy A Horner **67bl** M/Thomas Hoepker **67br** KP/JB Pics/Mark Cardwell **68–69** Z **71** NP/Matrix/Quesaola **72–73** KP/JB Pics/J Nordell **73** PP/Neil Cooper **74** TSW **75** M/James Nachtwey **76** TRIP/Richard Powers **76–77** M/Salgado Jnr **78–79** IP/Michael Mirecki **80** M/Susan Meiselas **81** PP/Ron Giling **82–83** TRIP/Dave Saunders **83** HL/Edward Parker **84** IP/Rhonda Klevansky **84–85** SAP/Dr Peter Francis **86** Knudsens Fotosenter **89t** Z/Icelandic Photo **89b** Knudsens Fotosenter/Ziesman **90** Knudsens Fotosenter **90–91** IP/Peter Menzel **92–93** Svenskt Pressfoto/Bjorn Larsson Ask **94–95** SP/Dario Mitidieri **96–97** TRIP/Jeremy Hoare **98–99** IB/Terry Williams **99** M/Stuart Franklin **100** CPL **101** SPL/Simon Fraser **102–103** TRIP/Bob Turner **104–105** A/Richard Bryant **106–107** TRIP/Helene Rogers **108–109** E/Francis Jalain **109** FSP/Patrick Aventurier **110** E/Thierry Borredon **111** M/Richard Kalvar **112–113t** E/Philippe Roy **112–113b** M/Patrick Zachmann **114–115** COP **116** SP/Alexander Caminada **116–117** TRIP/Eye Ubiquitous/David Cumming **118–119** N V Luchthaven, Schiphol **119** COP **120–121** KP/REA/Van Cappellen **123** RHPL/Thierry Borredon **124–5** Z/K Kerth **125** COP **126** IP/Alain le Garsmeur **127** COP **128** E/Stephane Frances **128–129** RHPL/Duncan Maxwell **130–131** TRIP/Sefton Photo Library **133** HL/Robert Aberman **134–135** RHPL **135** M/Fred Scianna **136** M/Fred Scianna **137** M/Zecchin **138** Marka/Mazzola **139** Marka/Benzi **140–141** SP/Dario Mitidieri **142** E/Walter Geiersperger **144** NP/Doran **144–145** M/Thomas Hoepker **146–147** IB/Brett Froomer **148** NP/Michael Engler **148–149** RHPL/Steve Barister **150–151** Sygma/Regis Bossu **152** TRIP/Martin Barlow **154** KP/Ben Gibson **155** Eye Ubiquitous/Yiorgos Nikiteas **156** TRIP/Christopher Rennie **156–157** TRIP/Christopher Rennie **158–159** TRIP/Christopher Rennie **159** KP/Richard Baker **160** C/Martti Kainulainen Lehtikuva Oy **162–163** TRIP/Igor Burgandinov **163** PP/Chris Stowers **164** C/Dilip Mehta **165** KP/Jeremy Nicholl **166** C/Black Star/Peter Turnley **167** C/Black Star/Peter Turnley **168–169** TRIP/Igor Burgandinov **170–171** M/Rene Burri **172** COP **173** TRIP/Helene Rogers **174** M/Abbas **175** KP/A Morkovkin **176** M/Abbas **176–177** C/Black Star/Christopher Morris **179** PP/Neil Cooper **180–181** COP **181** HL/Trevor Page **182** PP/Betty Press **183** COP **184** COP **184–185** HL/Sarah Errington **186–187** IP/Caroline Penn **188–189** M/Jean Gaumy **190** M/Abbas **191** HL/Anna Tully **192** HL **193** PP/Jeremy Hartley **194–195** PP/Jeremy Hartley **195** HL **196** TRIP/Dave Saunders **198–199** PP/Trygve Bolstad **199** M/Gideon Mendel **200** HL/Robert Aberman **201** HL/Nancy Durrell **202–203** HL/Sarah Errington **204** CPL **206–207** CPL **207** CPL **208** PP/Jimmy Holmes **209** PP/Trygve Bolstad **210** IP/Alain le Garsmeur **210–211** CPL **212–213** CPL **214** KP/REA/SABA/Bradshaw **216–217** IB/Steve Niedorf **216** TRIP/Sefton Photo Library **218** TRIP/Eye Ubiquitous/Frank Leather **218–219** PP/Sean Sprague **220** KP/JB Pics/Peter Charlesworth **220–221** M/Steve McCurry **222** HL/R Ian Lloyd **224** IP/David Corio **225** HL/Nancy Durrell **226** M/Philip Jones Griffiths **227** Eye Ubiquitous/David Cumming **228–229** M/Philip Jones Griffiths **230** RHPL/Nigel Blythe **232–233** IB/Andy Caulfield **234** M/Hiroji Kubota **234–235** NP/Lewis **236–237** PP/Ron Giling **237** HL/Crispin Hughes **238–239** Z/Fields **240** HL/Hilly James **242–243** HL/Michael MacIntyre **244** TRIP/Dave Saunders **244–245** TRIP/Helene Rogers **246–247** Z/Dr David Holdsworth

Editorial, research and administrative assistance
Nick Allen, Brad Bates, Mike Brown, Joanna Chisholm, Penny Commerford, Marian Dreier, Reina Foster-de Wit, Claire Gabbey, Matthew Kneale, Jo Rapley, Lin Thomas, Claire Turner

Artists
The Maltings Partnership, Derby, England

Cartography
Sarah Phibbs, Richard Watts
Maps drafted by Euromap, Pangbourne, England

Index
Barbara James

Production
Clive Sparling

Typesetting
Brian Blackmore, Niki Moores

Color origination
Scantrans pte Ltd, Singapore

INDEX

Page numbers in **bold** refer to extended treatment of the topic; in *italic* to illustrations or maps